TROUBLE SPOTS

The World Atlas of Strategic Information

TROUBLE
SPOTS

The World Atlas of
Strategic Information

ANDREW DUNCAN & MICHEL OPATOWSKI

FOREWORD BY FRANÇOIS HEISBOURG

SUTTON PUBLISHING

First published in 2000 by
Sutton Publishing Limited · Phoenix Mill
Thrupp · Stroud · Gloucestershire · GL5 2BU

British Library Cataloguing in Publication Data
A catalogue record for this book is available from the British Library

ISBN 0 7509 2171 4

Typeset in 10/13pt Sabon.
Typesetting and origination by
Sutton Publishing Limited.
Printed and bound in England by
J.H. Haynes & Co. Ltd, Sparkford.

CONTENTS

LATIN AMERICA: OUTSIDE THE MAINSTREAM

SPACE: THE NEW BATTLEFIELD

STOP PRESS

LIST OF MAPS

FOREWORD

BY FRANÇOIS HEISBOURG
CHAIRMAN, GENEVA CENTRE FOR SECURITY POLICY
FORMER DIRECTOR OF THE INTERNATIONAL
INSTITUTE FOR STRATEGIC STUDIES

Ten years after the end of the Cold War, it is possible to measure and set in perspective the elements of change, but also of continuity, which characterise the global strategic situation. This new Atlas of strategic information does this not only by displaying the broad picture, but also by providing the relevant level of precision: in many of today's trouble spots, the devil does indeed hide in the detail.

The changes vis-à-vis the Cold War period are awesome. In contrast to more than four decades of a tense but stable stand-off, Europe has once again become the seat of open warfare, with the complex, protracted and frequently gruesome conflicts of the Balkans. The former Soviet Empire has witnessed a more or less peaceful transition from communism to a range of successor regimes, extending from the vibrant new democracies of Central Europe to the lawlessness and violence characteristic of major parts of the ex-USSR. Simultaneously, a new Great Game is being played out in the Caspian Basin and the Transcaucasus: it only remains to be seen whether it will retrospectively prove to be as unimportant as the original Great Game was a century ago. But if the new contest doesn't appear to have found its Kipling, it certainly has its cartographers. Change yet again with the unbottling of the nuclear genie in South Asia, with India's and Pakistan's multiple nuclear tests in 1998. And in East Asia, the winds of change have blown away the dictatorships of countries such as Indonesia, South Korea, Taiwan: but, it remains to be seen whether these positive developments will help cope with the ominous rise of dangerous rivalries in the region, complicated by the uncertain prospects of national unity in China or Indonesia. Finally, we have the strategic challenges flowing from the development of transnational criminal organisations, notably the drug cartels of Latin America, in contrast to the Cold War polarisation between military regimes and left-wing insurgency.

Yet, and here the *Atlas* is no less illuminating, one cannot but be struck by the elements of continuity which transcend even as earth-shaking an event as the collapse of the Soviet Empire. The arc of crisis, stretching from Algeria to Kashmir by way of the Middle East, had been recognised as such by observers a quarter of a century ago, along with the rise of religious militancy and transnational terrorism.

The Middle East in particular seems to have been stuck in a strategic rut even since the end of the First World War, notwithstanding the global transformations which have been occurring in the interval. The miseries and misfortunes which afflict what used to be called the Dark Continent have something of the same timeless air; the only basic change seems to be that Africa's plight appears to be getting even worse. Bloodier civil wars – including the massive genocide in Rwanda – wrack an Africa that has generated a new category in the political vocabulary: 'failed states', in much the same way that the Middle East has spawned the notion of 'rogue states'. On a more positive note, we have the gradual but unceasing process of European integration which began nearly half a century ago among six continental European countries and which is now poised to embrace more than two dozen countries extending from Ireland to Estonia. At the same time, this European Union is tentatively entering the scene as a military and strategic player, in tandem with NATO, which has not only survived the Cold War but has preserved its standing and its relevance. Continuity, finally, in a different way, in the military uses of outer space: some of the technofantasies of President Reagan's 'Star Wars' scheme are now poised to move from virtuality to reality for better or for worse.

The new atlas also renders a considerable service in laying out some of the factors which will shape war and peace during the coming years and decades, including the strategic implications of global warming. Similarly, violent transnational challenges, whether criminal or terrorist, will not diminish, certainly not in view of the trends affecting the proliferation of weapons of mass destruction. The advances in bioengineering and biochemistry have already begun to make biological and chemical weapons accessible to non-state actors. And, if nuclear weapons appear to remain firmly in the grip of states, the combination of regime instability, as in Pakistan, with the spread of nuclear weapons, is not a reassuring one. The twenty-first century may well witness the first deliberate use of city-destroying weapons since the obliteration of Hiroshima and Nagasaki in 1945.

Against this backdrop, the United States of America will be with us as the sole superpower for many decades. Its reach and grip will be constantly challenged: but there is on the horizon no contender with even remotely similar weight. How the US will cope with the security challenges portrayed in the atlas remains to be seen. In particular, America's capability to deal constructively and effectively with regional powers – not least of which an ambitious China, and in a considerably more benign (and probably less cohesive) mode, the European Union – is open to question.

Today's world is more interdependent than the old world; global challenges loom in importance vis-à-vis a number of essentially regional contingencies; and peaceful non-state actors, from transnational corporations to NGOs, play an increasing role compared to the prerogatives of sovereign, occasionally war-making, states. However, and the pages of this book amply prove the point, this is not going to be a particularly peaceful world. Violent cross-border non-state actors; savage civil wars; the collateral damage from collapsing states alongside ferociously assertive dictatorships are going to be the hallmarks of our planet. Given these prospects, it is imperative to step up efforts towards global governance, including international peacemaking and peacekeeping operations along with measures aiming to curb the spread of the most destructive arms – not only nuclear weapons but at the other end of the spectrum, anti-personnel mines. Such initiatives, which figure prominently in the following pages, deserve to be a growing part of the strategic agenda.

INTRODUCTION

During the Cold War the world faced the threat of an all-out nuclear conflict that would bring catastrophic results not just to the participants but possibly everybody; fortunately, the chance of such a war breaking out was remote once the reality of deterrence had been established. However, the possibility of global nuclear war had a limiting effect on conflict elsewhere in the world in countries where the superpowers usually supported opposing sides but themselves managed to avoid direct confrontation. In the post-Cold War world many more conflicts have broken out and without the limiting effect of superpower involvement they have become as bloody and horrific for the contestants and their civil populations as a nuclear war would have been for the US and USSR. At the same time, wars between states have become less frequent while those within states have become very much more common.

This atlas illustrates the many problems that face the world: some have recently been resolved but may reappear, and others have not yet erupted but may have to be faced in the future. These problems do not inevitably lead to military conflict but can involve political confrontation, the imposition of sanctions of various kinds, and economic rivalry and competition.

The maps are supported by accounts of the historical background to each problem area and, where applicable, of the actions of the contestants and the efforts of the international community to halt fighting, deliver essential aid and broker a lasting solution. However, it is not the aim of this atlas to describe in detail the course of each war or civil conflict (such an attempt would soon be out of date), to distinguish between right and wrong, or to prescribe policies to solve problems. The main objective is to explain why the conflicts, problems and issues have arisen.

There are many reasons for confrontation and conflict: the most fundamental of these is the subject of land and its ownership. This is essentially a question of natives versus immigrants – the former being the descendants of the original or earliest inhabitants and the latter being any later arrivals, however long ago they appeared and regardless of how their settlement may have been legalised since. These disputes are often made more intransigent by religious differences, whether of faith, such as between Muslim and Jew in the Middle East, or of factions of the same faith, as in Northern Ireland and Croatia. Ethnic differences are also cited as a reason for discord but in many of the current trouble spots the parties come from the same ethnic base: Celts in Ireland, Semites in the Middle East and Slavs in Former Yugoslavia. Family quarrels are, of course, more vicious than those between strangers.

In its efforts to halt conflict, the world has not yet managed to reconcile quite contradictory principles. Article I (section 2) of the United Nations Charter states that the purpose of the UN is to ensure 'friendly relations among nations based on respect for the principle of equal rights and self-determination'. On the other hand, Article 2 (section 7) declares that 'nothing contained in the present charter shall authorise the United Nations to intervene in matters which are essentially within the domestic jurisdiction of any state'. Most intra-state conflicts are caused by the lack of human rights and the desire for self-determination. NATO's intervention in Kosovo, a conflict prompted by just such reasons, would appear to be in violation of Article 2, however justified the intervention was under Article 1. Nor can the right to self-determination, also set out in the 1966 International Convention on Civil and Political Rights, co-exist with the principle of the inviolability of modern international borders set out in Basket I of the Helsinki Final Act of 1975. This contradiction is at the heart of the disputes in Cyprus, Kashmir and, once again, Former Yugoslavia, for example. In most cases the inviolability of borders is given priority because other states foresee the granting of self-determination as having unwanted repercussions for themselves. There is no international law governing secession and many of today's international crises are concerned with the secessionist aims of one party. Drafting such a law would be difficult but perhaps it has become necessary.

In addition to examining a number of problems that involve only one or a few countries, this atlas also looks at several much wider potential problems, such as the shortage of resources like water, the influence of drugs, the effects of terrorism, and perennial topics including nuclear disarmament and the proliferation of chemical and biological weapons. It is divided into sections covering geographical regions, but in addition it examines Global Concerns, Weapons of Mass Destruction and Space. There is a brief further reading list for each individual topic and, where applicable, details of useful web-sites. In a volume as short as this it is not possible to cover every topic of security concern, nor is it possible to devote as much space to any one topic as it might deserve.

Research for this work was completed on 31 December 1999 but a 'Stop Press' section lists new 'trouble spots' that have recently appeared and updates for the period 1 January to 1 June 2000 problems already discussed.

GLOBAL CONCERNS

T here are a great many topics that could be chosen to fill this section, of which general stability is probably the most important, and with the end of the Cold War the world has become much less stable as the piece entitled 'A World at War' illustrates. The work of the United Nations is described in two of the many areas in which it works: Peacekeeping and Refugees. Other topics chosen are the Environment, Freedom of the Seas, Terrorism, Anti-Personnel Mines and Drugs. Many more issues could have been included had space allowed, such as International Crime, Aids, Globalisation and even Morality.

A WORLD AT WAR: A VIOLENT POSTWAR HISTORY

After the Second World War another – but violence free – confrontation which became known as the 'Cold War' was soon created. The dangers inherent in another, this time nuclear, world war were such that peace between the superpowers and the two alliances, NATO and the Warsaw Pact, was maintained. The two superpowers usually supported opposing sides in third-world conflicts and both remained determined to prevent such disputes escalating into direct confrontation between themselves; this determination led them to control local conflicts, with the consequence that few were ever resolved. Now that the threat of an all-out nuclear war has receded so has the enthusiasm of the US and Russia to back and control warring factions. The result is that local clashes have become more frequent, more bloody and more dangerous for the populations involved, who previously had not faced the danger of nuclear extinction.

The world has experienced a number of different forms of conflict since 1946: all-out war, such as Operation Desert Storm launched to recover Kuwait from Iraq; minor, mainly border wars with fighting restricted to a limited area of territory as in the Peru–Ecuador dispute; internal armed conflict, probably the most frequently occurring category, some incidences of which have continued for many years – for example, the Sri Lankan and Angolan civil wars; and terrorist campaigns that fall short of war, examples being Northern Ireland, Colombia and the Israeli-Palestinian dispute. Over 19 million people

Casualties and Costs			
War	Date	Killed	$US (bn)
Korea	1950–3	3m	340
Vietnam	1966–75	2m	720
Yom Kippur	1973	16,000	21
Falklands	1982	1,000	5
Iran/Iraq	1980–8	500,000	150

INTER STATE WARS

Europe
Soviet invasion of Hungary 1956
Soviet invasion of Czechoslovakia 1968

Middle East and North Africa
French/British/Israeli invasion of Egypt 1956
Arab Israeli War 1967
Arab Israeli War 1973
Israeli invasion of Lebanon 1978
Israeli invasion Lebanon 1982
Iran Iraq War 1980-88
Iraqi invasion of Kuwait 1990-91
Libya-Egypt 1977
North-South Yemen 1979-82

Asia
Soviet invasion of Afghanistan 1978-92
Chinese invasion of India 1962
India Pakistan War 1947-48
India Pakistan War 1965
India Pakistan 1971
Vietnam War 1965-75
Korean War 1950-53
Chinese invasion of Vietnam 1979
Malayasian Indonesia confrontation 1963-66
Vietnam-Cambodia 1977-79

Africa
Kenya-Somalia, (Shifta War) 1963-67
Portuguese attack on Guinea 1970
Morocco-Western Sahara 1976-
Ethiopia-Somalia(Ogaden War) 1977-78
Libya-Chad 1973-94
Burkina Faso-Mali 1985
Ethiopian-Eritrean border dispute 1998-
Eritrea-Yemen (Hanish Islands) 1995

Americas
El Salvador-Honduras 1969
US invasion of Grenada 1983
US invasion of Panama 1989
Argentine invasion of Falkland Islands 1982
Peru Ecuador border dispute 1995
Peru Ecuador border dispute 1997-98

WARS OF INDEPENDENCE

Algeria (from France) 1954-62
Guinea-Bissau (from Portugal) 1961-74
Angola (from Portugal) 1961-76
Bangladesh (from Pakistan) 1971
Indo-China (from France) 1946-54
Israel (against the Arabs) 1948-49
Indonesia (from the Netherlands) 1945-49
Mozambique (from Portugal) 1962-74
Namibia (from South Africa) 1966-90
South Yemen 1962-67
Zimbabwe (from Rhodesia) 1971-80
Tibet 1959, 1989

CIVIL/INTERNAL WARS

Europe
Albania 1997
Bosnia-Herzegovina 1992-95
Croatia 1991-95
Serbia (Kosovo) 1998-99
Greece 1945-49
Turkey (Kurds) 1984-
Russia (Chechnya) 1994-96, 1999-
Georgia 1990-96

Cyprus (Enosis) 1955-60
Cyprus (Greek-Turkish) 1964-

Middle East
Algeria 1992-
Lebanon 1958
Lebanon 1975
Jordan-PLO 1970-71
Israel-Palestinians (Intifada) 1987-90
Oman (Dhofar) 1964-67, 1970-75

Asia
Brunei 1962-63
Cambodia 1970-75 (Pol Pot)
Cambodia 1979-93 (Khmer Rouge), 1997-99
China 1945-49
Philippines 1969
Malaya 1948-60
Sri Lanka 1983-
Maldives (Indian Intervention) 1989
Bangladesh (Chakmas insurgency) 1992
Tajikistan 1992-97
Afghanistan (Pashtun v Uzbek/Tajik) 1993-1995
Afghanistan (Taleban takeover) 1995-
Kashmir 1990-
East Timor 1975-99
Papua New Guinea (Bougainville) 1988-98
Indonesia (West Irian) 1957-62
Myanmar 1947-54, 1975-80, 1982-

Africa
Angola 1975-
Burundi 1965-66, 1969, 1972, 1988, 1993-
Djibouti 1994
Ethiopia 1977-1991
Liberia 1980, 1985, 1989-97

Madagascar 1947-48
Nigeria (Biafra) 1967-70
Zaire (Katanga) 1960-65
Zaire (Shaba) 1977-78
Zaire/Republic of Congo 1996-
Rwanda 1959-1962, 1990-
Kenya (Mau Mau) 1952-56
Kenya (Holy Spirit Movement)
Sierra Leone 1991-98
Somalia 1988-98
Sudan 1955-72, 1983-
Niger/Mali (Touareg revolt) 1990-95
Mozambique 1976-1989
Uganda 1978-79

Americas
Cuba (Bay of Pigs) 1961
Colombia (FARC/ELN/drugs) 1976-
Colombia (La Violencia) 1948-58
Dominican Republic 1965-66
Guatemala 1954-96
Honduras 1981
Nicaragua 1978-79
Nicaragua 1982-89
Paraguay 1947
Paraguay 1954
Paraguay 1959-60
Peru 1948
Peru (Shining Path) 1980-
El Salvador 1977-92
Venezuela 1945
Venezuela 1958
Mexico 1994-

A history of the world at war since 1946.

have died as a result of armed conflict since 1946. But the financial cost of these wars is harder to quantify, particularly as the expense of rebuilding shattered states should be included. The annual price (in millions of US$) of conflict has been estimated as: Bosnia (1992–5) 840, Sri Lanka (since 1983) 380, and Papua New Guinea (since 1988) 27. Full-scale war is much more expensive and comparative costs (in billions of 1995 US$) are: Korean War 340, Yom Kippur War 21, and the Gulf War 102.

A new form of conflict has recently emerged, described by some as 'virtual' war. The bombing campaign against Serbia was the first example of the genre, although the same tactics have since been employed in some retaliatory raids. By using air attack only, and by employing stand-off weapons or keeping manned aircraft at altitudes above surface-to-air missile range, it is almost possible to guarantee no casualties to one's own side. By selecting only military or high-value industrial and infrastructure targets and using only 'smart' weaponry, it is possible to keep the casualties to the other side to a minimum. It is doubtful whether this sort of war will be successful in other circumstances. Certainly in undeveloped regions where the fighters whom the world wants to stop use only small arms and machetes it would be most inappropriate.

While there is only one inter-state war at present – between Ethiopia and Eritrea – there are sixteen intra-state wars of varying intensities and several countries are plagued by terrorism with the possibility of new conflicts erupting at any time as long-standing differences remain unresolved. There are numerous reasons why wars and terrorist campaigns break out: fear of a neighbour's growing military strength (Arab-Israeli war in 1967); ethnic and tribal differences (Rwanda and Burundi); desire for self-determination (Kurds, Kosovo); so-called religious wars (Algeria, Sudan); loss of strategic access (Iran-Iraq war); maltreatment of minority populations (Iraqi Sh'ia); shortage of vital resources (Israeli attacks on Syria); profit from drugs (Colombia, Myanmar). Probably the most fundamental reason for conflict is ownership of land, particularly for those who have lost their traditional land through history. As the accompanying map shows there are few territories that have escaped all conflict since 1946, possibly only Australia and New Zealand and, of course, their soldiers have taken part in several wars away from home. North America has not witnessed actual war but the US has seen several large-scale terrorist incidents and in Canada the Quebec secessionists refuse to give up their cause. Europe, until the Balkans erupted, was free from war but there are few countries that have not experienced terrorist activity, some, Britain and Spain for example, for a considerable length of time. All these countries have sent their soldiers to fight or to take part in peacekeeping missions, for some on numerous occasions.

Web Sites

Centre for Security Studies and Conflict Research: www.isn.ethz.ch/cwa
Initiative on Conflict Resolution and Ethnicity (INCORE):
    www.incore.ulst.ac.uk/cds/countries/index

UNITED NATIONS PEACEKEEPING: GLOBAL INVOLVEMENT

The United Nations, established in 1946 as a successor to the League of Nations, has many tasks, of which maintaining peace is the most important. There are two provisions in the UN Charter that allow the deployment of military forces in pursuit of peace. Chapter VI lays out the conditions for what has now come to be known as traditional peacekeeping where the UN or another organisation is invited by both parties in a dispute to assist them in maintaining peace while the problem is solved. The peacekeeping force is totally impartial and may only use force in self-defence. The number of UN peacekeeping operations rose dramatically at the end of the Cold War: in 1980 there were only 5, all are still in operation; by 1990 the total had risen to 13 while since then 20 other missions have been established and today there are 19 in operation. They vary in size from the 24 military observers of the UN Mission of Observers in Prevlaka (Croatia) to the 4,500 troops in the UN Force in Lebanon. A number of operations began many years ago: the UN Truce Supervision Organisation in Israel and its neighbouring Arab states was established in 1948, the UN Peacekeeping Force in Cyprus in 1964, and the UN Disengagement Force on the Golan Heights in 1974.

Chapter VII operations, the second kind of peacekeeping provided for under the UN Charter, allow 'the use of all necessary means', that is military force, to accomplish the UN's aim. Rarely is the operation conducted by a UN force; it is usually undertaken by an alliance or a coalition, such as that organised to recover Kuwait after its invasion by Iraq, authorised by a UN Security Council (UNSC) Resolution. There have been occasions where what began as a Chapter VI operation has had to be reinforced by a Chapter VII mandate; this occurred in Bosnia when NATO was authorised to mount air attacks in support of the UN Protection Force there.

There is a growing trend for peacekeeping operations to be carried out by coalitions or alliances, partly because so many more operations have become necessary and partly as a result of lack of UN funds or, on occasion, lack of UNSC consensus. Operations in Georgia, Sierra Leone and Bosnia are recent examples: the first two operate alongside UN observer missions. Another trend is for there to be few, if any, new peacekeeping missions in the traditional style. Today's situations need what is known as 'wider peacekeeping', peace support operations or peace enforcement. As yet there is little international agreement on exactly how these 'in-between' (between the impartiality and force in self-defence-only traditional operations on the one hand and all-out, no holds barred war fighting on the other) missions should be conducted although a great deal of work has been done in developing national doctrines and attempting to rationalise these. In some cases national military history and experience lead to quite different policies being adopted by different national contingents working to the same UN mandate. Recent experience shows that a coalition 'of the willing' led by an established military headquarters is more effective in the first

Current UN mission strengths			
	Troops	Observers	Police
MINUGUA	NIL	20	60
MINURCA	1,180	NIL	24
MINURSO	NIL	29	64
MIPONUH	NIL	NIL	286
MONUA	87	NIL	NIL
MONUC	NIL	37	NIL
UNAMSIL	NIL	207	NIL
UNDOF	934	NIL	NIL
UNFICYP	1218	NIL	35
UNIFIL	4,562	NIL	NIL
UNIKOM	NIL	209	NIL
UNMIBH	890	NIL	1,789
UNMIK	NIL	35	1,729
UNMOGIP	NIL	46	NIL
UNMOP	NIL	24	NIL
UNMIT	NIL	36	1
UNOMIG	NIL	87	NIL
UNTAET	NIL	111	193
UNTSO	NIL	138	NIL

As at 31.10.99

States that have submitted planning data for standby peacekeeping forces

Argentina	Lithuania
Australia	Malaysia
Austria	Mongolia
Bangladesh	Nepal
Belgium	Netherlands
Bolivia	New Zealand
Bulgaria	Nigeria
Canada	Pakistan
Chad	Paraguay
Chile	Poland
Czech Republic	Portugal
Denmark	Romania
Finland	Singapore
France	Syria
Germany	Tanzania
Ghana	Tunisia
Greece	Turkey
Guatemala	Ukraine
Ireland	United Kingdom
Italy	Uruguay
Jordan	Zimbabwe
Kirgyzstan	

▲ Ongoing UN mission
△ Completed UN mission
● Non-UN forces ongoing mission
○ Non-UN forces completed mission

NON-UN OPERATIONS

NNSC (1953-)
Neutral Nations Supervisory Commission

MFO (1981-)
Multinational Force and Observers

IFOR (NATO) (1995-1996)
Implementation Force

SFOR (NATO) (1996-)
Stabilisation Force

TIPH (1994)
Temporary International Presence in Hebron

KFOR (NATO) (1999-)
Kosovo Force

AFOR (NATO) (1999-)
Albania Force

Op Alba (NATO) (1997)
Operation Alba

ECOMOG
Economic Community (of West Africa) Monitoring Group
Liberia (1990-1997)
Sierra Leone (1998-)

CISPF
Commonwealth of Independent States Peace Force
Georgia (1992-)
Tajikistan (1992-)

INTERFET (1999-)
International Force for East Timor

PMG (1997-)
Bougainville Peace Monitoring Group

AMERICA

UNMIH (1993-1996)
UN Mission in Haiti

MIPONUH (1997-)
UN Civilian Police Mission in Haiti

DOMREP (1965-1966)
Mission of the Representative of the Secretary-General in the Dominican Republic

MINUGUA (1997)
UN Verification Mission in Guatemala

ONUSAL (1991-1995)
UN Observer Mission in El Salvador

ONUCA (1989-1992)
UN Observer Group in Central America

EUROPE

UNTAES (1996-1998)
UN Transitional Administration for Eastern Slavonia, Baranja and Western Sirmium

UNCRO (1995-1996)
UN Confidence Restoration Operation in Croatia

UNMIBH (1995-)
UN Mission in Bosnia and Herzegovina

UNMOP (1996-)
UN Mission of Observers in Prevlaka

UNPREDEP (1995-1999)
UN Preventive Deployment Force

UNPROFOR (1992-1995)
UN Protection Force

AFRICA

MINURSO (1991-)
UN Mission for the Referendum in Western Sahara

UNOMSIL (1998-)
UN Observer Mission in Sierra Leone

UNOMIL (1993-1997)
UN Observer Mission in Liberia

MINURCA (1998-)
UN Mission in the Central African Republic

ONUC (1960-1964)
UN Operation in the Congo

MONUC (1997-)
UN Operation in the Congo

UNOSOM 1 & 2 (1992/3-1995)
UN Operation in Somalia

UNAMIR (1993-1996)
UN Assistance Mission for Rwanda

UNOMUR (1993-1994)
UN Observer Mission Uganda-Rwanda

UNOMOZ (1992-1994)
UN Operation in Mozambique

MONUA (1997-1999)
UN Observer Mission in Angola

UNAVEM 1,2 & 3 (1989/91/95-1997)
UN Angola Verification Missions

UNTAG (1989-1990)
UN Transition Assistance Group

MIDDLE EAST

UNOMIG (1991-)
UN Observer Mission in Georgia

UNIIMOG (1988-1991)
UN Iran-Iraq Military Observer Group

UNIKOM (1991-)
UN Iraq-Kuwait Observation Mission

UNYOM (1963-1964)
UN Yemen Observation Mission

UNTSO (1948-)
UN Truce Supervision Organisation

UNFICYP (1964-)
UN Peace-keeping Force in Cyprus

UNEF 1&2 (1956-1967, 1973-1979)
UN Emergency Force

UNDOF (1974-)
UN Disengagement Observer Force

UNIFIL (1978-)
UN Interim Force in Lebanon

UNOGIL (1958)
UN Observer Group in Lebanon

ASIA

UNMOT (1994-)
UN Mission of Observers in Tajikistan

UNGOMAP (1988-1990)
UN Good Offices Mission in Afghanistan and Pakistan

UNGOMIP (1949-)
UN Military Observer Group in India and Pakistan

UNIPOM (1965-1966)
UN India-Pakistan Observation Mission

UNAMIC (1991-1992)
UN Advance Mission in Cambodia

UNTAC (1992-1993)
UN Transitional Authority in Cambodia

UNSF (1962-1963)
UN Security Force in West New Guinea (West Irian)

UNTAET (1999-)
UN Transitional Administration in East Timor

instance in a peace support operation situation such as Kosovo or East Timor than a UN-led mission that could deploy later when the situation is calmer. The coalition should, of course, be authorised by a UN mandate.

One major problem encountered during the establishment of a new mission is the time taken to raise and deploy the force when, often, speed is of paramount importance. In an effort to improve deployment time the UN has established a standby scheme whereby states place forces at short notice to react to UN calls for peacekeeping units. To date, 61 countries have earmarked a total of 147,500 troops and police and others will make available transport to deploy the force. Roughly 50 per cent of the earmarked forces will be able to deploy within 30 days. Some states may decline to make their standby contingent available for a particular operation because of political reasons.

A record of peacekeeping missions.

*Opposite, top: Refugees and others
of UNHCR concern.*

Another growing trend is the tendency for the US and on occasion its Allies to dispense with a UN mandate for use of force, albeit in support of internationally desired aims. There was no UN mandate for the US cruise missile strikes against Usarra Bin Laden's training camps in Afghanistan after the bomb attacks on US embassies in 1998. Nor was there specific authority for the 78-day bombing campaign against Serbia over its treatment of Albanians in Kosovo. The rift between the US and the UN is, in fact, more a rift between the US and the Secretary General. Relations would be improved if the US were to pay its outstanding debts to the UN, most of which are on account of peacekeeping costs.

As important as peacekeeping is the provision of humanitarian aid and the two often go hand-in-hand. Aid has become the responsibility of the UN High Commission for Refugees, which is operating in 118 countries. In several recent peacekeeping operations there has been a complete breakdown of government and an essential part of the mission has been a civil police contingent to assist in maintaining law and order, to investigate crime and to train a new police force. While most armies are not permanently engaged on operations and, therefore are available for peacekeeping, police forces are established and funded for the policing needs of a city, province or country. There are, therefore, no surplus police forces that can be readily dispatched to a peacekeeping mission, as in Kosovo where only roughly one-third of the 6,000 police authorised by the UN have been deployed.

Bibliography and Web Site

Otunnu, Olara, and Michael Doyle Lanham (eds), *Peacemaking and Peacekeeping for the New Century*, Rowman & Littlefield, 1998

Parsons, Anthony, *From Cold War to Hot Peace: UN Intervention 1947–1994*, Michael Joseph, 1995

The Blue Helmets: A Review of United Nations Peace-keeping, UN, 1996

www.   UN Department of Peacekeeping: www.un.org/Depts/dpko

REFUGEES: NOT JUST THE UNHCR'S PROBLEM

The United Nations High Commissioner for Refugees (UNHCR) is probably the busiest of the UN's agencies with 244 offices in 118 countries, a budget of over $1 billion a year, and responsible for over 22 million 'people of concern'. The UNHCR was preceded by the League of Nations High Commissioner for Refugees established in 1920 to cope with the aftermath of the First World War. Repatriation of 500,000 prisoners of war, the famine in the USSR where 30 million were starving, the return or settlement of 1.5 million refugees and in 1922 the population exchange between Greece and Turkey were the High Commissioner's first tasks. When the United Nations was established in 1945 it set up the International Refugee Organisation (IRO) to help the repatriation of the 21 million refugees created by the Second World War. The IRO was replaced by the Office of the UN High Commissioner for Refugees in 1951.

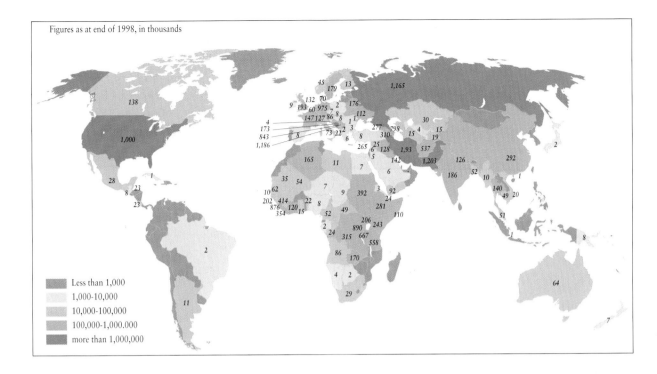

Figures as at end of 1998, in thousands

Less than 1,000
1,000-10,000
10,000-100,000
100,000-1,000.000
more than 1,000,000

Location of Palestinian refugees.

Armistice line, 1948
Territory occupied by Israel in 1967
Cease-fire line, 1973
Palestinian Authority since 1995
■ Refugee camp

The UNHCR is concerned with a number of different categories of people who need help. A 'refugee', as defined by international law, is a person who has left and cannot return to his country for fear of persecution or who has escaped from conflict. Today there are nearly 12 million refugees. However, the UNHCR warns that collecting precise figures for refugees in any particular circumstance is difficult and so these estimates should be treated with caution. 'Returnees' are refugees who have returned to their home country but who are still in need of assistance. The UNHCR monitors their well-being on return, but normally for no more than two years. Currently the UNHCR monitors over 3.45 million returnees. Asylum seekers are those who leave their countries and then apply for refugee status elsewhere; while the UNHCR is concerned for asylum seekers, it is the prerogative of the receiving country to grant refugee status. Finally, there are 'internally displaced persons' (IDP) to whom the UNHCR extends protection or assistance when requested to do so by the UN Secretary General or the UN General Assembly as this category was not included in the UNHCR's original mandate. The latest figure for IDP and others of concern to the UNHCR is 5.97 million, of whom the largest number are in Bosnia-Herzegovina (816,000) and Sierra Leone (670,000); one source claims there are as many as 20–22 million IDP in 55 countries. Not all IDP are created by war or civil conflict; large numbers are displaced by natural disasters, including famine, and by development projects, such as the Chinese Yangtze River 'Three Gorges' project and Turkey's Ilisu hydro-electric scheme on the Tigris.

The 1951 Convention on the Status of Refugees and the 1967 Protocol define who is considered a refugee and lay down the commitments that the contracting parties make in respect of the treatment of refugees. There are 132 parties to the convention and 53 states have yet to join. The Statute of the UNHCR, adopted by the UN General Assembly in December 1950, lays out the responsibilities of the Office: its main duty is to provide international protection for refugees and to 'seek permanent solutions to the problems of refugees by assisting governments . . . to facilitate voluntary repatriation of such refugees or their assimilation within new national communities'. Originally, refugee relief was seen as the responsibility of the state granting asylum but the UNHCR has found in many cases that it must provide the food and shelter needed by large-scale refugee movements. It normally takes the lead role in coordinating the work of other UN agencies and of non-governmental organisations (NGO) that also play a significant role in refugee relief; there are over 1,000 NGOs.

The refugee camp at Bojane Macedonia, May 1999. (OSCE Verification Mission)

The UNHCR is not responsible for the 3.6 million Palestinian-registered refugees in the Near East – these are the responsibility of the UN Relief and Works Agency for Palestine refugees (UNRWA). (See page 171 for Palestinian refugee statistics.) The refugee status of these people originated in the 1948 Israeli War of Independence when Palestinians fled, in some cases encouraged to do so, from Israeli-occupied land to the West Bank and Gaza Strip. When Israel overran the West Bank in 1967, some fled from the area first to Jordan and then to Lebanon. Their Arab hosts kept most of the refugees in camps; today more than thirty years later over 1 million Palestinian refugees are still in camps. Once a solution is found to the Palestinian issue the question of the right to return will arise. Israel is most unlikely to accept any of the refugees and the West Bank and Gaza cannot house them all. Many may not wish to return but host countries may well want to shed the burden of their presence.

Despite the work of the UNHCR mass refugees place a heavy burden on receiving countries that are often ill-equipped to cope with the influx. Refugee communities can be destabilising; they may alter the political or ethnic balance in the host country, are a breeding ground for crime and may be used as cover by guerrillas or terrorists fighting the government from which they fled and so cause security problems for the host country. Large-scale refugee populations also cause environmental problems, particularly the destruction of trees as wood is sought for fuel. Many remain in the host country for several years; others are unwilling to return home and must be assimilated by their hosts. On some occasions countries agree to accept populations before they become refugees, one example being the Kenyan Indians expelled by Idi Amin and taken in by the UK.

Bibliography and Web Sites

Cohen, Roberta, and Francis Deng, *Masses in Flight: The Global Crisis of Internal Displacement*, Brookings Institute, 1998
Hampton, Janie (ed.), *Internally Displaced People: A Global Survey*, Earthscan, 1998
Loescher, Gil, *Refugee Movements and International Security*, IISS Adelphi Paper 268.1992

UNHCR: www.unhcr.ch
UNRWA: www.unrwa.org

Refugees by origin	
Afghanistan	1,200,000
Angola	121,000
Burundi	279,000
Congo (DRC)	108,200
Eritrea	147,800
Liberia	353,400
Sierra Leone	340,400
Somalia	480,600
Sudan	416,200

Refugees by refuge country	
Algeria	165,000
Armenia	310,000
Azerbaijan	221,000
Canada	135,000
China	292,000
Congo (DRC)	240,000
Côte d'Ivoire	119,000
Ethiopia	262,000
Germany	949,000
Guinea	414,000
India	185,000
Iran	1,931,000
Iraq	104,000
Kenya	238,000
Liberia	103,000
Nepal	126,000
Pakistan	1,202,000
Russia	128,000
Sudan	391,000
Sweden	179,000
Tanzania	544,000
Thailand	138,000
Uganda	204,000
United Kingdom	116,000
United States	660,000
Yugoslavia	502,000
Zambia	168,000

Source: UNHCR as at end 1998, numbers over 100,000 only (pre-Kosovo)

WWW.

ENVIRONMENTAL CHANGE: STRATEGIC IMPLICATIONS

Everyone agrees that the world's environment is changing but as yet there is little agreement about how much and what the long-term implications of that change will be. There are several reasons for the changes and mankind can do something to halt or reduce a number of these, but too often the likely costs of reform act as a brake on action.

The element of environmental change that is most worrying, and about which something can be done to reduce its rate, is generally known as global warming, an effect brought about by the build-up of 'greenhouse' gases in the atmosphere. The principle greenhouse gas is carbon dioxide

CO_2. Emissions increase with expanding populations and growing industrialisation since both lead to increased fossil fuel use and continued deforestation. Other greenhouse gases include methane, nitrous oxide, chloro-fluorocarbons (CFCs), and carbon tetrachloride; their emissions are also increasing due to human activity. CO_2 and other gases in the atmosphere act like the glass in a greenhouse: they let most of the rays of the sun through but then trap some of the resultant heat that would normally be radiated back into space.

The increase in global temperature over the last century is put at between 0.3° and 0.6°C. This could be the result of just natural variation or it could be created by greenhouse gas emissions. Whatever the cause, scientists are certain that further global warming will take place. It is forecast that if greenhouse emissions can be reduced by some 60 per cent, the temperature will rise another 0.2°C per decade but if emissions are not reduced, then the temperature rise is likely to be 1.0° by 2015 and about 3.0°C before the year 3000. The reason for the continued rise in temperature even if emissions are significantly reduced is that most greenhouse gases have a long atmospheric lifetime – over 50 years for CO_2.

One consequence of global warming is a rise in sea level caused mainly by the thermal expansion of the sea, and melting mountain glaciers, Greenland sheet ice and the West Antarctic Sheet. (Antarctica contains 90 per cent of the world's ice; most of this is land ice and less likely to melt than sea ice.) Over the past 100 years the rise in sea level has been estimated as being between 1 and 2 centimetres per decade. One prediction has it that without a reduction in greenhouse gases, the sea level could rise some 18 centimetres by 2030 and 44 centimetres by 2070; even with a reduction of emissions the sea will continue to rise at a rate about 30 per cent below these estimates. The warmer sea water becomes, the greater is its expansion due to temperature rise: a 1° rise at 5° will expand water by one part per 10,000; at 25° the expansion after a 1° rise will be by three parts per 10,000 and that could cause a 3 centimetre increase in sea level. The first areas to be affected by rising sea level will be populated river deltas and Pacific and Indian Ocean atolls and islands. Over 300 atolls could disappear but they will become uninhabitable earlier as they suffer more frequent storms and freshwater sources become saline: already some islets off Kiribati have been submerged. The problem for deltas is accentuated by the fact that land there is often sinking due either to excessive extraction of drinking water or loss of soil as up-stream dams trap the silt that formerly replenished the land. Most of the coastal cities at risk can probably afford the sea defences to protect themselves and to adapt their ports to the changed conditions, but the work will be expensive. One estimate puts the cost of protecting North America from inundation by a 1 metre rise in sea level at $106 billion; for the Northern Mediterranean coast, $21 billion. Other consequences of a higher sea level are increased shoreline erosion, more coastal flooding, flooding of coastal wetlands, increased salinity in estuaries and aquifers. Bangladesh is the country most at risk: some 6 million of its people there live below 1 metre above sea level.

The effect of global warming inland will be more mixed: some areas will gain from it and others will lose. There will be little change at the

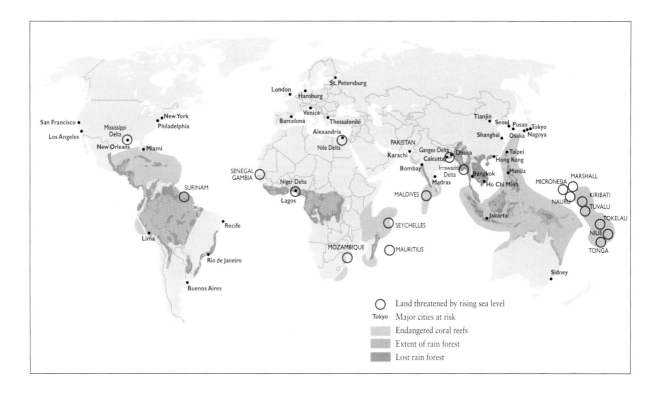

Land threatened by rising sea level

Tokyo Major cities at risk

Endangered coral reefs

Extent of rain forest

Lost rain forest

equator, more to its north and south. Winters will become shorter while summers will be longer. In high northern latitudes it will be wetter in the winter but drier in the summer. There will be more rain in the tropics but less in the sub-tropics. There will be drier soil over wide areas. One estimate predicts that the harvest from Midwest America could be cut by a third causing a reduction of grain exports of 70 per cent. New land for crops will appear in Canada and Siberia. Arid areas in North Africa and the Horn of Africa are likely to become drier still. No conclusive opinion has yet been published on whether global warming will assist or hinder world food production overall. Agriculture already contributes some 14 per cent of greenhouse gases; methane is produced by rice cultivation and by cattle and sheep, while nitrogen fertilisers contribute to nitrous oxide emissions. With the fast growing world population agriculture will have to expand dramatically and this could lead to increased global warming. However, increased levels of CO_2 stimulate extra growth in crops such as wheat, rice and soya bean.

Another factor contributing to global warming is the loss of rain forests cut down to make way for agriculture or to provide timber and fuel. This has a number of malign effects, one of the most serious being the total extinction of large numbers of plant, animal, bird and insect species. In relation to global warming, deforestation generates an increase in CO_2 emissions from the burning of cleared vegetation and timber waste. It also reduces the environment's ability to absorb CO_2 through photosynthesis. In addition, deforestation inevitably causes erosion particularly where rainfall is heavy and tons of soil are washed away. The loss of forest also causes a loss of evapotranspiration, which results in less cloud cover and therefore less rain. Finally, without forest wood

The possible effects of global warming.

people turn to burning animal dung and crop residues, thus depriving the soil of nutrients.

In addition to global warming, the ozone layer is being damaged. Ozone is found in the atmosphere in varying concentrations between sea level and 60 kilometres altitude. Ozone at around 25 kilometres altitude filters out ultra-violet C radiation that causes sunburn, eye-damage and skin cancer. But the gas is being depleted by the action of chloro-fluorocarbons (CFCs). The main effect of CFCs has been the creation of an ozone 'hole' over the Antarctic each spring, a hole that is increasing in size each year. There has also been a general reduction of about 5 per cent in ozone over the mid-latitudes of both hemispheres. CFCs are produced by solvents such as methyl chloroform, carbontetrachloride and CFC 113 (25 per cent) and by aerosols, foams, refrigeration and air-conditioning which employ CFC 11 and 12 (71 per cent). Halon 1301 in fire extinguishers (4 per cent) has the same effect. CFCs release chlorine that combines with ozone; it remains in the atmosphere for some 100 years.

Action is being taken in three areas to redress the harm being done to the environment. The Montreal Protocol of 1987, which came into force in 1989, required that the manufacture of CFCs be ended by 1996 in industrialised countries and by 2006 in developing countries. Halting the destruction of the rain forests is more difficult as the countries where they are situated are among the poorest in the world.

Establishing the parameters of global warming is the task of the Intergovernmental Panel on Climate Change set up by the World Meteorological Organisation and the United Nations Environment Programme. In 1990 it published reports on 'Climate Change: IPCC Scientific Assessment', 'IPCC Impact Assessment' and 'IPCC Response Strategies'. From these the Framework Convention on Climate Change (FCCC) was negotiated at Rio de Janeiro in 1992 and came into force in 1994. The convention was reinforced by a protocol agreed at Kyoto in 1997 and is the subject of annual follow-up meetings. The aim of FCCC is to achieve a 5 per cent improvement on 1990 levels of greenhouse gas emissions. How to achieve this aim has been the subject of many debates which have resulted in the introduction of a number of mechanisms. Full agreement on what should be done and how it should be reached is expected to be decided at the year 2000 meeting.

The situation is improving gradually. Nevertheless, global warming and its associated rise in sea levels will continue, land will be lost and populations will have to be relocated but the numbers involved will be small compared with the forecasts of the rise in the world's population. This reached 6 billion on 12 October 1999 and is forecast to rise to 8 billion by 2028. Populations in the developed world are expected to decline and the largest increases will occur in the least developed countries. Refugee problems, accusations of failing to meet environmental targets and the cost of feeding, providing fresh water for and educating the extra millions will cause local discontent and international disagreement but should not lead to war.

Estimated annual loss of natural tropical forest (millions of hectares)			
	Loss	%	Total in 1990
Africa	4.1	0.72	527
Continental Asia	1.9	1.2	139
Malay Archipelago	2.0	1.1	171
Central America	1.2	0.97	115
South America	6.2	0.7	803

Source FAO 1993

Global carbon dioxide emissions (1,000 million tonnes)	
5.5	1950
9	1960
15	1970
20	1980
22	1990
24	1996

Source: CDIAC 1999

It must be stressed that accurate data, on which to base exact predictions, is not available. However, at the two ends of the spectrum, there are those that claim that the ecological crisis is a myth and those who are so committed to the cause of environmentalism that they pursue policies that may also damage the eco-system. Overreaction is normally counter-productive and can lead to unforeseen consequences. Examples of this include the release by animal activists of farmed mink that devastated neighbouring wildlife and the Greenpeace action that stopped an oilrig from being sunk in deep sea, leading to more pollution when it was dismantled on shore.

Bibliography and Web Sites

Grainger, Alan, *Controlling Tropical Forest*, Earthscan Publications, 1993

Houghton, J.T.H., Jenkins, G.J.J. and Ephraums, J.J.E. (eds) *Climate Change: The IPCC Scientific Assessment*, Cambridge, 1990

Houghton, John, *Global Warming: The Complete Briefing*, Lion Publishing, 1994

Rootes, Christopher (ed.), *Environmental Movements*, Frank Cass, 1999

Sorrel, Steve, and Jim Skea (eds), *Pollution for Sale: emissions trading and joint implementation*, Edward Elgar, 1999

Greenhouse Gases, UNEP/GEMS No. 1, 1987

The Impact of Ozone Layer Depletion, UNEP/GEMS No. 7, 1992

The Ozone Layer, UNEP/GEMS No. 2, 1987

Global warming and climate change: www.cru.uea.ac.uk/tiempo

Greenpeace: www.gn.apc.org

Oxford Centre for the Environment, Ethics and Society: http//users.ox.ac.uk/~ocees

The UN Framework Convention on Climate Change: www.unfccc.de

United Nations Environmental Programme: www.unep.org

Estimated changes by 2030, warming in °C		
	winter	summer
Central North America	+2–4	+2–3
Southern Asia	+1–2	
Sahel	+1–3	
Southern Europe	+2	+2–3
Australia	+2	+1–2

Precipitation % change		
	winter	summer
Central North America	+0–15	-5–10
Southern Asia	little	+5–15
Sahel	–	marginal +
Southern Europe	some+	-5–15
Australia	–	+10

Source IPCC model

FREEDOM OF THE SEAS: VULNERABLE ROUTES AND PIRACY

Freedom of the High Seas is a cardinal principle of international law. However, it is not an unrestrained freedom as measures are necessary to ensure navigational safety, the protection of the marine environment, and the orderly exploitation of the seas' resources. There are a number of maritime arms control agreements, notably the Nuclear Weapon Free Zones, described on pages 35–7 and the Russian/US agreements on limiting the numbers of nuclear ballistic missiles deployed on submarines. The Partial Test Ban Treaty that prohibited nuclear test explosions in outer space and under water was signed by 121 states in 1963; it will be replaced by the Comprehensive Test Ban Treaty when this eventually comes into force.

In 1958 the UN agreed a number of conventions and in 1982 completed the Comprehensive Convention on the Law of the Sea that defines the jurisdiction of coastal states and the 'Freedom of the Seas'. The Convention came into force in 1994 after 60 states had ratified the treaty; to date 132 states have joined the regime but the US has still not ratified its signature.

The baseline between internal waters and the sea is normally the low-water mark along the shore. Coastal states may claim a zone of territorial sea up to 12 miles offshore through which all ships have the right of innocent passage (any passage not prejudicial to the peace, good order and security of the coastal state). Shipping is afforded unimpeded right of transit (this applies in straits) where territorial waters extend across an international strait (one that connects two areas of high seas). Coastal states may also enforce their customs, fiscal, immigration and sanitary laws over a further 12-mile zone, known as a contiguous zone, where the same freedoms apply as to the high seas. States have the right to exploit resources of the sea and the seabed in a 200-mile Exclusive Economic Zone (EEZ). Military activity is not forbidden in EEZs. The Convention has ruled that the continental shelf shall also be 200 miles wide and that where it is wider then the International Sea-Bed Authority (ISBA) will delineate it in accordance with agreed guidelines. The waters of an EEZ or above a continental shelf are governed by the same rules as the high seas.

The Convention also grants archipelagic states the right to establish perimeter baselines and to have sovereignty over the waters within them.

Incidents of piracy in 1996.

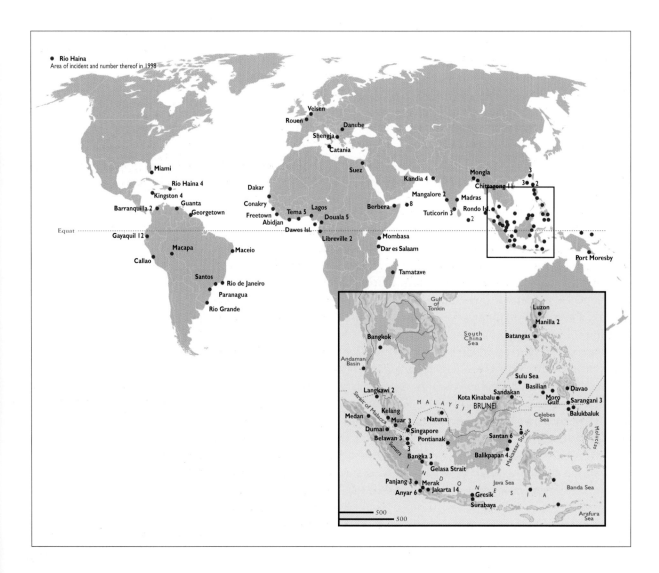

To maintain the freedoms of navigation and overflight in archipelagos, archipelagic sea lanes, where there is a right to transit, are created. Outside the lanes, ships have the right of innocent passage through archipelagic waters. The seabed beyond national jurisdictions is known as 'the area' and the ISBA is responsible for regulating the exploitation of resources there.

Problems over maritime borders naturally arise when the waters between two states have to be divided – the case of the Greek-Turkish dispute is covered on pages 99–101. Normally the division is based on the median line.

Although there are still maritime 'choke points' which if blocked would cause considerable inconvenience, most countries can be reached by alternative sea-routes, overland or by pipeline, by air or by a combination of these. The blocking of 'choke points' by naval forces employing submarines or mines is possible but the level of retaliation that can be mounted today could make this counter-productive and the threat of shore-based missiles against shipping would swiftly be opposed by air power. The sea is still a vital component in the enforcement of sanctions, the utility of which is discussed at pages 62–4.

Today, the old threat of piracy has returned and the number of incidents grew substantially in the early 1990s. However, the number of incidents in 1998 decreased by 17 per cent from 1997 with only East Africa showing an increase. The two regions most affected by piracy are the South China Sea, followed by South America and the Caribbean. In 1998 a total of 210 incidents were reported to the International Maritime Organisation and in the first nine months of 1999 there were 180 reported incidents were reported. The scale of acts of piracy varies considerably from the hijacking of ships and the theft of their complete cargo, down to armed robbery from private yachts often at anchor. Hijacking appears to be on the increase with ten cases reported between June 1998 and December 1999. Roughly $200 million worth of goods are taken by pirates each year. But one report suggests that only about half the total acts of piracy are reported. Reasons for not reporting include: avoiding delay while making the report; avoiding accusations that negligence allowed the attack to be successful; offending host countries; and incurring higher insurance premiums. Smugglers are unlikely to report becoming victims of piracy.

In territorial waters the responsibility for countering piracy lies with the government concerned and on the high seas each government is responsible for the safety of its own ships. Little, therefore, is done to prevent piracy on the high seas and unless coastal states cooperate and allow 'hot-pursuit' into their territorial waters, pirates can escape relatively easily. The best example of anti-pirate operations is in the Malacca Strait where the International Maritime Bureau has established a Regional Piracy Centre giving a 24-hour service in both receiving reports and providing warnings. Indonesia, Malaysia and Singapore have established coordinated patrols. These measures have proved effective and the number of incidents dropped from thirty-two in 1991 to six in 1998.

Freedom of the high seas: major choke-points

Bab el Mandab
Baltic Exits
Barents Sea
Korean Straits
Panama Canal
Straits of Gibraltar
Straits of Hormuz
Straits of Malacca
Suez Canal
Sundra and Lombak Straits

Major non-signatories of the Law of the Sea

Albania
Ecuador
Eritrea
Germany
Israel
Peru
Syria
Turkey
United States

Bibliography and Web Sites

Churchill, R.R., and A.V. Lowe, *The Law of the Sea*, third edition, Juris Publications, 1999

Goldbla, Jozef (ed.), *Maritime Security: The Building of Confidence*, UN Institute for Disarmament Research, 1992

Report on Acts of Piracy and Armed Robbery at Sea, 1999 (Annual) International Maritime Organisation

International Maritime Organisation: www.imo.org

Ocean and Law of the Sea Homepage: www.un.org/depts/los/index

TERRORISM: WARFARE OF THE UNDERDOG

The world is becoming increasingly concerned about terrorism as it becomes more likely that terrorists could acquire and use nuclear, chemical and biological weapons. Terrorism is not new. There are many instances throughout history of terrorist tactics being employed for a variety of reasons: the Assassin Sect in the Middle East in the twelfth and thirteenth centuries and the Thugs in India, to name but two. The statistics of international terrorism have been relatively consistent for the last decade, bar one or two horrific incidents, such as the attacks on US embassies in East Africa, which distort the figures. Statistics on domestic terrorist operations are more difficult to quantify and obviously vary more significantly as terrorist campaigns are defeated or initiated. In December 1999 the UN General Assembly voted to establish the International Convention for the Suppression of the Financing of Terrorism, which will aim to deny terrorist groups funds held in other countries.

There is no globally accepted definition of terrorism. The United States employs the following descriptions: 'the term terrorism means premeditated, politically motivated violence perpetrated against non-combatant targets by subnational groups or clandestine agents, usually intended to influence an audience'; 'the term international terrorism means terrorism involving the citizens or territory of more than one country'; 'the term terrorist group means any group practicing, or that has significant subgroups that practice, international terrorism'. A British definition is more succinct: 'Terrorism means the use of violence for political ends, and includes any use of violence for the purpose of putting the public or any section of the public in fear.' Once, the main aim of terrorism was to gain publicity for whatever cause was espoused; terrorists realised that causing too horrendous a scale of casualties was usually counter-productive in that it revolted public opinion and provoked the authorities into taking more effective action. (Of course, this counter-action sometimes actually helped the terrorist cause.) Modern terrorism is less easy to define but there is certainly now no restraint on the scale of its atrocities. It is conducted far more by ideological extremists, often with a strong if misguided religious belief. Where 'old' terrorists had a political or national cause that they cited as the motivation for resorting to action, today's terrorists have a more fanatical desire to punish rather than to influence and they rarely claim their successes. Groups are much harder to penetrate and tend to be much more professional in their operations.

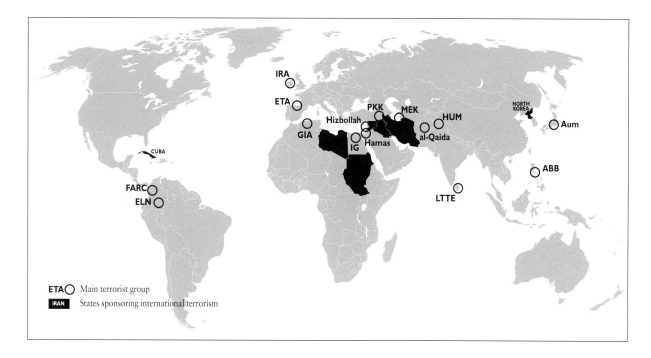

ETA ◯ Main terrorist group
IRAN ▪ States sponsoring international terrorism

Main terrorist organisations and the US assessment of states sponsoring international terrorism.

Before examining terrorism further, it is necessary to distinguish between the phenomenon and the legitimate use of force. The use of force by a state is legitimate if it is used as the law permits. It should strengthen the public's confidence in the rule of law and aim to improve both personal safety and the security of possessions. It should also prevent the formation of vigilante groups and the carrying of weapons for personal protection. The statement 'one man's terrorist is another man's freedom fighter' is often true. However, 'freedom fighters' who employ terrorism must expect to be labelled terrorists; there is a fine line between the two. For example Hizbollah rocket attacks on Israeli towns and settlements are clearly terrorism while Hizbollah ambushes of Israeli troops in South Lebanon can be considered legitimate military operations.

Most democratic governments apply the following policy principles in combating terrorism: there must be no concessions to hostage-takers or other terrorists; the fight against terrorism needs close international cooperation; the fight against terrorism requires the highest standards of human rights behaviour; the rule of law applies equally to suspected terrorists and the security forces. These principles are not always followed, often with unfortunate results for the authorities concerned. Certainly negotiating for the release of hostages only encourages further hostage-taking. The temptation to fight terrorism with terrorism is great but it usually leads to the discredit of the government authorising such tactics.

Countering terrorism is not easy; overreaction is what the terrorist wants. The Israeli policy of responding to terrorist attack by bombing suspected terrorist camps usually leads to civilian casualties and in the storm of adverse publicity the original terrorist attack, which may have killed women and children, is forgotten. Israel's policy of an eye for an

Terrorism: Warfare of the Underdog	
Acronym	Terrorist Group
ABB	Alex Boncayao Brigade
Al-Qaida	Usama Bin Laden
Aum	Aum Shinrikyo (Supreme Truth)
ELN	Ejército Liberación Nacional
ETA	Euzkadi Ta Askatasuna
FARC	Fuerzas Armadas de la Revolución Colombiana
GIA	Groupe Islamique Armée
Hamas	Islamic Resistance Movement
Hizbollah	Islamic Jihad (Party of God)
HUM	Harakat ul-Mujahedin
IG	al-Gama'at al-Ismamiyya
IRA	Irish Republican Army
LTTE	Liberation Tigers of Tamil Eelam
MEK	Mujahedin-e Khalq
PKK	Partiya Karkaren Kurdistan
SL	Sendero Luminoso (Shining Path)

US Embassy, Nairobi, Kenya. The bomb killed 250 people, November 1998. (US Department of Defense)

eye (or rather twelve eyes for an eye) has not yet succeeded in halting terrorist attacks on Israeli targets. In fact, aerial bombing in retaliation for terrorist activity is usually internationally condemned, as the US found out when it took action against Colonel Ghadaffi's Libya in 1986 after an attack on US servicemen in Berlin. The reaction was the same after cruise missile strikes on a factory in Sudan and training camps in Afghanistan linked to Usama Bin Laden, who was strongly suspected of organising the bomb attacks against the US embassies in Kenya and Tanzania in 1998. On only one occasion have sanctions imposed after a terrorist attack proved successful – those imposed on Libya over the involvement of Libyan nationals in the bombing of the PanAm flight over Lockerbie in December 1988. They took nearly ten years to have an effect.

The only proven method of defeating terrorists is by infiltration of the group and by patient intelligence and police work; this is a long and often painful process. However, other measures that can aid the international fight against terrorism include: preventing fund-raising for terrorist causes; freezing assets; sharing intelligence; allowing extradition; assistance with counter-terrorist training; urging all states to comply with the eleven, soon to be twelve, United Nations conventions on counter-terrorism. The US takes terrorism seriously, particularly as it is aware that it is seen as 'the Great Satan' by many opposed to US policies. The financial year 2000 Budget provides $11 billion for counter-terrorism. Plans are in hand to establish civil defence in 120 US cities to react to the effects of terrorist use of chemical or biological weapons.

The United States has taken the lead in countering international terrorism. Each year it publishes a list of those states it considers to be sponsors of terrorism and in 1999 seven states were named: Cuba, Iran, Iraq, Libya, North Korea, Sudan and Syria. The US also publishes descriptions of some thirty terrorist groups. One Islamist terrorist organisation, Harakat ul-Mujahedin, which operates in Kashmir, is claimed by press sources to be funded by the Pakistani Intelligence Services.

The number of international terrorist attacks varies each year and ranged between 440 in 1995 and 273 in 1998; the number of attacks in each region does not alter significantly, other than in Western Europe where 272 attacks were recorded in 1995 and only 48 in 1998. Western Europe, Latin America and the Middle East are the regions most affected by international terrorism.

The most difficult type of terrorist to defeat is the suicide bomber and this type of activist often achieves the most dramatic results. Three car bombs in Lebanon in 1983 killed 241 US marines, 58 French and 60 Israeli soldiers, and in February and March 1996 four suicide bombers killed 56 Israelis in Tel Aviv and Jerusalem, influencing the May 1996 election, which ended Labour Party rule. So far, only Islam and the Sri Lankan Tamil Tigers have produced volunteers to carry out such attacks. However, a new development is the arrival of lone fanatics, often suffering from some feeling of injustice, who have carried out terrorist acts including the Oklahoma City bomb, that at the Atlanta Olympics, and most recently the explosions in London aimed at the Black, Indian and Homosexual communities. Another new development has been the

Selected major terrorist attacks		
Event	Year	Dead (injured)
Bologna railway station	1980	84
US Embassy, Beirut	1983	47
US barracks, Lebanon	1983	239
French barracks, Lebanon	1983	58
Israeli HQ, Tyre	1983	60
Pan-Am, Lockerbie	1988	270
Jewish Centre, Buenos Aires	1994	96
Chemical weapons on Tokyo subway	1995	10(5000)
Oklahoma office block	1995	168
Jerusalem bus	1996	26
Tel Aviv shopping mall	1996	20
Suicide bomber, Colombo	1996	90
US Embassy, Nairobi	1998	250
Omagh	1998	28

emergence of the 'millionaire' terrorist in the form of the Saudi Arabian Usama Bin Laden who it is claimed is conducting a personal vendetta against the United States. At the bottom end of the terrorist scale are the anti-abortionists, who have bombed clinics in the US, and animal rightists who release mink, attack experimental stations that use animals and disturb hunts. A new form of terrorism is expected to be employed in attacking information technology systems and is known as cyber-terrorism.

So far the use of weapons of mass destruction by terrorists has been limited, the best known example being the release of nerve gas into the Tokyo subway system by the Aum Shinrikyo cult. The attack killed ten and injured as many as 5,000 people in March 1995; a more professional attack could have caused thousands of deaths. Chemical and biological weapons are far easier to manufacture and to smuggle into a target country than nuclear or radioactive weapons. Known as 'catastrophic terrorism', the scale of casualties that could be caused by chemical and biological weapons requires their use to be forestalled and this means a much-increased covert intelligence effort.

However, of the many terrorist campaigns, there are few that can claim success. The lengthy campaigns waged and in some cases still being waged are witness to this. The Irish Republican Army (IRA), Euzkadi Ta Askatasuna (ETA), Kurdistan Workers Party (PKK), Liberation Tigers of Tamil Eelam (LTTE), Revolutionary Armed Forces of Colombia (FARC) have all still not achieved their political aims after over twenty years of violence. But then none of them has totally given up the struggle either.

Bibliography and Web Site

Patterns of Global Terrorism, United States Department of State, annually

Falkenrath, R., R. Newman, B. Theyer, *America's Achilles Heel; NBC Terrorism and Covert Attack*, MIT Press, 1998

Higgins, Rosalyn, and Maurice Flory (eds), *Terrorism and International Law*, Routledge, 1996

Hoffman, Bruce, *Inside Terrorism*, Victor Gollancz, 1998

Kegley Jr, Charles W., *International Terrorism: Characteristics, Causes and Controls*, St Martin's Press, 1990

Reich, Walter (ed.), *Origins of Terrorism: Psychology, Ideology and States of Mind*, Woodrow Wilson International Centre/Cambridge University Press, 1990

Roberts, Brad (ed.), *Terrorism with Chemical and Biological Weapons: Calibrating Risks and Responses*, Chemical and Biological Arms Control Institute, 1997

Tanter, Raymond, *Rogue Regimes: Terror and Proliferation*, St Martin's Press, 1998

www.   US State Department-Counter terrorism: www.state.gov/www/global/terrorism

ANTI-PERSONNEL MINES: CIVIL WAR'S LEGACY

The initiative to complete a treaty against anti-personnel mines was taken by Canada in October 1996, as UN efforts to achieve agreement appeared to be making no progress. Until 1999, international law on the issue was set out in the 1980 UN Weapons Convention, the full title of which is 'Convention on Prohibitions or Restrictions on the Use of Certain

Conventional Weapons which May be Deemed to be Excessively Injurious or to have Indiscriminate Effects'. The Convention covered not only mines and booby-traps but items such as dumdum bullets, weapons that fragment into pieces undetectable by X-rays and incendiaries. It was a follow-on to the 1949 Geneva Convention on the Protection of War Victims. Only forty-one states became parties to the Convention, which only covered clashes between states and not internal armed conflict, despite the fact that the latter most frequently generates the indiscriminate laying of mines. A Protocol to the Convention has been opened for signature and has been approved by the US Senate. The Protocol bans the use of non-detectable anti-personnel mines (some were used by the Argentinians in the Falklands) and of mines equipped with anti-handling devices. Non-self-destructing and non-self-deactivating mines may only be laid in marked areas and signatories are committed to not exporting anti-personnel mines.

The Convention on the Prohibition of the Use, Stockpiling, Production and Transfer of Anti-Personnel Mines and on Their Destruction, or Land Mine Treaty for short (also known as the Ottawa Convention), came into force on 1 March 1999, six months after the fortieth ratification. By the end of 1999 136 countries had signed the Treaty and 89 had ratified it. However, a number of significant states have not yet become signatories, including the US, China and Russia, the first two having ratified the 1980 Convention and Russia having signed but not ratified it. It is more understandable that countries which have

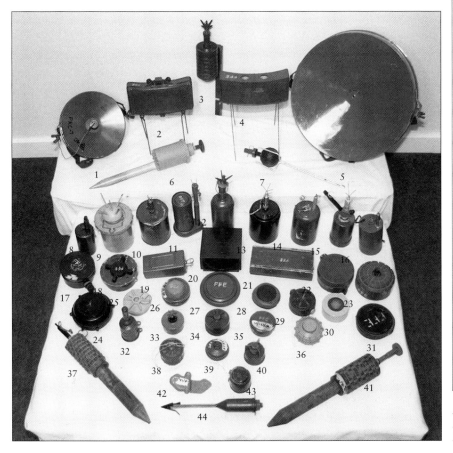

Anti-personnel mines. (Battlefield Engineering Wing, Royal Engineers)

Index of Mines		
1. Soviet	MON-100	
2. Soviet	MON-50	
3. Yugoslav	PMR 3	
4. Yugoslav	MRUD	
5. Soviet	MON-200	
6. Italy	P-25	
7. Vietnam	B-40	
8. China	Type 69	
9. Italy	V-69	
10. USA	M161A	
11. USA	M2A1	
12. Yugoslav	PROM 1	
13. Czech	PP-MI-SR	
14. Soviet	OZM 4	
15. Bulgaria	PSM 1	
16. Soviet	OZM 3	
17. Hungary	GYATA-64	
18. Soviet	PMN-2	
19. Israel	No 4	
20. Czech	PP MI-D	
21. Soviet	PMD-6	
22. Soviet	PMN	
23. Italy	VAR/100/SP	
24. Germany	PPM 2	
25. Belgium	PRB M409	
26. Italy	MAUS 1	
27. Italy	LORIE AP	
28. Italy	SB 33	
29. Argentina	FMK 1	
30. Germany	DM 11	
31. Yugoslav	PMA 3	
32. Vietnam	MBV-78A2	
33. Yugoslav	PMA 2	
34. Spain	P-4-B	
35. China	Type 72	
36. Italy	TS-50	
37. Yugoslav	PMR 2A	
38. South Africa	R2M1	
39. France	MI ID AP 51	
40. France	MI AD DV 59	
41. Yugoslav	PMR 2AS	
42. Soviet	PFM-1	
43. Vietnam	MD-82B	
44. France	MI AD DV PIQUET	

23

been involved in war in recent years have not signed; these include Egypt, Israel, India, Iran, Iraq, Pakistan, Saudi Arabia, Turkey, Vietnam and Yugoslavia. Neither North nor South Korea has signed as both rely heavily on the use of anti-personnel mines to protect their border from infiltration. The US cites the defence of South Korea as a reason why it has not signed; it is prepared to sign by 2006 if an effective replacement weapon can be developed.

There are sound military arguments for the use of anti-personnel mines in war by responsible states that record where and in what pattern mines have been laid, mark the perimeters of minefields and then lift the mines once there is no longer a need for the field. For example, during the Korean War 1950–3 when the Chinese and North Koreans employed attack by massed infantry, anti-personnel mines were essential to prevent the total over-running of defensive positions. Small forward observation posts that could be easily surprised gained a degree of protection from the weapon and anti-personnel mines laid among anti-tank mines made the task of clearing paths through a field slower and more dangerous. However, modern methods of laying minefields now include delivery from the air and from rocket and artillery delivered canisters; minefield maps of these cannot be drawn accurately. The British 'airfield runway attack' bomb not only cratered the runway but scattered anti-personnel mines to hamper repair work, and the US Gator system, which is delivered by aircraft, consists of 74 anti-tank and 22 anti-personnel mines all inter-linked by wire, which cover an area some 100 metres long. There are also 'smart' mines, which are deactivated after a set time; the new treaty bans these too although there had been efforts to have them excluded from its terms.

The overwhelming proportion of mine casualties result from mines laid without records or warning markers in a number of civil wars and in

Land mines: affected countries and the Ottawa Convention.

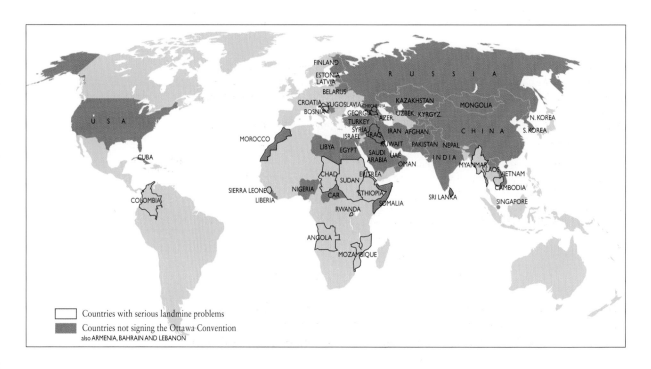

operations such as the Soviet Union's intervention in Afghanistan. There is now some controversy over the number of mines actually scattered in these wars and the organisations involved in mine clearance have reduced earlier estimates. The UN worldwide estimate indicates there are 110 million mines; the mine-clearing organisations say 2.2 million. There is no doubt that significant numbers of casualties are caused by anti-personnel mines. These are predominantly civilians and include a large number of children.

Mine clearance is taking place in virtually all the countries that have suffered from widespread use of the weapons. There is a thriving demining industry with non-governmental organisations and commercial companies supervising demining and training local people to clear the explosives safely.

There are still areas of the world, however, where anti-personnel mines are being laid indiscriminately. It is claimed that the Russians have dropped them in both Chechnya and Georgia; the Georgians too have used them in raids on Abkhazia. Both the Serbs and the Kosovo Liberation Army employed anti-personnel mines in Kosovo where over 200 civilians have been killed by them and by unexploded NATO bombs.

The effectiveness of the new treaty still has to be proven: there are large stocks of anti-personnel mines in many countries and treaty signatories have agreed to destroy them by March 2003. But no doubt attempts will be made to acquire stocks, hide them and create a black market. There is no provision for imposing sanctions on countries that have not signed the convention and continue to export mines.

Mines to be cleared: estimates		
Country	Red Cross	HALO Trust
Afghanistan	10m	400–600,000
Angola	10–20m	500,000
Abkhazia	–	20,000
Cambodia	4–6m	300,000
Chechnya*	(1–2m)	25–50,000
Mozambique	3m	250–300,000
Nagomo-Karabakh	–	25–40,000
Southern Sudan	(500k–2m)	40,000
Iran	16m	?
Iraq	10m	?
Bosnia-Herzegovina	6m	?
Vietnam	3.5m	?
Croatia	3m	?

? no estimates
* not including mines laid in 1999
– no Red Cross estimates

Bibliography and Web Sites

Cornish, Paul, *Anti-Personnel Mines: Controlling the Plague of 'Butterflies'*, Royal Institute for International Affairs, 1994

Smith, Chris (ed.), *The Military Utility of Landmines?* Centre for Defence Studies, King's College, 1996

Disarmament Forum, UN Institute for Disarmament Research, 1999

Hidden Killers, US Department of State, Office of Humanitarian Demining Programs, 1998

Landmines and the CCW Review Conference, UN Institute for Disarmament Research, 1995

Landmine Monitor Report 1999: Towards a Mine-Free World, Landmine Monitor Core Group, Human Rights Watch, 1999

Report for the Review Conference on the 1980 UN Convention, International Committee of the Red Cross, 1994

Cambodian Mine Action Centre: www.camnet.com.kh/cmac
Canadian Mine Action Centre: http://eagle.ucb.ns.ca/demine
International Campaign to Ban Landmines: www.icbl.org/lm/1999
Landmine Survivors Network: www.landminesurvivors.org
UN Institute for Disarmament Research: www.unog.ch/UNIDIR

DRUGS: A TRULY GLOBAL PROBLEM

Drugs, their use and distribution probably cause more problems in the world today than anything else. The list is endless: the impact on mental and physical health and its human and financial cost; the spread of AIDS;

crime to pay for drugs; turf wars between pushers at street level; outright war between producers at country level; terrorism to deter governments in producing countries from cracking down on trafficking; money laundering; bribery and corruption. The battle against drugs is fought on a number of levels. The eradication of crops, efforts to eliminate processing, interception during transit, seizure at ports of entry, action to stop street sales and education to deter use all play a part, but as yet without much success. The riches that can be gained by those involved in the production and supply chain are too tempting even in the face of the undoubted successes authorities achieve in interrupting production and intercepting consignments. Accurate statistics for illegal activity are hard to calculate but it has been estimated that over 160 million users spend some $400 billion on drugs each year.

There are five main types of drugs: narcotics, stimulants, depressants, hallucinogens and cannabis. Narcotics produce a general sense of well-being and euphoria. The narcotic heroin is sythesised from the opium poppy. Opium poppies are cultivated in the 'golden triangle' of the Shan states of Myanmar, Laos and north-west Thailand; in central Afghanistan; astride the Afghan/Pakistan border; and in Mexico and Colombia. In 1998 over 210,000 hectares were under cultivation with the potential of producing 310 metric tons of heroin sufficient for 31 billion 'bags' or single doses. The trade in heroin attracts dealers because addicts can take the drug for far longer than, for example, cocaine, which can kill a constant user within five years. High purity heroin can be sniffed and so its use could avoid the use of needles. Most heroin reaches Europe through Turkey and the Balkans. From there, mainly controlled by Turkish Mafia, it is transported either on the northern route via Romania, Hungary, Slovakia or the Czech Republic, or the southern route through Greece, Albania, Former Yugoslav Republic of Macedonia (FYROM), Croatia, and Slovenia.

The second group of drugs, stimulants, produce exhilaration; they also reduce appetite and help to keep the user awake. Cocaine is the most potent stimulant and is extracted from the leaf of the coca plant that is indigenous to the Andean highlands and is now cultivated in Bolivia, Peru and Colombia, where the size of the crop has doubled in the last ten years. The peak year for production was 1995 when close to 215,000 hectares were under cultivation, producing a potential 780 tons of cocaine. In 1998 190,800 hectares were cultivated producing a potential 555 tons of cocaine. However, Colombian cultivation doubled from a potential of 80 tons in 1995 to 165 tons in 1998; it also refines most of the crop from Peru and Bolivia. The US has cooperative programmes with producer countries to reduce the size of the annual crop; the programmes have been successful in Bolivia and Peru and the compensatory scheme in Bolivia has been ended. The reduced production in these two countries has encouraged Colombian syndicates to increase cultivation, despite spraying operations, for the last three years. Cocaine reaches the US through either Central America or the Caribbean, with the former being the current preferred route. Large-scale seizures have been achieved: in 1998 nearly 50 tons was intercepted by the Central American authorities and 9 tons in the Caribbean.

Countries determined by the US as major illicit drug producers or drug transiters	
Afghanistan	Hong Kong
Aruba	India
Bahamas	Jamaica
Belize	Laos
Bolivia	Mexico
Brazil	Nigeria
Burma	Pakistan
Cambodia	Panama
China	Paraguay
Colombia	Peru
Dominica	Taiwan
Ecuador	Thailand
Guatemala	Venezuela
Haiti	Vietnam

Source: White House, December 1998

Other types of drugs are abused on a far smaller scale. They are: depressants – mainly barbiturates and benzodiazepines; hallucinogens – mescaline produced from the peyote cactus and LSD (lysergic acid diethylamide); cannabis – derived from the hemp plant and containing tetrahydrocannabinol (THC) which can induce a sense of well-being and dreamy relaxation; marijuana and hashish are both derived from cannabis. Marijuana is the most commonly used drug in the US. In a 1996 national survey it was estimated that one-third of the population had used marijuana at least once, over 18 million at least once in the previous twelve months. Although most marijuana is smuggled into the US, it can be grown outdoors there either as a crop or in a domestic garden. Indoor growing allows production round the year. One outdoor operation in the US produced 16,000 plants estimated to be worth $27 million when seized; in 1997 worldwide some 4 million plants were eradicated which could have been processed into 1,820 tons of marijuana.

Estimating the international value of drug-trafficking is problematical because of the many variables involved. For example, there is a wide range of street prices in the US dependent on the city in which the purchase is made – the per gram price for cocaine in 1997 in Miami being half that in New York. 'Farmgate' prices naturally vary from crop to crop and country to country. Opium prices in Asia varied from $50 per kilo in Afghanistan to $627 in Vietnam, with the Colombian price being $580.

Opium poppies. (US Drug Enforcement Agency)

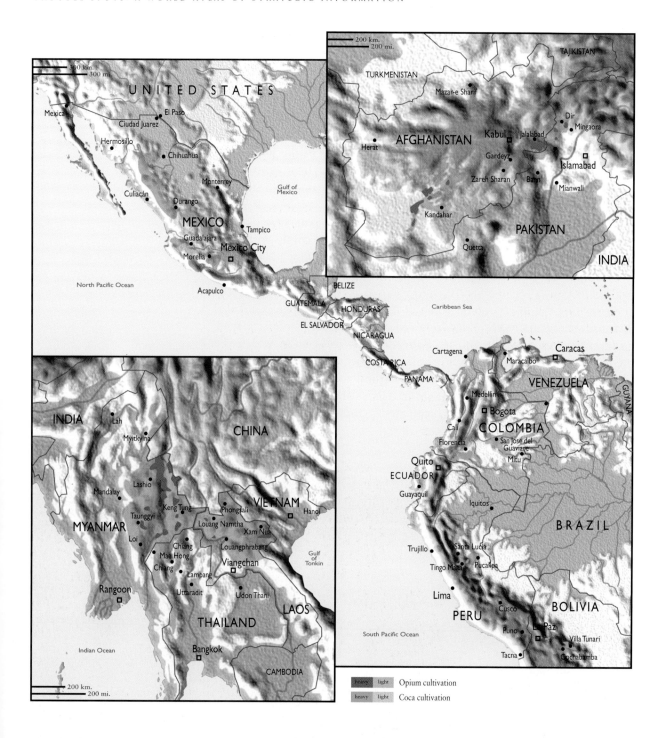

Main drug-producing areas in Asia and Latin America.

Some 200,000 families in Afghanistan were estimated to be involved in drug cultivation, earning $560 per annum; in Colombia there were 80,000 families earning $1,680. Both wholesale and retail prices of heroin and cocaine have been going down for twelve years. Heroin is about three times as expensive in the US than in Europe, while cocaine is twice as expensive in Europe as in the US. European retail prices for both cocaine and heroin are at least double the wholesale price. Estimates made in 1992 put the cost of 1 kilo of cocaine paste at between $200 and $775 depending on the source; 1 kilo of cocaine hydrochloride (HCI) was $800–$8,500. In Miami the wholesale price varied from $14,500 to $25,000 for 80 per cent purity and the street price for 1 gram of 55 per cent purity was between $40 and $175 (or $80,000 to $350,000 per kilo after dilution).

The two most important international measures against drug trafficking are the UN Convention Against Illicit Traffic in Narcotic Drugs and Psychotropic Substances and the Basel and Vienna Declarations regarding money laundering. The UN Convention requires parties, of which there were 150 by 1999, to institute legal measures to ban and punish all aspects of illegal drug production or trafficking, including drug-money laundering. Parties also answer annual report questionnaires (ARQ) so that the UN International Drug Control Programme can publish an analysis of trends in the illicit drug trade. In addition to governmental reports, the UN receives information from the International Criminal Police Organisation, the International Narcotics Control Board, the World Customs Organisation and its own field offices. In 1998 100 countries completed ARQs. The Basel declaration concerns the G7 countries and commits their central banks to attempting to identify customers suspected of drug-trafficking and the source of their funds and to refuse all dubious transactions. The Vienna declaration

Harvesting coca leaves. (US Drug Enforcement Agency)

commits ratifying states to introducing the crime of money laundering and to taking steps to identify, trace and confiscate the proceeds of drug trafficking.

The US has the most comprehensive system for tackling drugs. Each year the President reports to Congress on those he considers to be major illicit drug-producing or drug-transit countries. The December 1998 list contained 28 names, two fewer than a year earlier. Five other countries are considered to be major producers but are not listed as their production is consumed locally or not exported to the US. The President then certifies which of these countries has cooperated fully with the US or taken sufficient steps to comply with the UN Convention. The definition of a major drug-producing country is one that has 1,000 hectares or more of either opium or coca or 5,000 hectares of cannabis cultivated or harvested during a year. In 1998 the US identified forty-five major money-laundering countries, that is countries whose financial institutions engaged in transactions coming from the proceeds of serious crime. The list includes the US itself, Canada, France, Germany and the UK. Each year the US State Department publishes an International Narcotics Control Strategy Report. The 1999 edition is over 700 pages long and gives, in addition to data on cultivation and production, the action taken against drugs by each country during the year and the extent of cooperation with and assistance given by the US.

Bibliography and Web Sites

Drugs of Abuse, US Department of Justice, 1997

International Narcotics Control Strategy Report, US State Department, 1999

The National Narcotics Intelligence Consumers Committee Report 1997, US Drug Enforcement Administration, 1998

Supply and Trafficking in Narcotic Drugs 1996, United Nations International Drugs Control Programme, 1998

www. Drug Watch International: www.drugwatch.org/

The Drug Strategy Institute: www2.druginfo.org/orgs/dsi/

UN International Drug Control Programme: www.undcp.org/index

WEAPONS OF MASS DESTRUCTION

The term weapons of mass destruction has come to mean nuclear, biological and chemical weapons and long-range missiles that can deliver them. Nuclear weapons give rise to the greatest concern, possibly because they have been used less often than the others and possibly because the effects of a massive nuclear exchange, while unpredictable, are known to be catastrophic. In some ways nuclear weapons have had a positive effect in that it seems they contributed, though this cannot be proved, to the fact that there was never a war between democracy and communism, one that many thought likely fifty years ago.

Nuclear issues are dealt with here under three headings: proliferation, a continuing worry; weapons-free zones; and disarmament. Chemical and biological weapons are considered together and finally the delivery means for these weapons are discussed.

THE NUCLEAR DIMENSION: PROLIFERATION

The main weapon in the battle to prevent nuclear weapon proliferation is the Nuclear Non-Proliferation Treaty (NPT) which came into force on 5 March 1970. The background to the Treaty was the adoption by the UN General Assembly (UNGA) in 1959 and 1961 of resolutions calling for nuclear-weapon states to refrain from providing weapons to non-nuclear states and insisting that nuclear weapons should be subject to inspection and control. In 1965 the UN Committee on Disarmament was tasked by the UNGA to negotiate an international treaty to prevent the proliferation of nuclear weapons; the committee was co-chaired by the US and the USSR who, after intense negotiations, produced identical revised drafts. The Treaty was adopted by the UNGA in June 1968 and then opened for signature on 1 July 1968 when 62 nations agreed to it. The main elements of the treaty are:

I. Nuclear Weapon States agree neither to transfer nuclear weapons nor to assist non-nuclear states in acquiring nuclear weapons.
II. Non-Nuclear States undertake not to receive or manufacture nuclear weapons.

III. Non-Nuclear States undertake to accept safeguards and verification of their nuclear facilities by the International Atomic Energy Agency (IAEA).

IV. NPT parties have the right to develop nuclear energy.

V. Nuclear Weapon States are obligated to pursue agreement on a treaty on complete disarmament under international control.

At the time when the treaty came into force there were five nuclear weapon states: China, France, United Kingdom, United States and USSR. There are now only four UN members that are not parties to the NPT: Cuba, Israel, India and Pakistan. It is now known, following tests carried out in May and June 1998, that India and Pakistan are nuclear capable. Israel has long been considered a nuclear-armed state although it has always claimed that it will not be the first to introduce nuclear weapons into the region.

A large number of countries have the technical capability and the financial resources to develop nuclear weapons should they decide to do so. Programmes were initiated in South Korea and Taiwan but both countries were persuaded by the US to terminate the projects. In June 1975 the then South Korean President stated that 'Korea had the capacity to produce nuclear weapons' but Korea had no plans to do so unless the US withdrew its nuclear umbrella. Taiwan's President said in 1996 that it had the means to develop nuclear weapons and that, following Chinese naval and missile exercises, it would have to study whether it needed them to defend itself.

Argentina and Brazil undertook weapons development programmes. Both countries had safeguard agreements with the IAEA but these only covered a part of their nuclear activities. Unsafeguarded plants included a uranium enrichment plant and a plutonium separation plant in

Countries that have or have had nuclear weapons programmes.

Recognised nuclear powers
"De facto" nuclear powers
States developing nuclear weapons
States that have abandoned nuclear programmes

Indian Agni missile on Republic Day parade, January 2000. (Associated Press)

Argentina, and Braz[...]lutonium separation facilities. [...]1,050 feet deep in the Cachim[...]-in by the Brazilian President [...]ot develop nuclear weapons. La[...]ilitary had begun to design two [...] and Brazil made commitments to the exclusively peaceful use of nuclear energy in a number of joint declarations between 1985 and 1990. In 1991 they signed the Bilateral Agreement for the Exclusively Peaceful Use of Nuclear Energy which was ratified by both Congresses in December 1991. This led to the establishment of the Brazilian-Argentine Agency for the Accounting and Control of Nuclear Materials (ABACC). Argentina acceded to the NPT in October 1995 and Brazil joined in July 1998.

South Africa surprised the world in March 1993 when the then President, Frederick de Klerk, informed Parliament that South Africa had manufactured six nuclear fission devices, that these had been dismantled before the country had joined the NPT in July 1991 and that all other nuclear materials and facilities had been placed under international safeguards. The fact that South Africa had had a nuclear weapons programme was no surprise – a nuclear test site in the Kalahari Desert had been identified in August 1977 but US and Soviet pressure resulted in the test's cancellation. The news that weapons had been completed was totally

Countries that must join CTBT for it to come into effect	
Algeria	Italy
Argentina	Japan
Australia	Mexico
Austria	Netherlands
Bangladesh	North Korea*
Belgium	Norway
Brazil	Pakistan*
Bulgaria	Peru
Canada	Poland
Chile	Romania
China	Russia
Colombia	Slovakia
Congo (DRC)	South Africa
Egypt	South Korea
Finland	Spain
France	Sweden
Germany	Switzerland
Hungary	Turkey
India*	Ukraine
Indonesia	United Kingdom
Iran	United States
Israel	Vietnam

* non-signatories

Non-signatories of the NPT
Cuba
India
Israel
Pakistan
Yugoslavia (Serbia and Montenegro)

unexpected. De Klerk also stated that 'at no time did South Africa acquire nuclear weapons technology or materials from another country' and 'South Africa has never conducted a clandestine nuclear test'. The true nature of the double flash noted in the South Atlantic in September 1979 remains unconfirmed but no other evidence of a nuclear explosion has been found. In addition to the two shafts at the Vastrap test site, South Africa had both uranium enrichment and plutonium extraction plants and research and assembly facilities at Pelindaba, the dismantlement of which has been verified by the IAEA.

Details of India and Pakistan's nuclear programmes and tests are set out on pages 238–41. Those of Iraq's programme, its progress towards achieving a bomb before the Gulf War, and the measures taken to attempt to stop any future development are given at pages 154–6 and 185. North Korea has also come under suspicion of developing nuclear weapons although it was subject to IAEA inspection. Refusal to allow access to a suspected waste site led to a confrontation; the details of events and the measures being taken to halt the Korean programme are described on pages 282–60.

Iran is also suspected of having nuclear weapons ambitions. This suspicion is based mainly on energy-rich Iran's plans for nuclear power reactors which many consider the country does not need. Nuclear developments started under the Shah's regime in 1957 when an agreement was signed with the US on cooperation in the peaceful use of nuclear energy and a research reactor was completed in 1967. By the time of the 1979 revolution the most advanced project was the building of two 1,250 megawatt pressurised water reactors at Bushehr – were roughly 80 per cent and 65 per cent complete. A large number of Iranians have been sent abroad to study nuclear technology. Military research is believed to have comprised weapons design at the Amirabad centre, a laser enrichment programme and an uncompleted plutonium extraction plant at Tehran. In 1992–3 there were a number of unconfirmed reports of the smuggling of a small number of nuclear warheads from Kazakhstan to Iran. Kazakhstan denied the allegations but in April 1998 the Israeli newspaper, *Jerusalem Post*, claimed that it had been shown copies of Iranian government papers confirming the receipt of four warheads and supplies of enriched uranium from Kazakhstan in 1991. In January 1995 Iran signed a contract with Russia for the completion of the two reactors at Bushehr; later that month Iran commissioned a cyclotron accelerator at Karaj, ostensibly to produce radioactive material for medical scanners. The Russians resisted heavy US pressure not to complete the reactors but the US managed to dissuade Ukraine from supplying the turbines for plants. Chinese officials are said to have assured the US that the proposed sale to Iran of anhydrous hydrogen fluoride needed for a uranium enrichment process would not take place. The IAEA inspects a number of, but not all, Iran's nuclear facilities and, as yet, has not found any evidence of nuclear weapons development. Nevertheless, there is a strong body of opinion in the US and Israel that Iran is developing weapons and could have a nuclear capability in just a few years.

The NPT was extended indefinitely at the Review Conference held in May 1995 although there was some opposition to the form of words used. At the same time agreement was reached on 'Principles and Objectives for Nuclear Non-Proliferation and Disarmament. In all the agreement included twenty principles aimed at ensuring wider cooperation and greater transparency for nuclear matters. The nuclear weapon states 'affirmed their commitment to pursue in good faith negotiations on effective measures relating to nuclear disarmament'. Disarmament, or the lack of it, is a subject given a far higher priority by the non-nuclear states than those with nuclear weapons: the latter seem loathe to consider total nuclear disarmament that is required by the NPT.

Bibliography and Web Sites

Charpak, Georges, and Richard Garwin, *Will-o'-the-Wisp and Nuclear Mushrooms*, Udile Jacob, 1997

Kokoski, Richard, *Technology and the Proliferation of Nuclear Weapons*, SIPRI, 1996

Sokolski, Henry (ed.), *Fighting Proliferation: New Concerns for the Nineties*, Alabama Air University Press, 1996

Thomas, Raju (ed.), *The Nuclear Non-Proliferation Regime: Prospects for the 21st Century*, Macmillan, 1998

Arms Control Association: www.armscontrol.org/

Centre for Non-Proliferation Studies (Monterey Institute of International Studies): www.cns.miis.edu/

US State Department, Arms Control and Disarmament: www.acda.gov/

THE NUCLEAR DIMENSION:
NUCLEAR-WEAPON-FREE ZONES

The first nuclear-weapon-free zone (NWFZ) was established by the Antarctic Treaty, which covers the region south of the 60° south latitude and was signed on 1 December 1959. The Treaty contains an article prohibiting nuclear explosions and the dumping of radioactive waste in the zone. France, the UK, the US and the USSR were among the original governments involved in the drafting and agreement of the Treaty. China and India have since become parties to it.

The Treaty of Rarotonga covers a large part of the South Pacific and came into force on 11 December 1986. It became a blue-print for the subsequent NWFZs. The parties to the Treaty undertook not to manufacture or otherwise acquire, possess or control any nuclear explosive device; not to provide fissionable material or equipment for processing or producing fissionable material for peaceful purposes to any state unless it was subject to the safeguards required by the Nuclear Non-Proliferation Treaty or, in the case of nuclear weapon states, International Atomic Energy Agency safeguards; to prevent the stationing of nuclear weapons on their territory (but each could decide its own policy regarding the transit of foreign ships and aircraft); to prevent the testing of nuclear weapons in its territory; and not to dump and to prevent the dumping of radioactive matter in its territorial sea.

France, the United Kingdom and the United States were invited to be parties of three protocols to the Treaty; the USSR and China were invited

Parties to the South-East Asia NWFZ

Brunei
Cambodia
Indonesia
Laos
Malaysia
Myanmar
Philippines
Singapore
Thailand
Vietnam

Parties to the South Pacific NWFZ

Australia
Cook Islands
Fiji
Kiribati
Nauru
New Zealand
Papua New Guinea
Solomon Islands
Tuvalu
Western Samoa

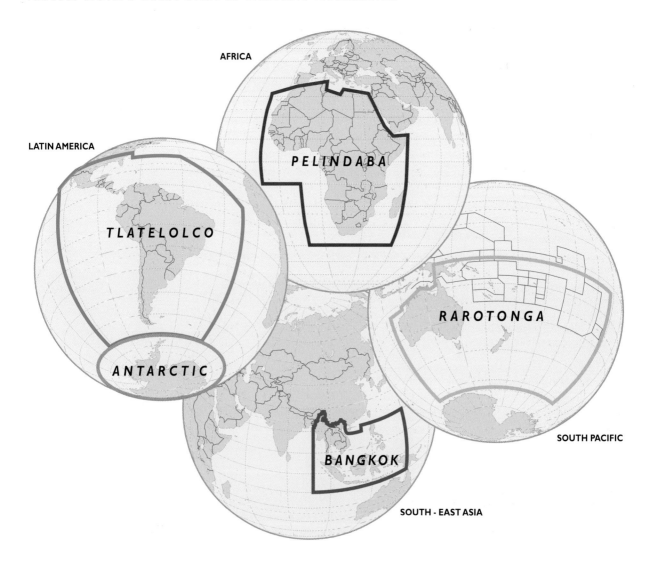

Nuclear-weapon-free zones.

to be parties to protocols 2 and 3. Protocol 1 concerned dependent territories in the NWFZ and the parties undertook to abide by the prohibitions of the Treaty covering manufacture, stationing and testing. Protocol 2 required parties not to use or threaten to use nuclear weapons against parties of the Treaty and not to contribute to any violation of the Treaty. Parties to Protocol 3 committed themselves not to test nuclear weapons within the NWFZ. France, the UK and the US signed the three protocols on 25 March 1996 at the meeting of the South Pacific Forum, two months after France had carried out its final nuclear test at Moruroa. China and the USSR had signed Protocols 2 and 3 in 1988.

The Treaty of Tlatelolco created the Latin American and Caribbean NWFZ. It has similar aims as the Treaty of Rarotonga but allows for the use of nuclear explosions for peaceful purposes. It had two additional protocols. Protocol 1 is similar to Protocol 1 of the Treaty of Rarotonga, covers territories of other states in the NWFZ and has been signed by France, the Netherlands, the UK and the US. Protocol 2 covers the use or threat of use of nuclear weapons by signatories against the parties to the Treaty: it has been signed by all five recognised nuclear-weapons states.

The Treaty was opened for signature in February 1965 but Argentina, Brazil and Chile did not become full parties until 1994. The last regional state to sign was Cuba which did so on 25 March 1995 and the Treaty came into force.

In Cairo on 11 April 1996, the heads of all fifty-three states in Africa signed the African NWFZ Treaty, also known as the Pelindaba Treaty (after the site where the Treaty text was drafted, which was also the base for South African nuclear weapons research). The agreement is very similar to the Treaty of Tlatelolco but also contains an article prohibiting armed attack on any nuclear installation in the NWFZ. Again there are three protocols, similar to those to the Treaty of Rarotonga, open for signature by the nuclear weapons states. The Organisation of African Unity recognises Garcia Diego as part of Africa though no African state controls it; the US may be storing nuclear weapons there.

On 28 March 1997 the South-East Asian NWFZ Treaty, which had been signed in Bangkok on 15 December 1995, came into force. The Treaty follows the same lines as the others but there is no article prohibiting armed attack on nuclear facilities. There is one coverall protocol open for signature by the nuclear weapon states; none has signed it yet.

So far only one state, Mongolia, has achieved NWFZ status; the UNGA adopted a resolution in December 1998 endorsing Mongolia's NWFZ status, which had been declared in 1972. The countries of Central Asia are negotiating a NWFZ treaty in Geneva but progress is slow.

Bibliography and Web Site

Alves, Péricles Gasparini and Dariana Belinda Cipollone (eds), *Nuclear Weapons-Free Zones in the 21st Century*, UNIDIR, 1997

US State Department: www.acda.org

`www.`

THE NUCLEAR DIMENSION: DISARMAMENT

The first nuclear arms control treaty agreed by the US and USSR did not reduce nuclear weapons but put a limit on them. The Strategic Arms Limitation Treaty (SALT) was agreed in 1972 and lasted three years; a second treaty, SALT 2, was signed in 1979 but was never ratified by the US Senate because of the Soviet invasion of Afghanistan. The US, however, said it would abide by the terms. The first agreement to achieve a reduction in nuclear weapons was the Intermediate Nuclear Forces Treaty (INF), which was signed by the US and USSR at the end of 1987 and came into force on 1 June 1988. The background to the Treaty was the USSR's deployment, starting in 1977, of the SS-20 missile which could only reach European targets; NATO's response was the 'two-track' approach of both deploying its own missiles and engaging in arms control negotiations. The Treaty required the elimination of all land-based missiles (both ballistic and cruise missiles, including those with conventional, chemical and biological warheads) with ranges between 500 and 5500 kilometres together with their launchers, support structures and equipment by 1 June

US strategic weapons (as at 1 January 2000)		
	1991	1999
ICBM		
Minuteman II	450	0
Minuteman III	500	500
MX Peacekeeper	50	47
SLBM		
Poseidon C-3	160	0
Trident C-4	384	192
Trident D-5	96	240
Bombers		
B-52 (ALCM)	172	93
B-52	38	0
B-1B	97	91
B-2A	0	20
Not including bombers at elimination site		

Soviet/Russian strategic weapons (as at 1 January 2000)		
	1991	1999
ICBM		
SS-11	326	0
SS-13	40	0
SS-17	47	0
SS-18	308	180
SS-19	300	150
SS-24	89	36
SS-25	288	360
RS-12M	0	20
SLBM		
SS-N-6	192	0
SS-N-8	280	64
SS-N-17	12	0
SS-N-18	224	208
SS-N-20	120	80
SS-N-23	112	112
Bombers		
Tu-95 Bear B	15	0
Tu-95 Bear G	49	2
Tu-95H6	0	32
Tu-95H16	62	34
Tu-160 Blackjack	15	8

1991. The Treaty was the first to include intrusive verification measures including on-site inspection. The US eliminated 165 Pershing II ballistic missiles and 443 Ground Launched Cruise Missiles (GLCM); the USSR eliminated a total of 899 ballistic missiles, which included 509 SS-20 and 106 mobile SS-23. The US also withdrew the nuclear warheads from 72 Pershing IA missiles manned by the German army.

The Strategic Arms Reduction Treaty (START) was signed by Presidents George Bush and Mikhail Gorbachev on 31 July 1991 and required significant reductions in strategic nuclear weapons – those delivered by inter-continental ballistic missiles (ICBM), submarine launched ballistic missiles (SLBM) and heavy bombers. Before the Treaty could be ratified the Soviet Union broke up and four of the new republics (Belarus, Kazakhstan, Russia and Ukraine) had strategic weapons deployed on their territory. At a conference in Lisbon the four republics and the US signed a protocol to START in which the four, as successor states, assumed the obligations of the USSR under the Treaty. Further, and most importantly, Belarus, Kazakhstan and Ukraine committed themselves to joining the Nuclear Non-Proliferation Treaty (NPT) as non-nuclear-armed states in the shortest possible time and so would give up all of their nuclear weapons (tactical as well as strategic). For a number of reasons the Ukrainian Parliament did not ratify its accession to the NPT until 5 December 1994 when the five signatories exchanged their instruments of ratification and START came into force.

The main provisions of START were that both the US and Russia would limit their deployed strategic nuclear forces to no more then 1,600 delivery vehicles with no more than 6,000 'attributable' warheads. ICBM and SLBM warheads were limited to 4,900 of which no more than 1,100 could be deployed on mobile ICBM. A limit of 154 was placed on 'heavy' ICBM (in effect only the Russian SS-18).

On 16 June 1992 Presidents Bush and Yeltsin signed a joint understanding on further nuclear cuts. This became START 2, which was signed on 3 January 1993. START 2 was ratified by the US Senate on 26 January 1996 but neither house of the Russian Parliament has yet done so. At first this delay was on account of NATO enlargement proposals. Now the Treaty is seen as unfair and too costly to implement. The NATO bombing of Serbia over Kosovo has been cited as another reason for not ratifying the agreement. START 2 requires both sides to reduce their forces within seven years of the Treaty coming into force to between 3,800 and 4,250 warheads, of which no more than 1,200 could be multiple independently targetable re-entry vehicle (MIRV) warheads, 650 'heavy' warheads and 2,160 SLBM warheads. In a second stage of the process, overall warhead numbers would be reduced to between 3,000 and 3,500, all MIRV ICBM warheads would be eliminated and no more than 1,750 SLBM warheads could be deployed. In both stages the limit on delivery vehicles would be 1,600. START 2 also improved the Treaty counting rules regarding warheads attributed to heavy bombers.

At their summit meeting at Helsinki in March 1997 Presidents Clinton and Yeltsin signed a protocol to START 2 which extended the date for completion of implementation to 31 December 2007. The two presidents also committed themselves to beginning negotiations on START 3 once the

Duma had ratified START 2. START 3 would further reduce warhead levels to between 2,000 and 2,300 for each side; the Treaty would also include measures for the destruction of warheads and would address the questions of long-range sea-launched cruise missiles, tactical nuclear weapons and transparency measures for holdings of nuclear materials.

A good deal of progress has been made in eliminating nuclear weapons. All Soviet nuclear warheads have been withdrawn to Russia – from Kazakhstan by May 1995, from Ukraine by June 1996; and the last SS-25 mobile ICBM with their warheads left Belarus in November 1996. Nor are there any delivery vehicles left in Belarus or Kazakhstan. Russia has taken into service the 54 SS-25 that had been deployed in Belarus. The 44 strategic bombers positioned in Kazakhstan have returned to Russia and many have been eliminated; all the ICBM and ICBM silos there have been destroyed. Also, 142 of the 176 ICBM, including the first SS-24s to be taken out of their silos, have been removed from Ukraine or eliminated and their silos destroyed. The future of the 32 bombers in Ukraine is unclear; they must either be destroyed there or be returned to Russia to count against its quota.

Weapons have not only been destroyed, however. Since September 1990 Russia has added one more train set of three missiles to complete the deployment of its rail-mobile SS-24 ICBM; production of the mobile ICBM, the SS-25, continued and a further 126, including those originally in Belarus, have been deployed. A new single warhead mobile ICBM, the RS-12M, has been developed and the first 20 deployed in former SS-19 silos at Tatishkevo. Russia has eliminated 413 ICBM of the older types (SS-11, SS-

Elimination of an SS-19 ICBM at Pervomaysk, Ukraine. (US On-Site Inspection Agency)

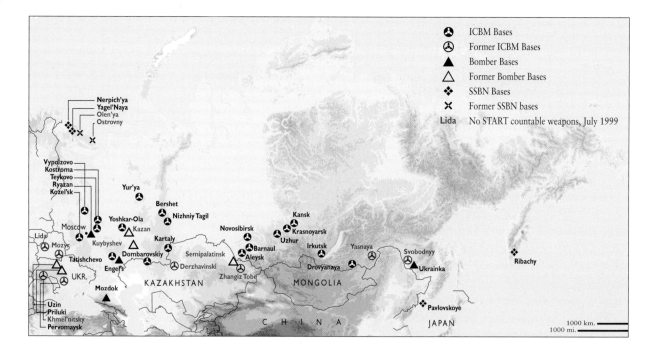

Russian strategic nuclear weapons sites and former Soviet sites.

13, SS-17) and destroyed all their silos. It has also eliminated 24 SS-18 and their silos and 20 SS-19. Thirty-three nuclear missile submarines have been decommissioned and the 476 SLBM with which they were armed eliminated or placed in storage. Two of the most modern ballistic missile, nuclear-fuelled submarines (SSBN), the Typhoon, have had their SLBM removed as they are no longer seaworthy. Seventy-five strategic bombers, including the forty from Kazakhstan, have been eliminated.

Little information on the progress of destruction of Russian non-strategic nuclear weapons is available but a number of pledges were made by President Gorbachev. All atomic demolition mines were to be eliminated by 1998; all nuclear artillery shells by 2000; half the stock of surface to air missile warheads by 1996; half all naval tactical warheads by 1995, with the remainder to be stored on shore; and half the non-strategic aircraft bombs by 1996.

The US has eliminated all its 450 Minuteman II (MM) ICBM and either destroyed their silos or converted them for Minuteman III; two ICBM bases have been closed and a third will be decommissioned shortly. In addition, 291 strategic bombers have been eliminated and a further 96 are non-operational and await elimination at Davis-Monthan airbase. Three B-1 bombers have crashed. Twenty B-2 bombers have been added to the inventory. Since 1990, 6 new Ohio class submarines each armed with 24 Trident D-5 SLBMs have been commissioned while 22 older missile submarines armed with Polaris SLBM have been eliminated. The US can now deploy 432 SLBMs as opposed to 640 in September 1990.

Non-strategic nuclear weapons have also been greatly reduced in number. The US is believed now to have only 750 free-fall nuclear bombs and 320 warheads for sea-launched cruise missiles, all of which are stored ashore. The US has eliminated all its nuclear artillery shells, short-range surface-to-surface missile warheads, all naval tactical nuclear weapons

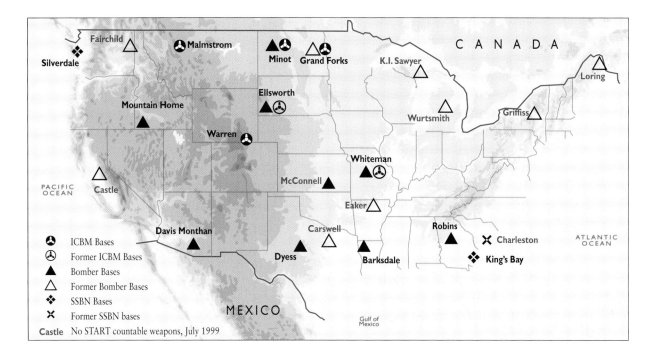

US strategic nuclear weapon sites and former sites.

(mines, torpedoes and depth charges), surface-to-air missile warheads and atomic demolition mines.

France and the United Kingdom, but not yet China, have also reduced their nuclear forces. The French have eliminated their intermediate range S-3 missiles, of which there were 18 deployed on the Plâteau D'Albion; 40 short-range Pluton missile launchers and their replacement, the Hadès missile, of which 5 were produced but never deployed. Only in the ballistic missile submarine field have there been any new deployments: the submarine force did consist of five boats each armed with 16 M-4 SLBMs, now there are two M-4 armed submarines which are being replaced by the Le Triomphant class with 16 M-45 SLBMs. Four Le Triomphant are planned; two have been commissioned.

The United Kingdom has ended its Royal Air Force nuclear role; there were eight nuclear-capable squadrons equipped with some 120 aircraft (Tornado GR-1 and Buccaneer) in 1990. The Polaris SLBM fleet of four submarines each armed with 16 SLBMs has been replaced by Vanguard class submarines each with the capability of carrying 16 Trident D-5 SLBMs. Currently three of four have been commissioned. Polaris SLBMs carried three warheads while Trident can be armed with as many as twelve; originally the UK announced it would arm each submarine with no more than 128 warheads (an average of eight per SLBM) but that was reduced to 96 in 1993, while in the 1998 Strategic Defence Review the number was further reduced to 48. Some of these warheads will be loaded on single warhead SLBMs so that they can be used in a sub-strategic role.

A number of states complain that the five recognised nuclear-armed powers are not doing enough to implement their commitment made when signing the Nuclear Non-Proliferation Treaty to work towards total nuclear disarmament. At the same time several groups (the Canberra Commission, International Generals and Admirals, Committee on Nuclear

Policy and Tokyo Forum for Nuclear Non-Proliferation and Disarmament), all made up of eminent former statesmen, academics and military officers, have published reports recommending total nuclear disarmament. It has been estimated that the US and USSR had a combined total of 61,000 nuclear warheads in 1990 and that today this number has been reduced by nearly half to around 35,000. However, even if all states were willing, total disarmament would still take some years to achieve.

Several sound reasons can be advanced in favour of retaining some nuclear weapons. These include the argument that nuclear weapons cannot be disinvented so there will always be a risk, in a nuclear-free world, of combatants racing to re-acquire them. Nuclear deterrence can be said to have worked in the case of NATO and the Warsaw Pact in that there was no war between these two major military alliances. Finally, it has been argued that there is no guarantee of stopping cheating and it would be possible for states to hide a number of nuclear weapons while professing to have disarmed; verifying total nuclear disarmament would require unacceptably intrusive and expensive measures.

It is likely to be a good many years before all the nuclear powers agree to total disarmament, let alone implement it. The best that can be hoped for is continued reduction in nuclear weapon holdings and an increase in measures to ensure that those which remain are subject to transparency regarding their deployment and alert status, and to agreed measures restricting their operational readiness.

Bibliography and Web Sites

Cochrane, Thomas B.C., William M.A. Arkin and Milton M.H. Hoenig, *Nuclear Weapons Databook*, Ballinger, 1984

Quinlan, Michael, *Thinking About Nuclear Weapons*, RUSI Whitehall Papers Series, 1997

Report of the Canberra Commission on the Elimination of Nuclear Weapons, Australian Ministry of Foreign Affairs, 1996

START Treaty Memorandum of Understanding Data (1990 to 1999), US Arms Control and Disarmament Agency (US ACDA)

Treaty on the Reduction and Limitation of Strategic Offensive Arms (START), US ACDA, revised October 1994

Treaty on Further Reduction and Limitation of Strategic Offensive Arms (START 2), US ACDA, 1993

www.

Arms Control Association: www.armscontrol.org

Bulletin of The Atomic Scientists: www.bullatomsci.org

Non-Governmental Committee on Disarmament: www.igc.apc.org/disarm

US State Department: www.acda.gov

THE CHEMICAL AND BIOLOGICAL DIMENSION: PROLIFERATION AND USE

Chemical weapons (CW) are man-made poisons. They can be disseminated by explosive charges (rockets, aircraft bombs, artillery shells, etc.) or by being dispersed from aircraft spray tanks (similar to crop spraying). There are four basic types classified by the effects they have on the human body. Choking agents cause damage to the lungs and include chlorine and phosgene. Vesicants burn the body both externally and internally; mustard gas is the best known example. Blood agents, such as hydrogen cyanide, block the passage of blood. The most modern and potentially most dangerous type is nerve agents, which can be absorbed through the skin and disable the nervous system; they include Sarin, Tabun and VX.

Biological weapons (BW) are living organisms that cause death or illness in man and animals and can destroy plants. They are disseminated in the same ways as CW but, because they multiply once they have infected a host body, much less of the agent is needed to cause the same level of casualties as a CW attack. BW agents must normally be inhaled but can also attack via contaminated food and water, open wounds or insect vectors. BW agents include bacteria (such as anthrax, plague and brucellosis), viruses, rickettsiae and fungi. Toxins, such as botulinum and ricin, lie between BW and CW as they are of biological origin and can be manufactured; they are not, though, living organisms.

A BW attack is far more effective than that by CW as it spreads far further and has a far higher lethality: CW potency is measured in milligrams, BW in micrograms and picograms. Given the right conditions BW can kill far more people than a nuclear attack but there is no material destruction.

Neither CW nor BW are new. CW were first employed by the Greeks in 600 BC and an early use of BW was the catapulting of bubonic plague casualties by the Tartars into the besieged city of Caffa in 1347. Gas was used extensively during the First World War but was not deployed in the

US Chemical Weapon Destruction Facility, Tooele, Utah. (US On-Site Inspection Agency)

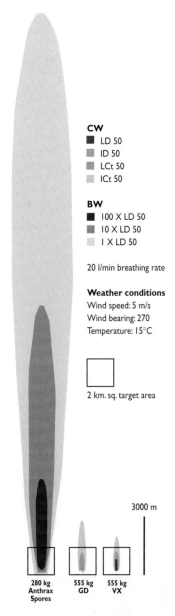

CW

- LD 50
- ID 50
- LCt 50
- ICt 50

BW

- 100 X LD 50
- 10 X LD 50
- 1 X LD 50

20 l/min breathing rate

Weather conditions
Wind speed: 5 m/s
Wind bearing: 270
Temperature: 15°C

2 km. sq. target area

3000 m

280 kg	555 kg	555 kg
Anthrax	GD	VX
Spores		

Comparison of BW and CW strikes using same delivery means.

Second, despite both sides being well supplied with CW. While not given such a high profile in the battle against proliferation as nuclear weapons, they can cause as many casualties, are much simpler and less expensive to produce, and do not require ballistic missiles or modern bombers to deliver them. The release of Sarin nerve gas in the Tokyo subway by the Aum Shinrikyo religious cult on 20 March 1995 demonstrated that CW and BW can be terrorist weapons. They can be disseminated from crop-spraying aircraft, through car exhausts and, in the case of BW, through municipal water supply systems.

While nuclear weapons have only ever been used twice operationally, both at the end of the Second World War, CW have been employed several times in recent years. They were used by Egypt in the Yemen in the 1960s; by Iraq against Iran in 1984 against exposed and unprotected troops making human wave attacks – later in the war, this provoked Iranian retaliation but on a much smaller scale; and by Iraq against Kurds at Halabjah in April 1988. CW were not used in the 1991 Gulf War although it was discovered afterwards that Iraq had stocks of 800 tons of mustard gas, Tabun and Sarin nerve agents. Delivery could have been by aircraft (over 1,300 bombs were found), artillery shells and rockets (9,000 found), and by surface-to-surface missile (30 warheads for Al-Hussein and Scud missiles).

The lethality of CBW agents is expressed as the dosage needed to kill 50 per cent of the exposed, unprotected population. For example, an agent with a LCt50 rating of 150 will be lethal to 50 per cent of those (assuming they breathe 10 litres of air per minute) who are exposed to a concentration of 15 milligrams per cubic metre for 10 minutes, or experience 30 seconds exposure to a concentration of 300 milligrams per cubic metre. Another measure is expressed in milligrams of agent per kilogram of body weight: a man weighing 100 kilograms would be killed by a 10,000 milligrams dose of an agent with a LD50 factor of 100. In both forms of measurement the lower the rating the more lethal the agent.

Just as weapons of this type have been around for centuries, so arms control in the CBW field is not new either: in 1675 the French and Germans agreed to prohibit the use of poisoned bullets. The first major treaty was the 1925 Geneva Protocol for the Prohibition of the Use in War of Asphyxiating, Poisonous or Other Gases and of Bacteriological Methods of Warfare, which was signed and ratified by the majority of the leading powers. It did not ban development or manufacture, nor was there any provision for verification. In 1972 a Convention on the Prohibition of the Development, Production and Stockpiling of Bacteriological (Biological) and Toxin Weapons and on their Destruction was signed and has since been ratified or acceded to by 144 countries; ratification is awaited from 16 other signatory countries. The Convention came into force after ratification by the depository states – the US, the UK and the USSR – on 26 March 1975. However, there are no measures to ensure compliance with the Convention and compliance and verification is now the subject of negotiations begun in 1994 for a legally binding protocol and being conducted by the Ad Hoc Group in Geneva. It is hoped that the protocol will be signed on the seventy-fifth anniversary of the Geneva 1925 protocol.

began negotiating a
oduction, Stockpiling
ion (CWC) but real
r a US-USSR chemical
adopted in September
General Assembly in
nuary 1993 when 130
n 29 April 1997, 180
d production facilities
e Organisation for the
includes an Executive
n of the world and a
140 inspectors and 100
ensive data exchange,
chemicals listed in the
nd analysis of samples
parties to the Treaty but

the US – had declared a
CW agent. Initially, as
gned a memorandum of
n experiment and an
d an agreement on the
uired the destruction of
eight years of the CWC
o 500 tons. Destruction
easy both for financial

reasons and on account of local opposition to destruction facilities for fear of environmental pollution.

CWC Challenge Inspection timetable

State claims inspection
Inspection Team assembled
Challenged state informed
Within 12 hours:
    Inspectors at point of entry
Within 36 hours:
    Inspectors at challenged site
Within 72 hours:
    Inspectors granted access
    Inspection takes place
Within 84 hours:
    Inspectors submit report to inspected
        state and leave
Final report submitted

Chemical-weapon-armed and suspect states.

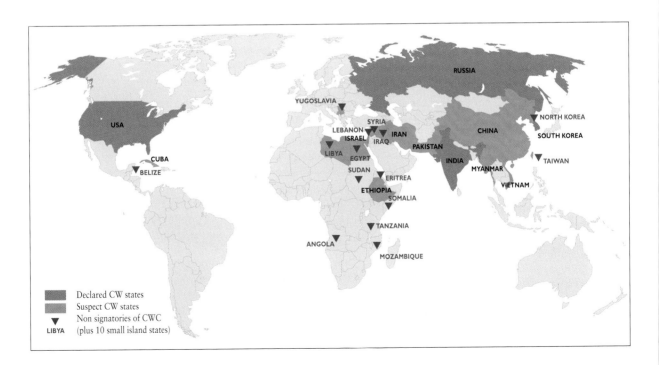

Declared CW states
Suspect CW states
▼ Non signatories of CWC
LIBYA (plus 10 small island states)

Members of the Australia Group	
Argentina	Italy
Australia	Japan
Austria	Luxembourg
Belgium	Netherlands
Canada	New Zealand
Czech Republic	Norway
Denmark	Poland
Finland	Portugal
France	Slovakia
Germany	Spain
Greece	Sweden
Hungary	Switzerland
Iceland	United Kingdom
Ireland	United States

Chemical weapon stockpiles (in tons)

United States

Mustard agent	17,234
Sarin nerve agent	8,902
VX (persistent nerve agent)	4,444
Lewisite	13
Tabun nerve agent	2
Binary components	680

Stored at nine locations, as declared 22 January 1996

Russia

Organophosphorous compounds

Sarin nerve agent	9,440
Soman nerve agent	3,238
V-Gas	5,994
General Ops	13,650
Lewisite	6,681
Mustard	865
Lewisite/Mustard mix	400

Stored at seven locations, revealed by Russia 1994

Another effort to halt the proliferation of CBW agents takes the form of controls agreed to by members of the Australia Group, formed in 1985, regarding the export of dual-use materials and technology. The Group has 28 members and has published detailed lists of the chemicals, biological agents and equipment of which export should be controlled.

There are a number of disadvantages to both BW and CW as battlefield weapons. Modern armies now equip their soldiers with protective clothing and so unless total surprise can be achieved casualties may not be high and conventional artillery fire would have to accompany any CBW attack. BW takes some time to take effect, up to several days, and so will not produce the instant casualties that would be needed to guarantee the success of battlefield attack. CBW is also affected by weather conditions. Although there is no wind speed that precludes the use of CBW, clouds of agent will be blown away from target areas more quickly by stronger winds and the rate of evaporation of liquid agent increases with increasing wind speeds. Winds rarely maintain a constant speed or direction and the more unstable atmospheric conditions are, the less effective will be the CBW attack. Turbulence, which depends mainly on changing air temperature at different heights, will mix vapour clouds with clean air and reduce the concentration of agent. On the other hand, rain has little cleansing effect on CBW; if it falls on contaminated ground then the evaporation rate of the agent will increase and the concentration of agent in the atmosphere will increase. The effectiveness of CW is not governed by temperature; however, high temperatures and humidity make the wearing of protective clothing even more uncomfortable. The wearing of protective clothing degrades troops' capability, particularly where tactile skills are needed.

A number of countries are known to have developed CW and BW weapons and others are strongly suspected of having done so; some of these are signatories of CWC. A number of Arab states are not prepared to join the CWC while, they claim, Israel has nuclear weapons.

Bibliography and Web Sites

Krutzsch, Walter, and Ralf Trapp, *A Commentary on the Chemical Weapons Convention*, Martinus Nijhoff, 1994

Roberts, Brad (ed.), *Terrorism with Chemical and Biological Weapons: Calibrating Risks and Responses*, Chemical and Biological Arms Control Institute, 1997

Chemical and Biological Institute (Washington): www.cbaci.org
Harvard Sussex Program: fas-www.harvard.edu/~hsp
Stockholm International Peace Research Institute: http://projects.sipri.se/cbw

DELIVERY: MISSILES, AIRCRAFT AND OTHER MEANS

Weapons of mass destruction – nuclear, biological and chemical (NBC) – can be delivered by a variety of means, depending on the weight of warhead, the range and accuracy needed, and the favoured option of the deliverer. Delivery can be by ground- and submarine-launched intercontinental ballistic missiles (ICBM and SLBM), intermediate- and short-range missiles (IRBM, SSM), cruise missiles launched from the ground, ships or submarines, and aircraft, aircraft bombs, artillery and rocket launchers, and by covert means by terrorists.

This analysis concentrates on missiles because they are seen as the main danger from proliferating countries – most modern combat aircraft can be adapted to carry nuclear and CBW weapons. There are advantages and disadvantages to employing either aircraft or missiles. Missiles are less expensive than aircraft and there is no danger to a pilot, but they can only be used once. In first and second generation missiles accuracy is poor and so they are only suitable for delivering nuclear warheads unless a large number can be fired. Range is of less importance if the target area is a nearby and small country, for example Syria only needs missiles with a range of some 400 kilometres to be able to strike any part of Israel – its SS-21 SSM can reach as far south as Tel Aviv. Aircraft can carry far heavier payloads than any missile and with in-flight refuelling can reach targets anywhere in the world. They can be recalled (as the bombers sent to attack Iraq in December 1998 were when Saddam Hussein agreed to US demands), while missiles can only be destroyed if they are not to reach their targets. Aircraft rely on the human factor, which can lead to the misidentification of targets, but missiles can and do go astray. Aircraft are more vulnerable to air defences though they can to some extent be protected by electronic means. A further disadvantage of missile attack is that the launch site can be readily detected whereas it could be possible to mount either an aircraft or terrorist attack without the attacker being identified. Anti-missile weapons are being developed and may soon be operational but this may only accelerate the production of missiles in an attempt to swamp defences.

Sophisticated cruise missiles that can 'jink' and follow contours will be harder to shoot down than ICBM. Cruise missiles do not need to be that sophisticated and very simple ones employing the same characteristics as unmanned aircraft (UAV) or remotely piloted vehicles (RPV) if fired in sufficient quantity could penetrate defences as the German V1 did in the Second World War.

The most worrying missile developments are in those countries known or thought to be developing nuclear weapons or CBW, and in countries eager to export their missiles or missile technology. Among the former are India, Iran, Iraq, Israel, Libya, North Korea, Pakistan and Syria; in the latter category are China, North Korea and Russia. India, Iran, Israel, North Korea and Pakistan are developing their own missiles, though Pakistan is believed to have had considerable help from China. In September 1999 Israel accused Syria of upgrading its Scud missiles so that they could reach all of Israel. Also in September 1999 the US made a deal with North Korea and agreed to lift a number of sanctions imposed some forty years previously in return for the North Koreans' promise not to carry out any more test flights of their long-range missile, the Taepo Dong 2. The US has agreed to assist South Korea in improving its missile capability in terms of quantity and range; since 1979 the US had restricted South Korea to having missiles with no greater range than 180 kilometres. Meanwhile, former Russian Prime Minister, Viktor

---

Elements in curbing missile proliferation

Export control measures
Arms control measures
International non-proliferation
  agreements
Cooperative non-proliferation
  agreements
Diplomacy
Deterrence
Defences

Nuclear delivery means (other than US and Russia, see page 84)

Weapon	Range in km
China	
CSS-4	15,000
CSS-5	7,000
CSS-2	2,700
CSS-5	1,800
CSS-N-3	3,000
H-6 bomber	2,180
France	
M-4 SLBM	6,000
M-45 SLBM	6,000
Mirage 2000	650
Super Etendard	650
With ASMP range	250
United Kingdom	
Trident D-5	12,000
Israel	
Jericho missile	1,500
F-15I aircraft	1,500
India	
Agni2 missile	2,500
Jaguar aircraft	850
Pakistan	
Ghauri 2 missile	2,000
F-16 aircraft	930

Members of the MTCR	
Argentina	Japan
Australia	Luxembourg
Austria	Netherlands
Belgium	New Zealand
Brazil	Norway
Canada	Portugal
Denmark	Russia
Finland	South Africa
France	Spain
Germany	Sweden
Greece	Switzerland
Hungary	Turkey
Iceland	United Kingdom
Ireland	United States
Italy	

Chernomyrdin, has said that NATO's bombing of Serbia will only encourage the proliferation of missiles and nuclear weapons by states that seek to defend themselves in the future against such bombing; he is not alone in this view.

In an attempt to halt the spread of missile technology the Missile Technology Control Regime (MTCR) was formed by seven states in 1987 and consists of a set of guidelines to govern members' export of missiles and unmanned aerial vehicles, their components and technology. Originally the regime covered only delivery vehicles for nuclear weapons, but after the Gulf War it was agreed to include delivery systems for CBW. In practical terms the agreement seeks to ban the transfer of missiles with a range of 300 kilometres carrying a 500 kilogram payload. The new guidelines included the statement that there is a 'strong presumption' to deny the export of components for missiles with ranges and payloads below the MTCR limits if they are intended for the delivery of weapons of mass destruction. The MTCR now has twenty-nine members and a further eight countries have said they will abide by its provisions. By signing the Intermediate Nuclear Forces Treaty, which came into force on 1 June 1988 the USSR and the US agreed to eliminate and not replace their ground-launched ballistic and cruise missiles with ranges between 500 and 5500 kilometres; other nations can and have deployed missiles of this type.

Countries armed with missiles over 100 kilometres range.

Developing long-range missiles is as much a demonstration of power projection as a necessity for the delivery of NBC weapons. Once countries have acquired the capability to produce BW or CW, they find it far cheaper to deliver them by covert means. What could potentially be achieved was shown by the inefficient use of CW by the Aum Shinrikyo cult on the Tokyo subway in March 1995: a more professional attack could have killed thousands.

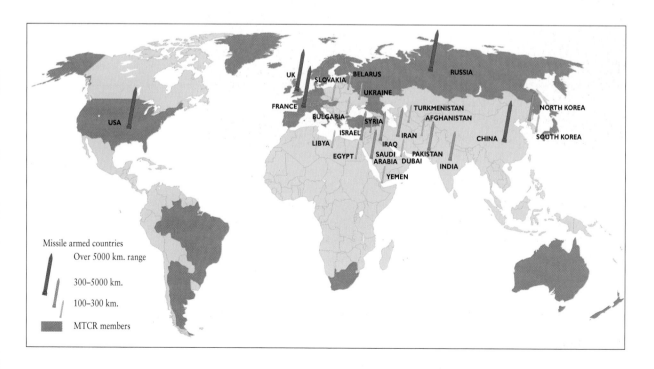

A Peacekeeper ICBM launched from Launch Facility O2, Vanderberg Air Force Base, as part of a test and evaluation programme. (US Department of Defense)

There is a growing realisation that major cities may face CBW attack by a variety of means and that passive defence by way of protective masks and clothing and antidote serums should be readily available in addition to active measures such as anti-ballistic missile defence, which is described on pages 58–62.

Web Sites

Centre for Non-Proliferation Studies (Monterey Institute of International Studies): www.cns.miis.edu/
US State Department: www.acda.gov

THE USA: THE ONLY SUPERPOWER

Nobody denies that the USA is the only remaining super power. It may still be threatened by Russian and Chinese nuclear weapons but not in any other military way, and it may be challenged economically in future – say, by Europe – but not at the moment. The first section below assesses the US's global military reach, which indicates the extent to which it is the only superpower. The second section reveals the ambivalence it shows in the use of that power. Since the US imposes sanctions more than any other country, their efficacy is considered next. Lastly, the analysis turns to a new topic giving concern to a growing number of states, both US allies and potential adversaries – anti-ballistic missile defence, the deployment of which could trigger a fresh nuclear arms race.

THE UNITED STATES: GLOBAL REACH

In recent years the US has shown that it truly has a global reach. Its intercontinental ballistic missiles (ICBM) and its submarine-launched ballistic missiles (SLBM) have been able to target any part of the world for many years, as can its network of satellites providing electronic and photographic intelligence, global positioning information and worldwide communications. Recently US bombers have been operating from bases in continental USA against targets in Serbia and before that during Operation Desert Storm against Iraq. US naval forces that can deploy across the high seas can launch cruise missiles against any inland target within their 1600 kilometre range and did so in 1998 against training camps funded by terrorist Usama bin Laden in Afghanistan. On earlier occasions they were launched against Iraq.

Despite this awesome capability, the US still needs permanently to deploy ground, naval and air forces around the world to be in position to deter and resist attack against its allies and on occasion to mount offensive operations. US ground forces are deployed, and have been so since the end of the Second World War, in Germany (although these are now at a much lower level than during the height of the Cold War), Italy, Japan and South Korea. A relatively small number of army personnel are deployed in Kuwait and Saudi Arabia. The US Army had a presence in Panama to protect the canal zone but this has recently been withdrawn. To allow continental US based units to deploy more quickly overseas a number of pre-positioned equipment packs are maintained. Some are land-based, as in Kuwait, Qatar (each sufficient for an armoured brigade) and in Europe; the stockpile in Kuwait has been manned on two occasions since the Gulf War in addition to during training exercises. There are also stockpiles at sea in maritime pre-positioning squadrons (MPS). Currently these are based at Diego Garcia in the Indian Ocean, Guam in the Pacific and in the Mediterranean. They can sail immediately to where they are needed. MPS carry equipment and stores for the US Marine Corps. Other ships carry equipment for an army brigade and for port operating units. The employment of pre-positioned stockpiles reduces the time required to move an army heavy brigade from between 20 to 30 days to one week and its stores lift from 27,000 tons to 2,000 tons.

The US Marine Corps is organised into three Marine Expeditionary Forces (MEF) that comprise a division supported by an air wing, each with over 100 combat aircraft. On rotation these MEF provide embarked forces in the Mediterranean and Western Pacific. Other forces can be embarked to meet crisis situations. The US has a considerable number of amphibious ships, over forty of which can lift a total of 39,000 troops and 1,500 tanks. Twelve of these ships embark helicopters and all bar one can embark six Sea-Harrier aircraft. In addition, the US is well supplied with military sealift shipping, including 8 fast ro-ro ships at 4 days' readiness

Amphibious shipping		
Quantity	Type	Men/Tanks
2	Amphibious Command Ship	700/-
6	Landing Dock Helicopter	1,900/60
5	Landing Ship Assault	1,900/100
11	Landing Platform Dock	900/4
16	Landing Ship Dock	500/40
2	Landing Ship Tank	347/10

Strategic sea lift capability	
Quantity	Type
7	Ammunition Carrier
8	Stores Ship
2	Hospital Ship
32	Tanker
41	Fast Cargo Ship, including 4 ro-ro and 27 Breakbulk
64	Other Cargo Ship, including 31 ro-ro

Strategic air lift capability	
Quantity	Type
126	C-5 (119,000kg or 345 men)
158	C-141 (40,800kg payload)
48	C-17 (76,660kg payload over 5,000km)
Plus	Civil Reserve Air Fleet
270	Long-range passenger aircraft
230	Long-range cargo aircraft

US Fast Sealift Ship Pollux, *Pusan Harbour, South Korea. (US Department of Defense)*

US B-2 strategic bomber takes off from Whiteman Air Force Base, Missouri. (US Department of Defense)

and some 120 ro-ro and dry cargo ships and 16 tankers at between 4 and 20 days' readiness.

The US Navy is divided into five fleets, one based in the Western Pacific, one in the Eastern Pacific, one in the Atlantic, one in the Mediterranean and a newly formed fleet in the Indian Ocean and Persian Gulf, to which ships are rotated from the other fleets. The Western Pacific Fleet is home-based in Japan. For power projection the US Navy mans 12 aircraft carriers each embarking 50 combat aircraft plus support aircraft and helicopters. The Navy has 76 surface ships and 57 submarines armed with cruise missiles.

The US Air Force is also deployed across the world with fighter wings permanently based in Europe (Germany, Italy and the UK) and the Far East (Japan and South Korea). Transport, tanker and special forces aircraft are also based overseas. In addition, there are currently a number of operational deployments: in Italy to support both SFOR in Bosnia-Herzegovina and KFOR in Kosovo; and in Saudi Arabia and Turkey to maintain the 'no-fly' zones over north and southern Iraq. A number of bases without deployed aircraft are maintained for use in emergency; these include Fairford in the UK and Diego Garcia for

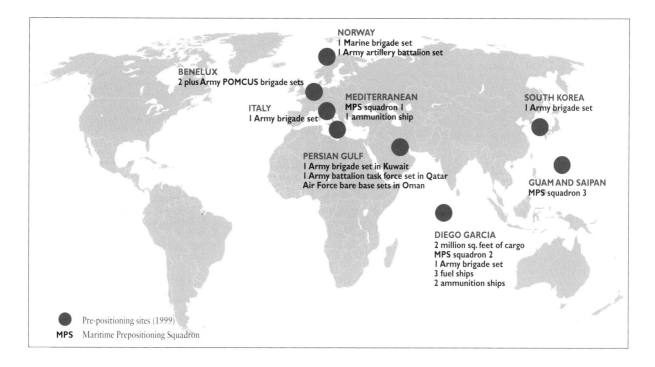

NORWAY
I Marine brigade set
I Army artillery battalion set

BENELUX
2 plus Army POMCUS brigade sets

ITALY
I Army brigade set

MEDITERRANEAN
MPS squadron I
I ammunition ship

SOUTH KOREA
I Army brigade set

PERSIAN GULF
I Army brigade set in Kuwait
I Army battalion task force set in Qatar
Air Force bare base sets in Oman

GUAM AND SAIPAN
MPS squadron 3

DIEGO GARCIA
2 million sq. feet of cargo
MPS squadron 2
I Army brigade set
3 fuel ships
2 ammunition ships

●   Pre-positioning sites (1999)
MPS   Maritime Prepositioning Squadron

strategic bombers. In addition to its over 2,800 combat aircraft, the Air Force has a strong transport force of 1,000 aircraft, including 48 C-17s that can lift a payload of 77 tonnes or a M-I Abrams main battle tank. There are 113 more C-17s on order for delivery up to 2003. Over 500 tanker aircraft capable of carrying out in-flight refuelling are also available.

In only one area is the US capability deficient: low intensity and peace support operations. The US Army and Marine Corps are highly armoured forces and only two divisions have been trained to fight on their feet: the 10th Mountain and the 101st Airborne. As recent experience in, for example, Kosovo and East Timor shows, these are just the kind of forces that the world needs most if it is to maintain peace and stability in the growing number of areas where outside intervention is required.

This combination of forces, some with global reach and others permanently deployed around the world plus a large force in continental USA, means that the US can react quickly to a crisis. That forces are already virtually on the doorstep of potential crisis areas helps to stabilise problems that could escalate.

Bibliography and Web Sites

Report of the Secretary for Defense to the President and the Congress (Annual), US Department of Defense
Strategic Assessment (Annual), US National Defense University

British American Security Information Council: www.basicint.org
Defense Link (US Department of Defense): www.defenselink.mil/
Defense News on Line: www.defensenews.com/
US Department of Defense: www.defenselink.mil/pubs/ofg/dod

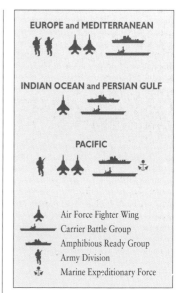

EUROPE and MEDITERRANEAN

INDIAN OCEAN and PERSIAN GULF

PACIFIC

Air Force Fighter Wing
Carrier Battle Group
Amphibious Ready Group
Army Division
Marine Expeditionary Force

US worldwide military deployment (map) and nominal US overseas presence (diagram).

THE UNITED STATES: THE RELUCTANT HEGEMON

US armed forces may not be the largest in numbers but they are more powerful in every other aspect than those of any other country. Its economy is the strongest in the world. It recognises its superiority and expects to retain it until 2015 when it considers a regional power may come to rival it. It is, therefore, not just a regional hegemony but a global one; why does it not always use this power and influence for the good of humanity?

The US appears reluctant to use its military power except when action suits its own policies. One explanation given for this is that US forces must be ready to fight two major wars simultaneously, Iraq and North Korea being quoted as possible examples. There is also the 'body bag' syndrome: virtually any US casualties are seen by the public as unacceptable, although this fear is qualified by some as only having effect when there is no national interest at stake. Certainly US casualties in the interventions in Lebanon in 1983 and Somalia in 1993 where there was no US national interest caused a relatively swift withdrawal from the operations. Lawlessness in Somalia continues seven years later. There was little risk of casualties in the NATO, but predominantly US, bombing of Serbia over Kosovo in 1999. In fact, there were none, but the restrictions placed on the air forces taking part in order to avoid casualties meant mistakes were made, unintended co-lateral damage and casualties were caused and few Yugoslav troops operating in Kosovo were destroyed.

There are other reasons for the US's apparent reluctance to commit forces. One is the built-in 'check and balance' of the constitution that can mean that the President may not command a majority in the Congress. An opposing majority can deny him the financial backing needed to commit troops or can invoke the 'war powers' act. (The American system is not well understood in countries where a parliamentary majority allows a Prime Minister to implement foreign policy virtually unquestioned.) In the case of the invasion of Kuwait it was essential to get UN authority before risking a vote in Congress. But there are advantages as well as disadvantages to the American way; when the Executive and Congress agree then long-term policies can be sustained. Congress approval also helps to gain the support of the general public. Members of the Congress are particularly vulnerable to special interest groups lobbying for their cause, whether it is a domestic or foreign policy issue. This can lead to policy decisions being held hostage to action on quite separate issues, for example the ratification of the Comprehensive Nuclear Test Ban Treaty (CTBT) and amendment of the Anti-Ballistic Missile Treaty. The President, too, is influenced by lobbies – the Irish and the Jewish to name but two.

Another reason for its hesitancy is the US's refusal to place its troops under the command of a non-American officer. In Bosnia this was avoided by the chain of command leading from the force commander (not always an American) up to NATO's Supreme Allied Commander Europe (SACEUR), an American officer. The United States forces are not designed, nor equipped, for peacekeeping and peace support operations. The Powell (Coln Powell, Chairman, Joint Chiefs of Staff, 1990–2) doctrine of using overwhelming force for the shortest possible time suits US resources. One of the country's criteria for taking part in operations is to have an exit strategy so that it cannot be trapped into committing forces, as in Bosnia, for an unknown number of years.

On occasion there can be three different foreign policies on the same issue depending on the views of The White House, the State Department, and the Department of Defense.

Of course, there are those who do not view the US as being reluctant to use its military power, which has been deployed unilaterally on a number of occasions – the bombing of Tripoli in 1986, the invasions of Grenada and Panama, the cruise missile attacks on targets suspected of being connected to Usama Bin Laden in Afghanistan and Sudan, for example. It is becoming more usual for the US to advocate aerial bombardment and cruise missile attack as the preferred tactic when military action must be taken, in order to avoid 'body bags'. Here Bosnia-Herzegovina, where the UN force commander opposed this option, and Kosovo, where there was no NATO consensus for ground force action, are the most recent examples.

The US has been described in many contradictory ways – arrogant, bully, paper tiger, satanic conspirator, interventionist, irrational, revisionist, quick on the trigger – none complimentary, and there is an example to confirm all of these. US foreign policy seems to be inconsistent, though others might describe it as pragmatic. The bully in the US is exemplified by its readiness to impose unilateral sanctions on numerous countries for relatively minor reasons; worse, it has passed legislation that allows it to take action against foreign firms that carry on trade where the US opposes it (major investment in the Iranian energy industry, for

US aircraft carrier USS John C. Stennis *with ammunition replenishment ship* Pacific, *August 1998. (US Department of Defense)*

US Tomahawk cruise missile fired at Iraq from USS Shiloh, *September 1996. (US Department of Defense)*

example). The branding by Iran and Iraq of the US as a satanic conspirator on account of its long-held policy of dual containment is understandable, but other Muslim countries have been dismayed by the lack of evenhandedness when the US invariably opposes any criticism of Israel at the UN Security Council. And it was undoubtedly quick on the trigger over the cruise missile attacks on a chemical plant in Sudan where it suspected chemical weapons for Usama bin Laden were being manufactured – a suspicion that was, it is now being alleged, not strongly held by the CIA before the attack.

At times, then, the US sets a bad example. Fortunately, the long-standing saga over US non-payment of dues to the UN appears to be over but only after it came dangerously close to losing its vote at the General Assembly under Article 19 of the UN Charter. This provision automatically removes the vote of any state that owes an amount equal to or more than its assessment for the previous two years. The US owes $1.52 billion; the Congress agreed to pay $926 million three years ago but attached strings to the payment that were unacceptable. President Clinton has now withdrawn his objection to the requirement that none of the money will go to fund the promotion or performance of abortions. Whether the UN will accept the $926 million as full and final payment of the US debt and whether it will agree to reduce the US share of the annual budget from 25 to 22 per cent (two other conditions put on the payment) remains to be seen. At the same time as it was withholding its fees, the US convinced the UN Security Council that it should impose sanctions on Afghanistan until Usama bin Laden was deported, and mounted a campaign and used its veto to ensure that Boutros Boutros-Ghali was not re-elected to serve a second term as Secretary General. Ghali, in his recently published book, has written 'the United States sees little need for diplomacy; power is enough'.

In the arms control field, on occasion the US sends out the wrong signal. The Senate's recent refusal to ratify the CTBT has horrified the non-nuclear-armed nations, especially as the Senate had the option of not voting on the issue. At least it cannot order the reintroduction of nuclear testing. Neither is the US stand against the Ottawa Convention on anti-personnel mines widely understood. One reason for its decision not to sign the treaty until 2006, and then only if other alternatives are available, is that it believes that anti-personnel mines are essential for the defence of South Korea. However, it should be noted that the US has played a major part in successfully negotiating bilateral treaties such as START 1 and 2 and multilateral agreements like the Conventional Forces in Europe Treaty. It cannot be accused of being anti-arms control.

Many Europeans cannot understand the US position on European defence. For some time the US has criticised Europe for not doing enough for its own defence; however, when Europe began announcing plans for the future (albeit without, as yet, promises to spend more or to invest in 'high tech' weaponry – the US's main complaint) the Americans quickly argued that the new scheme undermined NATO. President Chirac of France has rejected this criticism; the French Foreign Minister, Hubert Vedrine, put it slightly differently: 'The US has to make a choice. They have always been for sharing the burden. They've never been much for sharing the decision-making.' A genuine US complaint concerns the difficulty, or was it reluctance, European states exhibited in raising the 50,000 men needed for the Kosovo peacekeeping force from the total of nearly 2 million in the armies of the European NATO members.

The UN Charter clearly defines when military action may legally be taken, but the permanent members of the Security Council often vote contrary to the Charter's terms and to the humane course of action. Use of force is not authorised because of the possible implications for actions being taken in permanent members' own countries. Russia opposed action against Serbia as the Serbs were behaving in a similar manner to its own

US intervention worldwide since 1990.

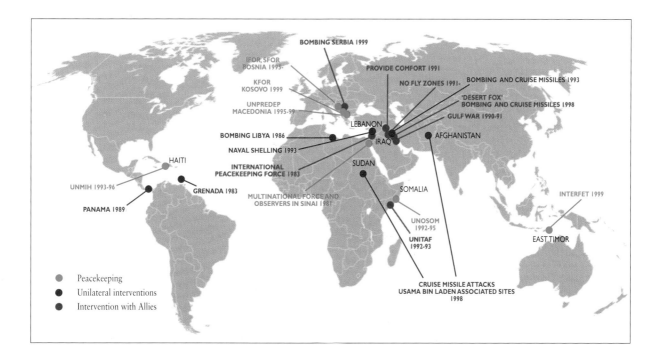

activity in Chechnya. (Russia is now using a version of NATO's tactics in Kosovo to destroy the Chechens.) Likewise, China opposes the use of force as this could, but is most unlikely to be, threatened over its treatment of Tibet. The US and, on occasion, its allies find it necessary to take military action without specific UN authorisation, normally finding suitable wording in the Charter to justify their actions. Recent examples include the bombing of Iraq in 1998, in retaliation for the obstruction of UN inspection teams, and of Serbia over Kosovo.

It is easy enough to criticise the US, either for doing too much or for not doing enough. Quite often it is criticised for both in respect of the same incident. But without US hegemony the world might well be a far more unstable place. Consider the implications of an alternative global hegemon – Russia or China, for instance.

Bibliography and Web Site

Boutros-Ghali, Boutros, *Unvanquished: A US-UN Saga*, IB Tauris, 1999

Haass, Richard N. (ed.), *Economic Sanctions and American Diplomacy*, Council on Foreign Relations, 1998

Kagan, Robert, and Charles William Maynes, 'US Dominance: Is It Good for the World', *Foreign Affairs* (Quarterly). Council of Foreign Relations

Foreign Policy (Summer 1998). Carnegie Endowment for International Peace

Survival Winter 1999–2000, International Institute for Strategic Studies, 1999

www.

Council for Foreign Relations: www.foreignrelations.org/public

BALLISTIC MISSILE DEFENCE: MYTH OR SURE DEFENCE?

One of the paradoxes of the post-Cold-War world is the new-found emphasis on ballistic missile defence. During the Cold War, when both sides faced large numbers of strategic nuclear missiles, the deployment of US and Soviet anti-ballistic missiles (ABM) was controlled by treaty. In the tactical field – where the Warsaw Pact was plentifully equipped with surface-to-surface missiles, such as Scaleboard, Scud and FROG, and NATO rather less plentifully with Pershing and Lance SSMs – there were no anti-SSM weapons at all. Now when the threat comes, or rather may come, from a handful of strategic missiles and more likely from improved SSMs in the hands of 'rogue' states, much effort and money is being expended on the development of both national and theatre missile defence (NMD and TMD).

The development of ABM was seen to lead to a race to procure more strategic missiles in order that any defence system could be overwhelmed. To avoid an accelerated arms race in ballistic missiles the ABM Treaty, signed by the US and USSR in 1972, prohibited the deployment of a nationwide defence against strategic ballistic missiles. Originally each side could deploy two systems, later amended to only one, to defend either the national capital or one ICBM launch area. The Soviet Union deployed a system around Moscow and the US deployed Safeguard to protect the Grand Forks, North Dakota, ICBM complex. The Moscow system is thought to be still operational though a number of the essential early warning radars have been shut down as they are no longer on Russian soil. The US ABM ceased to be operational in 1976.

A number of US-proposed new ABM systems would violate the ABM Treaty and Russia is adamant that the agreement should not be amended, even though America claims that its ABM would be limited to defend against 'rogue states' missiles and not Russian ICBM and SLBM. The Russians reaffirmed their opposition to altering the Treaty as recently as December 1999. China is also opposed to any ABM defences as the deployment of a theatre system in defence of Taiwan 'would only undermine security and stimulate the proliferation of missiles'. Taiwan, however, is determined to deploy TMD. America's allies are concerned too; there are radar facilities located in both the UK and Greenland that would have to be upgraded to allow them to contribute to missile defence and the two countries might be unwilling to allow the breaking of the ABM Treaty on their territory. Many Europeans believe that abrogating ABM would lead to the end of nuclear arms control and disarmament and could provoke China and Russia into improving their offensive capability in order to be able to swamp US missile defences. In December 1999 Secretary of Defense, William Cohen, told NATO that 'the threat from rogue states was real' and that 'the US might soon find it necessary to develop an anti-missile shield'. Russia and the US have agreed various parameters that demarcate between TMD and strategic missile defence. One parameter would only allow the deployment of TMD with an interceptor velocity of no more than 3 kilometres per second; however, short-range missiles could achieve this speed and more.

In March 1983 President Reagan embarked on the Strategic Defence Initiative and had spent over $30 billion before the concept was radically altered in 1993. After SDI the US turned to developing TMD and has recently returned to the concept of NMD. Among the concepts evolved for SDI were space- and ground-based surveillance and tracking systems, kinetic energy, laser and particle beam weapons, and space-based mirrors to reflect laser beams from a ground station to a target. One of the technically most ambitious parts of the project was 'Brilliant Pebbles', which was to consist of an array of autonomous space-based kinetic energy weapons, each with its own sensor, guidance, control and battle management capability. The weapons would be light (about 100lb), low-cost, and powered by solar rechargeable batteries. While SDI was expensive and never came to fruition it did have the effect of convincing the Soviet Union that it could not match US defence spending and so helped to lead to Mikhail Gorbachev's policies which ended the Cold War.

Of course, ICBMs are not the only way to deliver weapons of mass destruction and rather different defence systems would be needed to cope with long-range cruise missiles and with low trajectory missiles fired from submarines lying close to the target shore. Simple cruise missiles based on remotely piloted vehicles would be easier to intercept than ballistic missiles. However, sophisticated cruise missiles that can 'jink' and contour-hug will be difficult to acquire by ground-based radar and the US is experimenting with airborne radar to solve this problem. Defensive systems could be swamped by multiple warhead missiles and by decoys.

National Missile Defense mission

The Ballistic Missile Defense Organisation (BMDO) has balanced development, affordability, the potential threat, international treaty considerations and competing national defense priorities to establish the National Missile Defense (NMD) program. Expected Initial Operational Capability is 2005. The initial deployment will be limited to twenty missiles. [Now amended to 100 missiles.]

Elements of NMD Architecture

Ground-based Interceptors
Upgraded early warning radar
X-band radar (overseas and US-based)
Space-based infrared system
Battle management/command
Control and communications
In-flight interceptor communications

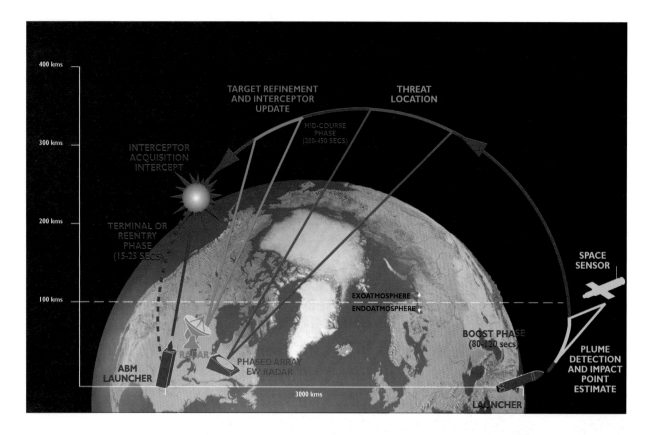

Theoretical capability of missile defence, figures 1 (above) and 2 (below).

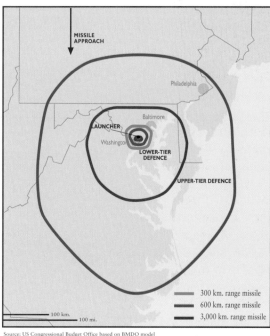

Source: US Congressional Budget Office based on BMDO model

Many consider that terrorist delivery of BW and CW would be achieved more successfully and far more cheaply than by missile delivery.

An issue that would need to be addressed before an ABM system was deployed would be the views of countries over which incoming missiles might be destroyed. The destruction of missiles, probably armed with chemical or biological agents (though BW germs may not survive the low temperature and aridity of the upper atmosphere), could result in the fall-out of agent.

Figure 1 illustrates a typical flight path of an ICBM. The best moment to attack incoming missiles is during the boost phase when burning fuel presents a target that is easily recognised by infrared sensors. Also, as the missile is still over the launcher's territory the risk of fall-out is avoided and multiple, independently targeted re-entry vehicles and decoys will not have been released. There is less than two minutes available to achieve a boost phase kill; interceptors need to be close, within 200 kilometres of launch sites, and fast. They would most likely have to be airborne or space-based.

Terminal defences are designed to destroy missiles once they have re-entered the atmosphere; they are either lower-tier weapons (such as the US Patriot) intercepting at up to 30 kilometres altitude or higher-

US Theatre High Altitude Air Defense missile on launch. (US Ballistic Missile Defense Organization)

tier weapons that can engage at between 30 and several hundred kilometres altitude. The area that can be protected by either tier depends on the speed of the incoming missile, and the speed of the missile in turn depends largely on its range. Figure 2 shows hypothetical footprints of the area that could be covered by lower- and higher-tier weapons. The terminal phase for incoming missiles lasts between 15 and 25 seconds only. Terminal defences can be based on land or on warships, the latter giving greater flexibility in deployment.

Apart from Israel, the US is the only nation developing ABM; it has an ambitious programme of both lower- and higher-tier weapons but, as yet, no boost-phase weapon. Lower-tier weapons for TMD are the Patriot Advanced Capability-3 (PAC-3), the Navy Area Defense programme employing a phased-array radar and an upgraded Standard Missile mounted on Aegis-equipped ships, to be in service in 2001 and 2003 respectively. The Medium Extended Air Defense System (MEADS) is being developed in cooperation with Germany and Italy. Upper-tier TMD weapons – the Theater High Altitude Area Defense (THAAD) and the Navy Theater Wide system – are designed to intercept medium- and intermediate-range missiles at high altitude and so will be able to defend larger areas than lower-tier weapons. A successful THAAD intercept was carried out in June 1999 after six earlier test failures; the system development has cost $3 billion since 1992. THAAD could be mounted on a warship. The Navy Theater Wide development is behind that of THAAD but a decision on which of the two systems will be procured is to be taken in 2002 with the aim of one entering service in 2007. A successful test of the Ground-Based Interceptor, which is a candidate for NMD, took place in October 1999 when the ABM hit a Minuteman ICBM 140 miles over the Pacific. An airborne laser (ABL) is also being developed that can intercept ballistic missiles early in their flight: the first in-flight lethality test is planned for 2003. The Israeli Arrow ABM was successfully tested against another missile on 1 November 1999.

NMD development is taking place but only in accord with the ABM Treaty and it is realised that NMD deployment may require modifications to that agreement. The aim is to produce a system that can intercept a small number of intercontinental missiles launched by a rogue state but is not capable of defending against a large-scale attack. One option being considered is the deployment of 100 ABM launchers in Alaska. The US administration was due to decide whether to deploy NMD in summer 2000 but there are recommendations that the decisions should be postponed. In Congress, pressure is mounting for early deployment of NMD. The Senate has voted in favour of deploying NMD 'as soon as technically feasible', while in the House of Representatives a bill endorsing the project, but without specifying a timetable or any conditions, was passed. The Russian Foreign Ministry has said that the votes 'pose a serious threat to the whole process of nuclear arms control, as well as strategic stability'.

Bibliography and Web Sites

Brown, Neville, *The Fundamental Issue Studies: Within the British BMD Review*, Mansfield College, Oxford, 1998

www.
Ballistic Missile Defense Organisation: www.acq.osd.mil/bmdo/
Federation of American Scientists: www.fas.org/spp/starwars/

SANCTIONS: DO THEY WORK?

Sanctions of any kind are a halfway house between diplomatic protest and military action. They can be imposed by the UN, by regional or ad hoc organisations or by individual countries. The most usual form of sanction is either a ban on arms exports to the state in question or on trade between the sanctioner and sanctioned. Other forms involve travel prohibitions, technology transfer and restriction of sporting activities. Just how successful sanctions are in altering the policies of the sanctioned party is open to question. They have had the desired effect on some occasions but more usually they only contribute to the outcome. The great advantage of imposing such measures is that 'something' is 'seen to be done' when public opinion demands this, but no military action has to be taken.

Arms embargoes and other trade restrictions imposed by the UN, for example, are not always upheld by all states. Therefore, sanctions may have to be backed by physical measures, normally naval to enforce a blockade. However, even these are often not totally successful. That a state is unable to obtain a commodity because of sanctions raises the value of that commodity to the state and this can encourage sanction 'busting' by the unscrupulous. Sanctions can also be counter-productive because of the injurious effects on the sanctioning parties – through loss of trade, for example. They can also cause the sanctioned state to take action that makes the ban relatively pointless – the best example of this being South Africa's creation of a thriving arms industry after the imposition of an embargo. Examples of the effects or failures of sanctions are often used to support or to denigrate their efficacy according to the policy inclination of the commentator; there is no clear agreement on what constitutes success. The threat of a particular ban can often be effective but overall there are more historical examples of the failure of sanctions than of their success.

Before 1990 the UN had only imposed sanctions twice – on Rhodesia and South Africa – whereas the US had initiated sanctions on some forty occasions. Since 1990 the UN has imposed arms embargoes on Angola, Haiti, Liberia, Libya, Rwanda, Sierra Leone and Yugoslavia; oil embargoes were also imposed on Angola, Haiti and Sierra Leone. The UN freeze on funds and embargo on aircraft landing in Libya is the most recent example of the successful use of sanctions: the two Libyan men suspected of causing the Lockerbie air disaster have now been handed over for trial in Holland under Scottish law. Libya's earlier refusal to hand over the suspects prompted sanctions that were at the lower end of the severity scale, but despite their relatively mild character, the measures worked. On the other hand, US sanctions imposed on Cuba in 1960 have still not had any effect on the Cuban leader, Fidel Castro, and have made little progress towards isolating Cuba, which now has a growing tourist industry. Most recently the UN has, at US insistence, placed a ban on international flights to Afghanistan and frozen its overseas assets. The reason for the sanctions is Afghanistan's continued protection of the terrorist sponsor, Usama bin Laden, and refusal to expel him.

The sanctions imposed on Iraq after the Gulf War in 1991 continue to generate considerable controversy. Here, as in other trade embargoes, the sanction has more effect on the general population than on the leadership or elite who are its prime target. To complicate the argument, Iraq is allowed to sell up to $4 billion worth of oil annually, the proceeds from which can be used to buy food and medical supplies. There should be no starvation or malnutrition and the fact that there is could be blamed on Saddam Hussein's failure to distribute the imports fairly and to his misuse of the funds generated. However, many attribute the suffering directly to sanctions and argue that they should be lifted. This argument is put forward particularly strongly by those owed large sums by Iraq and those eager to renew trading. The US has said it will veto the lifting of the embargo until Saddam Hussein has been removed from power. Meanwhile, the ban is bypassed on a regular basis.

The country that resorts most often to imposing unilateral sanctions is the United States. Currently there are US sanctions imposed on sixty-eight other countries, including a number of staunch American allies. In some cases embargoes are imposed on individual companies that have offended

Some reasons for US sanctions		
Imposed on	Date	Reason
Argentina	1944	Peron
UK and France	1956	Suez
Cuba	1960	Castro
Chile	1965	copper price
South Korea	1973	human rights
South Africa	1975	nuclear weapons
Nicaragua	1977	Samoza
Iran	1979	hostages
Iraq	1980	terrorism
Argentina	1982	Falklands
Angola	1986	Cuban troops
Sudan	1989	human rights
Libya	1998	terrorism

Some costs of imposing sanctions

Loss of exports, including services
Loss of transport and communications
Loss of cheap imports
Loss of imports not available elsewhere
Confiscation of funds
Loss of immigrant remittances
Return of migrant workers
Termination of joint ventures

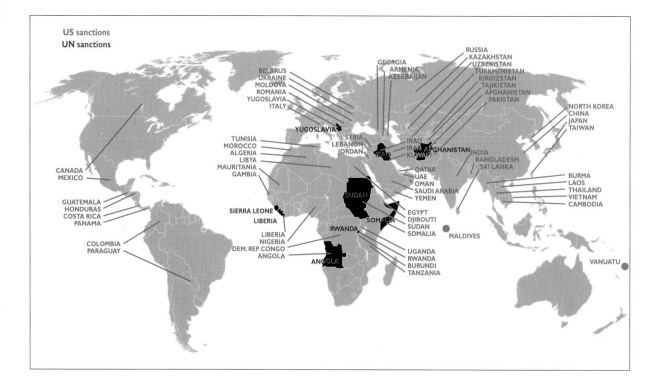

US and UN sanctions imposed around the world.

against US trade regulations or other sanctions. In November 1999 embargoes were imposed on one Kazakh and one Czech Republic company for arranging the sale of forty fighter planes to North Korea – the US had already placed an arms embargo on North Korea. A measure that affronts many is the US law forbidding foreign companies from investing more than $40 million in Iranian or Libyan energy projects or occupying any premises in Cuba that were formerly owned by US companies. Companies violating the law would be banned from trading in the US. The US argues that companies will prefer to trade with it than with Iran.

While the US is happy to impose sanctions, it is not prepared to accept decisions by others to restrict American exports. This has been clear in the recent 'banana' dispute with the European Union and the imminent confrontation over US hormone-fed beef and genetically modified crops.

Sanctions may not be guaranteed to work, but they must be tried before the drastic decision to employ military force is taken.

Bibliography and Web Sites

Doxey, Margaret P., *International Sanctions in Contemporary Politics*, Macmillan 1996
Freedman, Lawrence (ed.), *Strategic Coercion*, Oxford University Press, 1998
Hufbauer, G., J. Schott and K. Elliot, *Economic Sanctions Reconsidered*, 1990
Simons, Geoff, *Imposing Economic Sanctions: Legal Remedy or Genocidal Tool*, Pluto Press, 1999

United Nations: www.un.org
US Department of Treasury: www.ustreas.gov
US State Department: www.state.gov

END OF EMPIRE:
THE COLLAPSE OF
THE SOVIET UNION

The collapse of communism in the Soviet Union and in its satellite countries in Eastern Europe changed the world. The Cold War was over and a whole new series of international relations had to be created. This section is devoted purely to the former Soviet Union. It begins by describing how the Russian empire was built, acquired by the Soviet Union after the revolution and then broken up. Further sections examine the potential for future problems, including the possibility of further disintegration of the Russian Federation, first in the region most likely to be affected – the North Caucasus – and then elsewhere in Russia. The security of the Baltic States and their relations with Russia are also considered. At the other end of the country, the background to the problem of the Kuril Islands claimed by Japan is discussed. Finally, the very large-scale reduction in armed forces brought about not just by the break-up of the Soviet Union but also by the limitations imposed by the Conventional Forces in Europe Treaty is detailed.

THE SOVIET UNION: RUSSIA'S FORMER EMPIRE

It took Russia some 900 years to acquire an empire that was further expanded by the Soviet Union immediately after the Second World War; but the Soviet Union broke up in 1991 in only a matter of weeks. It is not at all clear that there will not be a further disintegration of the Russian Federation.

Although many different races had lived in the region in earlier times, the Russian nation seems to have been born when the East Slavs, who had settled in the river valleys of today's western Russia, Ukraine and Belarus, developed into a series of tribes during the fifth and sixth centuries. The Vikings who invaded in the ninth century and established themselves first in Novgorod and later in Kiev called the native people the Gadaraki. Through force of arms the Ryurikid family took control of what is known as Kievan Russia. In the 960s Svyatoslav attacked and defeated the Khazars to whom the Kievans had paid tribute. Orthodox Christianity was introduced in 988 after Svyatoslav's son Vladimir had thoroughly investigated the neighbouring religions – the Islam of the Volga Bulgars, the Judaism of the Khazars and the Christianity of Byzantium.

The Mongol Tatars first appeared in the region in 1223 on reconnaissance and in strength. They defeated a Russian army at the Kalka River before withdrawing. They returned in 1237 destroying Ryazan and other cities but as the spring thaw came they withdrew before reaching Novogorod. Then in 1240 the Tatars took the southern cities of Kiev and Chernigov and began their rule of the region.

Ivan III created Muscovy, as Russia with Moscow as its capital was known in the West. Tatar power ended in 1480 when the Russian army met the Tatars on the River Ugra and both took the decision not to fight. Ivan suppressed Novgorod in 1478, Tver capitulated in 1485 and Vyatka in 1489; only Pskov and Ryazan remained independent by the end of Ivan's reign. Vasiliy, Ivan's successor, took them both. Ivan IV defeated the last Tatar kingdoms, Kazan in 1552 and Astrakhan in 1554.

The next large-scale expansion took place in the sixteenth and seventeenth centuries when the Russians crossed the Urals and reached the Bering Sea in 1648. Russia's westward expansion was halted and at times reversed by the Poles and Lithuanians and later the Swedes whose King Charles XII made several expeditions deep into Russia in the early eighteenth century. Peter the Great established the capital at St Petersburg in 1703 and by the Peace of Nystad of 1721 gained Estonia, Livonia (Latvia) and part of Karelia. Under Catherine II, Russia gained control of the northern Black Sea coast, including the Crimea; Odessa was founded in 1794. Russia's conquests of the North Caucasus and Transcaucasus are described on pages 68–73 and 132–8.

In 1809 Sweden ceded the Grand Duchy of Finland to Russia and the latter gained the Grand Duchy of Warsaw in 1815. However, after a short period of control it failed to maintain its position in Montenegro and the Ionian Islands. Then Russia's attempt to gain secure access to the Mediterranean from the Black Sea was thwarted by the Crimean War and it turned its attention to Central Asia, crossing the Caspian and taking Tashkent, Bokhara, Khiva and Kokand between 1865 and 1876. During the same period Russia expanded in the far east by advancing to the River Amur and establishing Vladivostock. It also completed its conquest of Sakhalin. By 1900 it occupied all of Kazakhstan. It sold Alaska, occupied in 1774, to the US in 1867.

After the Russian Revolution of 1917 and the end of the First World War the new Bolshevik government had to fight hard to retain Russian territory because the counter-revolutionary army (known as the 'Whites' as opposed to the Bolshevik 'Reds') were supported by a number of west European allies, the Germans and the Turks. Fighting took place in the north, the south and the far east; as a result Poland, Finland and the Baltic States gained their independence. Armenia, Azerbaijan and Georgia briefly broke free but by 1921 they had become republics of the Soviet Union. Bessarabia became part of Romania.

The Second World War allowed the USSR to regain some of the territory lost after 1918: the Baltic States, Bessarabia, parts of eastern Finland and East Prussia, now known as Kaliningrad. Of course Soviet

Russian diaspora: % of population	
Ukraine	22
Belarus	13
Moldova	13
Turkmenistan	7
Uzbekistan	6
Tajikistan	2
Kazakhstan	32
Kirgyzstan	17
Georgia	6
Armenia	2
Azerbaijan	2

influence now extended much further west than the borders of the USSR because it was given post-war administrative responsibility for Eastern Europe where it ensured that communist governments came to power. The Soviet-led Warsaw Pact that faced NATO was formed in 1955 after West Germany was admitted to NATO; Soviet military forces remained in East Germany, Czechoslovakia, Poland and Hungary until the 1980s.

The break-up of the Soviet Union, a federation of fifteen Union Republics, and its empire was relatively quick. Mikhail Gorbachev became President of the USSR and Secretary General of the Communist Party in March 1985. He began by strengthening his position at home and then made a number of foreign policy statements including offers to reduce nuclear weapons. The Soviet economy was already in trouble made worse by increased defence spending, the oil glut and a drop in oil prices. In 1986 Presidents Gorbachev and Reagan held a summit meeting at Reykjavik at which no agreement could be reached over US plans for a Strategic Defence Initiative. However, Gorbachev did begin the Soviet withdrawal from Afghanistan and extended the USSR's moratorium on nuclear testing. The terms 'glasnost' (or openness) and 'perestroika' (or restructuring) now entered the world's vocabulary.

The year 1987 saw the start of nationalist movements in the Baltic States and in 1988 these developed in the Transcaucasus where the Nagorno-Karabakh issue erupted. The events leading to independence in the Baltic States are described on pages 77–81 and those in the Transcaucasus on pages 132–8. The challenge to the Soviet Union's cohesion had begun. Gorbachev addressed the United Nations in December 1988 and announced large-scale reductions in Soviet conventional forces. The Warsaw Pact adopted a defensive doctrine and further statements on Soviet intentions regarding arms reductions, withdrawals from Eastern Europe and military strength were made. The end of the Cold War appeared to be coming.

But despite his foreign policy successes Gorbachev was in trouble at home. There was growing opposition to his reforms from the Communist Party, the army and the KGB, but the changes were welcomed and copied in most Eastern European countries. During 1989 the unravelling continued, with Eastern European countries taking the lead in moving towards democracy. Gorbachev attended the fortieth anniversary celebrations in Berlin as Erich Honecker's government attempted to maintain the old regime while large numbers escaped from East Germany through Hungary and demonstrations took place. Gorbachev emphasised the need for reform, Honecker resigned and on 9 November the Berlin Wall came down.

There was also at this time violence in Moldova and in the Central Asian republics. Mass rallies were held in Ukraine. Changes were made to the politburo to strengthen Gorbachev's hand and there were those who wanted reform to go further but at the same time the number of influential opponents to perestroika grew. In August 1991 a coup failed to depose Gorbachev, much of the credit for foiling it being due to Boris Yeltsin, who had been elected President of Russia in June and who evaded arrest and mobilised both international and domestic opposition to the coup. A few days later Gorbachev resigned as General Secretary and the Supreme

Some Russian history	
c. 878	Kievan Rus, east Slav state formed
c. 988	Volodymyrl (Vladimir) converted to Orthodox Christianity.
1237–40	Mongol invasion
	Tatar suzerainty renounced
1533–84	Ivan 'the Terrible' expands eastwards
	Khanate of Kazan subjugated
	Khanate of Astrakhan subjugated
	Expedition east of the Urals
	Kamchakta and Pacific reached
1682–1725	Peter 'the Great'
	Annexation of Transbaikal
1762–96	Catherine 'the Great' expands to the south and west.
	Port on Black sea gained
	Khanate of Crimea annexed
	Napoleon's invasion
1853–6	Crimean War
	Conquest of east Caucasus
	Vladivostok
	Alaska sold to USA
	Sakhalin exchanged for the Kurils
	Russo-Japanese War lost
1917	Tsar abdicates, Russian Federation founded

▓	1462
▓	1598
▓	1689
▓	1815
▓	1914
┅┅┅	USSR 1990

The growth of the Russian Empire.

Soviet suspended all Communist Party activities. On 20 August the Baltic States and Belarus declared their independence and were followed over the next few days by Ukraine, Azerbaijan, Uzbekistan and Kirgyzstan. In October the Union Republics held a conference in Alma Ata but only eight signed a treaty on economic cooperation. On 14 November the Soviet constitution was abrogated. An unsuccessful attempt was made to establish a confederation but Gorbachev finally resigned on 30 December and the Soviet Union ceased to exist.

Bibliography and Web Site

Milner-Gulland, Robin, and Nikolai Dejevsky, *Atlas of Russia and the Soviet Union*, Phaidon, 1989

Starr, S. Frederick (ed.), *The Legacy of History in Russia and the New States of Eurasia*, ME Sharpe Inc, 1994

Institute for the Study of Conflict, Ideology, and Policy (Boston University): www.bu.edu/iscpi

NORTH CAUCASUS: THE NEXT TIER TO BREAK AWAY?

The Caucasian Mountains now form Russia's southern border while at the same time presenting a region of six republics all with greater or lesser ambitions for more independence. It is populated by some eighteen different ethnic groups; most have a long history of opposition to the Russians who have, over the years, introduced settlers. While Russia has no intention of losing control of this strategic region, the experience of the Chechen war could be repeated elsewhere in the North Caucasus, though the severity of the Russian reaction to the uprising in Chechnya should warn others not to try to break away.

The first significant contact between Russia and the Caucasian people came in 1556 when Ivan the Terrible conquered Astrakhan and a stretch of the Caspian coastline. At roughly the same time Cossacks arrived in the Terek region and set up settlements south of the river; the indigenous population of Chechens, who had lived there for centuries, kept to the mountains and forests. Two Russian army defeats in the early 1600s led to the Cossacks withdrawing north of the Terek. They returned as part of the Imperial Army a hundred years later and recolonised the area. Chechens who sided with the Russians against the East Caucasian leaders – Sheikh Mansur Ushurma, who revolted in 1785 and was captured 1791, and Imam Shamil, who led the opposition to the Russians from the death of Qazi Mullah in 1832 until 1859 when he surrendered but was allowed to go to Mecca – were rewarded with land north of the Terek. The period between these two East Caucasian revolts was one of relative peace punctuated by raids and counter-raids by the Russians and the Chechens and Dagestanis.

Russia needed to control Dagestan and Chechnya, and committed some 300,000 troops to doing so in the 1850s, for much the same reasons as it is trying to hold on to the territory today. The area lies on the edge of the two main routes from Russia to the Transcaucasus: the Caspian coastal road and the road from Vladikavkaz to Tbilisi in Georgia. Today the oil pipeline from Azerbaijan to Novorossiysk on the Black Sea also crosses Chechnya.

North Caucasian peoples	
Ethnic group	Approximate number
Chechen	957,000
Avar	601,000
Ossetians	598,000 (incl. South Ossetia)
Lezgi	466,000 (50 per cent in Azerbaijan)
Kabards	391,000
Dargin	365,000
Kumyk	282,000
Ingush	273,000
Karachai	156,000
Adygei	125,000
Lak	118,000
Abkhaz	105,000 (85 per cent in Abkhazia)
Tabarasan	98,000
Balkar	85,000
Nogai	75,000
Abaza	33,000
Rutul	20,000
Tsakhur	20,000 (65 per cent in Azerbaijan)
Agul	19,000
Mountain Jews	18,000

Also non-North Caucasian:
Russian 1.5 million, Armenian 150,000, Azeri 75,000

Source: 1989 Soviet census

The ethnic populations of the North Caucasus.

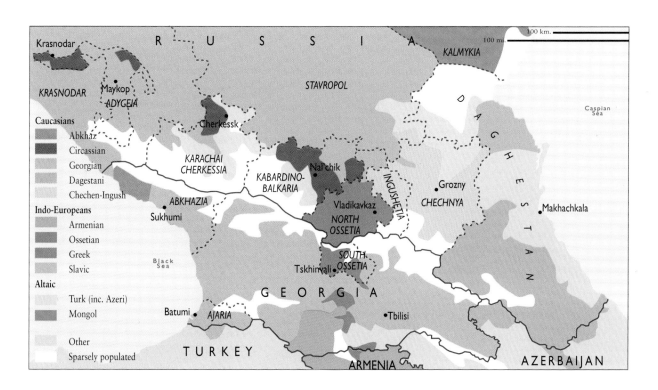

At the same time as the Russians were fighting Shamil, they were also conquering the West Caucasus where there was no such figure to unify opposition. By 1870 the Russians had driven out the majority of the mountain people and their lands were taken over by settlers from Russia, Georgia and Armenia. Islam had far less influence in the west than it had in the east.

The East Caucasians took the opportunities offered by the Russian-Ottoman War of 1877–8, the 1905 revolution and the collapse of tsarist Russia in 1917 to rebel and on the first two occasions were suppressed brutally. In May 1918 the Chechens and Dagestanis established a North Caucasus Republic and supported the Red Army against the White Russians who controlled most of the North Caucasus. Once the White Russians were defeated, the mountain people turned to fight the Bolsheviks who took nine months to subdue them. In 1921 the Soviets set up the Soviet Mountain Republic, which covered the whole region except Dagestan, but it was soon broken up into separate autonomous regions; the Chechen-Ingush region became an autonomous republic in 1936.

During the Second World War the Germans invaded the Caucasus and were only halted by the Red Army within artillery range of Grozny; the Chechens rebelled again but relatively few crossed over to join the Germans. In 1943 Stalin decided to deport the Balkar, Chechen, Ingush, Kalmyk and Karachai populations to Kazakhstan and Kirgyzstan; the Karachai were sent in November 1943, the Kalmyks followed in December and the Balkars in March 1944. It was the turn of some 478,000 Chechens and Ingush in February 1944; it is suspected that some 78,000 Chechens died on the journey. The Chechen-Ingush autonomous republic was broken up; its land was divided and handed to its neighbours. The Chechens were allowed back to the Caucasus in 1958 and the Chechen-Ingush autonomous republic was re-established but with two traditionally Cossack districts of Stavropol added. The Russian settlers remained mainly in the towns and in the north of the republic.

In August 1991, the (then) Chechen-Ingush autonomous republic, under the leadership of Air Force General Dzhokhar Dudayev, demanded complete independence. Little action was taken other than the declaration of a state of emergency – a decision quickly reversed by the Supreme Soviet – and the imposition of an economic blockade. In 1994 a covert operation backed by the Russian Federal Counter-Intelligence Service, but fronted by Chechens opposed to Dudayev, was mounted. Despite reinforcement from the Russian Army it was unsuccessful. During an attack on the Chechen capital, Grozny, on 26 November 1994, a number of Russian soldiers were captured. They were then publicly paraded, much to the surprise of their divisional commander who did not know that any of his soldiers were in Chechnya. The parade was probably the final straw that decided President Yeltsin to order military intervention.

The operation came at a particularly bad time for Russian forces, which were still in the process of reorganising after the massive changes forced on them by the break up of the Soviet Union. Many divisions were either being disbanded or converted into independent brigades, and as a result virtually all were well under strength, soldiers' living conditions were abysmal and morale was understandably low. Little or no time was given for the preparation of the operation and the initial force, presumably chosen from those most readily available and up to strength, was hastily assembled. On 11 December it was deployed to Chechnya without any preliminary training. It comprised a miscellany of different units drawn from virtually every branch: mechanised troops, airborne forces, naval infantry and Ministry of Interior Troops – none of whom had ever operated together before.

This was the first time Russian (or Soviet) forces had had to operate watched by the world's media and this added weight to the political requirement for the operation to be completed as quickly as possible. This in turn led to the disastrous decision to try to take Grozny with an armoured dash. The attacking forces paid heavily for this major tactical error. The Russians had badly underestimated Chechen strength and determination. Before 1991 there had been an armoured training centre based at Grozny. To allow this to be withdrawn unhindered a deal was struck in which half its equipment would be left behind; this deal left the Chechens with some tanks, infantry fighting vehicles and artillery. Not that they used these in the battle for Grozny.

Grozny was captured in early February 1995, and in March and April the Russians took the area's remaining towns as the Chechens withdrew into the mountains. Fighting continued and peace talks arranged by the Organisation for Co-operation and Security in Europe broke down. On 14 June a group of 100 Chechens raided Budennovsk in Stavropol, capturing the hospital and taking 1,000 hostages; two attempts to recapture the hospital were unsuccessful and eventually the Chechens were allowed free passage. They took 100 hostages with them but released them on 20 June.

Destruction in Grozny after the Russian assault, December 1994. (Novosti)

Topography of the Caucasus and regional organisation in the north.

In January 1996 a group of 200 Chechens infiltrated Kizlyar in Dagestan and seized 3,000 civilians. Again free passage was agreed. Then the Chechen convoy was halted at Pervomaiskoye and attacked by Russian special forces. However, the Chechens escaped with some hostages. In April two ambushes resulted in the death of over 100 Russian soldiers. Dudayev was killed in a rocket attack. Following agreement on a ceasefire, President Yeltsin appointed General Lebed, who had successfully defused the Russian/Moldovan confrontation in Transdneistr in Moldova, with full powers to negotiate a peace settlement. On 31 August he and the Chechen commander, Aslan Maskhadov, signed an agreement that provided for the withdrawal of Russian troops and declared that the future status of Chechnya would be agreed by 2001. In May 1997 Maskhadov, now the elected President of Chechnya, visited Moscow. He and President Yeltsin signed a short peace treaty confirming the ceasefire agreement of August 1996 and committing both sides to rejecting the use or threat of force.

The autonomous republic of Chechnya.

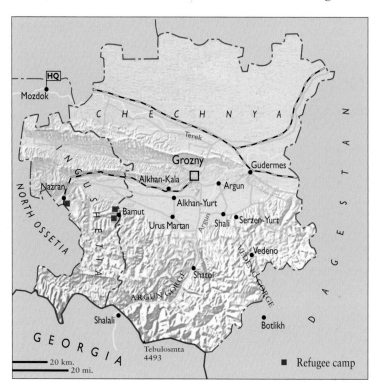

Chechnya, meanwhile, became a virtually lawless place; many of the fighters who had defeated the Russian Army turned to crime. In July 1998 the President narrowly escaped when his motorcade was damaged by a large car bomb. Kidnapping, including that of foreign workers, was rife; in October the head of the anti-kidnapping police was killed when his car was blown up. The whole region could have slipped out of control as the many criminal gangs, each from a different ethnic group (of which there are thirty-four in Dagestan alone), competed against each other. Four ethnic groups claim some form of autonomy: Avars, Dargins, Kumyks and Nogays. The disorder in Dagestan could have spread, threatening Russia's main transport link with the Transcaucasus, and had it broken away much of Russia's Caspian shoreline would have gone with it, so reducing Russia's share of Caspian resources. The Cossacks, too, are looking for the creation of a Cossack Federal Republic, a move that is opposed by all the peoples of the North Caucasus.

The Russian fear that Chechnya's revolt could be repeated across the whole North Caucasus has not been realised. The main threat lies in Dagestan, which is also lawless. Fighting there between Chechen-backed Dagestanis and the Russian government broke out in August 1999. The Russian government took the opportunity to teach the Chechens a lesson and entered the country, first as far as the Terek River. The Russian Army was eager to take its revenge on the Chechens and to restore some of its prestige. It seems to have been given the go ahead to subdue Chechnya and it set about this task with massive air and artillery attacks, aping somewhat NATO's tactics against Serbia. By the end of 1999 Grozny was still holding out, the Russians were remorselessly clearing the mountainous forests in the south of the country and many Chechens had fled as refugees into Ingushetia.

At the western end of the Caucasus are the autonomous republics of Karachevo-Cherkessia and Kabardino-Balkaria which both have split populations and where regional disputes could emerge. The Circassians called for an autonomous republic which would also include the Adygei autonomous region (whose population is of the same ethnicity as the Cherkess) and the coastal districts of the Russian Krasnodar region. The Karachai leaders demanded the restoration of the territory they had held before their deportation in 1943. The Russians decreed in 1995 that the Karachevo-Cherkessia should be abolished and incorporated into the Stavropol region, but this has not yet been implemented. In Kabardino-Balkaria both the minority Balkars and the Kabardins declared separate republics in 1991, a move backed by their parliament, but this plan was dropped because of strong opposition from ethnic Russians. One problem solved, temporarily at any rate, is the dispute between Ingushetia and North Ossetia; the territories fought in 1992 when the Ingush population in Ossetia was expelled. The two republics signed a treaty normalising relations in September 1997.

Bibliography and Web Sites

Bennington Broxup, Marie (ed.), *The North Caucasus Barrier: Russian Advance towards the Muslim World*, Hurst, 1993

Dawisha, Karen, and Bruce Parrott (eds), *Conflict, Cleavage and Change in Central Asia and the Caucasus*, Cambridge University Press, 1997

Fursberg, Thomas (ed.), *Contested Territory*, Edward Elgar, 1995

Gall, Carlotta, and Thomas De Waal, *Chechnya: A Small Victorious War*, Pan/Macmillan, 1997

Lieven, Anatol, *Chechnya: Tombstone of Russian Power*, Yale University Press, 1998

Trofimenko, Henry, *Russian National Interests and the Current Crisis in Russia*, Cambridge University Press, 1999

Smith, Sebastian, *Allah's Mountains: Politics and War in the Russian Caucasus*, IB Taurus, 1998

van der Leeuw, Charles, *Storm Over the Caucasus in the Wake of Independence*, Curzon Press, 1999

Central Asia-Caucasus Institute (Nitze School of Advanced International Studies): www.sais-jhu.edu/caci

WWW.

Government of Chechen Republic: www.amina.com/

North Caucasus Conflict Centre: www.cdi.org/issues/Europe/ncaucasus

PROBLEMS THAT COULD FACE THE RUSSIAN FEDERATION: UNREALISED FEARS

When the Soviet Union broke up into fifteen independent states in 1991 there were those who forecast further disintegration in the Russian Federation, which could face civil war between Russians and ethnic minorities. So far, with the exception of the revolt in Chechnya, this has not occurred. The main problems facing Russia are corruption and the economy: neither should lead to disintegration. If anything they should unite the country in its efforts to put things right. The division of Russia into regions and sub-regions is complicated and needs some explanation.

In the Soviet Union at the top level were the Union Republics. Within the Russian Federation there are four differently named sub-divisions. The six largest regions are called *krais* or territory, the next being the forty-nine *oblasts* or regions; there are also twenty-one autonomous republics and *oblasts*, mainly linked to an ethnic group but in only four is there a non-Russian ethnic majority, and the two major cities of Moscow and St Petersburg. Eight of the republics are in the Caucasus. Each entity sends two representatives to the Federal Council or upper house of the Federal Assembly or parliament. Election to the Duma, the lower house, is partly through regional constituencies and partly from party lists. Below this level come ten autonomous *okrugs* and the Jewish Autonomous Oblast in the far east; also with non-Russian ethnic populations, they are administratively subordinate to the region of which they form a part but constitutionally they are equal and also send two representatives to the Council. In 1992 all these entities, bar Chechnya and Tatarstan, signed the Federation Treaty. The *krais* and *oblasts* believed themselves disadvantaged by the treaty, which gave the republics greater economic autonomy, and so some declared themselves to be republics in the hope of gaining the benefits of that status. Many of the entities have signed bilateral treaties with Moscow. Some are power-sharing agreements, others are concerned with fiscal matters; all give different advantages to the regional partner but virtually all give them a share of Federal funding.

When the Soviet Union delineated its internal borders it often deliberately excluded a part of the local ethnic nationality from its natural region, as in the case of the split of the Ossetians between the Republic of North Ossetia in Russia and South Ossetia in Georgia or the Azerbaijan enclave of Nakichevan that lies between Armenia and Turkey. This issue is more pertinent in the North Caucasus than elsewhere; the problems there are described on pages 63–73. Problems could well materialise in Central Asia, particularly over the changes made to Uzbekistan in the past. Boundaries were altered and re-altered throughout the history of the USSR for a variety of reasons. By the end of 1991 some 164 territorial and boundary disputes had been identified in the territory of the former Soviet Union. Many of these had an ethnic or nationality aspect. Of the new independent states only Belarus and Russia, and Latvia and Lithuania, did not have disputes with each other; all the others had claims against their neighbours.

Disputed territory was not confined to within the former Soviet Union. Other states could have claims for land lost earlier to the Soviet Union but, with the exception of the Japanese claim on the Kuril Islands (see pages 85, 86), territorial demands have only been made by national extremists or provocative sections of the media. Potential issues concern Finland and Russia, Poland and Belarus and Ukraine. Slovakia, Romania and Mongolia could also make claims. Good progress has been made on resolving Chinese-Russian border issues.

In 1993 Boris Yeltsin abolished the regional Soviets and appointed governors to be the heads of the regional administration. His aim was to exercise control by his ability to appoint and dismiss governors. A number of governors were regionally elected and by 1995 Yeltsin had had to agree to the election of both governors and leaders of legislatures. Governors are now more concerned with their own power and the economy of their region than with following Moscow's policies. A larger threat to centralised rule comes from the so-called 'elites' formed in each region by leading politicians, industrialists and financiers who have been joined by, and to some extent taken control of, privatised business enterprises and criminal factions. They have managed to acquire major denationalised assets in their regions and have formed corporations that ensure they receive the profits. In the autonomous republics the 'elites' are usually members of the ethnic nationality. Governors and 'elites' are usually in alliance. The federal authorities still collect taxes and control the major utilities, such as the gas, electrical power industries and the railways, and so can influence regional economies to a degree by the level of subsidy each receives.

The two most separatist-minded republics, Tatarstan and Bashkortostan, are unlikely to declare total independence as they have no external borders and are so totally reliant on the central transportation system. Both have Muslim majority populations. Tatarstan has signed a beneficial bilateral treaty with Moscow. It is suggested that the Russian far east and north-west are the most likely to benefit from arrangements made directly with foreign powers, bypassing Moscow. A number of inter-regional economic zones have been established. However, even these more prosperous regions will still rely on the central government for subsidy. Nationalism is fuelled as much by economic prospects as by ethnic considerations. There have been some instances of ethnic violence in Tyva, Buratiya and Yakutia; demands for ethnic separatism are not strong as there has been a good deal of inter-marriage and it is becoming harder to differentiate between Russians and the original ethnic nationals.

Some see the resurgence of the Cossacks as a potential source of trouble. The Cossacks are most probably descended from the Mongol or Tatar horsemen who invaded the southern valleys of the Dnieper, Don and Volga in the mid-thirteenth century. Over the years they were employed on internal security and soon gained a reputation for ruthlessness and brutality. They enjoyed privileges, owning land and carrying arms, for example, not allowed to the peasants. The Tatar character of the Cossacks changed over the years as those fleeing from authority joined their ranks; the Cossacks, therefore, became more Russian but of a particularly independent nature. Two Cossack groups were established in 1990 – the Union of Cossack Russians and the Union of Cossack Hosts in Russia and Abroad – and they set about re-

---

Russian regional associations

Central Russia: Bryansk, Vladimir, Ivanovo, Kaluga, Kostroma, Moscow, Ryazan, Smolensk, Tver, Yaroslavi, Moscow City.

Black Earth: Voronezh, Belgorod, Kursk, Lipetsk, Orel, Tambov.

Greater Volga: Tatarstan, Mordovia, Marii-El, Astrakhan, Volgograd, Nizhny Novgorod, Penza, Samara, Saratov, Ulyanovsk.

North-West: Karelia and Koni, Arkhangelsk, Volgoda, Kaliningrad, Kirov, Leningrad, Murmansk, Pskov, Nenets, St Petersburg City.

Urals: Bashkortostan, Udmurtia, Kurgan, Orenburg, Perm, Sverdlovsk, Chelyabinsk, Komi-Permyak.

North Caucasus: Adygey, Dagestan, Ingushetia, Kabardino-Balkaria, Karachaevo-Cherkess, North Ossetia, Kalmykia, Krasnodar, Stavropol, Rostov.

Siberia: Buryat, Altai (Republic and Territory), Khakass, Krasnoyark. Irkutsk, Novosibirsk, Omsk, Tomsk, Tyumen, Kemerovo, Agin-Buryat, Taimyr, Urst-Orda Buryat, Yevenk, Khanty-Mansi, Yamal-Nenets.

Far East: Yakutia, Primorsky, Khabarovsk, Amur, Kamchakta, Magadan, Chita, Sakhalin, Koryak, Jewish Autonomous Region, Chukotka.

establishing Cossack traditions and way of life. Though Cossacks have been eager to volunteer for service in war zones, such as Chechnya, Ossetia and Tajikistan, they have not been as successful as in the past. They were often employed to do the government's 'dirty work', so allowing it to avoid responsibility. They have been employed as official vigilantes in Krasnodar and St Petersburg.

Russian populations living in the newly independent former Soviet Union republics were thought to be a possible source of confrontation. At one time it looked as though there would be a serious confrontation between Ukraine and Russia over the Crimea, which was handed to Ukraine by President Khrushchev in 1954, together with a sizeable Russian population, to mark the 300th anniversary of the Russian-Ukrainian union. When those deported by Stalin during the Second World War were restored to their original land by Khrushchev, the Crimean Tatars were not included. However, a large number are now returning; they are more separatist-minded than the Russian population there and would be the most likely cause of trouble within Ukraine. As the base for

The internal divisions of Russia.

REPUBLICS
1. Adygeia
2. Bashkortostan
3. Chechnya
4. Chuvash
5. Daghestan
6. Ingushetia
7. Kabardino-Balkaria
8. Kalmykia
9. Karachai-Cherkess
10. Khakasia
11. Marii El
12. Mordovia
13. North Ossetia
14. Udmurt
15. Tatarstan

AUTONOMOUS AREAS
16. Aga Buryat
17. Komi-Permyak
18. Ust-Ordyn Buryat
19. Jewish Region

Part of former USSR
Russian Federation 1999
Republics and Autonomous Areas
Region boundary
Territory boundary

the Soviet Black Sea Fleet, which had to be shared between Russia and Ukraine, settlement of the Crimea issue had some urgency: the Russians demanded to retain and have been given control of major docks and naval facilities in Sebastopol.

The expected problems of the Russian population in Kazakhstan have not materialised, nor those concerning the Russians in eastern Ukraine. Though many Russians might prefer to return to Russia this is not easy, because of the cost and shortage of housing. Only in Transdniestr has the Russian, or rather the Soviet, population declared and fought for its right to remain Russian but then this area had never been part of Romania, having had a Slav population for over a thousand years and having been taken by the Russians from the Ottomans.

The first task of Vladimir Putin, once elected Russian President, will be to attempt to restrict the power of the self-appointed 'elites' and to be able, once again, to appoint regional governors. In the longer term he may try to renegotiate bilateral treaties and amend the constitution and/or redraw regional boundaries and reorganise the entities thus voiding the treaties. It will not be an easy task as the 'elites' are well entrenched. However, restoring the economy and eradicating corruption, virtually the same task, are the greatest priorities.

Bibliography and Web Sites

Alexseev, Mikhail (ed.), *Center-Periphery Conflict in Post-Soviet Russia: A Federation Imperiled*, Macmillan, 1999

Kolossov, Vladimir, *Ethno-Territorial Conflicts and Boundaries in the Former Soviet Union*, International Boundaries Research Unit, 1992

Nicholson, Martin, *Towards a Russia of the Regions*, International Institute for Strategic Studies, Adelphi Paper 330, 1999

Shevtsova, Lilia, *Yeltsin's Russia: Myths and Reality*, Carnegie Endowment for International Peace, 1999

Ure, John, *The Cossacks*, Constable, 1999

Russian Ministry of Foreign Affairs: www.diplomat.ru/
Russian Embassy in Washington: www.russianembassy.org/

WWW.

THE BALTIC STATES: CAN THEY REALLY EXPECT TO JOIN NATO?

The three Baltic States – Estonia, Latvia, and Lithuania – only gained their independence at the end of the First World War. Before then the territory had been fought over since the twelfth century. It had been the objective of early crusades. The Teutonic Order, the Swedes and the Poles have ruled the region, as have the Lithuanians, who created their own empire in 1316, extending it further with the marriage of the Grand Duke to a Polish princess in 1386. After the partition of Poland in 1795 the three states became part of Russia, except for the southern part of Lithuania which became Prussian. Estonians differ ethnically from Latvians and Lithuanians in that they are of Finno-Urgic origin. Their ancestors arrived on the east Baltic coast around 2,500 BC, while the Latvians and Lithuanians are Balts who arrived in 600 BC and later inter-bred with East Slavs.

The Baltic States defence forces	
Estonia	
Men	4,800
Tanks	NIL
Artillery	33
Combat aircraft	NIL
Warships	7
Latvia	
Men	5,700
Tanks	NIL
Artillery	54
Combat aircraft	NIL
Warships	15
Lithuania	
Men	12,100
Tanks	NIL
Artillery	36
Combat aircraft	NIL
Warships	6

During the First World War the Baltic states were overrun by the Germans – Lithuania in 1915, and Latvia and Estonia in 1918. Only Estonia had suffered from Bolshevik administration since the 1917 revolution. Immediately after the end of the war the Estonians supported the White Russians and advanced into Russia, taking territory that was then incorporated into an independent Estonia by the 1920 Treaty of Tartu. The land was recovered by the USSR in 1945, although Estonia still claims it. In December 1918 Latvia was overrun by the Bolsheviks who were opposed by Germans and Latvians separately; eventually with Estonian assistance Latvia defeated both the Bolsheviks and the Germans. Lithuania was the scene of fighting between the Poles and Bolsheviks that finally resulted in Vilnius being left in Polish hands. It was not returned to Lithuanian control until 1940. In 1923 Lithuania occupied the Klaipeda district of East Prussia which remains part of its territory. Peace treaties were signed with the USSR and the three states were admitted to the League of Nations in 1922.

Baltic independence came to an end in 1940 following the Molotov-Ribbentrop pact of 1939 which placed the three states in the Soviet sphere of influence. Estonia, Latvia and Lithuania were forced to sign military agreements and the Soviet Army moved in. Elections were held and the new parliaments each requested their state's inclusion in the USSR.

In June 1941 the Germans attacked the USSR and soon overran the Baltic States, helped to some extent by the Balts who hoped they would regain their independence by revolting against the Soviets: they were disappointed. When the Soviet Union re-occupied the region Balt partisans waged a campaign from the forests, which continued in Lithuania until 1953. The Western Allies did nothing to aid the Baltic States other than refusing to recognise Soviet sovereignty. Although there had been a Russian minority population in the Baltic States for centuries – mainly refugees from persecution in Russia – it was virtually exterminated by Stalin and a wave of new Russian settlement began in 1945. By 1989 the ethnic origins of the three populations were as follows: Lithuanians 79.6 per cent, Russians 9.4 per cent; Latvians 52 per cent, Russians 34 per cent; Estonians 61.5 per cent, Russians 30 per cent. The remaining percentages were made up of Poles, Jews, Belarussians, Ukrainians and Swedes.

Movement for independence began in Latvia on 14 June 1987 when a group of dissidents, the 'Helsinki 86', demonstrated at the Freedom Monument in Riga. Other demonstrations were held on 23 August, the anniversary of the Molotov-Ribbentrop Pact, and on 18 November, the anniversary of the Latvian declaration of independence in 1918. After the police attacked 2,000 protesters at Tallinn in November, demonstrations spread to the other two states until attendance reached hundreds of thousands. By early 1990 all three supreme councils had passed a number of declarations but had not yet proclaimed full independence from the Soviet Union.

Then on 11 March 1990 the Lithuanian Supreme Council declared its full independence from the USSR and Vytautas Landsbergis was elected head of state. The Soviet reaction was to arrest Lithuanian deserters from the Soviet Army and to take over a number of Communist Party buildings; on 18 April it cut off shipments of oil to Lithuania. The Soviet economic blockade was only called off after the Supreme Council agreed a moratorium on the declaration of independence. On 30 March the Estonian parliament voted for gradual secession from the USSR, and the Latvian Supreme Council made a declaration 'On the Restoration of Independence' on 4 May. The run-up to independence witnessed a number of attacks by Soviet Airborne and OMON (Ministry of Interior) troops. In January 1991 paratroopers stormed the Press Centre and, leaving fifteen dead, the TV Centre in Vilnius. OMON troops seized the Ministry of the Interior in Riga and continually attacked Baltic border posts. The Baltic States did not help to stabilise the situation by passing a number of laws discriminating against the ethnic Russian populations.

Following referenda in March 1991, Estonia and Latvia declared their independence on 20 and 21 August 1991 and Lithuania redeclared its independent status. These declarations were recognised by the USSR on 6 September. The three states were also admitted to the UN in September.

For several reasons, the withdrawal of Russian forces from the Baltic States took place slowly. First, there was a lack of suitable accommodation elsewhere. Secondly, as no fresh soldiers could be brought in, the remaining manpower was needed for labouring jobs. And thirdly, there was a desire to maintain pressure on the Estonian and Latvian governments to grant full civil rights to the Russian minorities there. Russian interests in the Baltic included the early warning radar at Skrunda, the decommissioning of nuclear reactors for training submarine crews at Paldiski in Estonia, and arrangements for transit rights for Russian forces through Lithuania to Kaliningrad. Russian forces had withdrawn from Lithuania by the end of 1993 and from Estonia and Latvia by 30 August 1994; agreement was reached for the Skrunda radar to continue to operate until 1998 and then 18 months was allowed for its dismantlement. Decommissioning was completed on 19 October 1999 and Latvia took over the site two days later.

Russian influence during the Soviet Union's occupation of Estonia was greater than in the other two Baltic States. The Russian language had been described as essential in the running of the country and so there was no incentive for Russians to learn Estonian. Twenty-eight per cent of the population are native Russian speakers but to achieve Estonian citizenship they must meet the requirements of the language law passed in 1995; they must also have been resident in Estonia for five years and pass an elementary test on Estonian history. Russians see the law as discriminatory. Estonia has come under considerable criticism and some people in Russia have called for sanctions to be imposed. There is no movement of Russians out of Estonia as their standard of living is better than it would be in Russia even if they do not have Estonian citizenship. On independence Estonia looked to recover the land around Pskov and Ivangorod that had been awarded to it by the 1920 Treaty of Tartu and that the Russians took away in 1940. The claim appears to be in abeyance as Estonia agreed in 1994 to drop its insistence on the Tartu treaty being upheld. A border agreement has been negotiated and initialled.

The present situation in Latvia is that those eligible for citizenship have to pass a language test and know the basic principles of the constitution; their children, if born in Latvia, get automatic citizenship. There are about

Population percentages			
	Nationals	*Russian*	*Other*
Estonia	65	28	7
Latvia	56	34	10
Lithuania	81	9	10

Others include Poles, Ukrainians, Belarussians

The Baltic states and transfers of land.

600,000 non-citizens in the country at present. Latvia has also agreed to Russian sovereignty over Pitlavo which Russia annexed from Latvia in 1940; a border agreement has been initialled but not yet formally signed by Russia. The public use of the Russian language is banned.

Lithuania has passed a law on the rights of national minorities that guarantees all citizens – regardless of ethnicity – equal political, economic and social rights and freedom. Minorities can be educated in their native language and may establish cultural organisations. There are also minority language radio and television programmes. It will be interesting to see which policy – that of demanding linguistic integration or of perpetuating minority language and culture – is the most successful and the least troublesome.

The Baltic States feel threatened by Russia and know that, with their very limited defence assets, they would be unable to halt any Russian invasion. They are, therefore, keen to be allowed to join NATO. This move would be opposed strongly by Russia, which is against any further enlargement of NATO and would see the inclusion of any parts of the former Soviet Union as a hostile act. NATO has not ruled out further enlargement but would be chary and probably divided over membership for the Baltic States. It is not clear what action NATO could take should the Baltic States be invaded, given their geographical circumstances and the fact that, apart from the short stretch of border with Poland, there is no direct access from NATO territory.

There is, of course, a fourth Baltic State, the Russian *oblast* of Kaliningrad which is cut off from Russia by Lithuania. Kaliningrad also has a troubled history, having been at times Polish, Lithuanian and East Prussian. Its current population of nearly 1 million is totally Russian, the German population having either fled or been massacred in 1944–5. There has been some return of an ethnically German population but they have come from elsewhere in the former Soviet Union; however, tourism from Germany is increasing. There are no German ambitions, apart from among some extreme neo-Nazi groups, to reclaim the region. Nor does Lithuania, which calls the territory 'Little Lithuania', have any serious intentions of claiming it, mainly for fear of Polish and German reactions and the undesirability of taking over 900,000 ethnic Russians into Lithuania. Indeed, in 1999 the Lithuanians and Russians signed an agreement on cooperation between the Kaliningrad region and Lithuania. Much has been made of the military strength deployed in Kaliningrad, but in fact it is as much reduced as that elsewhere in Russia and does not of itself pose any threat to its neighbours' security.

Bibliography and Web Sites

Knudsen, Olav (ed.), *Stability and Security in the Baltic Sea Region*, Frank Cass, 1999

Herd, Graeme, *Crisis for Estonia? Russia, Estonia and a Post-Chechen Cold War*, Centre for Defence Studies, 1995

Lieven, Anatol, *The Baltic Revolution: Estonia, Latvia, Lithuania and the Path to Independence*, Yale University Press, 1993

Estonian Ministry of Foreign Affairs: www.vm.ee

Latvian Ministry of Foreign Affairs: www.mfa.gov.lv/eframe

Lithuanian Ministry of Foreign Affairs: www.urm.lt

www.

RUSSIA'S DWINDLING MILITARY CAPABILITY AND THE CONVENTIONAL ARMED FORCES IN EUROPE TREATY

As the Cold War ended a significant arms control treaty was agreed between NATO and the Warsaw Pact. It is known as the Conventional Armed Forces in Europe Treaty (CFE). The requirements of CFE together with the disbandment of the Warsaw Pact and then the break-up of the Soviet Union resulted in a dramatic reduction in the armed strength controlled by Moscow. When the treaty was signed on 19 November 1990 (by which time German unification had been achieved) the Warsaw Pact had 31,700 tanks in Europe; today the Russians have 5,500. Similar-sized reductions have taken place in the other categories of treaty-limited equipment (TLE) – artillery, armoured combat vehicles, attack helicopters and combat aircraft.

The CFE is a bloc-to-bloc treaty and its aim is to reduce greatly the numbers of offensive armaments in Europe while at the same time

Forces west of the Urals, 1999		
	Soviet	Russian
Tanks	20,725	5,510
ACVs	28,040	10,064
Artillery	11,490	6,299
Attack helicopters	1,240	761
Combat aircraft	5,710	2,870
	Divisions	
Tank	24	3
Motor rifle	56	7
Artillery	8	1
Airborne	7	4
	Brigades	
Tank	0	1
Motor rifle	0	11
Artillery	40	12
Airborne	5	0

ACV=Armoured combat vehicle

bringing the numbers of weapons held by each alliance to equal levels. As long as the geographical sub-limits are followed, each alliance can decide its own national limits. The treaty covers the whole area from the Atlantic to the Ural mountains (ATTU) and this territory has been divided into a number of zones, each of which has been given a sub-limit for TLE. These zones are sequential; that is to say the limits for the innermost zone are also counted in the totals allowed in the next largest zone. The zones are:

Zone 4: (The Central Region) Belgium, Czechoslovakia, Germany, Hungary, Luxembourg, Netherlands and Poland

Zone 3: Zone 4 plus Denmark, France, Italy, the UK and the Baltic, Belorussian (now Belarus), Carpathian and Kiev (both now in Ukraine) Military Districts

Zone 2: Zone 3 plus Portugal, Spain and the Moscow and Volga/Urals Military Districts of the USSR

Zone 1: The whole ATTU

There is also a 'flanking' zone also known as Zone 5, with separate sub-limits, which consists of Bulgaria, Greece, Iceland, Norway, Romania, Turkey, and the Leningrad, Kiev (Ukraine), North and Trans-Caucasus (now Armenia, Azerbaijan and Georgia) Military Districts. There are no separate limits for either the north or south flank, only a single limit for both together. Numbers counted in any country include the equipment of both that country within its borders and any 'stationed' equipment of other countries, such as US installations in Germany or Soviet *matériel* in Poland, etc. There are no zonal limits for attack helicopters and combat aircraft on account of their range and speed of redeployment.

The Treaty also contains other provisions designed to improve confidence and transparency. Each year there is detailed data exchange, setting out where and in which units TLE are deployed. There is also provision for inspections to be carried out to ensure the verification of TLE elimination and of the data submitted. The terms of the Stockholm document, produced by a conference of the Organisation for Cooperation and Security in Europe and agreed in September 1986, require states to give prior warning of certain military activities and to invite observers to large-scale military exercises. Confidence that CFE is not being violated is thus assured.

The USSR had actually held far more tanks and artillery in the ATTU but before the treaty was signed it transhipped large numbers of the oldest types of armament to the east of the Urals in order to avoid the cost of elimination. This equipment now lies, unmaintained and unusable in eastern Russia, Kazakhstan and Uzbekistan.

The task of meeting CFE's commitments was far greater for the USSR and then Russia than for any other country because the end of the Warsaw Pact and the reunification of Germany required the withdrawal of all Russian forces from Eastern Europe. These comprised nineteen divisions in the former East Germany, two in Poland, four in Czechoslovakia and four in Hungary. All had returned to Russia by the end of August 1994. When the Soviet Union broke up further withdrawals became necessary: five divisions from the Baltic states, two from Moldova and twelve from the Transcaucasian republics, although agreement was reached later for Russia to station troops in Armenia and Georgia (today roughly four brigades) and there is still a small force in the Transdneistr district of Moldova. The divisions in Belarus (ten) and Ukraine (twenty-two) became the basis of the armies for these countries. After the break-up of the Soviet Union its TLE limits had to be apportioned between the new republics and this was agreed at a meeting at Tashkent on 15 May 1992. (As was the division of the TLE of Czechoslovakia when it divided in 1993.)

Manpower was added to the CFE's limits in 1992 but this did not include naval forces other than marines and naval air personnel who were based on land, nor strategic rocket forces. There was no negotiation over national limits, countries purely committing themselves to having no more manpower than the figure they then declared. Russia's limit was 1,450,000; in January 1999 it reported having 748,776 men in the limited categories.

The CFE Treaty was revised by the Review Conference held in Vienna in May 1996. The changes made allowed Russia to station additional

Tank turrets and barrels after dismantlement at a Russian elimination site. (US On-Site Inspection Agency)

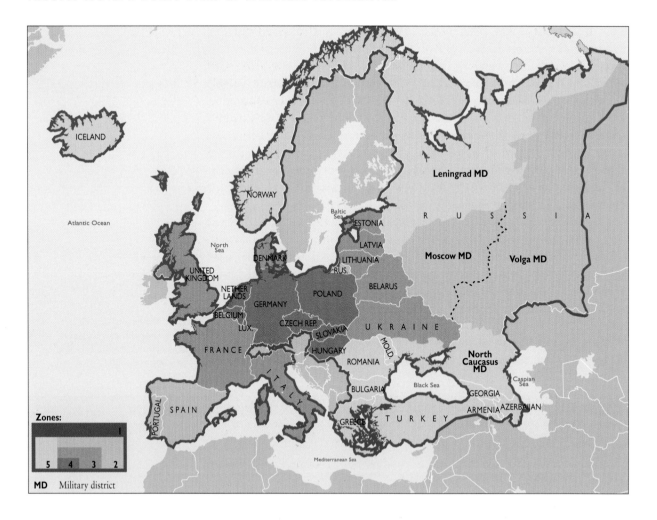

ICELAND

NORWAY

Atlantic Ocean

Leningrad MD

R U S S I A

North Sea

Baltic Sea

ESTONIA

LATVIA

LITHUANIA

Moscow MD

Volga MD

DENMARK

UNITED KINGDOM

NETHER LANDS

GERMANY

BELGIUM

LUX.

POLAND

CZECH REP.

RUS.

BELARUS

UKRAINE

FRANCE

SLOVAKIA

HUNGARY

ROMANIA

MOLD.

North Caucasus MD

I T A L Y

PORTUGAL

SPAIN

BULGARIA

Black Sea

Caspian Sea

GEORGIA

GREECE

T U R K E Y

ARMENIA

AZERBAIJAN

Mediterranean Sea

Zones:

				1
5	4	3	2	

MD Military district

The limitation zones of the Conventional Forces in Europe Treaty.

forces on its southern flank in the North Caucasus Military District. Changes were also made to the Flanks Zone in Ukraine. CFE had to be revised again to take account of NATO's enlargement to include Poland, Hungary and the Czech Republic. As the Treaty is no longer controlling a bloc-to-bloc situation, a new system of national and territorial limits has been devised; national ceilings limit TLE of each signatory deployed anywhere in the ATTU, while territorial ceilings limit the TLE of any signatory deployed in that country. Russia will still be constrained by sub-limits on its flanks. A revised treaty was signed by thirty nations at Istanbul in November 1999.

Bibliography and Web Sites

Odom, William, E., *The Collapse of the Soviet Military*, Yale University Press, 1998

A Review and Update of Key Treaty Elements (Annual) US Arms Control and Disarmament Agency

Concluding Act of the Negotiation on Personnel Strength of Conventional Armed Forces in Europe 1992

Final Document of the First Conference to Review the Operation of the Conventional Armed Forces in Europe, 1996

Treaty on Conventional Armed Forces in Europe, Treaty Document, 1990

Arms Control Association: www.arms control.org/

US Mission to NATO: www.nato.int/usa/info/cfe

www.

THE KURILS OR THE NORTHERN ISLANDS?

Fifty-five years after the end of the Second World War the ownership of a number of islands lying between Japan and the Kamchatka Peninsula is still the subject of a dispute between Japan and Russia which currently occupies the islands and has done so since 1945. The disputed islands are the three closest to Japan: Shikotan, Kunaishiri, and Etorofu and a group of smaller islands the Habomais group. There is no dispute over the islands further to the north-east, which are known as the Kurils. Japan always refers to the islands that it claims as the Northern Islands.

The basis of the Japanese claim is that the islands are historically part of Japan and that Russian influence had never been exercised south of Uruppu. Also, the Japanese-claimed islands are different from those further north in terms of fauna, flora and climate, all of which equate to those found in Japan. The more northerly, Russian islands are subarctic in character. Japan points to the Treaty of Commerce, Navigation and Delimitation of 1855 and the 1875 treaty in which Japan conceded Sakhalin Island to Russia in exchange for the Kurils. Both treaties confirm Japan's claim to the islands. The Russians argue that the treaties have no standing today and that they made concessions under duress; further, they say the agreements were nullified when Japan attacked Russia in 1904. In this war the Japanese gained the southern half of Sakhalin and the Kurils. At the Allied conference at Yalta it was agreed that 'the former rights of Russia violated by the treacherous attack of 1904 shall be restored' including Sakhalin and the Kurils. The Soviet Union declared war on Japan forty-eight hours after the first nuclear bomb had been dropped on

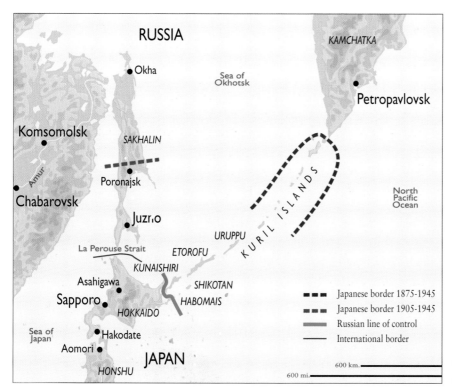

The changing control of the Kuril or Northern Islands.

Hiroshima and immediately occupied southern Sakhalin and all the islands between Kamchakta and Hokkaido.

Japan also claims – and has been supported in this claim by the US – that the Yalta agreement statements have no international legality and were purely statements of intent. Further, it says that Kunaishiri and Etorofu are not part of the Kuril Islands group. The US note to Japan also stated that 'the final disposition of territories as the result of war is to be made by a peace treaty'. The Soviet Union was not party to the 1951 Treaty of San Francisco which was signed by forty-eight of the fifty-one wartime Allies and Japan. Negotiations for a Soviet-Japanese peace treaty were held in 1956 and although the Soviets were prepared to hand over the Habomais and Shikotan they would only do so in return for retaining Kunaishiri and Etofuru and so no agreement was reached. Russia and Japan did sign a joint declaration that ended the state of war between them. It included a paragraph stating agreement on continuing negotiations for a peace treaty and noting that after its conclusion the islands of the Habomai and Shikotan would be handed over to Japan. In 1960, following the signing of the US–Japanese Security Treaty, the Soviets said it was impossible for them to return the Habomais and Shikotan to Japan.

Kunaishiri Island, occupied by Russia. (The Hutchison Library)

Soviet-Japanese relations improved when Gorbachev became President and it was rumoured that a large financial package of loans and grants had been offered for the return of the Northern Islands; however the Soviet military was totally opposed to any handover. On coming to power, Boris Yeltsin expressed his desire to settle the dispute and Georgy Yavlinsky, then Vice-Chairman of the interim cabinet, suggested that the 1855 Treaty should be respected and the islands returned. His opinion was reinforced by the discovery of documents which revealed that in 1853 Tsar Nicholas I acknowledged Japan's sovereignty over all four islands. At the Russian-Japanese summit held in Siberia in November 1997 both sides pledged to achieve a peace treaty by 2000, but immediately before the next summit meeting in April 1998 the then Russian Prime Minister designate told the Duma that Russia would not hand over the islands.

Bibliography and Web Site

Goodby, James, Vladimir Ivanov, Nobuo Shimotamai (eds), *'Northern Territories' and beyond: Russian, Japanese and American Perspectives*, Westport, 1995

WWW. Japanese Ministry of Foreign Affairs: www.mofa.go.jp/region/europe/russia/territory/index

EUROPE: BETWEEN UNIFICATION AND FRAGMENTATION

At the same time as western Europe was aiming to increase its integration by the establishment of a common currency and a common foreign and security policy, the south-east of the continent was breaking up and discarding federalism. First came the 'velvet divorce' of the Czechs from the Slovaks. This was followed by the violent break-up of the Yugoslav Federation, an episode that may well not yet be over.

This chapter begins by examining rival defence organisations under the headings 'Enlarging the Atlantic Alliance' and 'A European Security and Defence Identity'. The next three topics concern borders that are considered inviolate by international law but that often provoke problems. The many European border changes are described first, with a number of potential trouble spots being identified as a result of earlier border alterations and population movements. The two case studies examined are the fault line between the Greeks and Turks, which has existed for many centuries, and the more recent split of the island of Cyprus, which also involves both Greeks and Turks. The chapter ends with the historical background to the Northern Ireland issue that, as we go to press, appears possibly to have been solved.

There is no space to include accounts of other problem areas such as the renewed campaign of violence by the Basque separatist party, ETA, which has threatened to widen its campaign into France, or the Spanish claims to Gibraltar, which are being resisted by both the UK and the people of Gibraltar.

ENLARGING THE ATLANTIC ALLIANCE

The North Atlantic Treaty Organisation (NATO), established in 1950 by the Washington Treaty, was formed as a counter to the perceived threat of communist expansion following the coming to power of communist governments throughout Eastern Europe. It has always been both a political and a military organisation.

The collapse of communism, the disbandment of the Warsaw Pact and the break-up of the Soviet Union ended the Cold War and meant that the

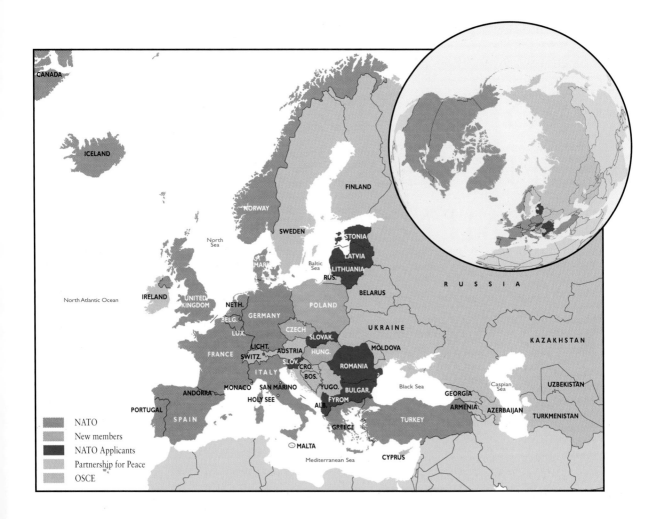

The enlargement of NATO.

main purpose of NATO no longer pertained. However, the organisation was seen as a great stabiliser and few voices called for its abolition. Indeed, almost immediately there were demands for enlargement of both its membership and its responsibilities. Former members of the Warsaw Pact feared that at some unspecified time in the future Russia could become an aggressive and expansionist threat – a view that some Westerners also hold – and they were keen to join the western alliance. Once Russia has solved its economic ills it could again become a military power, but whether it would be an expansionist one is uncertain. It was difficult even at the height of the Cold War to identify the circumstances in which the Warsaw Pact might have made a deliberate attack on NATO when it was clear conflict would have led to a nuclear war that no one could have won. War could only have broken out as a result of a miscalculation after preparatory military measures were taken to reinforce political initiatives and were misinterpreted: this nearly happened at the end of the Arab-Israeli War in 1973 when the US and USSR backed their political aims in the Middle East with military moves in Europe. It is often forgotten that Russia – and before it the Soviet Union – has always been deeply concerned over defence; it has in its history been invaded on four occasions, by Charles of Sweden, Napoleon, the Kaiser and Hitler, all of whom reached the gates of Moscow and caused millions of Russian casualties. The Soviet/Russian military doctrine of offence being the best form of defence can lead to intentions being misread.

There has been considerable debate on the wisdom of enlarging NATO's membership and those opposed to the move make a number of valid points:

- Enlargement would antagonise Russia, which could become less co-operative with the West – for example, delaying the ratification of START 2 – and it would improve the political standing of reactionaries and radical nationalists in Russia.
- Decision-making within NATO would become more difficult as the number of members rose.
- The security of countries not admitted would be less certain and this could lead to a strengthening of the Commonwealth of Independent States (CIS).
- The cost of bringing new members' defence capability up to NATO standards would be large.
- Enlargement would damage NATO's other measures for improving security and stability in Europe, namely the Partnership for Peace (PfP) programme and the NATO-Russia Founding Act.

Arguments in support of NATO enlargement – other than the benefit derived by those countries that are admitted – are less easy to formulate. The US Administration sees the issue as a choice between appeasing Russia and showing solidarity with the East Europeans. Enlargement became inevitable in January 1994 when President Clinton stated that 'the question is no longer whether NATO will take in new members but when and how'.

At its Madrid Summit on 8 July 1997, NATO formally invited Poland, Hungary and the Czech Republic to join the Alliance – an invitation that had to be ratified both by all NATO's current members and by the new members. The three countries were formally admitted to NATO on 12 March 1999. The Russian Duma has still not ratified START 2 but no other actions have been taken in reaction to the enlargement.

At Madrid NATO made it clear that further enlargement was possible. A number of countries are keen to join in the next wave but NATO members may have differing views on their suitability for membership. Slovakia, Slovenia and Romania are seen as the most likely states to be admitted; before the July decision was taken France had been pressing for Romanian membership and Italy for Slovenia's. The countries that would benefit most from NATO security guarantees are the three Baltic States but their membership would be resisted strongly by Russia and the practicalities of their defence are likely to lead to their exclusion. Russia has also said it was 'categorically against' the admission of any former Soviet states, while NATO has made it clear that it does not believe any nation should be excluded if it meets the criteria and seeks membership.

New NATO membership is not restricted to former Warsaw Pact members and a number of neutral countries have considered joining. NATO would find Austrian membership an advantage as this would

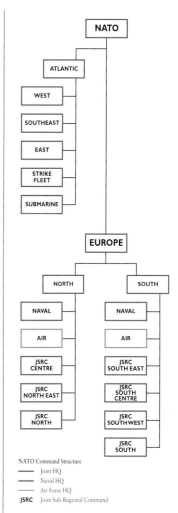

NATO Command Structure
—— Joint HQ
—— Naval HQ
—— Air Force HQ
JSRC Joint Sub-Regional Command

NATO's nuclear policy

'The fundamental purpose of the nuclear forces of the Allies is political: to preserve peace and prevent coercion and any kind of war. They will continue to fulfil an essential role by ensuring uncertainty in the mind of any aggressor about the nature of the Allies' response to military aggression.

'The Alliance will therefore maintain adequate nuclear forces in Europe. These forces need to have the necessary characteristics and appropriate flexibility and survivability, to be perceived as a credible and effective element of the Allies' strategy in preventing war. They will be maintained at the minimum level sufficient to preserve peace and stability.'

The Alliance's Strategic Concept, April 1999.

create a land-link with Hungary whose territory is currently not adjacent to that of any NATO member. However Austria, a member of PfP, has ruled the possibility out. In December 1998 the Irish Foreign Minister began to advocate Ireland's membership of PfP and it joined in late 1999. In Sweden, which is particularly concerned about Baltic security, an opinion poll held in late 1997 found a majority in favour of NATO membership; however, officials appear to be keener on the idea than politicians. In the Washington Summit communiqué of April 1999 recognition was given to the efforts and progress towards eligibility for membership made by Bulgaria, Estonia, Latvia, Lithuania, Romania, Slovakia and Slovenia. In the same paragraph gratitude was expressed for the cooperation given by the former Yugoslav Republic of Macedonia and by Albania during the Kosovo crisis.

On 27 May 1997 Russia and NATO members signed the Founding Act on Mutual Relations, Cooperation and Security between NATO and the Russian Federation. It begins 'NATO and Russia do not consider each other as adversaries'. The NATO states also reiterated that 'they have no intention, no plan and no reason to deploy nuclear weapons, nor establish nuclear weapon storage sites, on the territory of new members'. NATO's intentions on conventional forces were less precisely stated and were expressed as 'relying on reinforcement' rather than the additional permanent stationing of substantial combat forces. The Founding Act also established the Joint Permanent Council where security problems and issues can be discussed.

Calculations of the economic cost of NATO enlargement have generated widely varying estimates from as high as $110 billion to as low as $10 billion, both spread over a 10–15 year period and dependent on the defence posture to be achieved.

The other aspect of NATO enlargement – the addition of new responsibilities – is equally contentious and is generating a growing difference of opinion between the US and the European members of the Alliance. The US is looking to expand NATO's area of responsibility to allow it to engage in peacekeeping and military operations on a global basis. NATO's peace-enforcement operation in Bosnia-Herzegovina and peacekeeping in Kosovo are already considered to be 'out of area' operations, but it must be remembered that the Europeans were less keen to join the Coalition assembled to evict Iraq from Kuwait. In Operation Desert Storm only Britain and France joined the US in providing both ground and air forces, with Italy providing air forces; other NATO countries committed naval units but none entered the Persian Gulf.

The Alliance's Strategic Concept was approved at the summit held in Washington in April 1999. The concept reaffirms the Alliance's main purpose as 'to safeguard the freedom and security of all its members by political and military means'. The concept confirmed that NATO was open to further new membership and that nuclear weapons remained a key part of its deterrent strategy but that their use was considered to be extremely remote. There was no specific mention of new roles nor of 'out of area' operations other than support for the Mediterranean Dialogue and in 'developing further contact with the United Nations in the context of conflict prevention, crisis management, crisis response operations including peacekeeping and humanitarian assistance'. Considerable emphasis was given to NATO's operating in the Euro-Atlantic area. The Mediterranean Dialogue is a policy aimed at creating security and stability throughout the Mediterranean. NATO has six partners in the dialogue – Egypt, Israel, Jordan, Mauritania, Morocco and Tunisia.

Web Site

NATO: www.nato.int/

www.

A EUROPEAN SECURITY AND DEFENCE IDENTITY

For the last fifty years Western Europe has relied on the North Atlantic Treaty Organisation for its security and defence. At the same time there have always been voices calling for a European Defence Identity. Today, the voices appear to be growing louder despite the end of the Cold War ten years ago. There is in fact a plethora of European fora in which defence issues are debated but as yet none has the military capability built up by NATO over the years. NATO's capability relies on the US to provide several essential elements such as satellite-derived intelligence and strategic air transport lift. Is a separate European Security and Defence Identity (ESDI) necessary or even achievable?

The main contender to be the ESDI is the Western European Union (WEU), an organisation first established as the Western Union by the Brussels Treaty in March 1948 with Belgium, France, Luxembourg, the Netherlands and the UK as members. The Union was designed to provide security guarantees to its members. However, it was quickly superseded when NATO was formed by the Washington Treaty in 1949. The Brussels Treaty never lapsed. In 1954, after the failure to form a European Defence Community, Germany and Italy joined the Union which then became the WEU. On the WEU's thirtieth anniversary it was agreed that it should play a more important role in the defence of Europe. The first EU 'supreme head' of foreign and security policy, Javier Solana, was appointed secretary general of the WEU in June 1999.

The first military activity coordinated by the WEU was the minesweeping operation in the Persian Gulf towards the end of the Iran-Iraq war. Since then it has coordinated other naval operations during the Gulf War and in the Adriatic to enforce sanctions imposed on former Yugoslavia. It has not yet commanded any ground or air operations. It has no permanent military headquarters but it does have a small military planning staff.

A number of European military formations have been established. The first was the Franco-German Brigade formed in 1989. It was deployed to Bosnia as part of NATO's Stabilisation Force (SFOR). In 1992 it was agreed to form a Franco-German Corps that could form the core of a future European army. The role of the Corps was described as 'contributing to the Allies' joint defence, peacekeeping and peacemaking tasks, and humanitarian assignments', but the two tank divisions in the Corps were hardly suitable for the last two tasks. Since 1992 the Corps

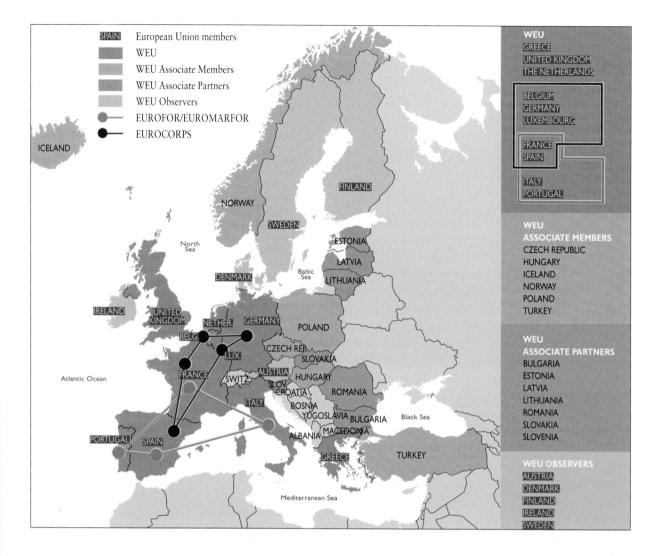

European security architecture.

has been expanded to include the Franco-German Brigade, a Spanish mechanised brigade and the Belgian mechanised division. It is now known as Eurocorps. In May 1999 the French and Germans announced their intention to remodel Eurocorps into a rapid-reaction force with a European Union defence role, but until Germany can field a professional, as opposed to a conscript, division it will not be able to react rapidly.

Two southern European forces have been formed: Euro Force (EUROFOR) and the European Maritime Force (EUROMARFOR). EUROFOR became operational in November 1997. It comprises a permanent international HQ in Florence and has units earmarked by the member nations, France, Italy, Portugal and Spain. The same countries have earmarked naval ships for EUROMARFOR. Neither force has yet been committed to operations. To some extent they were formed as a reaction to the fears of mass immigration from North Africa. More recently a South-Eastern Europe Multi-National Force (SEEMNF) has been agreed; Albania, Bulgaria, Greece, Italy, Macedonia, Romania and Turkey resolved on 12 January 1999 to form a brigade-sized peacekeeping force.

At the European Union summit on 3 June 1999 it was decided that there should be a common policy on security and defence and that there should be a 'capacity for autonomous action, backed up by credible military forces'. The EU will absorb the WEU and has appointed a High Representative for Security and Foreign Affairs; the first incumbent is the former NATO Secretary General, Javier Solana. How easy it will be for him to obtain agreement from the very diverse countries of the Union, each with different foreign policy priorities and domestic concerns, remains to be seen.

France is in a special position because while it is a political member of NATO, its military forces do not form part of the NATO command structure. France has, though, taken part in a number of NATO-led operations, such as those in Bosnia and Kosovo. There are those who think that France's support for European defence structures is aimed at reducing the US's influence in Europe.

The Euro-Atlantic Partnership Council is the consultative body for NATO's Partnership for Peace programme, which has been joined by all former members of the Warsaw Pact, by all former republics of the Soviet Union, and by Albania, the Former Yugoslav Republic of Macedonia and Slovenia. PfP was first proposed at the NATO summit of January 1994. Membership of PfP involves a partnership between individual states and NATO; the extent of involvement is entirely up to the partner. Partner states are, however, committed to the following: transparency in defence planning and budgeting; ensuring the democratic control of forces; maintaining a capability to contribute to UN or OSCE operations; developing in the longer-term forces able to operate with those of NATO.

The Conference for Security and Cooperation in Europe (CSCE) was held in Helsinki in August 1975. The event was attended and its Final Act signed by all members of NATO and the Warsaw Pact as well as by the neutral and non-aligned states of Europe. The Final Act includes three baskets covering political/military, economic and cultural/humanitarian matters. For the first time a number of confidence-building measures (CBMs), including notification of large-scale military activity and the invitation of observers to attend military exercises, were established. However, the measures were only applicable in a zone covering 250 kilometres from Soviet European borders. Between 1984 and 1986 a follow-up conference to improve the package of CBMs, now called confidence- and security-building measures (CSBMs), was held at Stockholm. Agreement was reached to extend the area covered by CSBMs to the Ural mountains, the threshold for notifying military activity was reduced, annual forecasts of military activity were introduced and for the first time provision was made for 'challenge' inspections which could not be refused. In 1990 agreement was reached on the exchange of military force data.

When the Soviet Union broke up, all the new states, including the Transcaucasian and Central Asian ones became members of CSCE. Towards the end of 1992 the CSCE began sending missions to areas of conflict, usually with the aim of promoting negotiations between the parties. Missions have been sent to Georgia, Estonia, Moldova, Latvia and Tajikistan. A mission to gather information on human rights sent to Kosovo, the Sandjak and Vojvodina was suspended when Yugoslavia refused to prolong its mandate. For some years CSCE has

> **ESDI: separable but not separate?**
>
> 'For NATO and the EU the next few years will be a juggling act, as both institutions try to tackle the two fundamental challenges that lie ahead: stabilising the European continent and redefining the transatlantic partnership. These goals are not contradictory – provided both organisations keep focused on their common strategic objectives and refrain from engaging in petty rivalries.'
>
> Peter Schmidt, *NATO Review*

ESDI and NATO: the three Ds

Duplication
Decoupling
Discrimination

had plans ready for the deployment of a peacekeeping force to Nagorno-Karabakh but Armenia and Azerbaijan have never agreed to its implementation. The Conference became known as the Organisation for Security and Cooperation in Europe at the Budapest conference in December 1994. By then a permanent secretariat had been established in Vienna. The OSCE organised the unarmed force of observers, known as the Verification Mission, sent to Kosovo in 1998. It was withdrawn before the bombing campaign began but has now returned to help NATO's Kosovo Force (KFOR) in monitoring the situation there.

On 15 November 1999 the European Union held its first joint meeting of foreign and defence ministers to discuss the essential increase to military capability needed for the conduct of operations such as that in Kosovo without US assistance. European forces lack strategic airlift, satellite-derived intelligence and precision-guided weapons – all expensive items. In November 1999, British Prime Minister Blair proposed the establishment of a European army wearing a common cap-badge by 2003; it should be capable of putting 30,000 men into the field in 60 days, though smaller elements could deploy much quicker. Next, at the Anglo-French summit in London, also in November 1999, it was decided that to improve Europe's ability to react to crisis, logistic and transport assets would be pooled when necessary. Then at the European summit at Helsinki in December 1999 it was agreed to form an EU rapid reaction force: it is to be 60,000 men strong, organised into 15 brigades, by 2003. Members will have to commit forces but troops will remain in their national locations and will not change their badges. The force will have air and naval components, is to develop its own satellite reconnaissance system and its aim is to be capable of operating independently of NATO should that become politically necessary. In the event, there will, of course, be no new troops, only existing forces that will now be 'double, or even treble, hatted'.

There is, therefore, no shortage of defence-oriented organisations in Europe but security is being challenged far more by the difficult-to-deal-with threats of refugees, drugs, terrorism and, further afield, the spread of weapons of mass destruction and their delivery means. European efforts to establish a parallel organisation may well reduce the US's willingness to lead NATO. It has already expressed its concern over European plans which it fears may undermine NATO. Former British Foreign Secretary, David Owen, believes that a United States of Europe will never achieve the cohesion, purpose or resolve to act as decisively as NATO did over Kosovo because it will lack the US's binding power. For the present NATO still remains Europe's premier defence organisation.

Web Sites

WWW.

European Union: www.europa.eu.int/
Organisation for Co-operation and Security in Europe: www.osce.org
Western European Union: www.weu.int

CHANGING BORDERS: 1914–99

As this book demonstrates, border disputes are one of the commonest causes of war, particularly when changes to territorial limits have been enforced. Probably no other region of the world has experienced more redrawing of borders over the centuries than Europe. The analysis that follows concentrates on changes made in the twentieth century after the First World War but, of course, there were many more in the preceding centuries. The implications of some, particularly in the Balkans, are still being suffered today. The various border movements in the Balkans laid down by the 1878 Treaty of Stefano, the Congress of Berlin and the 1913 Treaty of Bucharest are shown in the maps in the section on the Former Yugoslavia on pages 111–31.

Europe's borders were probably first drawn with the arrival of the Germanic tribes in the fifth century AD but they were soon altered, for instance by the Treaty of Verdun in 843 and the Partition of Meersen in 870. In medieval times land was often given as a dowry when royal marriages took place. In the next thousand years there were numerous border changes mainly brought about by war. The Holy Roman Empire, the Habsburgs, the Napoleonic era and the Austro-Hungarian Empire rose and fell. In the nineteenth century territorial divisions were redrawn by diktats issued after meetings of the Great Powers: Britain, France, Germany and Russia. The century also witnessed the unification of Germany (1815–71) and Italy (1859–70), and Belgian independence (1830–9). The Congress of Paris in 1856 after the Crimean War decreed reform in Turkey, which did not take place, the neutralisation of the Black Sea, which lasted until 1871, and the freeing of the Danubian Principalities, which led to an independent Romania. The Franco-Prussian War in 1870 ended with the French losing Alsace and Lorraine.

The early years of the twentieth century saw the Italian war with Turkey, in which Italy took Libya and the Dodecanese Islands, and the two Balkan Wars followed by the Treaty of Bucharest, which broke up Macedonia between its neighbours.

The First World War witnessed the end of two European empires – the Austro-Hungarian and the Ottoman. The collapse of the latter led to border changes far beyond Europe. The Austro-Hungarian empire broke up into Austria, Czechoslovakia and Hungary, while Romania, Ukraine and the new Kingdom of Serbs, Croats and Slovenes gained territory. Austria also lost land – its access to the Adriatic at Trieste, to Italy, an area that was contested at the end of the Second World War and was divided between Italy and Yugoslavia. Also included in the Yugoslav Kingdom was a Hungarian minority population in Vojvodina. Czechoslovakia also included the Sudetenland which had a German population and was a reason for the German invasion in 1938.

The end of the First World War also witnessed the Russian Revolution and the founding of the Soviet Union which also caused border changes. The growth of the Russian Empire into the Soviet Union and the latter's break up are illustrated on pages 65–8. Russia's collapse at the end of the First World War allowed Estonia, Latvia and Lithuania to gain their independence. This they lost again, first to the Soviet Union in 1939 and then to Germany. The Soviet Union recaptured the three Baltic States in

1914

1923

1950

1999

Europe's changing borders

1944 and held them until its break-up. Over the years since 1919 the Baltic States have lost and gained territory which could possibly lead to future disputes. France regained Alsace and Lorraine in 1919.

Poland has probably suffered more border changes and exchanges of territory than any other European country and these are illustrated in the maps below. While there have always been Polish people there has not always been a Polish state. At various times the Germans, Prussians, Russians and Lithuanians have absorbed its territory. Towards the end of the tenth and in the early eleventh centuries Poland was at its most powerful after its occupation of Pomerania, Bohemia, Moravia and its progress as far east as the River Bug. By the start of the First World War it was part of the Russian Empire and had no access to the Baltic Sea. It became independent

Poland's changing borders, 1772–1999.

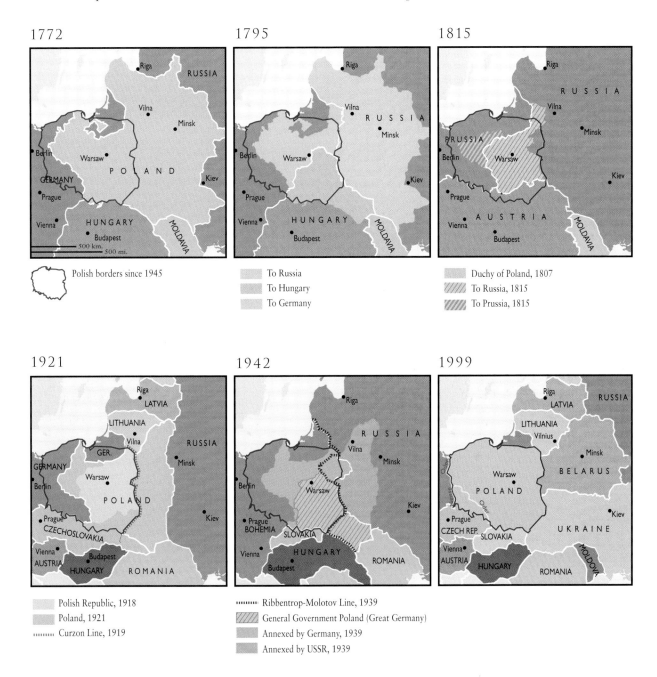

1772	Polish borders since 1945
1795	To Russia / To Hungary / To Germany
1815	Duchy of Poland, 1807 / To Russia, 1815 / To Prussia, 1815
1921	Polish Republic, 1918 / Poland, 1921 / Curzon Line, 1919
1942	Ribbentrop-Molotov Line, 1939 / General Government Poland (Great Germany) / Annexed by Germany, 1939 / Annexed by USSR, 1939
1999	

in 1918 and was awarded more territory by the Treaty of Versailles in 1921, including the Danzig corridor and a broad strip to the east of the Curzon Line (a Polish-Soviet border suggested at the Versailles Conference and to the west of which Lord Curzon suggested the Poles should withdraw in 1920). During the Second World War it was divided initially between the Germans and Russians until the Germans occupied it all after their attack on Russia. The most recent border changes came at the end of the Second World War and gave Poland territory that had been German before 1939. However, it had to surrender land in the east to the Soviet Union; this land is now part of Belarus. In 1946 some 12 million Germans were displaced from Silesia and Pomerania and had to find new homes in East and West Germany. The refugees included nearly 2 million from East Prussia which was divided between Poland and the Soviet Union whose portion is now the *oblast* of Kaliningrad. Not surprisingly some of the descendants of those displaced still consider their homeland to be in Poland. There has also been a growing number of German tourists visiting former East Prussia. In the 'Four + Two' Treaty that reunified Germany, the Germans recognised the Oder-Neisse line as the permanent border between Germany and Poland.

The 2.5 to 3 million Germans who lived in Sudetenland were expelled in 1946 and their representatives still meet each year in Bavaria, demanding that their expulsion be recognised as a crime. Some hope to regain their property. Before the Second World War Czechoslovakia also contained Ruthenia which, when the Germans broke the country up in 1939, gained its autonomy as Carpatho-Ukraine. After it declared its independence, it was annexed by Hungary. At the end of the Second World War when Czechoslovakia was re-formed it did not get the region back and Carpatho-Ukraine was incorporated into Ukraine and the Soviet Union.

There are Hungarian minorities in Romania (1.6 million, mainly in Transylvania), the Vojvodina province of Serbia (400,000) and in Slovakia (560,000). Hungary signed a Treaty of Good Neighbourly Relations and Friendship with Slovakia in 1995 but has been unable to reach a similar agreement with Romania. The Romanian-populated Republic of Moldova has changed hands and names over history. Russia gained Bessarabia, the land between the Prut and Dniester, from the Ottomans in 1812. It occupied Moldavia and Wallachia in 1853 – one of the causes of the Crimean War. Bessarabia remained in Russian hands when Romania became independent while Romania annexed the province of Dobruja in 1878. Bessarabia declared its independence as the Democratic Republic of Moldavia in 1917 and in 1918 joined Romania; Russia did not regain it until 1939. Russia altered the borders of the territory by transferring Northern Bukovina and Southern Bessarabia to Ukraine. At the same time it added a strip of land to the east of the Dniester to Bessarabia. The country became independent as Moldova in 1991 when the USSR ceased to exist, but the left bank territory of Transdniestria, backed by the Russian garrison, attempted to break away. The question of the region's sovereignty is still unresolved and a small Russian army garrison remains there. A complicating factor for Moldova is the minority Gauguz population in the south-west.

Web Site

WWW. International Boundaries Research Unit: www.ibru.dur.ac.uk/

GREECE AND TURKEY: A DANGEROUS FAULT LINE

Greece's involvement with Asia Minor began long before the creation of the modern Turkish state. History is responsible for much of the controversy that exists today when the main differences between two NATO allies are over Cyprus, which is discussed at pages 102–5, and the question of sea and airspace control off the Turkish coast and around the Greek islands in the Aegean.

The first Greek settlers arrived in the region after the collapse of the Mycenean Empire in 1200 BC and some 2000 years before the Seldjuk Turks. They established Ionia along the western coast of Asia Minor and other settlements took place, such as those by the Aeolians and the Dorians. Greek centres of population stretched around the Black Sea coast but further Greek expansion was halted by the Phrygians who inhabited the Anatolian plateau.

In the sixth century BC Asia Minor was part of the Persian Empire, which stretched into Thrace where its advance was halted by the Scythians. In 496 BC the Ionians revolted against the Persians but were defeated despite help from Greece. This led to the wars in which the Persians were defeated by the Greeks in naval battles at Marathon and Salamis. In 334 BC Alexander began a campaign during which he conquered most of Asia Minor, Syria, Mesopotamia, Lower Egypt and Persia, even reaching the Indus and Samarkand. The split after his death in 323 BC of Alexander's empire put Cyprus and the settlements on the eastern and southern coast under Ptolemy, while the remainder of the southern half of Asia Minor fell to the Seleucids. Next followed the Roman conquests and the establishment of Byzantium, now Istanbul; after the split from Rome, the Eastern Empire adopted the Orthodox faith. The Ummayids, the founders of the first Arab Islamic empire, twice failed to capture Byzantium, nor did Asia Minor form part of the empire of the Abbasids, their successors. On the break up of the Abbasid Empire there was a Byzantine revival which recovered Cyprus from the Arabs and for a short time took part of the Levant. The Seldjuk family were the leaders of a Turkmen tribe called the Ghuzz who migrated to Bokhara at the end of the tenth century and embraced Islam. In 1071, under Alp Aslan, they broke through the Byzantine defences and, after the battle of Manzikert, occupied over half Asia Minor.

In the second half of the fourteenth century the Ottomans crossed the Dardenelles and first took Gallipoli and then Salonika, Sofia and the Black Sea. In 1389 the Turks defeated the Serbs at Kosovo Polje. It was not until 1453 that the Ottomans, after a long siege, finally took Constantinople. Before then the Ottomans had occupied Bulgaria and the eastern half of Greece, completing their conquest of the latter by 1460. The Turks ruled Greece until the War of Independence which ended in 1829 after the British, French and Russian defeat of the Turkish navy at the battle of Navarino (Pylos Bay) in 1827. However, at that stage the Greeks had not recovered Macedonia or Crete. The Congress of Berlin, which met to revise the Balkan borders instituted by the Treaty of St Stephano after the Russian defeat of Turkey in 1878, also left Salonika, Crete and the Eastern Aegean islands under Turkish rule. Then major revolt broke out in Crete in 1897 and a Greek force landed on the island. This resulted in the island being given autonomous status and both Turkish and Greek troops withdrew.

The Italian-Turkish war of 1911–12 was fought mainly over Italy's conquest of Tripolitania and Cyrenaica. The 1915 Treaty of London, in a secret clause, gave Italy the Dodecanese Islands that it had occupied in the 1912 war. They were to be handed back to Turkey when 'the conditions of peace had been fulfilled' (Turkish troops withdrawn from Libya). They never were and Turkey gave up all claims to the islands under the Treaty of Sèvres which also granted Greece the islands of Imbros and Tenedos. Crete united with Greece in 1913 after most of the Muslim population had emigrated.

After the First World War Greece was given a mandate to administer Smyrna for five years after which time a plebiscite would be held to decide whether it would remain Greek or not; Greece landed troops at Izmir. In 1921 the Greeks decided to launch an attack against Kemal Ataturk who opposed the Greek occupation. The Greek army advanced towards Ankara but was defeated by a combination of an unusually severe winter, over-extended communications and a much-improved Turkish Army. The Greeks were forced out of Asia Minor leaving 30,000 dead and taking 1.35 million refugees back to Greece. The Treaty of Lausanne of 1923 created new borders. The European land frontier was adjusted to give more territory to Greece. After a long siege Greek sovereignty over the islands of Límnos, Lésvos, Khíos, Sámos and Ikaria was recognised. Turkey gained sovereignty over the whole of Anatolia, the islands of Imbros and Tenedos and a maritime belt extending 3 miles from the coast. There was an exchange of populations.

Greek-Turkish maritime boundaries.

After the Second World War the Paris Treaty of 1947 transferred the Dodecanese from Italy to Greece.

There are three elements to the Greek-Turkish dispute: the continental shelf; territorial waters, with the possibility of Greece extending its to a 12 mile limit; and air traffic control. The continental shelf issue revolves around the status of islands: Turkey does not recognise that they have a right to a continental shelf and so claims that its continental shelf stretches to the west of the Greek islands. There is also disagreement on how the issue should be resolved, with Turkey arguing for a political settlement to partition the Aegean continental shelf, while Greece wants the dispute settled on legal interpretations of the Law of the Sea by the International Court of Justice. The Law of the Sea recognises that coastal states have the right of territorial waters up to 12 miles off their shores, including islands. At present Greece only claims a 6-mile territorial water but has stated that it will extend the limit to 12 miles when it sees fit to do so. In June 1995 the Turkish National Assembly resolved that the government should take military measures to protect Turkish interests should the Greek limit be extended; Greece considers this resolution a violation of the UN Charter. The internationally agreed Athens Flight Information Region (FIR) extends from the Greek mainland as far east as the edge of Greece's 10-mile national air space (Turkey only recognises a 6-mile Greek air space) to the east of the Aegean islands. In 1974 Turkey issued a notice to airmen (NOTAM) requiring aircraft flying over the eastern half of the Aegean, in which a number of Greek Aegean and Dodecanese islands lie, to report to the Istanbul FIR. The NOTAM was withdrawn in 1980 but since then Turkish military aircraft regularly violate the Athens FIR. A further element in the Greek-Turkish dispute is the question of the demilitarisation of certain Aegean islands which was required by the Treaty of Lausanne and of the Dodecanese islands as demanded by the Treaty of Paris. The Turks accuse the Greeks of fortifying the Aegean islands while the Greeks maintain that only partial demilitarisation was required and that the Montreux Convention of 1923 ended the demilitarised status of Límnos and Samothraki.

Imia Islet, scene of confrontation, December 1995–January 1996. (Greek Ministry of Press)

The most recent and dangerous incident in the Dodecanese concerned the uninhabited islets of Imia that lie halfway between the Greek island of Nisidha Kalymnos and the Turkish Cavus Ada. In December 1995, after a Turkish freighter with engine trouble was stranded on one of the islets, Turkey issued a statement claiming the islets belonged to it. Greece rejected the claim and the mayor of Kalimnos visited Imia and planted a Greek flag; a week later a group of Turkish journalists was filmed replacing it with a Turkish flag. At the end of January Turkish commandos landed on the islets but were soon withdrawn and the incident was settled peacefully but not until both sides had deployed naval forces.

Relations between Greece and Turkey continue to be tense and are not aided by the experiences of their joint history. However, Greece came quickly to Turkey's aid after the major earthquake of August 1999 and Turkey as rapidly helped Greece after the earthquake that hit on 7 September 1999. There has been a definite improvement in relations with Greece withdrawing its objections to Turkish membership of the European Union while also imposing tough conditions. Inter-government talks have taken place but as yet they have not addressed the key divisive issues of the Aegean and Cyprus.

Bibliography and Web Sites

Alford, Jonathan (ed.), *Greece and Turkey: Adversity in Alliance*, IISS Adelphi Library 12, 1984

Howard, Harry, *The Partition of Turkey: A Diplomatic History 1913–1923*, University of Oklahoma Press, 1966

The International Status of the Aegean, Ministry of Press and Mass Media, Athens, 1998

Greece: www.mfa.gr/foreign/bilateral
Turkey: www.mfa.gov.tr/grupa/ad/ade/default

WWW.

CYPRUS: A CASE FOR PARTITION

The earliest inhabitants of Cyprus are thought to have been Ionians who colonised it around 1400 BC and so there has always been a Greek influence on the island in terms of language, culture and religion. Despite the Greek presence, its early history was dominated by the Assyrians, the Egyptians and the Persians. In 330 BC the island's city states welcomed Alexander the Great and supported his campaigns; after his death Cyprus became part of the Ptolemaic empire. Rule by Rome until AD 330 was followed by Byzantine control until the Arab invasions between 649 and 965, after which Byzantium recovered the island. Captured by Richard I of England for the Crusaders in 1191 it was occupied by the knights and their descendants for nearly 300 years. The Venetians lost the island to the Ottomans in 1571 and the latter, as was their custom, brought in colonists who settled often in the same villages as the native inhabitants but always remaining quite separate. Until this point the language and culture of the whole population had been Greek.

The British came to Cyprus in 1878 after leasing the island from Turkey as a base for their support of the Turks in the war against the Russians. Britain annexed Cyprus during the First World War and British rule was recognised in 1923 by the Treaty of Lausanne; two years later it became a Crown Colony. The fact that the British had offered Greece the island in return for a Greek attack on Bulgaria during the First World War – an offer that was refused – later led to Greek Cypriots renewing their demands for *enosis* (union with Greece), a demand encouraged by the school teachers brought in from Greece. An uprising in 1931 was suppressed but both the Greek and Turkish communities were then given a small role in the government.

The movement for *enosis* became more militant after the Second World War and was encouraged by Greece which requested that the UK transfer the colony to it; the request was declined. In 1950 Makarios was appointed Archbishop and took over the leadership of the campaign for *enosis*. He organised a plebiscite which showed that 95 per cent of Greek Cypriots supported union with Greece. As UK influence in Egypt was reduced, Cyprus was seen as an essential base in the region should the British have to leave the Suez Canal Zone. In December 1954 Greece took its case to gain control of Cyprus to the UN General Assembly. The EOKA (National Organisation of Cypriot Fighters) campaign begun in 1955 to induce the British to withdraw was led by Colonel Grivas, a Greek Cypriot officer in the Greek Army.

In August 1955 the British held a conference in London with Greece and Turkey but without Cypriot representation. The Greeks repeated their call for self-determination while the Turks recalled their 400 years of sovereignty and claimed that Britain had no right to turn the island over to anyone but them. The British then offered a scheme for self-government, which fell far short of self-determination, and Archbishop Makarios rejected it. The Turks called for equality with the Greek Cypriot community should self-government be granted and demanded that *enosis* should be permanently excluded as a possibility. In 1956 Makarios, who was known to be actively involved in terrorism, was banished to the

Seychelles and British security forces waged a successful campaign against the EOKA guerrillas. Late in 1956 a new British scheme was proposed but was rejected by the Greek Cypriots because it did not meet their demand for self-determination. However, it was accepted by the Turks despite the unequal representation that the Turkish Cypriots would receive. The Turks were much assured by the Colonial Secretary's statement 'that any exercise of self-determination should . . . must include partition'.

In 1957 Greece again appealed to the UN for self-determination for Cyprus but agreed that this could not lead to joining another state. Makarios was released, just when the security forces were close to defeating EOKA, on the understanding that terrorism would end. By 1957 the UK had changed its position to one of requiring only bases in Cyprus rather than the whole island.

The next proposal, known as the Macmillan plan, was put forward as antagonism between the two communities increased; the scheme gave each community self-government but with a joint council chaired by the British Governor on which representatives of Greece and Turkey would sit. The council would be responsible for foreign affairs, defence and security. Turkey accepted the plan but Greece did not, while Makarios countered with a proposal for independence under UN supervision with guarantees for Turkish Cypriots as a minority but not as equals. Makarios' plan was not acceptable to either the UK or Turkey; Greece threatened to leave NATO if the Macmillan plan was implemented and returned to lobby the UN again but without success.

Greece and Turkey now worked to produce a formula, agreed at conferences at Zurich in 1959 and London in 1960, for independence; Turkey dropped its demand for partition and Greece its for *enosis*. The new Republic, which became independent on 16 August 1960, was a bi-communal federal state guaranteed by Greece, Turkey and the UK. A House of Representatives had most legislative powers with two communal assemblies having responsibility for religion, education and culture. Checks and balances were built into the constitution. The British retained a number of military assets located on Sovereign Base Areas. At the end of 1963 Makarios proposed a long list of changes to the constitution, many reducing Turkish Cypriot rights; it was rejected by the Turkish side and inter-communal fighting broke out, both sides committed atrocities and some 500 people were killed in the first few days. British troops managed to halt some of the violence but were unable to stop the flight of 25,000 Turks to areas with a Turkish majority and therefore safe. In March 1964 the United Nations Peacekeeping Force in Cyprus (UNFICYP) was established but the mandating UNSC resolution referred to the by now wholly Greek Cypriot government as the legal government of all Cyprus. UNFICYP established itself between the two sides in Nicosia, Kyrenia and Lefka. Elsewhere, UN troops were located across the island so that they could react quickly should a confrontation arise. The Greeks refused to allow the Turkish members to retake their seats in the House of Representatives. The Turks appealed to the British who refused to call a meeting under the Treaty of Guarantee, thus losing Turkish respect.

In August 1964, after a further proposal had been rejected, the enclave at Kokkina was attacked and the Turks responded with air strikes from

Cyprus: opposing forces	
Greek Cypriot National Guard	
Men	10,000
Tanks	145
Artillery	270
Warships	1
Greek Army	
Men	1,450
Tanks	60
Artillery	18
Turkish Cypriot	
Men	4,500
(infantry only)	
Turkish Army	
Men	30,000
Tanks	300
Artillery	360
Warships	1
UK garrison	
Men	3,200
Infantry Battalions	2
RAF Helicopters	
Aircraft on training	
UNFICYP	
Men	1,200
Infantry: Argentine, Austria, UK; plus Canada, Finland, Hungary, Ireland, Netherlands and Slovenia.	

the mainland. Makarios threatened an all-out attack on Turkish Cypriots unless the air attacks stopped. The Greek Cypriots formed a national guard from para-military groups, conscripts and mainland Greek officers; Greece covertly sent 10,000 men to join Grivas' command. The Turks also formed a defence force – *Mücahit* or fighters – under Turkish Army officers. A UN report and a further proposal came to nothing as the Greek 'colonels' junta came into power in Greece; it was even more determined to achieve *enosis*. The Turks dismissed their proposals. In October 1967, after twenty Turkish Cypriots were killed by the National Guard in two southern villages, the Turks mobilised but were unable to invade the island due to foul weather; they only demobilised when Greek troops were withdrawn. An autonomous Provisional Cyprus Turkish Administration was then declared. Inter-communal talks began in June 1968 and continued until they reached deadlock in the spring of 1971; the opportunity was taken to renew Greek–Turkish talks but the Turks proposals were unacceptable to Makarios who saw that autonomy for the Turkish Cypriots would lead to partition. Grivas, who had been under house arrest in Athens since 1967, escaped to Cyprus where he formed a new terrorist group, EOKA B, and started a campaign against the supporters of independence.

In November 1973 the leader of the Greek junta was overthrown and plans were made for a coup to overthrow Makarios and achieve *enosis*. The coup took place on 15 July 1974 but Makarios escaped to a British base while heavy fighting took place; the coup succeeded and a former EOKA terrorist, Nikos Sampson, became president. Although the Turkish Cypriots were not attacked, they feared that they soon would be and, after failing to get the British to join them, the Turks invaded

Cyprus since 1974.

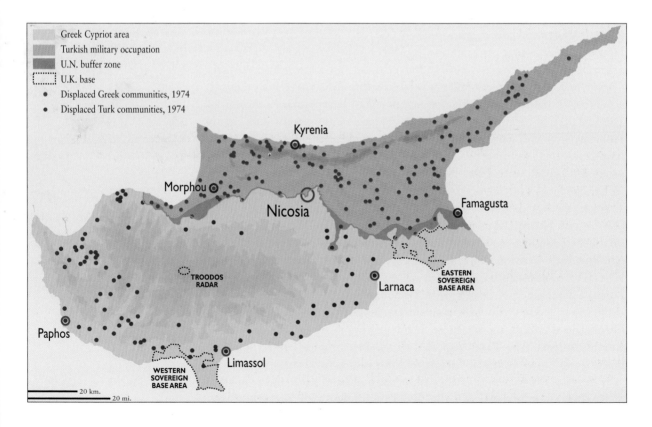

on the 20th, took Kyrenia and secured a corridor to Nicosia. Greek resistance was stronger than had been expected and the Turks agreed to a ceasefire but continued to build up their forces while talks on establishing a bi-zonal federation took place. In August the Turks broke out of the Kyrenia salient and established a line across the island from the north coast east of Kokkina to Varosha on the east coast south of Famagusta. About 150,000 Greek Cypriots who lived north of this line fled to the south and have been replaced by colonists from the Turkish mainland. A ceasefire was agreed. The UNFICYP was deployed in a buffer zone along the ceasefire line and has remained there ever since.

Since 1975 negotiations sponsored by the UN have taken place. In the earliest meeting Makarios and the Turkish Cypriot leader, Rauf Denktash, agreed guidelines for a solution that included provision for an independent, non-aligned, bi-communal federal republic with a central government to safeguard both the unity of the country and its bi-communal nature.

The basic difference between the two sides is that the Greeks stress the unity of Cyprus as an indivisible territory with a single citizenship. The Turks argue for two zones and two communities joined by a federal government responsible only for foreign affairs, tourism and some health matters; in the federal legislature and the Council of Ministers there would be equal representation. There have been numerous initiatives and the appointment of several special representatives, but a solution is not much nearer.

Bibliography and Web Sites

Dodd, Clement H., *The Cyprus Imbroglio*, Eothen Press, 1998
McDonald, Robert, *The Problem of Cyprus*, IISS Adelphi Paper 234, Winter 1988/9

Cypriot Press and Information Office: www.pio.gov.cy
Turkish Republic of Northern Cyprus: www.trncwashdc.org

WWW.

NORTHERN IRELAND: HAS PERMANENT PEACE BEEN ACHIEVED?

The Irish are a Celtic race and are of the same ethnic extraction as the Scots, Devonians and Bretons. Until the late twelfth century Ireland was divided into a number of chiefdoms whose rulers were constantly squabbling and attempting to acquire each other's land. The earliest invaders were Vikings. The English first became involved in the island in 1152; an Irish chief abducted another's wife which led to his losing his chiefdom and appealing to the Normans in England for help in recovering it. The Normans landed in May 1169 and captured the town of Wexford. Other Norman barons landed in 1170 and by 1171 had captured Dublin. The English king, Henry II, then stepped in to curb the power of the barons and to subdue the Irish chiefs. After a six-month campaign Henry had marked out an English-ruled province in south-east Ireland, known as the Pale, and had received submissions from most of the important Irish chiefs. English colonists became major landowners and were known as the Anglo-Irish.

Scotland's involvement in Ireland began when, after Bannockburn in 1314, it invaded and occupied Ulster for three years. Ireland had had no strategic value until the defeat and the eviction of the English from France, but with the growing utility of sea transport Ireland could be seen as another point from which England could be attacked. The first example of this was the invasion led by Lambert Simnel who was defeated by Henry VII at Newark in 1487. The English conquest of Ireland was a pre-emptive move to forestall attacks on England from Ireland by other enemies.

Henry VIII's predecessors had received their lordship of Ireland by papal grant given in 1155 and approved by the Irish Church. Henry, the Irish Church argued, had forfeited this by his break with Rome and the Papal Bull Rex Hibernia gave Ireland to Henry's daughter Mary and her husband Philip. Irish opposition to the English became both nationalistic and religious. English hatred of Catholicism was based on a combination of Queen Elizabeth's excommunication, the Spanish threat and Irish rebellion.

The Spanish Armada, which was defeated in 1588, had Ireland as a secondary objective; on its return journey some twenty-four ships were wrecked off the Irish coast. The Spanish armed and encouraged Irish rebellions but two other armadas en route for Ireland in 1596 and 1597 were both broken up by stormy weather. However, the Irish rebellion spread and Elizabeth dispatched an army of 20,000 men with instructions to subdue the country systematically. The Spanish sent another expeditionary force which successfully landed and captured Kinsale; there the English army beat both the rebels and the Spanish who surrendered in January 1602. There followed a protracted campaign to defeat the Irish rebels and this was achieved with the surrender of the Earl of Tyrone on 30 March 1603.

Queen Elizabeth died to be succeeded by the Scottish James I. James established a colony in Ulster and the 'plantation' of Ulster with Lowland Scots began. The settlers found that they became responsible for order and property rights and so began the history of Protestant domination of the Catholic population. The settlement also led to the rebellion of 1641 in which 2,000 settlers were killed and, not unnaturally, during the English Civil Wars Irish Catholics sided with the Royalists. After the execution of Charles I in 1649, Cromwell embarked on a bloody conquest of Ireland. Some 500,000 native Irish and 112,000 colonists out of total population of 1,448,000 are thought to have perished between 1649 and 1652; another 100,000 Irish were transported to the American colonies. Ethnic cleansing had begun but was halted once the new colonists realised that they needed the Irish workforce.

The restoration of Charles II in 1660 made little difference to the situation of the Irish. After succeeding to the throne in 1685 James II began to change matters with a parliamentary act that overturned the land settlement. However, its implementation was halted by the crowning in 1688 of the Dutch Prince William of Orange who was married to James's daughter. The Catholic Irish remained loyal to the defeated James and captured most of Ulster. But in 1689 they failed to win the siege of Derry and the next year were defeated by William at the battle of the Boyne (two notable landmarks in Northern Irish folklore). Although the Irish were treated as second-class citizens, denied the right to own property or to Catholic education or burial, they did not take advantage of the Jacobite uprisings in favour of James II's descendants in 1715 and 1745.

From the end of the seventeenth century until the beginning of the nineteenth Ireland was owned and ruled by Anglo-Irish Protestants although the Dublin parliament was subordinate to that at Westminster. Scotland, on the other hand, after the Union of 1707 became part of Great Britain. Both the French and American revolutions had an effect on Ireland in terms of land reform, religious toleration and the repeal of some oppressive laws. Ireland became part of the United Kingdom of Great Britain and Ireland and not part of Great Britain itself. However, it remained to all intents and purposes a colony with a separate parliament.

There were small-scale Irish rebellions in 1803, 1848 and 1867; while these established a tradition of revolution they failed to have any effect on the British government and the Protestant colonists blocked the political movements they represented. Ireland remained primarily an agricultural economy and only in Ulster was there any industrialisation; where it did occur, industrialisation bred discrimination in employment further alien- ating the Catholics. While the British did not deliberately cause the Great Famine of 1846 in the same way that hunger had been forced on Ireland by Cromwell and others before him, the British government did insufficient to counter the results of the disaster. In ten years the population was reduced by a quarter with a million dying and another million emigrating.

In another difference from the rest of the United Kingdom, the Irish police from its establishment in 1814 by Robert Peel, the then under-secretary for Ireland, was a centralised, armed, para-military force. By the mid- nineteenth century the churches had secured control of education and hatred of the other community became part of the curriculum.

The first instances of Irish terrorism in mainland Britain took place in 1867; though poorly carried out, they had the effect of persuading the Prime Minister, Gladstone, that reform in Ireland was necessary. In both 1886 and 1893 Gladstone introduced Home Rule bills: the first was defeated in the Commons and the House of Lords threw out the second.

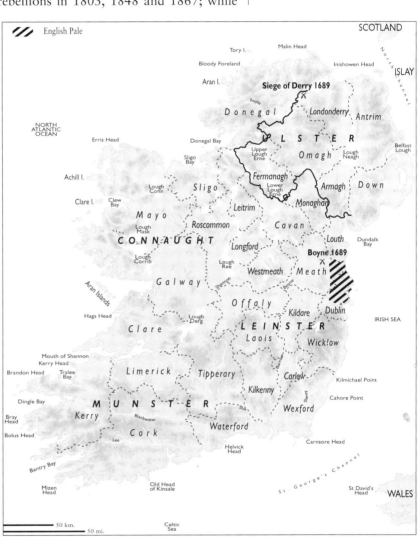

Ireland.

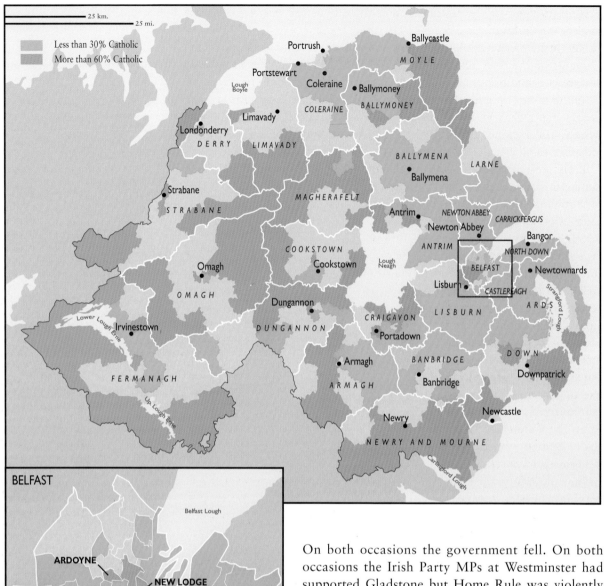

Protestant and Catholic majority areas in Northern Ireland.

On both occasions the government fell. On both occasions the Irish Party MPs at Westminster had supported Gladstone but Home Rule was violently opposed by the Ulster Protestants. A third bill did make progress through parliament. Passed twice in the Commons and rejected twice by the Lords in 1913, it was then amended to allow Ulster counties to opt out of Home Rule. Both the Ulster Volunteer Force and the Irish Volunteers landed arms and ammunition purchased from Germany and the Lords amended the bill to exclude all of Ulster. The start of the First World War postponed further consideration of Irish Home Rule; both Nationalists and Unionists supported the war effort and many died in the armed forces.

In 1916 the Irish Republican Brotherhood organised the Easter uprising which was swiftly crushed and its ringleaders executed. The Brotherhood then merged with the political party Sinn Fein which began to make electoral progress at the expense of the Irish Party; in the 1918 election it won seventy-three seats which its members refused to take up at

Westminster. An Irish parliament, the Dail, was set up, guerrilla warfare broke out and the Irish Republican Army was formed. In 1920 the Government of Ireland Act established two Home Rule parliaments, one in Dublin and one in Belfast, which became the capital of a six-county Ulster. The Anglo-Irish Treaty of 1921 gave Ireland Dominion status, a status that was quietly dropped in 1937 when the twenty-six counties became the Irish Free State. *(EIRE)*

(IRISH FREE STATE)

The Protestants of Northern Ireland enjoyed an electoral majority and ensured that their community was favoured at the expense of the Catholics. The latter suffered discrimination in many fields, particularly in employment and housing, while gerrymandering ensured they had little political influence. The minority community saw the police – the Royal Ulster Constabulary, which had few Catholic officers, and the B Specials, which had none – as fundamentally hostile.

A series of Catholic civil rights demonstrations were held in 1968 and the RUC over-reacted to provocation. Initially British Army reinforcements were welcomed by the Catholics whom they had come to protect but the mood soon changed to one of confrontation. The IRA took advantage of the situation, assumed the role of protector of the Catholic community and attacked both the army and police. Initially the IRA concentrated its activities in Belfast and Londonderry so that it could obtain the maximum publicity. By the beginning of 1972 the British Army appeared to be getting the upper hand, certainly in Belfast. In March the Northern Ireland parliament, Stormont, was prorogued and William Whitelaw was appointed Secretary of State. He instituted a policy determined to find a political rather than a military solution to the troubles. It was a brave decision but one which ensured that the violence continued for nearly thirty years.

Considerable progress towards achieving peace was made in the mid- and late 1990s. The taboo of involving the Irish government was dropped, and in December 1993 the British Prime Minister and the Irish Taoiseach drafted the Downing Street Declaration. For its part Britain stated 'it had no selfish strategic or economic interest in Northern Ireland', while the Irish affirmed that the principle of self-determination should be respected and that the Irish constitution would be changed. The IRA declared a ceasefire in August 1994 and this was followed by a similar declaration from the Combined Loyalist Military Command in October. Throughout 1995 the British linked political talks to terrorist disarmament. In January 1996 former US Senator George Mitchell, brought in to chair an international commission, recommended that disarmament and talks should take place simultaneously. In July 1997 a second ceasefire came into effect and after six weeks Sinn Fein – the nationalist party seen by many, though denied by its members, as the political wing of the IRA – was admitted to the peace talks. Sinn Fein also signed up to the 'Mitchell Principles' which required participants to the talks to agree to the verifiable disarmament of all paramilitary organisations during the course of the talks. At the same time the IRA declared it had no intention of disarming; the term disarmament was abandoned in favour of the word 'decommissioning'.

Despite some terrorist incidents and the continuance of punishment beatings, the talks carried on. A peace resolution known as the Good Friday Agreement

Northern Ireland: Casualties (dead)		
	Security Forces	Civilian
1969	1	13
1970	2	23
1971	59	115
1972	148	322
1973	79	173
1974	52	168
1975	31	216
1976	52	245
1977	43	79
1978	31	50
1979	62	51
1980	26	50
1981	44	57
1982	40	57
1983	33	44
1984	28	36
1985	29	26
1986	24	37
1987	27	68
1988	39	55
1989	23	39
1990	27	49
1991	19	75
1992	9	76
1993	14	70
1994	6	56
1995	1	8
1996	1	14
1997	5	17
1998	2	53
1999	0	7
Total	957	2342
Police	302	
Army	655	

Bomb damage in Omagh. Twenty-five were killed on 15 August 1998. (Associated Press)

was signed on 18 April 1998. Its main provision was the establishment of an assembly elected by proportional representation and a power-sharing executive to take over the responsibilities of the Northern Ireland government departments. Cross-border institutions were to be established, the police force and the judicial process reviewed. Disarmament was not mentioned. Not unnaturally the Unionists insisted that decommissioning must start before Sinn Fein could be admitted to the executive, while Sinn Fein maintained that decommissioning was not a 'Good Friday' commitment. Meanwhile, the release of convicted terrorists, both Republican and Unionist, had begun. Eventually the Unionist leader, David Trimble, was convinced that risks must be taken if peaceful progress was to be made and he persuaded his party to agree to let Sinn Fein participate in government in return for a pledge that decommissioning would take place. However, he stated that the Unionists would withdraw from the executive if they were not satisfied by the progress made in decommissioning by February 2000.

There are still risks that what has been achieved may be lost. New terrorist bodies – the 'Continuity IRA' and the 'Real IRA' – who may violate the ceasefire have emerged, and the IRA could still refuse to disarm or could fail to decommission sufficient weapons to satisfy the Unionists. As in other parts of the world there are still extremists who prefer violence to compromise.

Bibliography and Web Sites

Bardon, Johnathan, *A History of Ulster*, Blackstaff Press, 1992

Bew, Paul, and Gordon Gillespie, *A Chronology of the Troubles 1968–99*, Gill & Macmillan, 1999

Edwards, Ruth Dudley, *The Faithful Tribe: An Intimate Portrait of the Loyalist Institutions*, HarperCollins, 1999

Falls, Cyril, *Elizabeth's Irish Wars*, Constable, 1950

O'Farrell, Patrick, *Ireland's English Question*, Batsford, 1971

O'Leary, Brendan, and John McGarry, *The Politics of Antagonism: Understanding Northern Ireland*, Athlone Press, 1996

Sloan, G.R., *The Geopolitics of Anglo-Irish Relations in the 20th Century*, Leicester University Press, 1997

BBC News: http://news.bbc.co

Independent Commission on Policing for Northern Ireland: www.belfast.org.uk/report

THE BALKANS: EXCHANGING COMMUNISM FOR NATIONALISM

Europe and the US have been concerned by and involved in events in the Balkans for the last ten years. Their success rate at solving the problems has been mixed. Only in Macedonia can it be claimed that preventive diplomacy has been a success and in Albania the Italian-led intervention contributed to stabilising that country when it was in danger of imploding. Elsewhere it was either a case of doing too little too late or going to the other extreme and using massive air power to force the Serbs into halting their ethnic cleansing in Kosovo but at the risk of sending the wrong message to the watching world.

(Modern names have been used throughout so as to avoid misunderstanding even though these were not used until long after the events described.)

YUGOSLAVIA: BACKGROUND AND HISTORY

The federation called Yugoslavia, which started to disintegrate in 1991, was established in 1918 after the end of the First World War as an attempt to stabilise the Balkans. At first it was known as the Kingdom of the Serbs, Croats and Slovenes and was created by joining the previously independent states of Serbia and Montenegro and parts of the Austro-Hungarian and Ottoman Empires, both of which had been destroyed by the war. In 1920 the province of Vojvodina was added. In 1929 the bitterness of the ethnic divides within the federation encouraged the king to establish a strong dictatorial government in Belgrade and a system of *banovina* or governorships, which deliberately took account of neither historical boundaries nor the ethnicity of the population.

German occupation during the Second World War gave an added dimension to the centuries-old divisions as Yugoslavia was broken up by the Axis. The southern half of Slovenia became part of Italy, along with

Yugoslavia: ethnic population (thousands)			
	1918	1948	1981
Serbs	4,666	6,547	8,140
Croats	2,857	3,784	4,428
Slovene	1,025	1,415	1,754
Bosnian Muslim*	728	809	2,000
Albanians	442		750
	1,730		
Macedonian	586		810
	1,340		
Montenegrin	?	810	579
Hungarian	472	?	427

*1948/81 all Muslims less Albanians

Others in 1918	
German	513
Turks	168
Romanian	229
Jews	64
Sandjak/other Muslim	140

1878–1912

1914

1923

1999

Changes to Balkan borders,
1878–1999.

the Dalmatian coastal strip; Italy also took control of Montenegro, Albania – the latter had been expanded into Kosovo, which was mainly inhabited by ethnic Albanians – and parts of Macedonia. Hungary took the two northern districts of Croatia and the larger part of Vojvodina while the ethnic German population there took over the administration of Banat District. Bulgaria took eastern Macedonia and parts of southern Serbia. All that was left was a truncated Serbia directly governed by the Germans and an 'independent' state of Croatia, which included Bosnia and Herzegovina under the rule of Croat Ustashe, a puppet Nazi state. The Ustashe were violently anti-Serb. They forcibly converted many to Catholicism and are said to have massacred as many as 400,000.

Opposition to the German occupation was divided. The Serbian guerrillas, the Chetniks, were only nominally under the control of Draza Mihailović whose loyalty was to the government in exile; some collaborated with the Italians. The other main guerrilla group was the 'Partisans' organised by Tito and it drew its support not just from Croats but also from Serbs and others. Like the Chetniks, the Partisans spent as much time fighting rival Yugoslav groups as they did the occupation forces which relied heavily on non-German units and included a Muslim SS division. The Partisans are believed to have killed as many as a million fellow Yugoslavs during and immediately after the war including 18,000 prisoners of war returned from Austria.

After 1945 Tito held Yugoslavia together by a combination of an emphasis on communism as an alternative to nationalism, centralised bureaucracy and a high degree of ruthlessness. The country was redivided into six republics and two autonomous provinces, Vojvodina and Kosovo, both of which were within Serbia; the post-war borders left many communities, particularly the Serbian, on the wrong side of the boundary lines. The only difference between the provinces and the republics was that constitutionally the former could not secede while the latter could. Slowly centralisation withered and a new constitution imposed in 1974 left the Federal government responsible only for defence, foreign affairs and some economic matters.

Tito died in 1980 leaving a rotating leadership for the Federation as his legacy. As decentralisation developed so did nationalism, which was given a new purpose with the collapse of communism throughout eastern Europe.

The new states of former Yugoslavia.

In 1987 Slobodan Milosević gained the leadership of Serbia and with a new constitution in 1990 he abolished the autonomous status of Vojvodina and Kosovo, much to the dismay of the Hungarian and Albanian populations there and also of the Republics of Slovenia and Croatia who foresaw an unacceptable rise in Serbian nationalism and power.

Today Yugoslavia comprises only Serbia and Montenegro. Milosević and Serbia are seen as the direct cause of the break-up of the Federation and of the fighting that has taken place since. Serbia has had to absorb a large number of refugees, mainly from the Serbian enclaves in Croatia, and a number of these had been housed in Kosovo. The conflict in Kosovo is dealt with separately on pages 124–9. While the Serbs consider the fighting throughout former Yugoslavia as a civil war within the independent republics, many believe that the level of military support given to the Serb communities in Croatia and Bosnia-Herzegovina justifies the conflicts being described as inter-state wars. For this, rump Yugoslavia has had sanctions imposed on it by the United Nations.

It is a matter of debate whether Montenegro will remain part of Yugoslavia. The Montenegrins must know that separatist moves will be reacted to forcibly by Serbia but they might gamble that NATO forces now in Kosovo and Bosnia-Herzegovina would come to their immediate aid. The republic has already made itself economically independent by adopting the D-mark as the Yugoslav dinar loses value. In response Serbia has blocked cross-border payments, leaving Montenegro to fund pensions and government workers' salaries. Serb police stopped fresh food from entering Montenegro in early December 1999. Alternative supplies from Croatia and Slovenia are 20 per cent more expensive. However, only roughly half the population supports the idea of independence. If Montenegro did declare its independence then Serbia would lose its access to the sea and its only naval base at Kotor. Serbia is most unlikely to allow Montenegro to break away peacefully.

Bibliography and Web Site

Carter, F.W., and H.T. Norris (eds), *The Changing Shape of the Balkans*, SOAS/GRC Geopolitical Series, UCL Press, 1996

Glennie, Misha, *The Balkans 1804–1999: Nationalism, War and the Great Powers*, Granta Books, 1999

Silber, Laura, and Alan Little, *The Death of Yugoslavia*, Harmondsworth, 1995

The Former Yugoslavia: Chronology November 1996–May 1998, Foreign and Commonwealth Office Background Brief, 1998

www.

Helsinki Committee for Human Rights in Serbia: www.helsinki.org.yu *and* www.ihf-hr.org.serbia

Serbian Ministry of Information: www.serbia.info.com

SLOVENIA AND CROATIA: TOURISM HAS RETURNED

Slovenia

Slovenia was the least Balkan-oriented element of Yugoslavia. It had had a long experience of association with its Italian and Austrian neighbours but had maintained its language and Slavonic identity. It was the only republic of the Yugoslav Federation to have a homogeneous population with a common religion, Roman Catholicism. It was eager to join Yugoslavia in 1918 to escape the influence of its much larger neighbours. Throughout the inter-war years it was a moderating influence in Yugoslav politics and its people had no desire, unlike the Croats, for separatism. During the Second World War it was split between Italy and Austria, but after 1945 it was expanded by being given most of the Slovene-populated areas of north-east Italy.

Until the collapse of communism Slovene nationalism was hardly an issue but in the late 1980s it became the most critical part of the Yugoslav situation. In the first multi-party elections in 1990 the centre-right coalition, DEMOS, campaigned for independence and won. In July the National Assembly voted for a declaration of sovereignty giving precedence to Slovene over Federal law and resolving to develop its own foreign and defence policy. Next it took control of the Territorial Defence Force, the Yugoslav-wide system for mobilising and arming the country in the event of war. In December 1990 in a referendum the country voted overwhelmingly for independence and in March 1991 it stopped sending conscripts to the Federal Army.

The Serbs were not concerned by Slovene independence other than with regard to the effect that it would have on Croatia by complicating Serbian efforts to stop the latter leaving the Federation. Slovenia declared its independence on 25 June 1991 and the Federal Army immediately sent in armoured forces but without infantry support which was essential for operations in the heavily forested mountainous area. The Serbian aim was

Dubrovnik, Croatia. (The Hutchison Library)

Slovenia and Croatia post-independence, showing Serb-dominated areas.

to reach and seal off the external borders of the Federation. However, few of the columns got through because they were held up on narrow roads which were either in gullies or on embankments with the result that tanks could not deploy off the roads. The European Community (EC) managed to broker an agreement but the Slovenes failed to meet their commitment to lift the blockade of army barracks; on 18 July the Federal Army was ordered to pull out of Slovenia. Casualties in the fighting had been light; nineteen Slovene men and forty-five Federal soldiers killed. In January 1992 the EC, at German insistence, recognised Slovenia as an independent state.

Croatia

The historical splits and border changes of history have seriously affected Croatia, as they have Bosnia and Herzegovina (see pages 118–21). After the split of the Roman Empire, the Croats became Catholics and used Roman script, while the Serbs adopted Orthodox Christianity and the Cyrillic alphabet. Large numbers of Serbs fled the Ottoman Empire and came to inhabit the Croatian/Bosnian and Croatian/Vojvodina border areas.

Croatia formed the main part of the Austro-Hungarian Empire's military frontier region with the Ottoman Empire, which stretched from northern Dalmatia to Transylvania. During the Second World War Croatia was greatly enlarged, incorporated the whole of Bosnia-Herzegovina and was ruled as a Nazi puppet state by the violently anti-Serb Ustashe. After the war, Croatia was also given parts of Italy, including the Istrian peninsula and Italian Dalmatia; the post-war borders left many Serbs within Croatia.

The multi-party elections in Croatia in April 1990 brought Franjo Tudjman, a former communist, partisan and army general, to power as leader of the right-wing Croatian Democratic Union (HDZ). Tudjman reintroduced the old Croatian flag and the new constitution made no mention of the Serbs, who for their part organised the Serbian Democratic Party (SDS) and boycotted the National Assembly. By October they had declared regional autonomy in the regions (Krajina, Eastern and Western Slavonia) in which the Serbs pre-dominated. After a referendum in May 1991 in which Croats voted overwhelmingly in favour, Croatia declared its independence on 25 June 1991. Even before that there had been frequent violent clashes between Serbs and Croats. Now there was open war as the Serbs began to expand their enclaves and to force the Croatian minorities there out in what has now become known as ethnic cleansing. The Croats had been unable, unlike the Slovenes, to take over the Territorial Defence Force armouries and so were poorly armed, while the Federal Army gave support to the Serbs. Vukovar in Eastern Slavonia was taken and destroyed, the ancient port of Dubrovnik was shelled, and many other towns and villages were badly damaged as their Croat populations were driven out by the Serbs.

In mid-January 1992 the EC recognised Croatia's independence. The UN envoy Cyrus Vance arranged a ceasefire and got agreement for the deployment of a UN peacekeeping force, the United Nations Protection Force (UNPROFOR). The peacekeeping plan required the withdrawal of the Yugoslav People's Army (PLA), the demilitarisation of the UN Protected Areas, the return of refugees and the establishment of a Croatian police force. The UN authorised a force of nearly 14,000 men, including police, but only 9,700 initially deployed; the UN so misjudged future events that according to its original plans Sarajevo was to be the UNPROFOR HQ and logistic base. In the event fighting around the airport required the transfer of a battalion from Croatia to Sarajevo.

No progress was made in returning the Serb-held areas, Eastern and Western Slavonia and Krajina, to Croat control during 1993 and 1994. By mid-1994 there were some 250,000 Croats displaced from Krajina and up to 420,000 Croat refugees from Bosnia in Croatia. During this time the Croatian Army was being established, armed with smuggled weapons and trained and advised by an American commercial company employing retired US Army officers. Then in May and August 1994 in two swift, well-planned operations the Croats recovered first Western Slavonia and then Krajina, which resulted in some 200,000 Serbs fleeing as refugees to Bosnia and Serbia. Few of these refugees have returned to their homes.

In a move to prevent a Croatian assault on Eastern Slavonia which could escalate into a war with Serbia, the Contact Group (a negotiating team of

Opposing forces, Croatia, August 1995		
	Croatian	Serb
Men	70,000	50,000
Tanks	220	250
Artillery	325	320
Aircraft	25	20

UNCRO (the follow-on force to UNPROFOR, established in November 1995): Total 12,150, plus 418 police. Infantry Battalions from: Argentina, Belgium, Canada, Czech Republic, Denmark, Jordan, Kenya, Nepal, Poland, Russia, Ukraine.

UNTAES ORBAT		
	No. of Men	Type of Force
Argentina	73	Recce Company
Belgium	668	Mech Battalion
Czech Republic	39	Field Surgical Team
Indonesia	71	Medical Company
Jordan	863	Mech Battalion, Tank Company, Artillery Battery
Pakistan	981	Mech Battalion, Artillery Battery
Poland	53	Police Group
Russia	842	Mech Battalion
Slovakia	553	Engineer Battalion
Ukraine	323	Helicopter Squadron, Light Infantry Company
Plus 100 observers from 22 countries		
Total	4,880	
March 1997		

representatives from France, Germany, Russia, the UK and the US) negotiated an agreement in November 1995 that would allow the UN to implement the peaceful return of the region to Croatian rule. The UN Transition Authority in Eastern Slavonia (UNTAES) was established and the UN troops already deployed there increased in strength from 1,600 to about 5,000 and were reinforced with tanks, artillery and attack helicopters. These heavy weapons had on occasion to be deployed in a show of force to induce Serb elements to withdraw. Demilitarisation of Eastern Slavonia began in May 1996; Serb heavy weapons were taken to Serbia and soldiers disbanded. A programme to 'buy back' the many small arms and ammunition held by most adults was instituted, funded by the Croat government; it resulted in nearly 10,000 weapons being handed in. UNTAES's civilian component supervised the establishment of local government and a Serbo-Croat police force. In April 1997 the region took part in the Croat national and local elections. On 15 January 1998 the UN handed full control of Eastern Slavonia back to the Croatian authorities. Both before and since then there has been movement of Serbs, mainly those who had fled from the other two Serb enclaves, out of Eastern Slavonia; Serbs complain of discrimination.

A small UN operation, the UN Mission of Observers in Prevlaka (UNMOP), still continues to monitor the demilitarised zone and heavy weapons exclusion zone on the Prevlaka Peninsula, which controls access to the Bay of Kotor. In 1995 the Croats agreed to demilitarisation in return for the withdrawal of Yugoslav artillery from around Dubrovnik.

Bibliography and Web Sites

Tanner, Marcus, *Croatia: A Nation Forged in War*, Yale University Press, 1997

Croatian Government: www.vlada.hr/english
Slovene Ministry of Foreign Affairs: www.gov.si/mzz/ang

BOSNIA AND HERZEGOVINA: WAITING TO RE-EXPLODE

The origins of the Bosnian people are buried in ancient history; they are most likely the descendants of the Illyrian tribes which lived in the mountainous and forested area between the two main north–south routes – along the Dalmatian coast and from Belgrade down the Morava valley. The Romans conquered them in AD 9. Since then the purity of Bosnian blood has been diluted by the various invaders of the region – settlers from other parts of the Roman Empire, the Goths who drove out the Romans in the fourth century, Mongol-Turkic Huns and Iranian Alans in the fourth and fifth centuries, Slavs and Avars in the sixth century. Finally, in the 620s the Slavic Serb and Croat tribes arrived, the latter said to have been invited in by the Byzantine Emperor to evict the Avars.

Bosnia was situated on the western side of the boundary between the eastern and western parts of the Roman Empire when it was divided in 284. Then, after the expulsion of the Goths, it came under Byzantium which was only able to exercise direct control infrequently. The Emperor Constantine made the first known reference to Bosnia, as the territory of Bosona, in 958. Byzantine control was re-established by Basil II in 1018 and Bosnia was then ruled alternately by Serb and Croat governors. Hungary, after taking Croatia, extended its rule into Bosnia in 1102 and periods of both Hungarian and Byzantine rule followed until 1180 when Bosnia achieved a form of independence. This it maintained, thanks to its difficult terrain, until conquest by the Ottomans in 1463. It then became the border region between the Ottoman and Austrian-Hungarian Empires.

During the Ottoman period, conversion to Islam took place slowly over more than 100 years with some 40 per cent of the population being Muslim in 1548. There was no forced conversion, other than of boys who were conscripted into the Janissaries, though it was obviously advantageous in many ways to be Muslim. Both the Ottomans and the Hapsburgs brought in Serbs and Vlachs to settle their border areas with martial peoples, further muddling the population of Bosnia. The Ottomans also settled *spahi* or cavalrymen with estates in return for guaranteed availability for military duty which included, depending on the size of the estate, providing additional manpower; naturally *spahi* were Muslims. After a series of wars between the Ottomans and the Austrians and Venetians, Bosnia was occupied by Austria in 1878 and annexed in 1908. It remained so until the First World War. By then three groups peopled Bosnia: Orthodox and Catholic Christians and Muslims. Only since the late nineteenth century have the Orthodox begun describing themselves as Serbs and the Catholics as Croats, regardless of their actual descent.

After the war Bosnia became part of the new Yugoslav kingdom. When that country was reorganised in 1921 into thirty-three *oblasts* or provinces, six were Bosnian and together they conformed to Bosnia's previous borders. In 1929 the bitterness of the ethnic divisions led the king to re-divide the country into *banovina* or governorships that deliberately took no account of historical boundaries; Bosnian territory was divided between four *banovina*. German occupation during the Second World War gave an added dimension to the centuries-old divisions as Yugoslavia was broken up; Bosnia and Herzegovina were included in a puppet Nazi state ruled by the Croat Ustashe. The Ustashe directed most of their efforts against the Serbian population and to a lesser extent the Muslims who formed a Muslim Volunteer Legion for their defence. In late 1942 the Muslims appealed to the Germans to halt Ustashe action against them and offered to expand the legion under German control. The Germans would not agree to Bosnian autonomy but took the opportunity to raise a Muslim SS division that later carried out reprisals against Serbs. By the end of the war many Muslims had also joined Tito's Partisans.

In post-war Yugoslavia, Bosnia-Herzegovina was one of the six Federal Republics. Its borders now included an area in the north that consisted of the Muslim-populated enclave around Bihac and a Serbian-dominated strip along the border with Croatia. The first step towards the recognition of Muslim national status came in May 1968 when the conference of the Central Committee of the League of Communists of Bosnia and Herzegovina concluded that 'the Muslims are a distinct nation'. The new Yugoslav constitution of 1974 passed a great deal of power to the individual republics and also recognised the Bosnian Muslims as a nationality; by then the Muslim proportion of the population had risen from 30.7 per cent in 1948 to nearly 40 per cent.

UNPROFOR, September 1995

Total 19,000, plus 30 civil police. Infantry Battalions from: Bangladesh (Bihac), Canada, Egypt, France (3), Jordan, Malaysia, Netherlands (Srebrenica), Nordic States, Pakistan, Russia, Spain, Turkey, Ukraine, United Kingdom (2 and an armoured recce squadron), Infantry Company New Zealand.

Plus (not included in total) Rapid Reaction Force: France (tank, scout, 120mm mortar, engineer companies, helicopter battalion); UK (brigade HQ, infantry battalion, 105mm artillery battalion, helicopter regiment, 12 RAF helicopters); Netherlands Marine Company.

SFOR 1999: Three Multi-national Divisions (MND)

Force Troops

Engineer battalions: Hungary and Romania
Logistic battalions: Austria, Bulgaria, Greece
PSYOPS battalion: multi-national
Signal battalion: multi-national
Aviation regiment: US
Military police company: multi-national

MND South-West

HQ and Commander: UK
Infantry battalions: Belgium, Canada, Czech Republic, Netherlands and UK
Armoured cavalry battalion: UK
Artillery battalion: UK
Engineer battalion: UK
Helicopter squadron 2 x: UK
Signals battalion: UK
EW squadron: UK

MND South-East

HQ multi-national, Commander: France
Infantry battalion 2 x: France, Germany, Italy, Morocco, Portugal, 2 x Spain, Ukraine
Engineer battalion: France/Spain
Helicopter battalion: France
Artillery battery: Italy

MND North

HQ and Commander: US
Infantry battalion: Denmark, Finland, Norway, Poland, 2 x Russia, Sweden, Turkey, 2 x US (Task Force) (all arms)
Artillery battery: Russia, Turkey
Engineer battalion: US
Engineer company: Russia, Turkey
Helicopter regiment 2 x: US
Infantry company: rotated between Estonia, Latvia, and Lithuania
Signal battalion: US
Air defence battalion: US

When the Communist Party collapsed in early 1990 nationalist parties, all with different agendas, replaced it. Both Serbia and Croatia were seen as threatening to Bosnia and Herzegovina, though the Croatian President, Franjo Tudjman, opposed border changes mainly on account of the Serbian enclaves in Croatia. The Bosnian President, Alija Izetbegovic, a Muslim, opposed Croatian and Slovenian independence as this would leave Bosnia at the mercy of Serbia. In May 1991 three Serbian-dominated areas of Bosnia declared themselves as 'Serb Autonomous Regions' and Serbia began secretly supplying the Bosnian Serbs with arms. In September the Bosnian Serbs called on the Federal Army for protection and the army assisted in establishing the borders of the Serb Autonomous Region of Herzegovina. The European Community's Badinter Arbitration Commission recommended that a referendum be held in Bosnia before the EC considered its recognition. In the referendum, which most Serbs boycotted, 64 per cent voted virtually unanimously for independence and the EC recognised this in April 1992.

The Serbs then began the process now known as ethnic cleansing, evicting the Muslim population from a number of towns. The main aim was to link up the Serbian enclaves by controlling the area between the army base at Banja Luka in Bosnia and the Serb-occupied areas of Croatia to the west and Serbia to the east as well as a strip of territory running down the eastern border to the Serb enclave in eastern Herzegovina. In April 1992 when Milosević declared a new federal state of Yugoslavia comprising only Serbia and Montenegro, he also transferred the Bosnian-Serb members of the Federal Army with their weapons to the Bosnian-Serb Army (BSA).

A great many lessons can be learnt from the way the Bosnian crisis was handled. Many countries based their policy not on what was best for Bosnia but on either domestic political concerns or the implications for other foreign policy matters. For example, initially the EC opposed the break up of Yugoslavia because of the effect this might have on the

Site of the historic bridge across the Neretva at Mostar. Destroyed by Croats, 1993. (US Department of Defense)

disintegrating Soviet Union. The US called for a policy of lifting the arms embargo on the Bosnian Muslims and carrying out air strikes against the Serbs but was not willing to commit ground troops; the Europeans, with troops on the ground in Bosnia, strongly opposed this policy. The Contact Group worked out its political settlement plan without consulting UNPROFOR and then presented it on a 'take it or leave it' basis. The UN gave UNPROFOR unrealistic mandates and then failed to provide the resources,

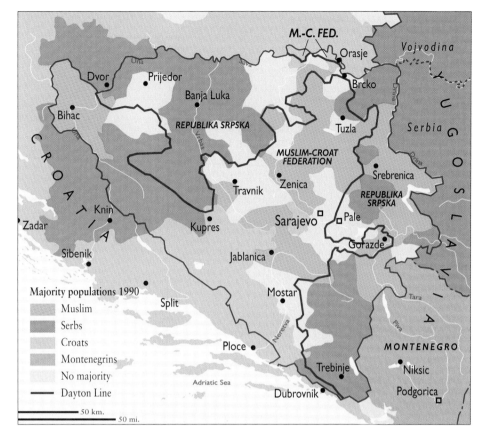

usually sufficient troops, to enable them to be carried out successfully – for example, as in the case of the 'safe' areas. Once bombing was accepted as necessary there was disagreement between NATO and the US, both of which wanted to carry out strategic bombing, and UNPROFOR, which needed bombing that was tactical and only sufficient to be counted as a minimum use of force.

A combination of the Croat success in recovering territory from the Serbs both in Croatia and in Bosnia, together with British and French artillery immediately engaging anyone firing on Sarajevo, NATO bombing and the effects of sanctions on Serbia, brought about the Dayton conference in November 1995. The military tasks set by Dayton were quickly achieved: NATO deployed a strong presence known as the Implementation Force (IFOR) and renamed the Stabilisation Force (SFOR) a year later, the two sides were separated and heavy weapons returned to barracks. The political clauses of the Dayton Agreement have still not been fully implemented; virtually no refugees have managed, or even dared, to return to their homes when these are in the territory held by the other side. The country is virtually partitioned between the Muslim-Croat Federation and Republika Srpska.

Bosnia-Herzegovina showing the population split in 1990 and the 1995 Dayton armistice line.

Bibliography and Web Sites

Bildt, Carl, *Peace Journey: The Struggle for Peace in Bosnia*, Weidenfield & Nicolson, 1998

Carter, F.W., and H.T. Norris (eds), *The Changing Shape of the Balkans*, SOAS/GRC Geopolitics Series, UCL Press, 1996

Holbrooke, Richard, *To End a War*, Random House, 1998

Judah, Tim, *The Serbs: History, Myth, and the Destruction of Yugoslavia*, Yale University Press, 1997

Malcolm, Noel, *Bosnia: A Short History*, Macmillan, 1994

O'Shea, Brendan, *Crisis at Bihac: Bosnia's Bloody Battlefield*, Sutton, 1998

Owen, David, *Balkan Odyssey*, Victor Gollancz, 1995

Rose, Michael, *Fighting for Peace*, Harvill Press, 1998

Silber, Laura, and Alan Little, *The Death of Yugoslavia*, Harmondsworth, 1995

Bosnia Report: www.bosnia.org.uk

Bosnian Ministry of Foreign Affairs: www.mvp.gov.ba/

NATO Stabilisation Force: www.nato.int/sfor

OSCE Mission to Bosnia: www.oscebih.org

MACEDONIA: AN EXAMPLE OF PREVENTIVE DIPLOMACY

(The Former Yugoslav Republic of Macedonia (FYROM) is referred to as Macedonia here.)

Former Yugoslav Republic of Macedonia.

The history of Macedonia is inextricably linked to that of Greece. However, the Macedonians never considered themselves to be Greeks, while the latter now claim that the former were a Greek tribe despite the ancient Greek view that they were barbarians. It was Philip II, father of Alexander the Great, who formed Macedonia into a strong state during the fourth century BC. He extended the state but not at the expense of the Greeks with whom he forged agreements so that among his titles was Hegemon of the Greek League. Alexander conquered a vast empire that broke up on his death. The various generals, who had inherited parts of the empire, were constantly at war from which Macedonia and Greece kept apart. The origins of the people living in Macedonia who now call themselves Macedonians are hard to define. For thousands of years the population of Macedonia and Thrace had a different culture to that of those living to the south, the area occupied by Greek-speaking tribes in the third century BC.

'Geographic' Macedonia refers to the area between the Sar Mountains and Mount Skopska Crna Gora to the north, the Rila and Rhodope mountains to the east, the Aegean coast as far west as Mount Olympus in the south and the Pindus Mountains and Lakes Ohrid and Prespa in the west. The Bulgarian portion is known as Pirin Macedonia and the Greek as Greek Macedonia.

Geographic Macedonia fell to the Romans and on the split between Rome and Byzantium it became part of the Byzantine Empire. It was conquered by the Bulgars in the seventh century but was recovered and ruled by Byzantium from 1014 until 1230. The next 100 years witnessed several changes of rule and splits in the region with the Serbs taking Skopje in 1282. By 1346 the Serb Empire stretched from the Danube in the north to central Greece in the south and from the Drina in the west to Thrace in the east. The Ottomans gained control over Macedonia and the Balkans following their defeat of the Serbs at Kosovo Polje in 1389, and Macedonia was part of the Ottoman Empire until its collapse.

After the Turkish-Russian War, the 1878 Treaty of Stefano created a Greater Bulgaria which included Macedonia and part of Greece. A few months later the treaty was overturned; the Congress of Berlin redrew the borders and created Greater Macedonia. This new border arrangement pleased none of Macedonia's neighbours and was a constant source of friction and conflict. After the Balkan War of 1912–13, the Treaty of Bucharest divided Macedonia between its neighbours Bulgaria, Greece and Serbia. Then after the First World War Serbian Macedonia became part of the newly formed Kingdom of the Serbs, Croats and Slovenes, renamed Yugoslavia in 1921. Macedonia plus part of Serbia was one of the *banovina* created by the king in 1929 in an effort to end historical boundaries and ethnicities. During the Second World War Macedonia was split between Italian-controlled Albania and Bulgaria. After 1945 Macedonia became one of the republics of the Yugoslav Federation.

It is not surprising with such a history of changing borders and population movements that Macedonia should have very mixed population. According to a census, in 1994 it comprised a majority of Macedonians (70 per cent including about 40,000 Macedonian-speaking Muslims) and minorities of Albanians (22.5 per cent; they complain their numbers were under-represented in the 1991 census), Turks (4 per cent), Roma or Gypsies (2 per cent) and Serbs (2 per cent). There is also a small number of Bulgarians. People of Macedonian origin live in Bulgaria but the numbers registered at censuses there have dropped considerably since 1946, probably on account of the fact that Bulgaria no longer recognises a separate Macedonian nationality. Macedonians also live in Greece where there is controversy over the number of Slav Macedonians. It is also not surprising that there is controversy over who exactly the Macedonians are. The Macedonians of FYROM are certainly Slavs, more probably of the Bulgar line than of the Serb.

When the Yugoslav Federation broke up, Greek opposition to the use of the name Macedonia delayed its international recognition until the compromise title of the Former Yugoslav Republic of Macedonia was agreed upon. Greek opposition to the name may appear petty but there

Greater Serbia
State of Tsar Dusan, 1355

Serbia.

UNPREDEP, June 1995

1,127 troops, 23 civil police
Nordic Battalion (Denmark, Finland,
  Norway, Sweden)
United States Battalion

are valid reasons for it. There is bitterness stemming from the Greek civil war of 1948 in which many Slav-speaking Greeks joined the communist guerrilla army ELAS; many went into exile and gained positions of importance in Macedonia. Nor did FYROM help matters by printing bank notes showing a historic building in Thessalonika and by using Alexander the Great's symbol, the star of Vergina, on the national flag. The Greeks also fear that allowing the country to be called Macedonia might kindle expansionist flames for other parts of historic Macedonia.

In a worst-case scenario, civil war in FYROM could well involve Albania, Bulgaria and Serbia and even drag in Greece and Turkey. In November 1992 the FYROM President Kiro Gligorov requested the UN to deploy observers to the country. After reconnaissance it was decided to send a battalion of 700 men plus 35 military observers and 26 civil police monitors; in July 1993 the UN Nordic battalion was reinforced by 300 US troops. The UN force was known as the UN Preventive Deployment Force (UNPREDEP). There have been a number of border incidents but because of the UN presence none has been allowed to escalate. At the UNSC the Chinese vetoed the further extension of UNPREDEP's mandate following Macedonia's establishment of diplomatic relations with Taiwan in January 1999. UNPREDEP's role was then assumed, unofficially, by the troops assembled in Macedonia as an extrication force for the unarmed OSCE 'verifiers' in Kosovo.

A flood of some 300,000 refugees from Kosovo began to stream into Macedonia shortly after NATO's bombing campaign began in March 1999. There were some ugly scenes at the border as the Macedonian authorities tried to regulate the flow into the country and thousands had to spend days in the open waiting to be admitted. Humanitarian agencies helped by NATO troops erected a number of large camps for the refugees and organised measures to meet their feeding and medical needs. There were fears that this alteration to the ethnic balance in Macedonia, even if only for a short period, would destabilise the country. When Milosević finally gave in and the bombing stopped on 10 June some refugees began to return to Kosovo immediately, far sooner than was expected or planned. Within weeks virtually all the refugees had gone home.

Bibliography and Web Sites

Danforth, Loring, *The Macedonian Conflict*, Princeton University Press, 1995
Pettifer, James (ed.), *The New Macedonian Question*, Macmillan, 1999
Poulton, Hugh, *Who Are the Macedonians?*, Hurst, 1995

www.

International Crisis Group: www.crisisweb.org
Macedonian Ministry of Information: www.sinf.gov.mk

The memorial monument at the site of the battle of Kosovo Polje, 1389.

KOSOVO: THE SEEDBED OF ANOTHER BALKAN WAR

The region known today as Kosovo is the southernmost part of Serbia. Albania is to its south-west and Macedonia to the south and south-east. It is surrounded by mountains that give it a strategic importance because whoever holds it can threaten movement to both its south and its north. The region's name comes from Kosovo Polje, or plain, to the south-west of Pristina, and the battle fought there in 1389 between the Serbs under

Prince Lazar and the Ottomans of Murat. Little is known of the course of the battle other than that it was intense and both sides suffered heavy casualties with both Murat and Lazar being killed. Although the Ottomans were left in command of the field, they soon withdrew and so it is uncertain whether the outcome really was an Ottoman victory, a draw or even, as in some accounts, a Serbian victory. Ever since it was fought, the battle has had an emotional place in Serbian history – not exactly a myth but certainly an epic occurrence never to be forgotten and now the source of Serbian determination to keep control of the region.

It is not possible to say with any certainty who the original inhabitants of Kosovo were but they must have been assimilated by both Serbian Slavs and by Albanians who crossed into the region from neighbouring areas. Nor is there any certainty over the origins of the Albanians; one theory is that they could be the descendants of the Albanoi tribe referred to by Alexander's general, Ptolemy, in the fourth century BC. It has been argued that they could be descended from either the Illyrians or Thracians, two of the earliest inhabitants of the Balkans and its coastline. Counter-arguments refute both these possibilities. Whoever inhabited Kosovo first, it was not the Serbs whose control stopped at the Kopaonik Mountains and who did

Kosovo, showing its borders in 1919, 1939 and today.

not take control of Kosovo until the late twelfth century. Before then the area was under Bulgarian or Macedonian rule from the 850s to 1014 when Byzantine control was re-established by Emperor Basil. The Serbs only ruled Kosovo from the 1180s – when it was taken by the Grand Zupan, Stefan Nemanja – to the 1450s when the Ottomans conquered the region.

In 1689 the Austrians conquered and occupied Kosovo but were forced out the following year by the Ottomans who went on to take Belgrade. It is claimed that as many as 500,000 Serbs fled with the retreating Austrians, further adding to the Kosovo Serbian myth. In 1876 the Serbs in alliance with the Russians, who had declared war on the Ottomans, managed to advance into Kosovo and were only halted by the Ottoman-Russian armistice of January 1878. The Treaty of San Stefano, completed by Russia and the Ottoman Empire in March 1878, created a Greater Bulgarian state and gave northern Kosovo to the Serbs. The treaty was unacceptable to the other European powers who replaced it with the Congress of Berlin that cut Bulgaria down in size, restoring Macedonia and the *vilayet* of Kosovo to the Ottomans.

At a meeting of the Albanian clan chiefs a 'League' was formed in 1878 but initially it was totally loyal to the Ottoman Sultan. In September an official, Mehmet Ali, sent to demarcate the new border between Montenegro and Kosovo, was killed when fighting broke out; this brought to an end cooperation between the Ottoman government and the league which called for a single Albanian *vilayet* to be formed. During this time the Serbs had introduced ethnic cleansing and expelled some 60,000 Muslim families to Macedonia and 70,000 Albanians to Kosovo. As the Muslim population from Kosovo grew so Serbs emigrated.

Many of the important events leading to the Albanian declaration of independence from the Ottoman Empire in November 1912 took place in Kosovo. A revolt broke out aimed at overturning the 'Young Turk' regime; by late June 1912 the revolt had spread to many parts of Kosovo and to Tirana and Shkodra. By the end of July most of Kosovo had been taken and some 45,000 men assembled, a list of demands was submitted and when no reply was received the force marched on Skopje. In August the majority of the demands were agreed to and an Albanian state was to be formed within the Ottoman Empire. The Albanian success suggested to other Balkan states that a war against the Ottomans might be quickly won. The Serbs and Bulgarians agreed a secret division of the territory they proposed to capture; the Greeks and Montenegrins joined the alliance. The Serbs delivered arms to Kosovan Serbs, border incidents were manufactured and reports of Albanian atrocities spread. The Serbian attack began on 16 October. The Albanians resisted strongly but they and the Ottomans were heavily outnumbered and the Serbs and Montenegrins completed the conquest of Kosovo by early November. The Serbs pressed on until they reached the Adriatic; they had massacred thousands. The European powers then deliberated the future of the territorial changes; Albania became independent, but Serbia held Kosovo.

During the First World War the Albanians supported the Austro-Hungarians. Afterwards the Serbs took revenge for Albanian hostility during their withdrawal of 1915 and some 6,000 Kosovo Albanians were killed in the first two months of 1919. The Serbs did not allow Kosovan schools to teach in Albanian and refused to recognise Albanians as a national minority; at the same time Kosovo suffered a campaign of colonisation by Serbs from other parts of Yugoslavia and the confiscation of land. A number of revolts took place in the early 1920s but all were ruthlessly suppressed. In the 1929 redivision of Yugoslavia into *banovina* Kosovo was split between three: one that included Montenegro; one with eastern Serbia; and one with Macedonia. The *banovina* were governed by hard-line Serbs.

There is a legal argument against Kosovo being part of Serbia because the Treaty of London of 1913, which recognised this move, was never ratified by Serbia, nor, as required by the Serbian constitution of 1903, was a Grand National Assembly called to agree the new borders of Serbia. It is claimed the Treaty of Bucharest, also of 1913, cannot legalise the transfer of former Ottoman territory because the Ottoman government was not a party to the treaty. It is also argued that the 1925 Treaty of Ankara signed by Turkey and the newly formed Yugoslavia can be used as a basis for claiming that Kosovo is Yugoslavian rather than Serb. In fact, the Kosovans have been treated as Yugoslav citizens since 1918 but as Albanian-speaking Serbs rather than as Albanians.

During the Second World War most of Kosovo was incorporated into Albania which had been captured by the Italians. The Kosovans took the opportunity to drive out a number of Serbian and Montenegrin colonists. When Italy capitulated in September 1943 the Germans quickly took over the enlarged Albania, which they recognised as an independent state; the Kosovans again took advantage of the situation to expel more colonists. Kosovans played little part in the Yugoslav resistance movements. At the end of the war the German withdrawal route from Greece and Albania was through Kosovo and some 5,000 Albanians fought with the German rearguard against the advancing Bulgarian and Soviet forces.

Constitutional events immediately after the war also provided ground for legal argument over Kosovo's status. It was established as the Autonomous Region of Kosovo-Metohija by the People's Assembly of Serbia in September 1945, two months before the communist Popular Front won the Yugoslav-wide elections and then passed a new constitution confirming the six-republic federation with two autonomous provinces in Serbia. In the 1950s and early '60s Kosovo saw the Serb minority population of 27 per cent given preference in many fields: communist party membership, official positions and industrial employment. At the same time Kosovo received far less development investment than other areas. After Tito's first visit to Kosovo in March 1967 improvements were made and changes to the 1963 constitution established the territory as a federal legal entity. The constitution of 1974 awarded both Kosovo and Vojvodina equivalent status to the republics and direct representation on federal bodies, including one representative on the collective Presidency of Yugoslavia (the republics had two representatives).

The death of Tito in 1980 was followed by an Albanian revolt in Kosovo in 1981 which was brutally suppressed. Slobodan Milosević used the situation of the Serb minority in Kosovo in his campaign to be elected as President of Serbia in 1987. Kosovo then experienced a tightening of Serb control with the press being brought into line, the police presence increased, many professionals dismissed and politicians silenced or imprisoned. Milosević pressed for a new Serbian constitution, which abolished the autonomous status of Kosovo and Vojvodina, and in July 1990 the Serbs dissolved the Kosovan Assembly and government. The

Kosovo Force contributors			
Argentina	110	Luxembourg	2
Austria	470	Morocco	300
Azerbaijan	35	Netherlands	1650
Belgium	1,000	Norway	1,250
Canada	1300	Poland	615
Czech Republic	160	Portugal	330
Denmark	900	Russia	3,250
Finland	680	Slovakia	6
France	4,800	Slovenia	40
Georgia	35	Spain	1,230
Germany	5,600	Sweden	740
Greece	800	Switzerland	130
Hungary	300	Turkey	1,000
Iceland	2	UAE	1,250
Ireland	100	UK	3,500
Italy	5,850	US	6,100
Jordan	50	Ukraine	240
Lithuania	30		

local law court was abolished and the judges removed. In 1992 the Kosovans held their own elections, not recognised by the Serbs, and chose Ibrahim Rugova as the president of the 'Republic of Kosovo', which set up a parallel apparatus to the Serbian administration.

For the next five years Rugova campaigned for the return of the pre-1990 autonomy but was resolute in pursuing this without resort to violence, despite the growing militancy of the Serb police and the resettling of 19,000 Serbian refugees in early 1996. While there had been instances of Albanian attack on Serbian police earlier, the Kosovo Liberation Army (KLA) first made its presence known in February 1996 when it organised a number of bomb attacks at five camps for Serb refugees from the Krajina region of Croatia. Until December 1997 KLA operations were confined to isolated attacks on the police and their stations, but after the rebellion in Albania in March 1997 the KLA received many weapons from the hundreds of thousands looted from the arsenals there. KLA attacks became more daring and by early 1998 included the over-running of police stations and attacks on police patrols and road checkpoints. Over fifty police and officials were killed. By March 1998 Serbia had had enough and considered that the attacks it had suffered justified the taking of tough measures to suppress the KLA for whom complete independence had become the goal.

Strong contingents of the Yugoslav Army and the paramilitary police moved into Kosovo. Wherever there was an excuse villages were shelled, cleared of their remaining population, looted and set alight. While the KLA fought back as best it could, thousands of refugees fled into the hills and forests. The Western world was appalled but decided there was little it could do. Plans for a NATO force along the Albanian side of the border were abandoned as being both difficult to implement and probably aiding the Serbs more than the Albanians. On 15 June 1998, in a show of strength, a NATO force of over eighty aircraft from thirteen countries carried out air manoeuvres over Albania close to the border with Kosovo. It was thought likely that launching air strikes against Serb forces in order to stop the fighting would be seen as taking sides in the dispute.

In October 1998 US negotiator Richard Holbrooke, backed by the threat of NATO air strikes, persuaded both sides to maintain a ceasefire. The Serbs were to withdraw their special police forces and army units other than those normally based in Kosovo which were to return to their barracks. The OSCE was to establish an unarmed team of 2,000 observers to be called 'verifiers'. At the same time NATO agreed to deploy a force to Macedonia which would be on standby to rescue the verifiers should they become the targets of either side. The Holbrooke Agreement also included provisions for early elections. By December the ceasefire was in danger of breaking down completely as the Serbs set ambushes along the Albanian border and Serb officials were murdered in isolated incidents.

The discovery, on 15 January 1999, of the massacre of forty-five Albanian Kosovan men, unarmed and in plain clothes, outraged the US and European states. Two senior NATO generals were sent to Belgrade to warn President Milosević that Serbian behaviour was unacceptable. At about the same time the Serbs ordered the expulsion of the head of the OSCE verifiers and denied the Chief Prosecutor of the UN War Crimes Tribunal entry into Kosovo. An ultimatum was issued to both the Serbs and the Albanian Kosovans that they must agree a 'contact group' peace plan or suffer NATO air attack. The meeting began at Rambouillet on 14 February and had to be extended twice, first to the 20th and then to the 23rd. Meanwhile NATO air forces began to concentrate for operations that would be carried out if agreement could not be reached and advance units of a NATO peacekeeping force, to be deployed if agreement was reached, started to arrive in Macedonia. On the 23rd the Serbs were still refusing to allow NATO troops into Kosovo and the Kosovans were still unhappy about the lack of commitment to a referendum on independence in three years time. As the Kosovans had not signed the agreement (and as bombing them was impractical) the talks ended without a settlement but the Kosovans had agreed the plan in principle and were to return in two weeks time after it had been discussed in Kosovo.

The Kosovans then signed the peace agreement on 18 March but the Serbs showed no sign of agreeing to the deployment of NATO peacekeepers and the meeting was terminated. NATO, without a specific UN mandate as this would certainly have been vetoed by Russia, then embarked on a bombing campaign to force Milosević to agree to its terms. No doubt Milosević expected the Alliance to crack before he did, while some optimists believed bombing would give Milosević an excuse for caving in without losing face. In the event despite the adverse publicity NATO continued bombing for seventy-eight days. Milosević agreed to new terms not as intrusive for Serbia as those proposed at Rambouillet. By then some 840,000 refugees had been forced out of Kosovo into Albania and Macedonia and their homes destroyed. NATO troops and others, including Russians, entered Kosovo on 12 June 1999 and began the task of rebuilding the province. A fresh round of ethnic cleansing ensued as vengeful Albanians forced most of the Serb population out. The long-term future of Kosovo is not yet decided. The agreement made with NATO confirms that Kosovo is a constituent part of Serbia but it is likely to press for its independence. Should it gain independent status then calls for a greater Albania will be inevitable and that would destabilise the region again.

Weapons collected by KFOR			
Type	Handed in by KLA	Confiscated from KLA	Others
Rifles	6,831	1,313	2,149
Pistols	281	324	995
Machine-guns	737	75	62
Mortars	173	5	3
Anti-tank	306	17	153
Grenades	27,006	53	85
Mines	1,252	35	160

Source: KFOR September 1999

Bibliography and Web Sites

Malcolm, Noel, *Kosovo: A Short History*, Macmillan, 1998
Veremis, Thanos (ed.), *Kosovo: Avoiding Another Balkan War*, University of Athens, 1998
Vickers, Miranda, *Between Serb and Albanian: A History of Kosovo*, Hurst, 1998

American Muslim Assistance, Kosova Crisis Center: http://amahelp.com/kosova
Kosova Crisis Centre: www.alb-net.com/
NATO Kosovo Force: www.nato.int/kosovo/jnt.grdn

ALBANIA: A POTENTIAL TIME BOMB

In ancient times this region was inhabited by Illyrians: the identity of the original Albanians is disputed. They could have been descendants of the Albanoi tribe mentioned by Alexander the Great's general, Ptolemy, in the fourth century BC, or they could be descendants of the original Illyrians and Thracians. Alexander did not conquer the independent Greek state of Epirus that stretched over today's north-west Greece and south-west Albania. Epirus remained neutral during the Persian and Peloponnesian Wars; its king, Pyrrhus, twice defeated the Romans but with very heavy losses, giving us the term 'Pyrrhic Victory'. The region became part of the Roman province of Illyricum in AD 169 and then the Byzantine despotate of Epirus until 1347. For the next 100 years the whole area suffered a series of invasions by Bulgarians, Serbs, Venetians and finally the Ottomans who made Albania part of their empire after the battle of Scutari in 1478. The hatred between the Serbs and Albanians began when Orthodox Serbs began persecuting Catholic Albanians.

The Albanians converted to Islam during the Ottoman occupation but always retained their Albanian nationality. Christians and Muslims both preserved their language, customs and laws. After the Russian-Ottoman war of 1876–8, the Albanians beseeched the Congress of Berlin to give them independence but they were to remain under Ottoman rule. The clan chiefs formed the League of Prizren in 1878: initially loyal to the Ottoman Sultan, it ended cooperation with the government after fighting broke out in Kosovo. The League called for a single Albanian *vilayet* to be formed but only Britain supported the claim and the leaders of the League were arrested and either executed or exiled.

Turkish control of education, Turkish schools for Muslims and Greek for Christians, ended with the 'Young Turks' revolution. An Albanian uprising began in 1910 and fighting continued for three years until the Turks agreed to autonomy for Albania, then including Kosovo. Albanian success encouraged other Balkan states to throw out the Turks; the Serbs and Bulgarians secretly agreed a division of the territory they intended to capture. Greece and Montenegro joined the alliance. The Serb attack on the Turks and Albanians began in October 1912 and carried on until they had reached the Adriatic. The First Balkan War would have ended in December 1912 but for the overthrow of the Turkish government by the 'Young Turks'; in fact it was concluded in April 1913. The settlement agreed at the Treaty of London gave Albania its independence as Austria was determined that Serbia should not have access to the sea. Albania was not affected by the second Balkan War and the Treaty of Bucharest, also in 1913.

Albania.

During the First World War the Albanians sided with the Austro-Hungarians who drove the Serbian Army south until it had withdrawn through Albania and was taken off by Allied shipping to Corfu. When the Serbs returned they killed over 6,000 Albanians in early 1919. The Italians invaded and annexed Albania in April 1939 and most of Kosovo was incorporated into Albania. On Italian capitulation in 1943 the Germans occupied Albania and treated it as an independent state. The communists under Enver Hoxha formed a guerrilla resistance force and took over the country in 1946. Rural collectivisation, nationalisation of industry, the closure of mosques and churches and one-party control were effected. Hoxha chose isolation and Albania became a closed country. Albania broke off relations with the Soviet Union and left the Warsaw Pact in 1961; it broke with China in 1978. The Albanian population became impoverished. In 1967 it was declared the world's first atheist state.

Rioters capture a tank in Tirana during the uprising of September 1998. (Associated Press)

There was some improvement in trade relations after Hoxha's death in 1985 but internal opposition to the regime did not develop until 1990 when plans were agreed to hold elections. The communists were returned to power in March 1991 and set about introducing reforms but not much was achieved. Elections in March 1992 saw the Democratic Party with a two-thirds majority and Dr Sali Berisha became President. He was one of few who had been allowed to travel outside Albania, had enjoyed post-graduate studies in Paris and so had some experience of Western democracy. By the summer of 1993 some improvements had been achieved with the majority of the population feeling that it was better off. At the same time there had been widespread fraud and corruption, the main manifestation of this being the 'pyramid' sales that lost many thousands their life savings and helped to precipitate the violent upheaval in 1997 when army barracks and ammunition dumps were looted. Over 750,000 weapons and 1.5 billion rounds of ammunition are believed to have been stolen.

Currently 3 million people live in Albania and there are approximately another 3 million Albanians elsewhere in the Balkans – 2 million in Kosovo, 50,000 in Montenegro and 500,000 (maybe more) in Macedonia. A number, some 50,000, live close to the border in Greece in an area known to Albanians as Cameria; there are also a large number, perhaps as many as 300,000, Albanian illegal immigrants elsewhere in Greece. There is a Greek minority living in southern Albania in the area they call Northern Epirus, a region that Greek nationalists consider should be theirs. Following the NATO operation in Kosovo there must be a growing possibility of new demands for a greater Albania which would continue to destabilise the Balkans.

Web Site

Albanian Ministry of Information: http://mininf.gov.al/english

THE CRESCENT OF CRISIS

The crescent of crisis arcs from the Kurdish-populated areas at the junction of Turkey, Iraq and Iran across the Transcaucasus and Central Asia to Afghanistan. This section examines the issues arising from Turkey's plans to utilise better the waters of the Euphrates and the Tigris, the plight of the Kurds who have little chance of achieving independence, the continued quarrels in the three Transcaucasian states, the pipeline issue for exporting Central Asian oil and gas, and the long-lasting saga of Afghanistan.

THE TRANSCAUCASIAN NEXUS: HISTORY REVISITED

The territory now forming the three Transcaucasian republics – Georgia, Armenia and Azerbaijan – was taken into the tsarist Russian Empire in the first half of the nineteenth century. Before this time the peoples of the region had inhabited a much wider area and today a good number of ethnic Transcaucasians live beyond their national borders. Each of the three republics has its own modern problems deriving from ethnic minorities who are demanding a degree of self-determination, if not independence.

The Romans and Persians contested the region from the first century BC. Armenia and Georgia adopted Christianity under the Romans in the fourth century AD. After the Arab invasion of 642 the Azerbaijanis and the North Caucasians became Muslims. The Transcaucasus has always provided the route for invading forces marching between Central Asia and Asia Minor; many invaders conquered and partitioned the region regardless of the wishes of the indigenous population. The Seldjuks ruled it from 1071 and were followed by the Mongols and then the Turks. Finally, the Russians began penetrating the area in the early 1700s.

Armenia

Armenia has a long history as a nation, going as far back as the eighth century BC, and was once a much larger country than now. At the height of its power, in 65 BC it stretched from the Caspian to the Mediterranean. It ruled the north-eastern part of Asia Minor. It was then split between the Byzantine and Persian Empires. By the start of the First World War

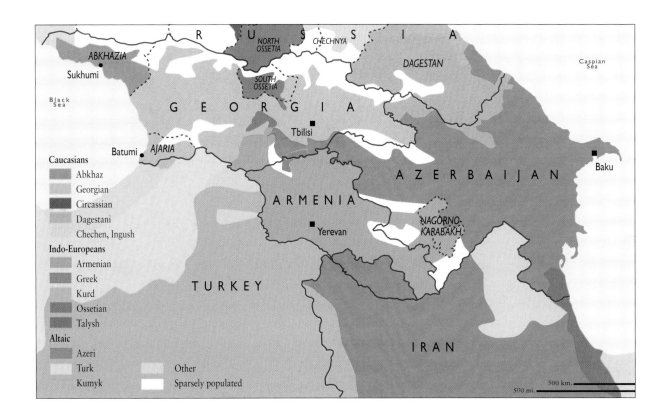

The topography of the Transcaucasian region.

Armenians were split between Russian rule, which had controlled the country since the early nineteenth century, and Turkey. The war gave the Armenians the opportunity to support one side or the other in an attempt to regain Armenian territorial unity. However, they decided to support their respective governments. Neither government repaid their loyalty. The Russians conscripted 150,000 soldiers and deployed some far away on the Polish and Galician fronts. The Turks blamed the Armenians in part for their defeat by the Russians and in 1915 began a massive ethnic cleansing operation which is believed to have resulted in the deaths of some 600,000 Armenians and the flight of 300,000 to 400,000 into Russia, Persia and Mesopotamia.

The ethnic populations of the Transcaucasus.

Caucasians
- Abkhaz
- Georgian
- Circassian
- Dagestani
- Chechen, Ingush

Indo-Europeans
- Armenian
- Greek
- Kurd
- Ossetian
- Talysh

Altaic
- Azeri
- Turk
- Kumyk

Other

Sparsely populated

At the end of the war it was thought that the Armenians would receive special treatment from the victorious powers but none was prepared to accept a mandate for governing Armenia. The powers compelled the Turkish government to recognise an independent Armenian state and the US was appointed to arbitrate on its borders. In 1920 President Wilson gave Armenia virtually all the territory taken by Russia during the war; but his arbitration came too late. In January 1920 the Turks had attacked the French garrison in Cilicia and driven the population out of Marash, massacring some 50,000 Armenians. In May the Bolsheviks had taken control of Erivan and in September handed the area to the Turks with another massacre of Armenians. In October France withdrew from Cilicia. The Treaty of Lausanne, which finalised the peace between Turkey and the powers, made no mention of an independent Armenia.

Azerbaijan

Azerbaijan or the land of the Azeris (it only became a state in 1918) has had changing borders throughout its history; the Azeris, who for most of their history have been associated with Persia, were originally Zoroastrian and became converted to Islam after the Arab invasion in the mid-seventh century. In the eleventh century, when they were part of the Seldjuk Empire, they became fused with a number of Turkic tribes who arrived, over many years, from Central Asia; gradually their language changed to become a distinct tongue. The Mongols under Hualagu conquered the Azeris in the thirteenth century. The region witnessed much of the fighting between the Ottoman Turks and the Iranians; in 1747, after the death of Nadir Shah, the Iranians lost control and the Azeris broke up into a series of khanates.

In the second half of the eighteenth century attempts were made to form a single nation. North-eastern Azerbaijan was dominated by Fath'Ali Khan of Kuba who aimed to unite the whole region under his rule but he was forestalled by the Russians who viewed Kuba's expansion as a threat to their own ambitions. The Russian commander, Pavel Tsitsianov, a Georgian, as part of his conquest of Georgia decided that he must first control the Azeri khanates as far as the Caspian Sea; some accepted the Russian terms peacefully while others had to be conquered. The Treaty of Gulistan gave Russia control of a large amount of Iranian territory stretching from Baku to Georgia. However, it did not end Russian-Iranian fighting. The Iranians invaded in 1825 but were defeated at the battle of Ganja and the Russians went on to capture Tabriz. The Treaty of Turkmanchai, signed in 1828, gave Russia more Azeri territory and divided it between Russia and Iran along the line of the Araxes river. After the formation of the Soviet Union, the Azerbaijan region became the Republic of Azerbaijan and on the break up of the USSR it gained its independence.

Nagorno-Karabakh

Armenia and Azerbaijan are both affected by the Armenian-populated enclave of Azerbaijan known as Nagorno (Russian mountainous)-Karabakh (Azerbaijani black garden). There are Armenian historical claims that Nagorno-Karabakh was part of Armenia as early as the

Russia: garrisons	
Georgia: HQ Tskhinvali and 3 bases – Vaziani, Akhalkaki, Medzhnistskari/Batumi	
Men	5,500
Tanks	140
ACVs	400
Artillery	155
Armenia: 1 base, Gyumri	
Men	3,000
Tanks	75
ACVs	150
Artillery	85
Peacekeeping: 1,500 men in 3 battalions	

seventh century BC. For their part Azeri historians believe that the indigenous Albanian population was assimilated by Armenian settlers in the eighth century. It became part of the Persian province of Albania (not to be confused with Balkan Albania) (Arran) after the partition between Byzantium and Persia in AD 387; the inhabitants remained Christian. It fell to the Russians in 1805. The main settlement of Armenians in Karabakh took place in 1828–30 and again in 1877–8 following the Russo-Turkish war. There were no borders dividing Georgia, Armenia and Azerbaijan between the Russian conquest of the Transcaucasus in 1828 and the Russian revolution in 1917. The three states materialised after the revolution and before their occupation by the Bolsheviks in 1920; during this time the Armenians fought the Azerbaijanis over territory including Nagorno-Karabakh. The Bolsheviks allocated Azerbaijan both Nagorno-Karabakh and Nakhichevan, an Azeri enclave on the border with Iran; the former had the status of 'autonomous region' and the latter 'autonomous republic'. At the same time Armenia was awarded the Azeri-populated regions of Zangezur and part of Gazakh. Separatist aims were encouraged in 1987 when Gorbachev's economic advisor, an Armenian, advocated that the enclave should become part of Armenia. Also in February 1988 after a series of strikes and demonstrations, the regional soviet of Nagorno-Karabakh appealed to the Supreme Soviets of the USSR, Armenia and Azerbaijan to agree to its transfer to Armenia. In February some 2,000 Azeri refugees from Stepanakert arrived in Sumgait, sparking off two days of rioting in which both Armenians and Azeris were killed and this led to large-scale deportations from both Armenia and Azerbaijan.

The collapse of the Soviet Union exacerbated the situation and both Armenian and Azeri national forces gained in strength by inheriting weaponry from departing Soviet units. The scale of fighting increased dramatically with the Armenians taking over more Azeri villages and establishing a corridor at Lachin from the border to Nagorno-Karabakh, which had declared itself an independent republic but was not recognised as such. A stalemate was reached after the Azeris managed, in 1992, to recover some territory. It was hoped the issue could be resolved but nothing was agreed, despite the efforts of Russia, Turkey (who backed the Azeris), Iran and the Organisation for Cooperation and Security in Europe, which has prepared an, as yet undeployed, observer force.

Georgia

Since independence Georgia has suffered far more disruption and is more likely to lose territory to ethnic minorities than Armenia or Azerbaijan despite being the oldest nation of the three. Georgia is divided in two by the Likhi mountains, which in the past served as the frontier between Byzantium and the Arab Empire and later the Ottoman Empire and Persia. The East Georgians were converted to Christianity around AD 330 and the West Georgians in the sixth century. With staunch Muslim neighbours on either side, religion probably held the Georgians together and led to their looking to Russia for support.

National forces	
Armenia	
Men	42,000
Tanks	100
ACVs	200
Artillery	230
Combat aircraft	6
Attack helicopter	7
Azerbaijan	
Men	69,000
Tanks	260
ACVs	330
Artillery	300
Combat aircraft	50
Attack helicopter	15
Georgia	
Men	27,000
Tanks	80
ACVs	110
Artillery	110
Combat aircraft	7
Attack helicopter	3
Nagorno-Karabakh	
Men	20,000–25,000
Tanks	300
ACVs	300
Artillery	300
(estimates)	

The Russian Empire first invaded Georgia in 1801 but did not complete its conquest until 1864, after two wars had been fought against the Turks. From 1918–21 Georgia regained its independence and was the scene of fighting between Red and White Russians and between Bolsheviks and Mensheviks. In 1921 the Bolsheviks took control and Georgia became part of the Soviet Union. The Soviets gave Abkhazia (a separate kingdom from the eighth century which merged with West Georgia at the end of the century) and Adjaria (inhabited by Sunni Muslims) the status of autonomous republics and made South Ossetia (an area settled by Ossetians from across the Caucasus in the seventeenth and eighteenth centuries) an autonomous *oblast*.

On independence in 1991 Georgia found it had inherited three separate territorial/ethnic problems and a population of whom 30 per cent were not ethnic Georgians. The President, Zviad Gamsakhurdia, attempted to abolish the autonomous status of the three areas. Georgian nationalists deposed him in an armed coup in January 1992. A period of civil war followed until the end of 1993 when government forces took Gamsakhurdia's last stronghold, Zigdidi, and he committed suicide. Eduard Shevardnadze, the former Soviet Foreign Minister, was invited back to Georgia to lead it in March 1992 and he was elected head of state in October.

There had been friction between the Georgian government and the South Ossetians some years before Georgian independence. In August 1988 the Ossetian Popular Front protested to Moscow that Georgia's intention to make Georgian the only official language was unacceptable; the group called for South Ossetia's unification with North Ossetia. In September 1990 the front declared an 'Independent Soviet Democratic Republic' which was shortly followed by the abolition by the Georgian parliament of South Ossetia's autonomous status. Violent clashes followed and Soviet Interior Ministry troops were sent to the region. In June 1992 the situation was defused after agreement between Yeltsin and Shevardnadze and a joint Russian-Georgian-South Ossetian peacekeeping force was established. It is still deployed.

Abhkazia was briefly a full union republic from 1921 until its status was downgraded to autonomous republic within Georgia in 1931. Then followed a period of 'Georgianisation' with the forced resettlement of Georgians in Abkhazhia reducing the Abkhaz proportion of the population. In 1978 an attempt to secede failed but Russian policy allowed Abkhazians to gain a disproportionate influence in the Supreme Soviet and the local Communist Party. In the Soviet referendum of March 1991, which the Georgians boycotted, the Abkhazians voted overwhelmingly to remain in the Union. After Georgian troops had captured Sukhumi in August 1992 the Abkhazians appealed to Russia for protection. Fighting continued, interrupted for short periods by ceasefires until the Abkhazians recaptured Sukhumi and the rest of the region in September 1993. Some 200,000 or more ethnic Georgians fled from their homes. In July the UNSC had agreed to the deployment of observers who established the UN Observer Mission in Georgia (UNOMIG) which began to deploy in August but this was suspended following the breakdown of

Opposite: *Lachin on the corridor from Nagorno-Karabakh to Armenia. (Associated Press)*

the ceasefire. Georgia joined the Commonwealth of Independent States (CIS) in October and obtained Russian assistance in exchange for the use of port facilities and agreement over the stationing of Russian troops.

A Russian peacekeeping force deployed along the Inguri in June 1994 and established a demilitarised zone 12 kilometres wide on either side of the river. There is also a heavy weapons exclusion zone stretching a further 20 kilometres beyond the demilitarised zone. Despite the presence of Russian troops and UN observers, both sides have infiltrated armed groups from time to time into each other's territory; nor have the bulk of the refugees from either side managed to return to their homes. The most recent flare-up of the conflict occurred in May 1998 when Abkhazian forces launched an offensive against Georgian infiltrators; this caused 30,000 ethnic Georgians to become refugees for a second time.

The situation in the Muslim region of Adjaria has been far more peaceful, probably due to the presence of the Russian bases at Batumi and Medzhinistskari. However, though recognising Georgian sovereignty in principle, it is virtually independent and its President, Aslan Abashidze, is a potential political rival to Shevardnadze for the Georgian presidency. Elsewhere in Mingrelia, which borders Abkhazia, the population remains loyal to the late Gamsakhurdia and in the Armenian-populated area around Akhalkalaki, where there is another Russian base, there could be a further problem. Just how much Russia is influencing events in Georgia is unclear but it is strongly suspected by the Georgian government of provoking trouble. In October 1999 Shevardnadze said that he intended to apply for NATO membership for Georgia. Russian border troops were withdrawn in November. Four Russian military bases remain but Georgia has rejected Russian requests for the troops there to be used against Chechnya.

Bibliography and Web Sites

Croissant, Michael, *The Armenian-Azerbaijan Conflict: Causes and Implications*, Praeger, 1971 and 1998

Gachechiladze, Revaz, *The New Georgia: Space, Society, Politics*, UCL Press, 1995

Hoiris, Ole, and Sefa Martin Yurukel (eds), *Contrasts and Solutions in the Caucasus*, Aarhus University Press, 1998

Hunter, Shireen T., *The Transcaucasus in Transition: Nation-Building and Conflict*, Centre for Strategic and International Studies, 1994

Wright, John, Suzanne Goldberg and Richard Schofield (eds), *Transcaucasian Boundaries*, SOASD/GRC Geopolitics Series UCL Press

WWW.

Armenian Embassy: www.armeniaemb.org/
Georgian Parliament: www.parliament.ge
President of Azerbaijan: www.president.az

CENTRAL ASIA: GETTING THE OIL OUT

Three former republics of the Soviet Union – Azerbaijan, Kazakhstan and Turkmenistan – are all rich in oil or gas resources. One problem faces all three – how to get their oil to market. There is no shortage of potential routes but virtually all suffer from a major political or security objections.

As much of the oil is under the Caspian Sea, another difficulty arises over assembling offshore rigs there. It can be done by towing dismantled sections along Russian rivers and canals but this is expensive. Getting all the other essentials for modern oil drilling to the Caspian is equally difficult, not only because of poor transport links but also on account of widespread corruption and inefficiency.

There are a number of existing pipelines; from Baku via Tbilisi to Supsa on the Black Sea, from Baku to Novorossiysk via Grozny, and on the east of the Caspian from the Tengiz field to Samarra. These last two pipelines connect up with the main Russian network. Naturally all neighbouring countries – Russia, Turkey and Iran – are keen to see the new, essential pipelines transit their territory, for both political and economic reasons. Politics will play a crucial part in the decision-making process with the US adamant that the pipes should not cross Iran so that it cannot hold oil companies to ransom in any future crisis, nor is the West eager to rely on the use of Russian pipelines. On the other hand, it has always been said that commercial advantage will be the main deciding factor for those who ultimately pay for any pipeline. It has been estimated that the pipelines will be needed by 2004 and so decisions on routes must be taken by October 2000 if they are to be ready in time.

On 18 November 1999 Azerbaijan, Georgia and Turkey signed an agreement to build a pipeline from Baku through Georgia and then south through Turkey to the Mediterranean port of Ceyhan. But the line will not be built unless the oil companies decide that it will be profitable. At the moment Azerbaijan only produces a tenth of what would be needed to make it so – one million barrels a day – and Azeri production is forecast to only reach 800,000 barrels a day by 2008. It is claimed that the Turkish route would be over three times as expensive as the Novorossiysk pipeline, and it would cost over $2.4 billion to construct. Pipelines traversing either the North Caucasus or the Transcaucasus could be liable to interruption by the various civil wars in progress there, however; the Turkish route avoids crossing Abkhazia while a Tbilisi–Novorossiysk pipeline has to cross it. Another, and cheaper, option is to pump oil to Iran for use in the north of the country, exchanging it for Iranian oil from the Iranian oil wells close to the Persian Gulf.

The Russians naturally favour pipelines going north from Baku to Machachkala and then to Novorossiysk. The existing pipeline crosses Chechnya and is currently closed, but the Russians have announced the construction of a bypass line skirting Chechnya. Who will pay for the new pipeline is not yet clear.

Kazakhstan oil could easily be exported either via the Russian system, which it joins at Guryev, or across the Caspian from Baku. There is also the possibility of an expensive new pipeline crossing all of Kazakhstan to western China. The Chinese have signed a memorandum of understanding to build the line as part of a deal in which they would buy two Kazakh oilfields. Using a pipeline to China would be more expensive by about $2 a barrel than sending it by tanker via Iran's Kharg terminus.

Turkmenistan already has a gas pipeline into northern Iran, opened in late 1997 and scheduled to deliver 12 billion cubic feet a year. It would

Caspian oil reserve estimates (billion tons)

	IEA	BP	National
Azerbaijan	0.5–1.5	1.0	2.5
Kazakhstan	1–3	1.1	2.1–3.1
Turkmenistan	0.15–0.2	na	6.7
Uzbekistan	0.03	0.1	0.6

Oil production (million tons)

	1990	1995	1998
Azerbaijan	12.5	9.2	11.4
Kazakhstan	25.8	20.5	25.9
Turkmenistan	5.7	4.7	6.3
Uzbekistan	2.8	7.6	8.0

Gas production (million cubic metres)

	1990	1995	1998
Azerbaijan	9.9	6.6	5.6
Kazakhstan	7.1	5.9	6.2
Turkmenistan	87.8	32.3	13.2
Uzbekistan	40.8	48.6	54.8

Source: DIW database

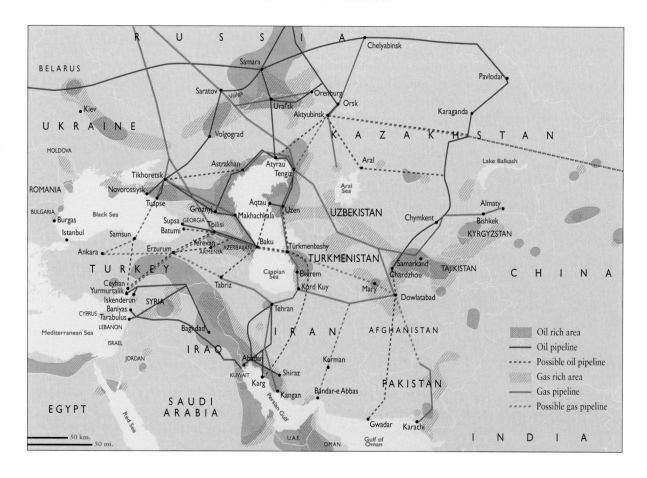

The present and possible pipelines from the Caspian oil fields.

like to see this linked to Turkey. Turkey, ignoring US opposition to the project, has already begun a gas pipeline from Erzurum to the Iranian border and will extend it to Ankara later. An American oil company prefers a route from Turkmenistan through Afghanistan to Pakistan and perhaps later to India. The security of such a route is doubtful.

Pipelines are not the only cause of disagreement. The division of the Caspian Sea also provokes dispute. Azerbaijan, Kazakhstan and Turkmenistan, who all have oil deposits close to their shore, want national sectors from which they would be allowed to drill all the oil. However, Russia and Iran have proposed that they, Azerbaijan, Kazakhstan and Turkmenistan should share the Caspian's resources equally on the grounds that it is an enclosed body of water and so is jointly owned by all five and should be shared under international law. Much to Iran's annoyance, the Russians have signed a deal dividing the northern Caspian into Russian and Kazakh sectors, though they have agreed to share fishing equally.

The energy reserves are not as large as originally thought but they are nevertheless substantial. The Central Asian/Caspian basin oilfields have proven reserves of 28 billion barrels and the equivalent of 70 billion barrels in gas (243 trillion cubic feet). These reserves are twenty times less than those in the Persian Gulf.

Web Site

www.

US Energy Information Administration: www.eia.doe.gov/emer/cabs

THE KURDS: A PEOPLE WITHOUT A COUNTRY

The Kurds are probably the descendants of the Indo-European tribes that migrated westwards during approximately the second millennium BC; some claim they are descendants of the Medes who lived in the area north-east of Persia, between the Zagros Mountains and the Caspian Sea, until they were conquered by the Persians in 550 BC. The wild tribes settled in the mountainous region, which now covers eastern Turkey, south-west Armenia, north-west Iran, northern Iraq and north-east Syria. From the relative safety of the mountains their communities survived unassimilated under the various empires that controlled the area in turn, but were probably joined by both Arab and Turkoman tribes that came to be considered Kurds later. The tribes are not ethnically identical and have no common language. The term Kurd has had a number of meanings: including 'Cyrtii' or mercenary slingers in the Seleucid regime of 300 BC, then being used to describe the nomads of the Iranian plateau at the time of the Islamic conquest in the seventh century. Kurdistan was first used as the name for the region inhabited by the Kurds by the Seldjuks in the twelfth century, but it has never had identified borders and its extent has changed over the centuries.

By the time of the First World War the Kurds were mainly living under Ottoman rule; the creation a Kurdish state was promised, but never implemented, by the 1920 Treaty of Sèvres (which also recognised the Kurds claim to exist as a people). The Treaty of Lausanne in 1923, which realigned Turkey's borders, made no reference to the Kurds, however. The Europeans considered that a Sunni Kurdish state would act as a useful buffer between Turkey and the Turkmen people of

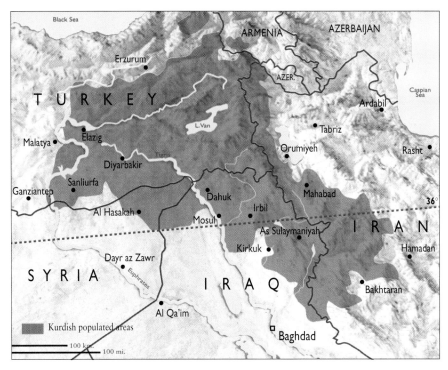

The lands predominantly populated by Kurds.

Central Asia; Turkey and the newly formed Soviet Union republic of Azerbaijan; and the Shi'a populations in Azerbaijan and the Azeri provinces of northern Persia. In the event British control of the newly independent Iraq and the exploitation of oil in Mosul Province would have been threatened by Kurdish nationalism and the plan was dropped.

Since then the Kurds, who number as many as 25 million, have been unhappy residents of the region. There have been many Kurdish uprisings, for example against the Turks in 1924, 1930 and 1937, in Iran in 1880, 1920 and 1944, and in Iraq from 1931 to 1935, in 1945 and from 1961 to 1970. With few exceptions the Kurds in neighbouring countries have never managed to cooperate against their rulers. Indeed, often the ruling power has enlisted the help of a neighbouring Kurdish population against its own rebelling Kurds.

Kurdish rebellions led to a number of officially agreed border changes in the region (borders arbitrarily imposed by the Allies after the defeat of the Turks in 1918). Following the 1930 rebellion, during which Turkey accused the Persians of supporting the Kurds, the Turks exchanged strips of land near Kotur and Bazirgan (and later near Maz Bicho) in return for the eastern slopes of Mount Ararat, which had been a Kurdish stronghold during the rebellion.

In 1945, for a period of one year, the Soviet Union during its occupation of northern Iran established a small Kurdish Republic of Mahabad (south of Lake Urmia). Mahabad lay within the separatist province of Azerbaijan, which was populated by ethnic Azeris initially supported by the Soviet Union. Once the Soviets confirmed their intention of withdrawing, the Azerbaijani soon came to terms with the government. There were some skirmishes between Kurds and the Iranian Army but Kurdish unity was fragile and began to break up; in December 1945 Iranian control was re-established. The importance of this event was to bring the Kurdish question to international notice again. However, it was then to be forgotten for some years.

Turkey

In more recent times the Kurds have been highly active in opposing their rulers but once again they have not acted in concert. Turkish Kurdish militancy increased throughout the 1980s as the Partiya Karkaren Kurdistan (Kurdistan Workers' Party) (PKK) intensified its insurgency and the government took counter-measures. With Iraq busy conducting its war against Iran, the Turkish Army, which was concerned by the growing liaison between Kurdish nationalists and left-wing political parties, staged a coup and took control of Turkey. An alliance between the PKK and the Iraqi-based Kurdistan Democratic Party (KDP) led to a Turkish incursion into Iraq with the agreement of the Iraqi government.

Since 1984 the Turkish authorities have battled against the PKK both in eastern Turkey and across the border in northern Iraq. During that time some 30,000 people, mainly PKK guerrillas but also some civilians, have died. A large proportion of the Turkish Army has been deployed in south-eastern Turkey in its efforts to suppress the revolt. Ironically, this region coincides to some extent with the portion of Turkey excluded from the Conventional Forces in Europe Treaty, an exclusion granted in recognition of the threats faced by Turkey from its southern neighbours. The PKK receives assistance from both Syria and Iran; Syria allows PKK camps and training to take place over the border from Hatay (the province returned to Turkey in 1938 after being part of the French mandate and which Syria claims), and in Lebanon. Syria also remains suspicious of Turkish plans for the use of Euphrates waters in the GAP irrigation project (see pages 150–3); this could reduce Syria's supply.

In February 1999 the PKK leader, Abdullah Ocalan, was extradited to Turkey from Kenya where he had been hiding in the Greek Embassy. He was tried by a military court and sentenced to death; the sentence has not yet been carried out. Ocalan then called for an end to the Kurdish rebellion, a move that was supported by the PKK but the party considered it depended on the government's response. PKK guerrillas have started to pull out of Turkey but at the end of September 1999 the Turkish Army sent 5,000 men, backed by air support, into northern Iraq to hunt down those who had vowed not to give up the struggle.

Iraq

Iraqi Kurds came to prominence after the Gulf War of 1991 when, with encouragement from US President George Bush, they rebelled against Saddam Hussein only to be viciously repressed by the remnants of the Iraqi Army because they received no military support from the Coalition. The uprising began in Ranya on 4 March 1991 and rapidly spread across the Kurdish region. Within a fortnight Kurds had taken control of virtually the whole area including the city of Kirkuk. Iraqi reaction was swift and a major offensive backed by a whole spectrum of heavy weapons was launched on the 28th; within a matter of days the Iraqis had recovered control and hundreds of thousands of refugees fled to the mountains on the Turkish/Iraqi border and into Iran.

The plight of the Iraqi Kurdish refugees caused a public outcry that 'something must be done'; the British Prime Minister, John Major, was responsible for persuading the Coalition to set up a 'safe haven' protected by troops. Mainly from the UK and the US, they deployed on Operation Provide Comfort, which also helped to deliver food aid and to construct camps. A 'no-fly' zone, north of the 36th parallel was established to protect the Kurds from Iraqi air attack and this is still monitored by British and US, but no longer French, aircraft based at Incirlik in Turkey. By July 1991 the bulk of the refugees had returned home, most of the Coalition ground forces had withdrawn leaving a 'rapid reaction force' based at Silopi in Turkey and a UN 'guard' force set up along the southern edge of the 'security zone'. Both have now been withdrawn.

Iraqi Kurds are split between the supporters of Massoud Barzani and the Kurdistan Democratic Party and those of Jalal Talibani and the

---

**The Treaty of Sèvres, 1920
(never implemented)**

Article 62. A commission . . . shall draft within six months . . . a scheme of local autonomy for the predominantly Kurdish areas lying east of the Euphrates, south of the southern boundary of Armenia as it may hereafter be determined, and north of the frontier of Turkey with Syria and Mesopotamia . . . and decide what rectifications, if any, should be made to the Turkish frontier where, under the provisions of the present Treaty, that frontier coincides with that of Persia.

Article 64. If within one year . . . the Kurdish people . . . show that a majority . . . desires independence . . . Turkey hereby agrees to execute such a recommendation and to renounce all rights and title over these areas. If . . . no objection will be raised by the Principal Allied Powers to the voluntary adhesion to such an independent Kurdish State of the Kurds inhabiting that part of Kurdistan which has been hitherto been included in the Mosul Vilayet.

The mountains of Northern Iraq. (The Hutchison Library)

Patriotic Union of Kurdistan (PUK). KDP members live in the northeast of Iraq and are mainly tribal Kurds, whereas the PUK supporters live further to the south and are mainly townspeople. By the second half of 1996 the KDP had lost the support of Turkey, because of the truce with the Turkish PKK, and of Iran. The KDP had invaded the PUK region to attack the Kurdistan Democratic Party of Iran (KDPI); in 1994 it lost the city of Arbil to the PUK. Fighting between the two factions escalated in August and Barzani called on Saddam Hussein for help, which was willingly supplied. Some 30,000 Iraqi troops overran Arbil and turned it over to the KDP; the KDP went on to take the city of Sulaimaniya. Iraqi security forces hunted those who had backed a secret US CIA operation based in Arbil and who had not been hurriedly evacuated by the Americans. The US swiftly mounted a series of cruise missile attacks on air defence targets in southern Iraq and strongly reinforced its forces in the Gulf. However, they found little support for further military action against Saddam, the French withdrawing their contribution to the force monitoring the northern no-fly zone. The US took the opportunity to extend the southern no-fly zone northwards to the 33rd parallel, bringing a number of air bases into it.

Iran

In Iran the Kurdish Democratic Party (KDPI, to distinguish from the Iraqi KDP), formed in 1945, hardly existed until 1951 when the Shah lost much of his power to the liberal Prime Minister, Muhammed Musaddiq, and membership then rose. The US-backed army coup in 1953 restored the Shah to power and the KDPI lay low. When Qasim came into power in 1955 in Iraq he courted the Kurds and Mustafa Barzani returned there from exile in Iran. He proposed the amalgamation of the Iraqi KDP with the KDPI but before anything could be arranged the Shah's secret police arrested some 250 Kurdish activists and once again the KDPI was reduced to a few exiles in Iraq. Mustafa Barzani now made his peace with the Shah in return for aid against the Baghdad government. A new Kurdish campaign began in 1967 but with no support from the KDP it was soon defeated by the army.

The Kurds, who are Sunni Muslims, welcomed the overthrow of the Shah but got involved in fighting with local Shi'a forces within weeks of Ayatollah Khomeini's return. The new Iranian government employed the Pasdaran or Revolutionary Guard Militia rather than the regular army against the Kurds and this resulted in a brutal pacification campaign in which some 10,000 Kurds were killed in fighting or were executed. Nearly half Iran's population is not Persian and so giving autonomy to the Kurds was not considered an option. The Kurds are divided: a second major group materialised in 1978 (though they claim they were formed in 1969), called Komala or the Organisation of Revolutionary Toilers of Iranian Kurdistan. Komala was a Marxist organisation but was more democratic than the KDPI and aimed to provide education and health services. It was more determined to fight than the KDPI which attempted to negotiate with the government.

The KDPI and Komala agreed to cooperate in late 1982 and enjoyed two years of military success, but when they split again after a killing, four years of bitter infighting helped the Iranian forces to drive the KDPI into Iraq. Komala began to disintegrate after joining the Communist Party of Iran and lost members as it was no longer a Kurdish entity. Both KDPI and Komala continue to maintain camps in Iraq where they have been attacked but have not been evicted by the Iraqi Kurds, just as the PKK was earlier.

The prospect of Kurdish freedom and a Kurdish state is highly improbable at present but if the world community takes a stronger interest in minority rights, as it did in Kosovo and East Timor, that situation could change.

Bibliography and Web Sites

Arfa, Hassan, *The Kurds: An Historical and Political Study*, Oxford University Press, 1966
Gunter, Michael, *The Kurds and the Future of Turkey*, Macmillan, 1997
MacDowall, David, *A Modern History of the Kurds*, IB Tauris, 1997
——, *The Kurds: A Nation Denied*, Minority Rights Publications, seventh edition, 1997
O'Ballance, Edgar, *The Kurdish Revolt 1961–1970*, Faber & Faber, 1973
Olsen, Robert, *The Kurdish Question and Turkish-Iranian Relations*, Mazda, 1998
Pelletiere, Stephen, *The Kurds: An Unstable Element in the Gulf*, Westview, 1992

Kurdistan Regional Government: www.krg.org
Turkish Ministry of Foreign Affairs: www.mfa.gov.tr/ac/acf
Washington Kurdish Insitute: www.clark.net/kurd

www.

Afghan population by ethnicity	
Pashtun	38 per cent
Tajik	25 per cent
Hazara	19 per cent
Uzbek	6 per cent

Afghan population by religion	
Sunni Muslim	84 per cent
Shi'a Muslim	15 per cent

Afghan population by language	
Afghan Persian	50 per cent
Pashtun	35 per cent
Turkic	11 per cent

AFGHANISTAN: DOOMED TO PERPETUAL CIVIL WAR

Afghanistan is another country that suffers from having an ethnically and religiously mixed population. The dominant ethnic group is the Pushtuns who inhabit the southern half of the country (and also northern Pakistan); they are mainly Sunni Muslims. The Hazaras in central Afghanistan are Shi'a Muslims. In the north there are three ethnic groups, each related to their neighbours in Central Asia; Turkomen in the north-west, Uzbeks to their east and Tajiks in north-east Afghanistan.

Afghanistan has always been made up of small, fiercely independent tribal kingdoms. The country has seen a series of invaders over the centuries, some more successful than others at controlling the region. Darius, Alexander the Great, Genghis Khan and Tamerlaine all held sway here for periods as did the Persians and Moghuls. In 1719 it was the turn of the Afghans to become the conquerors. At various times they held Persia, northern Pakistan and India, and Kashmir. At the end of the eighteenth century the 'Great Game' began, with Russia and Britain seeking to gain influence, but neither conquered the region though Russia took control of what are now the Central Asian Republics.

The British invaded Afghanistan on a number of occasions, the best known ending when the force that occupied Kabul for two years from 1838 withdrew and was annihilated during its winter retreat. Other invading forces purely carried out punitive measures before withdrawing. After the war of 1878–80 Afghanistan became a buffer state between the British and Russia who agreed Afghanistan's borders and forced the Amir to take responsibility for the Wakhan corridor so that there would be no common border between the two. The British supplied the Pushtun Amir with arms and finance, which enabled him to crush tribal revolts and establish a totalitarian state. Afghanistan severed its ties with Britain in 1919.

During the Cold War Afghanistan received aid from both East and West but the Soviets provided nearly five times as much as the US and trained and equipped the army. The US did not supply military aid as Pakistan, a member of both the Central Treaty Organisation (CENTO) and South-East Asia Treaty Organisation (SEATO) US-led alliances, opposed this. Both superpowers attempted to influence the ruling regime rather than, as elsewhere, supporting rivals. In 1973 the ruler Mohammed Zahir Shah was deposed by his cousin Daoud Khan, who was supported by Soviet-trained army officers and the Parcham wing of the communists – People's Democratic Party of Afghanistan (PDPA). Daoud proclaimed himself president. The abolition of the monarchy before a tested alternative was put in place worried both the superpowers and Afghanistan's neighbours who feared a period of instability could overflow their borders.

Jamiat-I-Islami, the Islamic movement led by Burhanuddin Rabbani and Ahmad Masoud, was suppressed and its leaders fled to Pakistan where they received support from both Pakistan and the CIA. They attempted an uprising in 1975 that was quickly put down. The Islamists then split into two parties: the Jamiat-I Islami, composed mainly of those with a Tajik background, and the predominantly Pushtun Hizb-I Islami led by

Gulbuddin Hekmatyar. In April 1978 the communist PDPA took power in a military-backed coup following the arrest of a number of its leaders; US aid was suspended and Soviet influence was greatly expanded. The communist coalition soon split and the Khalq wing took charge and imposed a brutal regime that led to a number of revolts across the country, some aided by Islamist refugees in Pakistan. In March 1979, following the overthrow of the Shah in Iran, an attack by Jamiat-I Islami captured Herat and killed the Soviet advisers there. The Soviets decided on a limited intervention into Afghanistan to forestall an expected American move in reaction to the Shah's fall (in fact none was contemplated) and to assist in controlling the internal disorder. The Soviets secured Kabul, killing the Khalq leader, and installed the Parcham leader, Babrak Karmal. Restoring government control required large-scale Soviet military reinforcement so that by 1981 there were over 100,000 troops deployed. The Soviets initially employed the wrong troops and the wrong tactics: motor rifle units that were neither trained nor equipped for counter-insurgency operations.

The invasion automatically provoked US assistance for exiled Afghan groups known as mujahedin (meaning 'holy warriors') and weapons were soon reaching them through Pakistan. As the number of opposition parties increased dramatically, the Pakistan government decided to restrict the supply of arms to only seven groups which formed, in May 1985, the Ittehad-i-Islami Afghan mujahedin and later the Afghan Interim Government. The Soviet Army never managed to pacify the country and suffered heavy casualties; the supply of US Stinger SAMs ended Soviet air-superiority. Soviet policy changed when Gorbachev became president in 1985. President Karmal was eased out office in 1986 and was replaced by Muhammed Najibullah. In April 1988 agreement was reached at Geneva

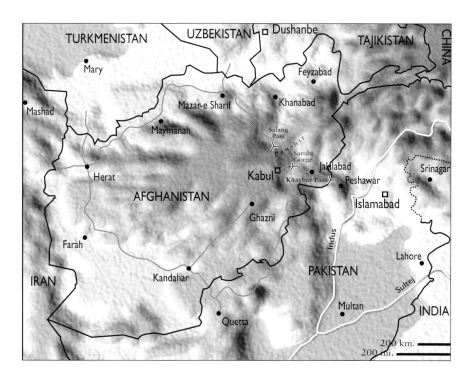

The topography of Afghanistan

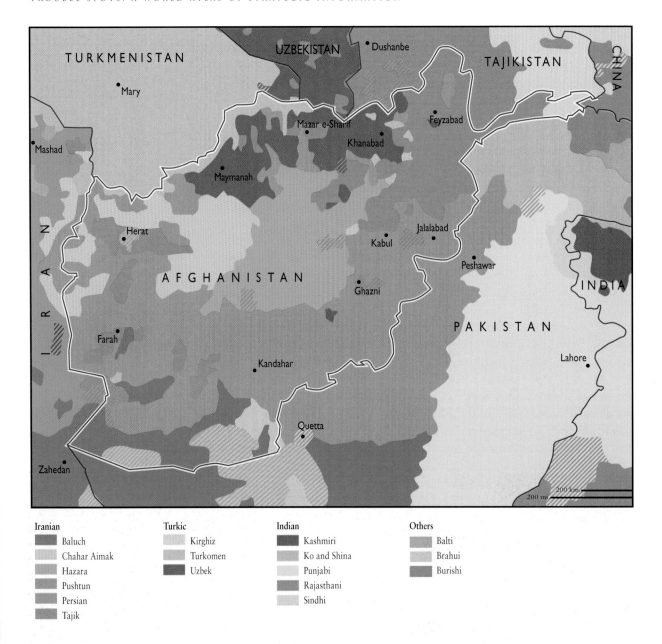

Iranian
- Baluch
- Chahar Aimak
- Hazara
- Pushtun
- Persian
- Tajik

Turkic
- Kirghiz
- Turkomen
- Uzbek

Indian
- Kashmiri
- Ko and Shina
- Punjabi
- Rajasthani
- Sindhi

Others
- Balti
- Brahui
- Burishi

The ethnic populations of Afghanistan and its neighbours

over Soviet withdrawal and by 15 February 1989 the Soviet Army had left, admitting to having lost 13,300 men killed and 35,500 wounded.

The PDPA government was expected to fall quickly but it was three years before it gave up power, though it only had control of the main cities during this time. The Soviet withdrawal did not end the civil war as the Mujahedin coalition fractured and clashes occurred between Hizb-I Islami and other Mujahedin groups. Their backers, Iran and Saudi Arabia, accentuated the differences between the Persian-speaking and Pushtun Mujahedin. The government was forced to concentrate its forces on defending the major cities, allowing the Mujahedin to take control of most of the countryside where they reverted to their habitual rivalry and abandoned their fight with the government.

The entry into Kabul in April 1992 of the Uzbek militia of Rashid Dostam, who had deserted Najibullah, in alliance with Jamiat-I-Islami was peaceful but fighting soon broke out between the various parties and the destruction of Kabul began. Alliances were formed and broken; the main power struggle was between Rabbani, now President, and Hekmatyar, the Prime Minister, who had been joined by Dostam. They concentrated their efforts on Kabul while the other groups established their own territories across the country.

The strife and corruption within the Mujahedin movement is believed to have been the main reason behind the formation of Taliban in Kandahar in early 1994. They first came to notice in October when they rescued a Pakistani convoy that had been attacked by another group; they then went on to take control of Kandahar. Taliban appealed to the young and to the religious student community (talib is a student). Their initial progress was breathtaking and by February 1995 they had reached the outskirts of Kabul; they were then held up there for the rest of the year and most of 1996. They made progress elsewhere, though, taking Herat in September 1995. A year later they took Jalalabad, then after forcing their way through the Sarobi Gorge they attacked Kabul from the east and took it on 26 September. They continued their advance northwards until they reached the Salang pass held by Dostam and the Panshir Valley held by Masoud. Dostam and Masoud made a pact and pushed Taliban back to Kabul. Fighting continued in 1997 with as many as 200,000 refugees arriving at Kabul. The situation changed briefly when one of Dostam's lieutenants, Abdul Malik, defected to Taliban which quickly moved into Mazar-I-Sharif after the town had been taken by Malik. The Taliban then

> **The aims of Taliban**
>
> Restore peace
> Disarm the population
> Enforce sharia
> Defend the integrity and Islamic
>   character of Afghanistan

The gutted palace, Kabul. (The Hutchison Library)

attempted to disarm the Shi'a fighters who resisted and, aided by Malik, killed 300 Taliban and captured 1,000. Following this, Taliban began to be recognised by other states as the legitimate government of Afghanistan.

Taliban imposed a harsh but strict Islamist regime, turning back the clock in many respects but particularly in the treatment of women. In August 1998 they retook the northern city of Mazar-I-Sharif and then massacred perhaps as many as 5,000 Shi'a Hazara males as a reprisal for prisoners executed there in 1997. The murder in Mazar-I-Sharif of nine Iranians caused the Iranian government to mass troops and hold exercises on the border but it did not, as was expected, attack the Taliban. The Taliban now rules the country apart from the far north-east where Masoud's forces still hold out.

Bibliography and Web Sites

Magnus, Ralph, and Eden Naby. *Afghanistan: Mullah, Marx and Mujahid*, Westview, 1998

Maley, William (ed.), *Fundamentalism Reborn? Afghanistan and Taliban*, Hurst, 1998

Marsden, Peter, *The Taliban: War, Religion, and the New Order*, Oxford University Press/Zed Books, 1998

Rashid, Ahmed, *Taliban: Islam, Oil and the New Great Game in Central Asia*, IB Tauris, 2000

Rubin, Barnett, *The Search for Peace in Afghanistan*, Yale University Press, 1995

Jamiat-e-Islami: www.jamiat.com

Online Center for Afghan Politics: www.afghan-politics.org/

Taleban Islamic Movement: www.taleban.com

STRATEGIC WATER: THE TIGRIS AND EUPHRATES

There is as yet no international law covering the non-navigational use of transboundary surface or ground water resources. Legally binding commitments on water allocation and quotas can only be reached by treaty and each treaty only applies to a specific situation. The International Law Commission has been asked to develop international law on the non-navigational use of international watercourses and it has submitted a framework convention that is being negotiated at the UN. Articles of the convention include the following principles: transboundary rivers should be used in an equitable, reasonable and optimum manner; equity does not mean equal distribution, many factors have to be taken into consideration; riparian states must not harm others significantly, and must cooperate and regularly exchange information. Legal experts reject that any state can have absolute sovereignty over an international water system and support the concept of a community of riparian interests.

Syria depends on the River Euphrates and Iraq on both the Euphrates and Tigris for much of their water; both rivers originate in Turkey where the south-east Anatolian or Güneydogu Anadolu Projesi (GAP) project is claimed by Syria and Iraq to threaten their water supply. The GAP project, begun in the early 1970s, is ambitious; it aims to double the irrigated area of Turkey, provide nearly half its electricity and create 3.3 million jobs. Iraq (originally Mesopotamia which first introduced integrated water planning) has depended on Tigris and Euphrates waters for some 6,000 years.

There is no agreed data for the annual flow of the Euphrates, Tigris and their tributaries; for example, two experts have respectively calculated the Euphrates average annual flow at Hit in Iraq as 26.4 and 32.7 billion cubic metres. Turkey has provided the following data: of the average annual flow of the Euphrates of 35 billion cubic metres (it has been as high as 55 billion and as low as 15 billion), Turkey contributes 89 per cent, Syria 11 per cent and Iraq nil; of the Tigris flow of 49 billion cubic metres, 52 per cent comes from Turkey, 48 per cent from Iraq and none from Syria. These flows represent some 28.5 per cent of Turkey's total surface water. Iran contributes to the Tigris through the Lesser Zab and Diyalah. The three countries' claims for shares of the water total far more than what is available. Turkey plans to use 52 per cent of the Euphrates water leaving 37 per cent, which it contributes for the riparian states; similarly Turkey plans to use 14 per cent of the Tigris leaving 38 per cent for the others. However, Syria is claiming 32 per cent of the Euphrates to which it contributes 11 per cent, and 5.4 per cent of the Tigris to which it does not contribute at all. (The river constitutes the border between Syria and Turkey for about 20 miles and so allows Syria to claim to be a riparian state.) Iraq wants 65 per cent of the Euphrates, to which it does not contribute, and 92.5 per cent of the Tigris, to which it contributes 48 per cent. The combined demands of Iraq and Syria, if met, would mean that Turkey could use virtually none of the two rivers' waters.

All riparian states have constructed, or are still constructing, a number of dams and barrages on both rivers to provide very large water storage capacities. Upstream storage can seriously reduce the flow downstream but, on the other hand, in times of drought stored water could be allowed to flow downstream. In the droughts of 1974 and 1988–9 Turkey and Syria preferred to have filled their reservoirs and so reduced the amount of water available for Iraq. In 1988–9 the discharge at the Turkish–Syrian border was reduced from 500 to 150 cubic metres per second. All reservoirs suffer large-scale loss through evaporation; it has been estimated that when completed the Turkish reservoirs could lose up to 2 billion cubic metres a year.

In 1982 Turkey and Iraq set up a Joint Technical Committee which Syria joined the following year; the committee meets regularly to exchange data but has been unable to reach any agreement on the long-term sharing of the Euphrates and Tigris waters. Turkey, as part of a wider economic cooperative agreement with Syria, has committed itself to releasing an annual average of more than 500 cubic metres per second at the Turkish–Syrian border until a final agreement is reached. Syria and Iraq are calling for a larger release in the order of 700 cubic metres per second. Syria and Iraq have agreed an allocation of Euphrates waters that gives Iraq 58 per cent and Syria 42 per cent of annual flows regardless of quantity.

The GAP project, which may not be completed until 2010, comprises the development of 22 dams, 25 irrigation schemes and 19 hydroelectric power stations generating some 7,500 million watts. It is estimated that

Possibilities for a peace water pipeline	
Western pipeline	
Delivery point	*Quantity (cubic metres a day)*
Syria	
Aleppo	300,000
Hama	100,000
Homs	100,000
Damascus	300,000
Jordan	
Amman	600,000
Saudi Arabia	
Tabuk	100,000
Medina	300,000
Yanbu	100,000
Mecca	500,000
Jeddah	500,000
Eastern pipeline	
Delivery point	*Quantity (cubic metres a day)*
Saudi Arabia	
Jubail	200,000
Ad Damman	200,000
Al-Khobar	200,000
Al-Hofuf	200,000
Kuwait	600,000
Bahrain	200,000
Qatar	100,000
UAE	
Abu Dhabi	280,000
Dubai	160,000
Sharjah/Ajman	120,000
Ras Al-Khaimah/Fujairah	120,000
Oman	
Muscat	200,000

Source: Brown and Root, International inc. Feasibility Study

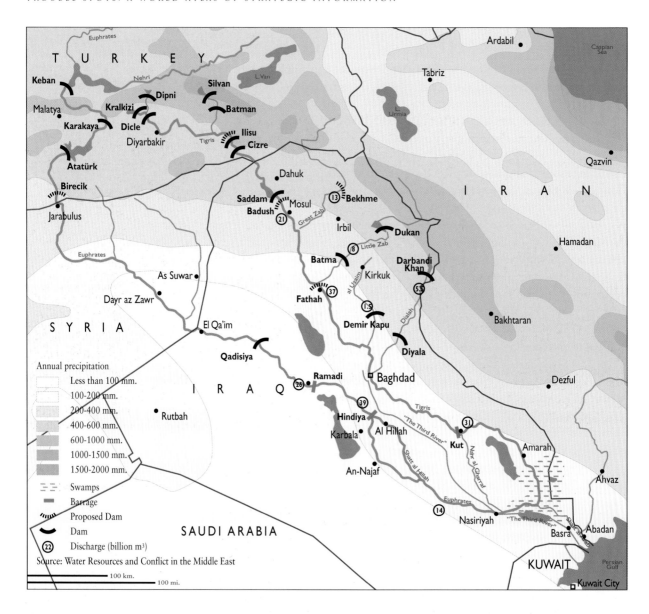

The Tigris and Euphrates

GAP will add 70 per cent to Turkey's energy output and an additional 1.7 million hectares of land will be irrigated. The reduction of flow caused by the additional irrigation and evaporation loss could be as high as 50 per cent. To compensate for the loss Turkey has proposed a 'Peace Pipeline' plan that would bring water, estimated as about 16 million cubic metres a day, from the Seyhan and Ceyhan rivers that now flow into the sea, not just to Syria and Iraq but also to aid Jordan, Saudi Arabia and the Gulf States. The cost of this water would be substantially less than the only other alternative, desalination.

Accurate figures are not available but it has been estimated that Iraq is likely to face water shortages by 2005 and Syria fifteen to twenty-five years later. This estimate does not take into account the possibility of serious drought and unless Turkey increases its annual commitment to release 16 billion cubic metres, shortages will occur earlier. The latest development – Turkey's plan for a dam at Ilisu – could threaten Iraq's Tigris water supply and at the same time make thousands of Turkish

Kurds homeless. The dam's reservoir will hold over 1 million cubic hectares of water and will cover 300 square kilometres.

Two other cross-border factors – support for Turkey's Kurdish rebels and the Hatay province controversy – heighten the disagreement between Turkey and Iraq and Syria. Turkey accuses both Syria and Iraq of giving support and safe havens to PKK guerrillas. The two countries nearly came to blows in June 1996 when Syria massed forces on its northern border following a spate of bomb attacks blamed on Syrian Turks. Hatay became a Syrian province after the break up of the Ottoman Empire but was ceded to Turkey in 1939 by France, then the mandatory power, following a unanimous vote by the Hatay assembly. Syria still considers Hatay to be its rightful territory. Turkey's increasing cooperation and alliance with Israel does not help matters. Given Turkey's military strength a water war is unlikely but shortages are bound to increase tension between the states.

The Ataturk Dam on the Euphrates. (Associated Press)

GAP objectives

Build 22 High Dams
Build 19 hydro electric plants
Generate 27bn kWh per year
Irrigate 1.7m hectares
Provide Turkey with food sufficiency
Create 3.3m jobs

Bibliography and Web Sites

Berschorner, Natasha, *Water and Instability in the Middle East*, IISS Adelphi Paper 273, 1992

Kliot, Nurit, *Water Resources and Conflicts in the Middle East*, Routledge, 1994

Soffer, Arnon, *Rivers of Fire: The Conflict Over Water in the Middle East*, Rowman & Littlefield, 1999

Facts About The Euphrates-Tigris Basin, Turkish Government

GAP Southeastern Anatolian Project, Turkish Ministry of Public Works, 1994

Turkish Ministry of Foreign Affairs: www.mfa.gov.tr
GAP: www.gap.gov.tr

THE MIDDLE EAST: THE WORLD'S MOST VOLATILE REGION

Two of the most worrying issues facing the world are rooted in the Middle East – the Arab-Israeli conflict, which has been the cause of five wars and numerous terrorist incidents, and the security of Persian Gulf oil, which has been threatened by two wars in the last twenty years. The section begins with an overview of the proliferation of nuclear, biological and chemical weapons (NBC), the so-called weapons of mass destruction, and the long-range missiles that can deliver them. The Arab-Israeli issue is dealt with in five pieces looking at: Lebanon, Israel's security, Israel's water, the Palestinians and Jerusalem. The Gulf situation is discussed in items on Iran, Iraq and Arabian border problems. There are also pieces on the Nile waters and on whether Islam is a threat.

Web Site

www. Middle East Network Information Center (University of Texas):
http://menic.utexas.edu/menic

MILITARY REACH: TOO LATE TO STOP PROLIFERATION

While the Middle East may not be the most dangerous place to live in the world at the moment, it does hold the record for the number of major wars fought in one region in the last forty years. Although several Middle Eastern states have had so-called weapons of mass destruction for some years, any fresh outbreak of war would be more than likely to see the use of long-range missiles with NBC and conventional warheads.

Range is not the most important requirement for missiles in the Middle East as the table in the margin opposite shows. Syria's current missiles can reach any part of Israel, while their most accurate SSM, the Soviet SS-21, can hit as far south as Tel Aviv. Tel Aviv is only 500 kilometres from Iraqi territory and just over 1000 kilometres from Iran. Similarly, Tehran is roughly 600 kilometres from Iraqi territory and Baghdad not more than 100 kilometres

Israel's anti-ballistic missile, Arrow, being tested on 1 November 1999. It is now in service. (Israel Aircraft Industries)

from the border with Iran. Jordan, Lebanon, Oman and Qatar have no SSM; nor do Bahrain and Kuwait but they have the 30 kilometre range US MLRS and the 70 kilometre range Russian Smerch rocket launcher respectively.

Israel is known to have a nuclear arsenal and has been suspected of having had operational nuclear weapons since at least the late 1960s. Whether it would ever use them in the 'Samson' mode is debatable. Nor have nuclear weapons deterred the Arabs from conventional war against Israel. If an Arab country or Iran were to obtain nuclear weapons, the situation would be quite different and would be as dangerous as that between India and Pakistan following their nuclear tests. Israel is not averse to employing pre-emption when it is threatened. Its nuclear weapons could be delivered by aircraft or by the Jericho missile; the range of the most recent version is thought to be over 7,000 kilometres. Its latest fighter bomber, the US F-15I, can reach Iran but not necessarily all its counter-force targets and this could cause Israel problems should Iran acquire nuclear weapons as is forecast – perhaps in as little as two years if it can get fissile material. Israel's new German-built class of submarines gives it the capability to launch cruise missiles and so could provide the country with a nuclear second-strike capability.

Several Middle Eastern countries are suspected of having nuclear ambitions and the fear is that some could purchase weapons stolen from the huge Russian stockpile. After the Pakistani tests in 1998 it is now known that there is an Islamic bomb. Only Iran and Iraq are likely to be able to introduce nuclear weapons into their armouries in the foreseeable future. Iran's potential capability and development efforts are described on page 34. The extent of Iraq's nuclear programme surprised the world when it was revealed soon after the end of the Gulf War; long suspected, it was far closer to fruition than ever imagined. With the know-how and the designers and engineers still available, it should not take Iraq long to regain its position once sanctions are lifted and international attention turned elsewhere. Now that UNSCOM, the UN inspection organisation, has been withdrawn, who knows what clandestine activities might have begun. There have recently been hints that Saudi Arabia may also be considering starting a nuclear weapons programme.

Chemical and biological weapons are far easier and less expensive to develop than nuclear armaments; they would be considered as frightening as nuclear weapons had the world experienced their full-scale use in modern war but they are unlikely to obtain the same political significance. The Middle East has already witnessed the use of chemical weapons (CW) on several occasions – Egypt in Yemen in 1960s, Iraq against Iran in the First Gulf War and later against Kurds at Halabaja, and Iran was forced to reply in kind against Iraq. Other Middle Eastern countries credited with a CW capability are Israel, Libya (with its construction of a chemical plant at Rabta and, after a fire at Rabta, the underground complex at nearby Tarhuna) and Syria.

Biological weapons (BW) have not yet been employed operationally, other than in assassination attempts, but it is believed that a number of Middle Eastern countries have BW programmes. Certainly Iraq was known to have BW under development and to have had some weapons loaded with biological agent, but not much of the programme was revealed by UNSCOM inspectors. Most information on the issue came from General Hussein Kemal Hassan who defected to Jordan in 1995, from an admission by Rihab Taha, a

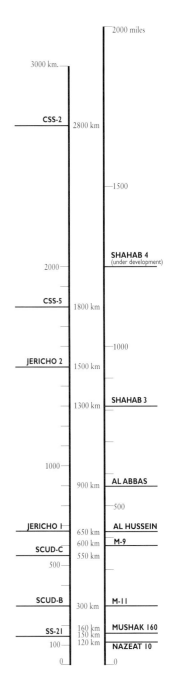

Missile ranges

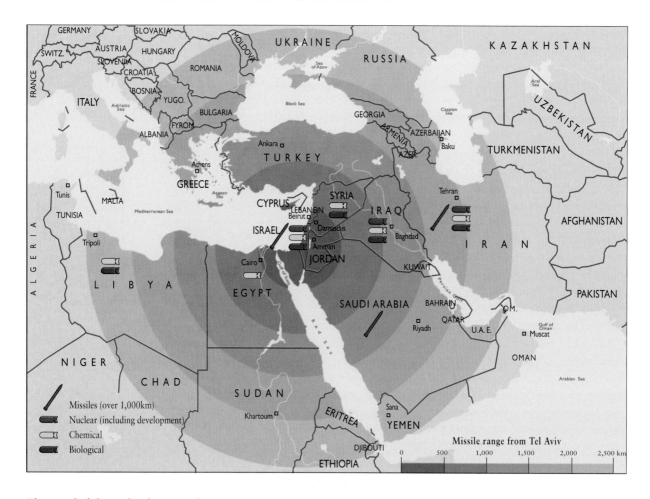

The spread of chemical and biological weapons, and long-range missiles in the Middle East.

leading Iraq germ specialist. After the defection Iraq made further admissions as to its BW activities, which had included producing anthrax and botulinum toxin, testing delivery means, and loading missile warheads with BW. It is strongly suspected that biological weapon programmes are in progress in Iran, Israel, Libya, Syria and possibly Egypt. BW production can be carried out in small, hard-to-recognise facilities; far less agent is required than for CW attack and it disperses over a much larger area than CW. BW lend themselves to terrorist use, are more easily smuggled than CW or fissile material and can be effectively disseminated through water supplies.

In terms of future Middle Eastern wars, it has to be emphasised that those most at risk from either nuclear weapons or CBW will be civil populations and not fighting forces.

Web Sites

www. Center for Strategic and International Studies, Middle East Programme: www.csis.org
Centre for Non-Proliferation Studies (Monterey Institute for Strategic Studies): www.cns.miis.edu

THE WATERS OF THE NILE

The Nile is critical to both Egypt and Sudan. The Egyptian population grows at the rate of about one million a year and it has been predicted that Egypt will be suffering a 16–30 per cent water deficit by the end of

The waters of the Nile that concern the riparian states.

	Swamps
	Barrage
	Proposed Dam
	Dam
	Dam and Power Station
	Irrigation Canal
㉒	Discharge (billion m³)

Source: Water Resources and Conflict in the Middle East

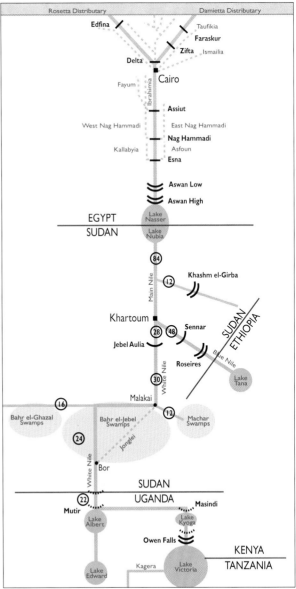

2000. There are two main sources of the Nile: the Blue Nile, which rises in Ethiopia and joins the other, the White Nile, at Khartoum. The White Nile flows out of Lake Victoria through Uganda. Uganda, Kenya and Tanzania share the coastline of the lake. Victoria is fed by the River Kagera, which crosses Rwanda and Burundi. The Albert, Edward and George Lakes also contribute to the White Nile and their western shores lie in the Democratic Republic of Congo (formerly Zaire). Thus there are seven riparian states which, except possibly Kenya, enjoy ample precipitation, have a relative surplus of water and do not use as much Nile water as they are entitled to by virtue of their share of and contribution to the river.

The Nile waters were first controlled in 3400 BC by the ancient Egyptians who aimed to improve irrigation, flood control and navigation. In more modern times Mohammed Ali in 1834 created a system of canals in the Nile Delta to enlarge the irrigated area. In 1861 British engineers constructed the first successful barrage. The first Aswan Dam was built in 1902 and after its height had been raised in 1934 it could store 6 million cubic metres. The first attempt to extend control of the Nile came in the early 1900s; the plan envisaged storing water in Sudan and further south for use in times of drought by building dams on both the Blue and White Niles and the River Atbara and constructing storage reservoirs on the lakes further south. British officials in Egypt and Sudan supported schemes that favoured the country in which they worked. Sudanese officials opposed the

The Aswan High Dam.
(Photographers' Library)

building of a canal through the Sudd swamps, which Egyptian officials saw as increasing the water flow northwards, because of the implications for the local population. With no agreed overall plan for the control of the Nile, the riparian states, especially Egypt, developed their own projects.

Egyptian plans for constructing the Aswan High Dam began in the early 1950s without taking its effect on Sudan into account. However, agreement was reached in 1959 on sharing the then available water reaching Aswan: Egypt was allocated 55.5 billion cubic metres and Sudan 18.5 billion. The agreement was based on the average Nile flow at Aswan being 84 billion cubic metres and the evaporation loss 10 billion. Construction began in 1960 and the project was completed in 1971. The aim was to store some 162 billion cubic metres of water and to generate 10 billion kWh of electricity per year. It was expected that water supply would be guaranteed, including for irrigation, throughout the year without seasonal fluctuations; 1.3 million hectares of extra cultivation would be provided. The dam has had some negative effects, the main one being the loss of the silt that used to be washed down the Nile, enriched the farming soil and provided the material for brick-making. Now large quantities of expensive fertilisers and pesticides must be used and they reduce the quality of the water significantly. Bricks now have to be made from productive soil.

The Sudd swamps cover between 20,000 and 30,000 square kilometres depending on the season. Some 30 billion cubic metres of water a year are lost from the area through evaporation and seepage or over 50 per cent of the inflow into the swamp. The Jonglei Canal scheme was planned to save and deliver to Aswan an additional 3.8 billion cubic metres. There have been several plans for the canal. The construction work that began in 1978 was for a 360 kilometre canal carrying 25 million cubic metres a day or 1.6 billion a year. A second canal was to be built doubling the capacity. Work was halted by the civil war in 1984 after 267 kilometres had been completed. The canal was not a cause of the war but it has become a symbol for the Nilotic population of the Sudd and southerners generally of the government's exploitation of their resources. The extra water the canal would provide is essential for Egypt but not for Sudan, which currently does not use all its quota.

Egypt's population is calculated to increase by around 2.5 per cent per year, reaching 70 million by the end of 2000. There will be a need for an increase in the area irrigated if the population is to be fed. (Already Egypt imports some two-thirds of its food.) One estimate is that water requirement will grow to 65 billion cubic metres in 2000. Another suggests that an additional 12.7 billion cubic metres will be needed to irrigate all the land that has been earmarked for reclamation. A number of measures are under way to employ the available water better. They include use of waste-water, improving the efficiency of irrigation schemes (traditional methods waste some 60 per cent) and reducing the amount of water-intensive crops. At best Egypt could recover up to 12 billion cubic metres by these measures. In the long term Egypt's water requirements can only be met by gaining more from Nile improvement schemes but these might only achieve an additional 18 billion cubic metres and then only if all the proposed schemes can be funded and implemented, and if Egypt is given priority in water allocation.

As yet other riparian states have made no plans that would jeopardise Egypt's and Sudan's water supply. The East African riparians have other

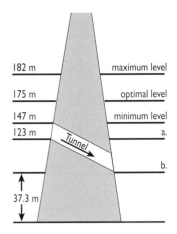

182 m — maximum level
175 m — optimal level
147 m — minimum level
123 m — a.
Tunnel
b.
37.3 m

a. Electricity production stops
b. Irrigation pumping stops
Live storage: 90 billion m³
Dead storage: 6.8 billion m³

The Aswan High Dam.

Nile sources	Drainage basin (square miles)	Mean discharge (billion cubic metres)
Blue Nile (Khartoum)	12,530	53.5
Atbara	38,764	11.8
Sobat	86,872	12.4
White Nile	514,312	24.0
Bahr al Razal	20,077	16.0
White Nile	38,610	30.0
Main Nile		
At Atbara	104,247	94
Khartoum to Med		
at Aswan	–	84

The Sudd	
Inflow (billion cubic metres)	
Bahr al Razal	16
Sobat	12
White Nile	24
Total	52
Outflow	30

water sources and use relatively little of the Nile's waters. At present Ethiopia has a poor system of water distribution and no funds to improve matters. Irrigated land could be increased by some 50 per cent. The Blue Nile has a high potential for generating electric power but massive funding would be needed. Egypt views any Ethiopian increase in the use of Blue Nile water as a hostile act but any large-scale additional use is unlikely in the short term. In the longer term any shortfall for Egypt could be more than compensated for by creating water storage capability in Ethiopia where the evaporation rate would be three times less than that at Aswan.

Bibliography

Berschorner, Natasha, *Water and Instability in the Middle East*, IISS Adelphi Paper 273, 1992
Kliot, Nurit, *Water Resources and Conflict in the Middle East*, Routledge, 1994
Soffer, Arnon, *Rivers of Fire: The Conflict Over Water in the Middle East*, Rowman & Littlefield, 1999

LEBANON: A DIVIDED COUNTRY UNDER OCCUPATION

Lebanon has a long history that begins with the Phoenician City States in the tenth century BC. It was then conquered by the Persians in the sixth century BC, by Alexander the Great in the fourth and by the Romans in the first. It was part of the Byzantine Empire until AD 641 and from then, apart from short periods of Crusader rule, was held by Islam; from 1516 until the end of the First World War it was part of the Ottoman Empire.

The country has a multiplicity of religious beliefs: the Romans introduced Christianity and the Arabs Islam; there are a number of branches and sects of each. The largest Christian sect is the Maronite, the next largest the Greek Orthodox. The most numerous Muslims are Shi'a but there are nearly as many Sunni. And there are the Druze who also live in northern Israel and southern Syria.

Lebanon: population by religion	
Muslim	60 per cent
Christian	30 per cent
Druze	6 per cent
Armenian	4 per cent
Non-Lebanese Population	
Syrian	300,000
Palestinian	500,000

A period of fighting between Druze and Maronites began in 1841 and eventually led to two multi-faith district councils, each with a member from the Druze, Greek Orthodox, Greek Catholic, Maronite and Sunni communities, being established to advise the governors – the first time religious persuasion was accorded formal representation. A peasants' revolt in 1858 developed into conflict between the Druze and the Maronites in which both Sunni and Shi'a Muslims supported the Druze while the other Christian sects joined the Maronites. The fighting spread across the whole country with the Muslims, aided by the Ottomans, gaining the upper hand until France intervened and saved the Maronites in the northern Chouf Mountains from the massacres that had occurred elsewhere. As a result of European pressure the Ottomans created an autonomous governorate of Mountain Lebanon in which the religious sects were represented on the council not equally but in proportion to their percentage of population.

The modern Lebanese state was created, along with other Middle Eastern countries, at the end of the First World War when the Ottoman Empire was broken up. Initially Lebanon was a French mandatory territory, as was Syria; border changes effected during the mandate have left a legacy of problems that persist today. In 1920 the French created Greater Lebanon which included Tripoli and the Akkar district in the north and the Bekaa valley in the east. While Mountain Lebanon had been predominantly Christian, in Greater Lebanon the Christian and Muslim communities were of roughly equal strength. Independence was granted in 1941 but not achieved until 1943 when a 'national pact' was arrived at: the Christians renounced the protection of Europeans powers, the Muslims the ambition of union with Syria. The multi-faith nature of the population was taken into account – the president was always to be a Maronite and the prime minister a Sunni Muslim.

Lebanon took little part in the Arab war against Israeli independence in 1948. There was some fighting along Israel's northern border but all territory won or lost was exchanged after the war. The Lebanese-Israeli border, though technically still an armistice line, follows the route of the Lebanese-Mandatory Palestine border. Lebanon did not carry out terrorist raids against Israel though the Palestine Liberation Organisation (PLO) continued its fight

Lebanon, as at 1 January 2000.

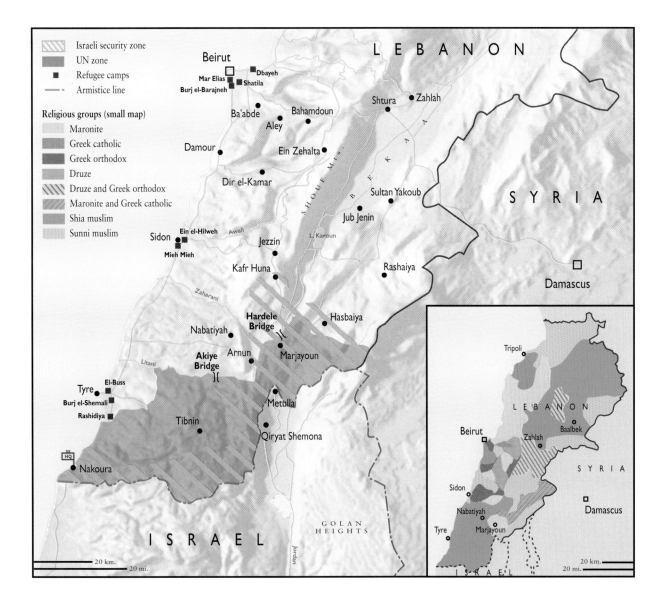

against Israel from Lebanese soil after its eviction from Jordan in 1970. Lebanon took no part in the 1967 or 1973 Arab-Israeli wars.

The massive increase in the Palestinian presence in Lebanon in 1970 had a number of consequences. First it led to much deeper Israeli raids into Lebanon as they sought to hit the PLO leadership. Secondly it brought about a strengthening of all the armed militia – the Christians purchasing arms in Europe and receiving training from the Lebanese Army while the Muslims received arms from the Palestinians. Clashes between the Palestinians and the Lebanese Army on the one hand and armed factions on the other had taken place since 1968, but full-scale civil war did not break out until 1975. Initially it was fought between Palestinians and left-wing Muslims against the Christian Phalangists. In 1976 an Arab peacekeeping force, mainly provided by Syria, deployed; the other Arab contingents soon withdrew while the Syrians have remained in strength ever since. PLO and later Hizbollah terrorist attacks across the border into Israel have provoked numerous retaliatory operations and several invasions by the Israelis. The Israelis still occupy a zone close to the border where there are frequent clashes between the Israeli Defence Force and the Israeli-backed South Lebanese Army (SLA) and Hizbollah guerrillas. The new Israeli Prime Minister, Ehud Barak, has said he will withdraw from Lebanon in July 2000.

The first Israeli invasion of Lebanon took place in March 1978 in response, the Israelis claim, to an increasing Palestinian build-up in the south of the country and not as a direct retaliation for a PLO seaborne raid that resulted in the deaths of thirty-four Israelis. Southern Lebanon was also the scene of conflict between Christian and Shi'a communities and the Israelis took the opportunity to destroy Shi'a villages and recruit the Christians into Major Haddad's militia. Israel withdrew its forces, which had penetrated as far north as the River Litani by the end of April, and handed over control to the UN Interim Force in Lebanon (UNIFIL) except for a 10 kilometre wide strip along the border where Major Haddad took charge.

The attempted assassination of the Israeli ambassador in London was cited as the reason for the much larger and longer-lasting invasion in 1982 when the Israelis advanced as far north as Beirut and eventually caused the PLO to withdraw from the country. Israel's forces remained in Lebanon for a further thirty months which resulted in many Israeli casualties and led to the formation of the Shi'a Hizbollah. Hizbollah originated in a breakaway group of Amal (a Lebanese faction) and was backed by Iran. It was initially supervised by the small contingent of the Iranian Revolutionary Guards who arrived in the Bekaa in July 1982 and was soon reinforced to some 2,000 strong.

Hizbollah was probably responsible for two suicide car bomb attacks in 1983 on the French and US Marine units which caused massive casualties. The withdrawal of the Western contingents from Lebanon was claimed as a victory by Hizbollah. Later a similar attack, which was certainly carried out by the group, was made on the Israeli HQ in Tyre. The Israelis' movements were continually harried by Hizbollah until they fought their way out of Lebanon in June 1985. After the Israeli withdrawal fighting continued in Lebanon with clashes between an alliance of the Shi'ite Amal and the Druze against the Christians, Amal against the Palestinians left in Beirut, and pro-Syrian militias against the fundamentalist Sunni in Tripoli. Civil war

---

Syrian Forces

Beirut: part-mechanised brigade; 5 Special Forces regiments

Bekaa: Mechanised Division HQ; part of 2 mechanised brigades; part of 1 armoured brigade

Special Forces regiments at *Tripoli, Batum, Kpar Fallus*

intensified in 1986; the tripartite agreement between the Maronites, Amal, and the Druze collapsed within two weeks and the Syrians had to deploy troops in Beirut to halt the fighting between Amal and Hizbollah.

The civil war was only brought to an end in 1990 after the surviving members of Lebanon's parliament met in Taif and later in Lebanon to agree a new constitution. Initially most parties rejected the Taif Agreement. Nevertheless a new president was appointed only to be killed two weeks later. This atrocity spurred the formation of a new government, composed equally of Christians and Muslims, which dismissed the army commander, General Aoun. Most of the army remained loyal to Aoun and it was not until October 1990 that the General surrendered to the Syrian Army. The armed factions all agreed to leave Beirut and eventually consented to disarmament; only Hizbollah was allowed to continue to be armed.

Opinion in Israel is divided over whether it should withdraw unilaterally from South Lebanon. Argument in favour of withdrawal points to the ever-growing list of Israeli casualties (39 killed in 1997 and 24 in 1998, not counting the 73 who died in a disastrous helicopter collision en route for Lebanon in 1997). Also, Israel always earns adverse publicity whenever it reacts to a terrorist attack (usually on the principle of ten eyes for one rather than an eye for an eye). Withdrawal could have a positive effect on negotiations with Syria which would no longer be able to use Hizbollah as a surrogate force to provoke Israel. (Syria could easily curtail Hizbollah activity if it wished – both Syrians and Hizbollah are based in the Bekaa Valley and most of Hizbollah's arms and ammunition are flown in from Iran through Damascus airport.) UNIFIL has said that it could redeploy up to the Israeli border within a week.

Looking west over the Lebanese border from Misgav Am in Israel. (Zev Radovan)

But withdrawal could also mean Hizbollah rocket attacks reaching further into Israel; they can already hit northern Israel from north of the Israeli security zone. Arrangements would have to be made to protect the members and families of the South Lebanese Army (SLA) against whom reprisals are likely to be taken, and, of course, Israel is also loathe to be seen to be making any withdrawal that could spur on its enemies. Israel will expect the Lebanese Army to ensure there are no terrorist attacks across the border after withdrawal but the Lebanese Army is unlikely to satisfy Israel in this respect despite the great improvements made to its capability over recent years.

Bibliography

Abul-Husn, Latif, *The Lebanese Conflict: Looking Inward*, Boulder, 1998

O'Balance, Edgar, *Civil War in Lebanon, 1975–92*, Macmillan, 1998

Sirriyeh, Hussein, *Lebanon: The Dimensions of Conflict*, International Institute for Strategic Studies Adelphi Paper 243, 1989

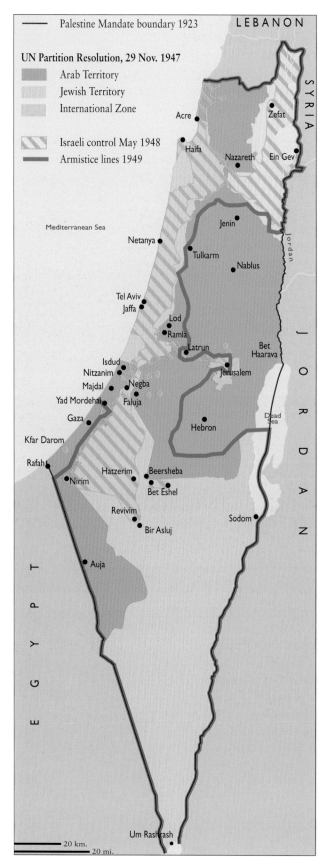

The division of land, 1923–49.

ISRAEL'S SECURITY SITUATION: LAND FOR PEACE

When Israel gained its independence on 15 May 1948 it was immediately attacked by five Arab armies. Since then it has only signed peace treaties with two of its attackers, Egypt and Jordan. Fighting between Arab and Jew had occurred much earlier – in 1920, 1929 and 1936; serious conflict broke out after the United Nations General Assembly passed a resolution in November 1947 to establish Jewish and Arab states in a partitioned Palestine. By May 1948 the Jews had roughly trebled the territory they controlled. The fighting ended after the Israeli capture of Elat on the Red Sea on 10 March 1949; as Armistice agreements were signed Israel withdrew from Lebanon and Iraqi troops from west of the Jordan. Some exchanges of land took place along the ceasefire line between Israel and Jordanian-controlled West Bank. The Israelis controlled the bulk of Palestine with Egypt taking the Gaza Strip. Syria had some small areas in the Yarmouk valley and along the border to the north, and Jordan occupied East Jerusalem and the West Bank.

There have been three major Arab-Israeli wars since 1949. The first came in 1956 when Israel, in collusion with France and Britain, invaded Egypt and then withdrew from the Sinai which it had overrun. In 1967, provoked by the closure of the Straits of Tiran and an Egyptian build-up in Sinai, Israel launched a pre-emptive air strike that destroyed most of the Egyptian, Syrian and Jordanian air forces. During six days of fighting Israel captured Sinai, the Golan Heights, the West Bank, Gaza Strip and East Jerusalem; it did not withdraw from these territories after a ceasefire was agreed. Surprised by the Arab attack in 1973 Israel nearly lost the Golan and the Egyptians managed to cross the Suez Canal; eventually Israel regained the Golan, crossed the canal and surrounded the Egyptian Army which was trapped on the east bank. Between the major wars there have been outbreaks of fighting on all of the armistice lines and terrorist attacks made mainly by Palestinians across all Israel's borders.

Israel has now signed peace treaties with Egypt and Jordan, and has made considerable progress towards reaching agreement with the Palestinians.

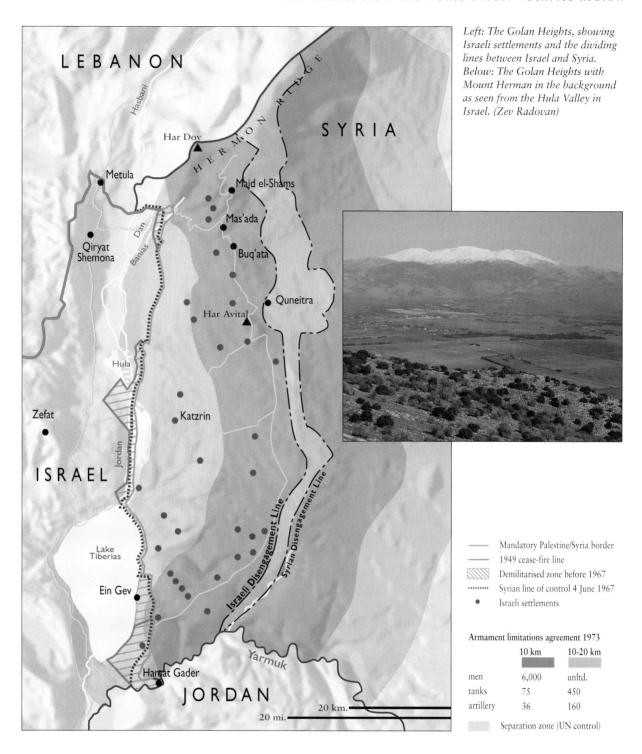

Left: The Golan Heights, showing Israeli settlements and the dividing lines between Israel and Syria. Below: The Golan Heights with Mount Herman in the background as seen from the Hula Valley in Israel. (Zev Radovan)

			Mandatory Palestine/Syria border
			1949 cease-fire line
			Demilitarised zone before 1967
			Syrian line of control 4 June 1967
•			Israeli settlements

Armament limitations agreement 1973

	10 km	10-20 km
men	6,000	unltd.
tanks	75	450
artillery	36	160

Separation zone (UN control)

Israel withdrew from the whole of Sinai and from small areas along the border with Jordan. After secret talks in Oslo, agreement reached with the Palestinians led to the establishment of the Palestinian Authority (PA) which had control of most of the Gaza Strip and an enclave around Jericho. The West Bank was divided into three zones: Area A in which the PA has total authority including security; Area B from which the Israel Defence Force (IDF) has withdrawn but retains overall responsibility for security and for the protection of Israeli settlements, with the PA police responsible for public order; and Area C where Israel has retained full control of security. The plan was to transfer areas progressively from category to category until the final status talks had been completed by 4 May 1999 (now scheduled for September 2000). The Israeli government under the late Yitzhak Rabin began talks with the Syrians on a peace treaty; although nothing was signed or formally announced it would appear that Rabin agreed to withdraw from the Golan in return for a return to normal relations. While the principles that it would follow were decided upon, no agreement was reached on matters such as: the final border; the timing and phases of withdrawal; separation and limitation of forces clauses; and confidence-building measures. Israeli-Syrian peace talks re-opened in December 1999.

Despite the progress made towards peace with all its neighbours Israel still feels threatened in three quite separate ways: conventional war, missile attack and terrorist attack. Each threat has to be countered by different forces with different equipment and training. At present Israel is best prepared to meet the least likely threat – conventional war launched by its Arab neighbours. Egypt remains an existential threat on account of its large armed forces which are increasingly equipped with more modern weapons paid for by US aid. The Limitation of Forces agreement means that Egypt can station few troops east of the Suez Canal and it is likely that Israel will act fast enough to meet any attacking force deep in Sinai and halt it there.

Israel's main fear is a surprise attack on the Golan but Syria could recover the Heights through negotiation. Syria would then be in an even better position to attack Israel despite the demilitarised zone and limitations on forces that would undoubtedly be included in any peace treaty. However, as long as Israel holds on to the Golan a Syrian attack is always a possibility. From the east Israel fears an Iraqi rather than a Jordanian attack. However, the Jordan Rift (not the river) is an effective tank obstacle and there are few crossing points nor are there many east–west routes through the West Bank. The Israeli air force could hold up any attempt to cross the Jordan Rift. Nevertheless, Israel has deployed an armoured division in the West Bank poised to cross the River Jordan and meet any Iraqi force in the desert east of Mafraq. Recently there have been suggestions that Saddam Hussein, as part of a programme to gain Iraq's rehabilitation in the region, could agree to a peace treaty with Israel and even to the resettlement of as many as a million Palestinian refugees.

Many Israelis see giving up the Golan as throwing away their country's security on the Syrian front but the situation has changed radically since the pre-1967 days when Syrian troops overlooked Israel's Hula Valley. Attacking up the Golan Heights would be less difficult now; there are many more tank-passable routes and tank engines have much greater power. Syrian artillery can, in any event, already hit targets in Israel from its present positions on the Golan. The peace treaty could include restrictions on the development of Syrian minefields and anti-tank obstacles on the Golan. The political fall-out in Israel of withdrawal would be far less than abandoning settlements in the West Bank. There are far fewer settlers – only some 17,000 live on the Golan – nor are there the same emotional ties as to the biblical areas of Judea and Samaria, though there was Israelite settlement on the Heights during the reigns of David and Solomon.

Opposing Forces	
Israel	
Active manpower	173,000
Tanks	3,800
Artillery	2,770
Combat aircraft	460
Armed helicopter	130
Syria	
Active manpower	316,000
Tanks	3,450
Artillery	3,120
Combat aircraft	590
Armed helicopter	70
Jordan	
Active manpower	104,000
Tanks	900
Artillery	870
Combat aircraft	90
Armed helicopter	15
Egypt	
Active manpower	450,000
Tanks	3,650
Artillery	3,240
Combat aircraft	580
Armed helicopter	130

Artillery includes guns, rocket launchers and mortars of 100mm calibre and over

A far more likely, more dangerous and more difficult to prevent threat is that of attack by long-range missiles armed with chemical, biological and even nuclear warheads. Iran is developing such a capability and Iraq could certainly produce one again when sanctions are lifted and it is not under an inspection regime. Syrian missiles can already reach any part of Israel and its short-range weapons can target Haifa and Tel Aviv. Israel is developing an anti-missile system, the Arrow, of which a small number are now operational, but how successful it would be in the event of a massed missile attack is unclear. Israel also has its own Jericho missiles and is receiving F-15I aircraft from the US; these have the range to reach Iran with an 11,000lb payload. Israel's nuclear capability deterred Iraq from using chemical weapons against it during the Scud missile attacks launched against Israel during the Gulf War. However, successful deterrence is less assured than it was in the NATO/Warsaw Pact context.

Until the Palestinian problem is satisfactorily resolved and a peace treaty is agreed with Lebanon and Syria which includes measures to disarm and disband Hizbollah, Israel will continue to suffer terrorist attack. A frightening aspect of Muslim terrorism is its ability to find volunteers for suicide bomb attacks which, short of draconian security measures that would virtually paralyse normal life, are hard to forestall. In the twelve months from March 1994 over 100 Israelis were killed in eight suicide attacks, all bar one in Israel proper. The most alarming threat that Israelis may face is terrorists armed with CBW agents that could be

Looking across the Jordan Rift, the egress on the Israeli side is as steep as that which can be seen on the Jordanian side.

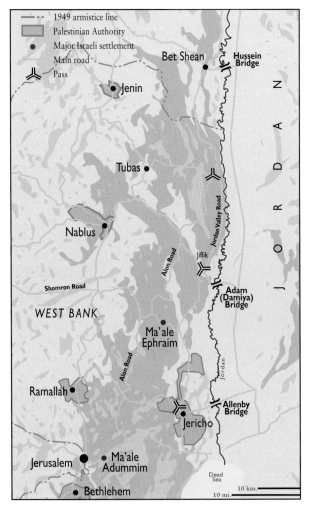

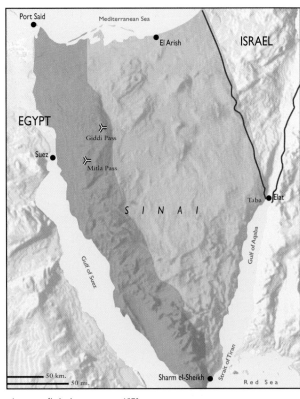

Armament limitations agreement 1973

	1 Division	Border Troops	Police Only
men	22,000	4,000	Police
tanks	230	—	—
artillery	126	—	—

There is a 5 km wide zone on the Israeli side of the border where only
4 battalions of 4,000 men, no tanks and only 180 APCs may be deployed

Above: *The approaches to Israel
from the east over the Jordan Rift.*

Right: *Sinai, showing the areas in
which armaments are limited.*

introduced into air-conditioning systems or released in crowded places. A captured Hamas activist has revealed during interrogation that recruits with scientific expertise were being sought, and it is suspected that Hamas, Islamic Jihad and Hizbollah have all considered the use of CBW.

At long last one can have some optimism that the Arab-Israeli confrontation may be close to an end but although Israel's immediate neighbours are in favour of peace, countries like Iraq and Iran are still implacably opposed to Israel's existence. After so many years of violence Israelis will continue to feel threatened even though peace treaties have been agreed. Of course, Israel's neighbours feel equally threatened because they have lost all wars with Israel. Sadly there are extremists both in Israel and the Arab world who do not want peace and who could upset the whole process.

Bibliography and Web Sites

Karsh, Ephraim (ed.), *Between War and Peace: Dilemmas of Israeli Security*, Frank Cass, 1996
Schiff, Ze'ev *A History of the Israeli Army: 1874 to the Present*, Sidgwick & Jackson, 1985

www.

Haaretz (newspaper): www.haaretz.co.il/eng
Israel: www.israel-mfa.gov.il/peace/basic ref
Jaffee Center for Strategic Studies: www.tau.ac.il/jcss/start
Jerusalem Report: www.jrep.com

A PALESTINIAN STATE: THE PRICE FOR PEACE

The name Palestine was given to the region lying between the Mediterranean and the River Jordan by the Romans after their conquest in 64 BC. Before then the indigenous population of numerous tribes had been generally known as Canaanites who were joined by the Israelite and Philistine invaders. The region was conquered or fought over on numerous occasions both before and after the Roman conquest but since then the original inhabitants have been known as Palestinians, whether Christian or Muslim, and these people included Jews until Israel gained its independence.

In 1880 the Jewish population of Palestine numbered some 24,000, compared to an Arab population of about 300,000. The Jewish repopulation of Palestine began in 1882 as a result of pogroms in Russia and persecution in Poland and Romania; 25,000 emigrated then and a second 'Aliyah' took place between 1904 and 1914 when 40,000 Jews came from Europe and Yemen. During the First World War the British Foreign Secretary, Arthur Balfour, in a letter to Lord Rothschild stated that the government would use its best endeavours to establish a National Jewish Home in Palestine; the homeland was not to prejudice the rights of the Palestinian population. After the defeat of the Turks in 1918, Britain received a mandate to govern Palestine. However, it restricted the emigration of Jews. In the 1920s there were several instances of Arab attacks on Jewish settlements, the worst being the killing of fifty-nine people including women and children in Hebron in August 1929.

The Arab revolt of May 1936 was aimed as much at the British authority as the Jewish population; by October 80 Jews had been killed and the British Army had killed over 100 Arabs in suppressing the revolt. A commission, the first of several and headed by Lord Peel, was tasked with examining the future of the British Mandate; the commission recommended partition but with a British-controlled sector from the Mediterranean up to and including Jerusalem. A number of other investigating organisations were appointed until finally a UN Commission reported in November 1947. This too recommended partition into

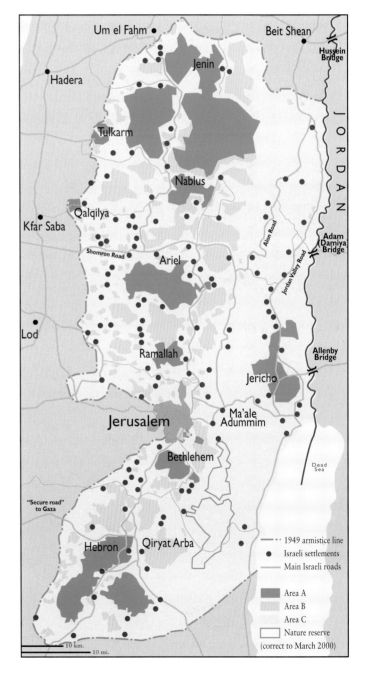

The divisions of the West Bank into Areas A, B and C, and Israeli settlements.

169

Arab and Jewish states but with a UN-controlled international territory around Jerusalem. The Jews accepted the UN recommendation but the Arabs did not. The UN General Assembly passed a resolution on 29 November 1947 recognising Israel's independence. Fighting between Jews and Arabs had begun well before this and after the resolution was passed elements of five Arab states entered Palestine to defeat the Israelis. The war continued until 10 March 1949 when Israel captured the Red Sea port of Um Rashrash, now called Elat; armistice agreements with Israel's four neighbours were signed between February and July 1949. In the war the Israelis had taken considerably more territory than had been recommended in the UN partition proposal but they had also lost the Jewish Quarter of Old Jerusalem and a number of settlements north and south of the city. The Egyptians gained control of a strip along the Mediterranean coast around Gaza, and Jordan controlled what became known as the West Bank. Large numbers of Palestinians left or were forced to leave the areas now controlled by Israel, many being housed in refugee camps in the West Bank and Gaza Strip. Only in the north did a considerable Palestinian population remain under Israeli control as did the Bedouin who lived in the Negev.

In 1967, following the withdrawal of the UN peacekeeping force in Sinai at Egypt's request, the blockading of the Straits of Tiran to Israeli shipping and a build-up of Egyptian forces in Sinai, Israel launched a pre-emptive strike against air force bases in Egypt, Jordan and Syria. In the ensuing war Israel captured the remaining parts of Palestine, the West Bank and the Gaza Strip, as well as Sinai and the Syrian Golan Heights. Many of the refugees in camps in the West Bank fled to Jordan. Despite the resolutions of the UN Security Council Israel remained in control of these territories and retained them after the 1973 war.

In the early days of the occupation the Israelis were seen as no worse governors than the Jordanians; many Palestinians were inured to occupation – 'Before the Jordanians it was the British, before them the Turks, so what's new?' The Gaza Strip became a hotbed for Palestinian terrorism until 1971 when General Ariel Sharon eradicated the terrorists using draconian methods. In the West Bank there were demonstrations from time to time and some amateur attempts at terrorist attack. The Israelis established a number of settlements in both Gaza and the West Bank; they were sited in such a way as to enhance the defence of the areas, mainly along the border with Egypt, in the Jordan Valley and on the high ground overlooking it. The 'Allon' plan avoided establishing settlements close to centres of Arab population. The Likud government changed this policy when it was elected in 1977; it was dedicated to the dogma that Judea and Samaria formed the 'God-given land' known as 'Erez Israel'. Settlement activity increased enormously from 33 settlements with 20,000 inhabitants in 1977 to the current 240 settlements and some 180,000 settlers (excluding East Jerusalem). Many are ardent supporters of 'Erez Israel' who are unlikely to leave settlements even when these are totally surrounded by Palestinian-controlled land.

By 1987 the Palestinians' resentment was growing. First, their problems appeared to have been relegated to a position of secondary importance at the Arab League summit in Jordan in November. Secondly, Palestinians in the Occupied Territories were feeling abandoned to some extent by the PLO hierarchy. Palestinian youth was becoming disenchanted with the apathy of its elders, particularly when compared with the success of the Southern Lebanese Shi'ites against Israeli forces there. The example of a lone Palestinian fighter who flew by hang-glider into northern Israel and killed six Israeli soldiers before being killed himself did much to encourage belligerency. The spark that led to the Intifada, or uprising, in December 1987 was a traffic accident at a Gaza crossing points in which four Arabs were killed by an Israeli vehicle. Initially, the Intifada was spontaneous and essentially homegrown; it quickly spread from Gaza to East Jerusalem and the West Bank. The Israelis were caught by surprise and reacted with ill-conceived measures of violence, which were soon broadcast across the world. Palestinian morale was boosted and a good deal of sympathy worldwide generated. Coping with the Intifada was not what the Israeli Army had been trained or equipped for, nor did it see it as its proper role; the general staff soon made it clear that there was no military solution and that a political one must be found. A number of Israelis realised for the first time that they could not occupy the territories forever.

The first moves towards solving the Palestinian problem came as part of the Camp David Accords of 1989, when the Egyptian-Israeli peace treaty was negotiated, in which the Israelis committed themselves to moving towards autonomy for the Palestinians. However, the Shamir government made no attempt to implement this. Next, at the end of the Gulf War a conference jointly chaired by the US and Russia was held in Madrid at which the Palestinians came as part of the Jordanian delegation. At the conference the US assured all parties that it sought a Palestinian autonomy agreement lasting five years and that in the agreement's third year talks on its final status would start. The main conclusion of the conference was that bilateral talks should be initiated between Israel and Arab countries, and it was agreed to hold a number of follow-on conferences, including one to be convened in Washington involving Israel, Jordan and the Palestinians. For all the effort, no progress was achieved.

At the end of August 1993 it was revealed that secret talks had been taking place between the Israeli government and the PLO in Oslo and that they had agreed to recognise each other. In September Prime Minister Yitzhan Rabin and Chairman Yasser Arafat exchanged letters in which the PLO recognised the State of Israel's right to exist in peace and security and renounced the use of terrorism and violence. Rabin responded that Israel recognised the PLO as the representative of the Palestinian people and would start negotiations with them. On the 13th, a 'Declaration of Principles on Interim Self-Government Arrangements' (Oslo I) was signed at the White House.

The aim of the declaration was to establish a Palestinian Interim Self-Government Authority and to hold elections for a council to govern the West Bank and Gaza in respect of all matters except those being reserved to the permanent status negotiations. These included: Jerusalem, settlements, refugees, security arrangements and borders. The transitional period was not to exceed five years. The principles also included provisions for the handover of certain civil responsibilities, such as health and education; the redeployment of Israeli forces; the formation of a

Palestinian refugees			
	Camps	Registered	In Camps
Jordan	10	1,541,405	277,555
Lebanon	12	378,440	205,233
Syria	10	378,382	110,427
West Bank	19	576,160	155,365
Gaza	8	808,495	442,542
Total	59	3,677,382	1,154,512

The Gaza Strip showing Israeli settlements and controlled roads.

Palestinian Police Force; and the withdrawal from the Gaza Strip and Jericho area. Despite a number of horrifying terrorist incidents, which included the killing of thirty Palestinians at prayer in the Hebron Tomb of Abraham Mosque by an Israeli extremist followed by two bombs which killed thirteen Israelis, an 'Agreement on the Gaza Strip and Jericho' was signed in Cairo on 4 May 1994. Israeli troops withdrew and Jericho was handed over to the Palestine National Authority (PNA) on the 15th and Gaza the next day.

'The Israeli-Palestinian Interim Agreement on the West Bank and Gaza Strip' (Oslo II) was initialled in Washington on 28 September 1995. The agreement divided the West Bank into five zones: East Jerusalem (annexed by Israel), Israeli settlements to remain under Israeli control and Areas A, B, and C. In Area A the PNA is responsible for security and all Israeli troops are withdrawn, in Area B responsibility for security is shared by Israel and the PNA, and in Area C Israel retains full security control. The PNA is responsible for civil administration in Areas A, B, and C. Initially Area A comprised six of the main Arab towns, which were handed over by the end of 1995. The inclusion of Hebron was delayed while negotiations on how much of the city Israel would retain in order to protect the small Jewish settlement in its centre were carried out.

The process was then interrupted by two events. First came the assassination of Prime Minister Rabin on 4 November 1995 by an Israeli extremist, following which his successor, Shimon Peres, decide to call elections. Secondly, there was the killing of leading Palestinian bomb-maker Yehiya Ayash, 'the Engineer', on 5 January 1996 by means of a booby-trapped mobile telephone; this led to a series of reprisal attacks by suicide bombers who killed fifty-six Israelis. Voting for safety rather than security, the Israelis elected Benjamin Netanyahu as Prime Minister and the Likud returned to government; the peace process virtually came to a halt. Not until January 1997 was the main part of Hebron handed over to the PNA, nine months after the scheduled date. Israel retained control of Abraham's Tomb and about 20 per cent of the city, where 30,000 Palestinians live, so as to protect 500 Israeli settlers. The Hebron agreement included, among other matters, the withdrawal of Israeli forces in three stages from the whole West Bank except for Israeli settlements, the security roads linking them to Israel and as yet undefined military areas. Two Israeli offers for the first stage of withdrawal were rejected by the PNA as being too small.

The deadlock appeared to be broken by the Wye Memorandum agreed by the Israeli Prime Minister and Chairman Arafat on 23 October 1998 after a week of hard negotiating at President Clinton's insistence at the Wye Plantation in Maryland. The agreement included: an Israeli release of several hundred Palestinian prisoners; a timetable for the arrest by the Palestinians, supervised by the CIA, of alleged terrorists and confiscation of illegal weapons; an Israeli troop withdrawal from a further 13 per cent of the West Bank, of which 3 per cent is to be declared a nature reserve; the opening of Gaza airport, which took place on 3 November. Most importantly for Israel the Palestinian National Council was to meet and vote to confirm the annulment of the anti-Israeli clauses in the PLO Charter; this took place in the presence of President Clinton on 14 December. Initially there was a two-week delay while Prime Minister Netanyahu insisted that the Wye Memorandum be ratified by the Israeli cabinet and then by the parliament, the Knesset. The memorandum was ratified in the cabinet by 7 votes to 5 with three abstentions and two absences and in the Knesset by 75 to 19 with 9 abstentions and 16 members not voting.

The first stage of the troop withdrawal took place on 20 November when the PNA took full control (Area A) of 7.1 per cent more of the West Bank. The Wye Memorandum was then halted following a speech by

The city of Hebron showing the area of Israeli control.

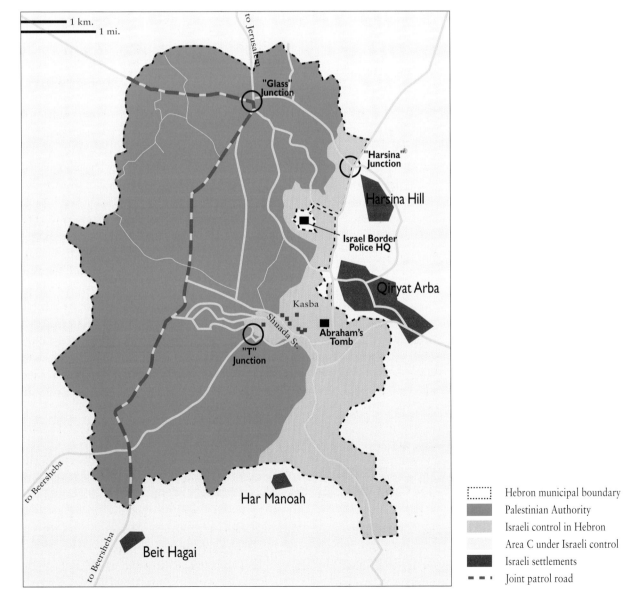

Map legend:
- Hebron municipal boundary
- Palestinian Authority
- Israeli control in Hebron
- Area C under Israeli control
- Israeli settlements
- Joint patrol road

Yasser Arafat in which he proclaimed his intention of declaring Palestinian independence on 4 May 1999, the date the five-year transitional period ended. Despite the efforts of President Clinton to hold the Israelis to the deal, the Israeli cabinet set three conditions for the resumption of the Wye agreements. The Palestinian Authority had to: renounce its intention of unilaterally declaring an independent state; halt violence and incitement; collect and destroy illegal weapons, and detain murderers and cooperate with Israel.

The Palestine peace process took on a new lease of life with the Israeli election of May 1999 which made Ehud Barak Prime Minister. A summit meeting was held at Sharm el Sheikh in September 1999 at which Barak committed Israel to carrying out the withdrawals agreed to at Wye by the Netanyahu government. The final-status talks were to begin straight away with the aim of creating a framework agreement by 15 February 2000 and getting final agreement by September. It is now clear that there will be a Palestinian state, but its borders remain to be decided. These will depend on Israeli demands to retain most but by no means all settlements under Israeli sovereignty; it is possible that land in Israel will be handed over to the Palestinians in exchange. The Palestinians have not rejected this idea. Israel must also decide whether it wants to have a 'hard' border with Palestine or one that allows freedom of movement for workers and for trade. In the latter case, Israel would want to have an element of control on the borders between Gaza and Egypt and the West Bank and Jordan (a much shorter distance to control).

Bibliography and Web Sites

Safieh, Afif, *The Peace Process: From Breakthrough to Breakdown?* Palestinian General Delegation to the UK, 1997

Schiff, Ze'ev, Ahmad Khalidi, Hussein Agha. *Common Ground on Redeployment of Israeli Forces in the West Bank*, Initiative for Peace and Cooperation in the Middle East, 1995

Israel, The West Bank and Gaza: Toward a Solution, Jaffee Centre for Strategic Studies, 1989

Report on Israeli Settlement in the Occupied Territories (Bimonthly), Foundation for Middle East Peace, Washington

Strategic Survey (Annually), International Institute for Strategic Studies

West Bank and Gaza: Israel's Options for Peace, Jaffee Centre for Strategic Studies, 1989

WWW.

Applied Research Institute for Jerusalem: www.arij.org
Foundation for Middle East Peace, Settlement Report: www.fmep.org
Israel/Palestine Center for Research and Information: www.ipcri.org
Palestinian Academic Society for the Study of International Affairs: www.passia.org

JERUSALEM: THE FINAL PROBLEM

The future status of Jerusalem, claimed by both Israelis and Palestinians as their historical capital, has been deliberately left as the final problem to be solved in the Arab-Israeli peace process. The hope is that if everything else has been satisfactorily concluded then all that has been achieved will not be thrown away because agreement cannot be reached over the city.

Jerusalem is holy to all three monotheist religions and all three have fought to regain it for their faith: the Crusaders recovered it from the

Fatimids for Christianity in 1099; Saladin and the Saracens regained it for Islam in 1190 following the defeat of Crusaders at the battle of Hattin; the Israelis held the western half of Jerusalem in 1948 during the War of Independence, completed its capture in 1967, and ever since have maintained it is the indivisible capital of Israel.

The origins of Jerusalem have not been firmly established. The earliest evidence of occupation is pottery found in tombs in the area now known as Ophel and dated to 3200 BC. It became a Canaanite city and at some stage was inhabited by people whom the Bible calls Jebusites. There is evidence that the city was called Rushalimum (inscriptions on broken vases found at Luxor and dated to 1878–42 BC). Any dispute over the ownership of Jerusalem must begin with its capture, probably around 1000 BC, by David who was the first king of both Israel and Judah, the two nations established by the Jews after their arrival in the 'promised' land.

Jewish control of Jerusalem, whether under a united Israel or a separate Judah, lasted until its capture by the Babylonian, Nebuchadnezzar, in 597 BC. Control of Jerusalem and the Holy Land then passed in turn to the Persians, Alexander the Great, the Ptolemies and the Seleucids. In 167 BC the revolt by the Maccabeans recovered Jerusalem for the Jews but only until 63 BC when it was taken after a siege by the Romans. With the exception of the two Jewish revolts – the first in AD 66 and the second, or Bar Kochba revolt, in AD 131 – the Romans and their Byzantine successors ruled the Holy Land until the Muslim conquest when Jerusalem fell in the winter of AD 636/7.

The Crusaders drove out the Muslims in 1099 and Christians ruled Jerusalem until 1187 when Saladin took the city. Muslim rule by the Ayyubids, Mamelukes and Ottomans continued until the First World War when General Allenby entered Jerusalem at the end of 1917. The British were given a mandate to govern Palestine and did so until May 1948 when

Jerusalem: population	
1948	
Jews	100,000
Muslim	40,000
Christian	25,000
1967	
Jews	199,000
Muslims	54,000
Christians	11,000
1999	
Jews	421,500
Arabs	180,630

Jerusalem, the walls of the old city with David's Tower to the left.

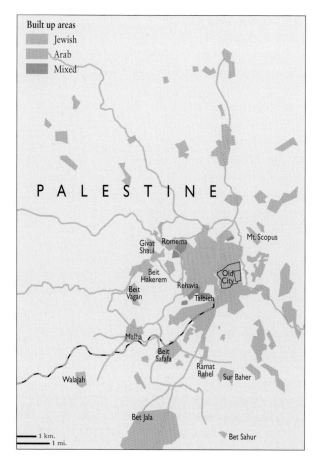

Left: *Jerusalem, 1948*; right:
Jerusalem, 1967.

Israel gained its independence. The United Nations partition plan envisaged Jerusalem becoming an international zone. In 1948 Jerusalem was the scene of bitter fighting both in the city and on the supply route from Tel Aviv, and was at times cut off from Israeli-held territory; the Arabs captured the Jewish quarter in the Old City. An armistice was reached with the Jordanians in 1949 which left Jerusalem divided: the western or modern part was held by the Israelis and the eastern half and the Old City by the Jordanians. It is claimed that some 60,000 Palestinians were displaced from their homes in West Jerusalem. A number of Jewish settlements around Jerusalem were overrun by the Jordanians and destroyed; they have now been re-established.

In 1967 the Israelis sent a message to the Jordanians: 'We shall take no action against Jordan unless Jordan attacks us first'. It was ignored: King Hussein said later that 'he knew he would lose but had no alternative but to join the Arab assault'. Nevertheless, after heavy fighting, Israel captured and reunited Jerusalem. In June 1967 Israel extended the municipal boundaries in all directions; the Jewish quarter was reoccupied, extended and rebuilt. The Haram Ash Sharif, or Temple Mount, was left under the charge of the Islamic Waqf and Jews were forbidden to pray on the Mount. Since then Israel has built a circle of dense housing virtually all round the city, most of which is on land that formed part of the West Bank and where some 176,000 Israelis now live. Israelis have also managed to buy property and land in Palestinian quarters of Jerusalem, such as Silwan and Ras al Amoud. In 1995 permission was given for development on one of the few remaining open spaces around Jerusalem – Har Homa (to Israelis), Jabal Abu Ghneim (to Palestinians) – between the outskirts of the city and Bethlehem. The Labour government halted the development after land clearance had begun but the Likud government gave the go ahead in late 1996. Building is still in progress.

That the international community does not share Israel's view of its right to rule over an undivided Jerusalem can be seen in the fact that virtually no foreign embassies have been opened in Jerusalem; these remain firmly in Tel Aviv requiring their ambassadors to make frequent journeys to Jerusalem. Most consulates in the city have always seen themselves as embassies to the Palestinian population whether in Jerusalem or the West Bank. The US Congress, however, supports Israel's claim and in June 1997 voted virtually unanimously in favour of a resolution declaring Jerusalem to be the eternal and undivided capital of Israel; it also voted $100 million to fund the move of the US Embassy from Tel Aviv to Jerusalem. As yet the embassy has not moved.

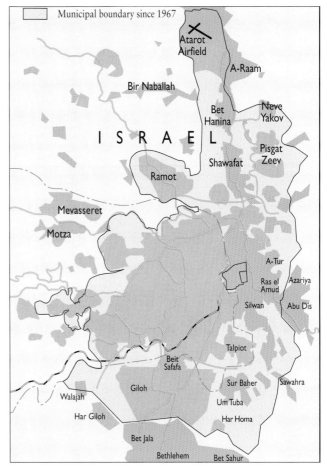

Jerusalem 2000.

There is no doubt that the Palestinian population of Jerusalem has been badly treated by the Israeli authorities. East Jerusalem has been starved of funds to update public utilities, planning permission for new building by Palestinians is hard to get and many unauthorised buildings have been demolished. A welcome development is the decision by the Israeli Interior Minister, Nathan Scharansky, to rescind the regulation that deprived Palestinian Jerusalemites of the right to reside there once they had been absent for seven years.

It will not be easy to mediate an equitable solution to the problem of Jerusalem which will be acceptable to both moderate Israelis and Palestinians, let alone any of the hard-liners. In mid-1999 it was rumoured that Prime Minister Barak and Chairman Arafat had reached a provisional agreement over Jerusalem in which no land would be handed to the Palestinians. They would, however, have authority over Jerusalem's 150,000 Palestinians and the Islamic holy sites. In return, Israel would not oppose Palestinian statehood and would agree that Abu Dis, which lies 2 miles east of Jerusalem, could be the Palestinian capital.

Bibliography

Armstrong, Karen, *A History of Jerusalem: One City, Three Faiths*, HarperCollins, 1996

Karmi, Ghada (ed.), *Jerusalem Today: What Future for the Peace Process?*, Garnet Publishing, 1996

Jerusalem File (Bimonthly), The International Campaign for Jerusalem

Israeli water use (million cubic metres)		
	Fresh	Recycled
1990		
Agriculture	860	380
Domestic	650	—
Industry	—	40
Overall Total		1,930
2000		
Agriculture	820	430
Domestic	768	—
Industry	100	45
Overall Total		2,153
2010		
Agriculture	550	767
Domestic	970	—
Industry	131	50
Overall Total		2,468

WATER: ISRAEL'S GREATEST SHORTAGE

Throughout the Middle East water is one of the scarcest resources. It is, therefore, a constant factor influencing every country's security. None more so than Israel where most sources of water originate beyond its pre-1967 borders. The problem is heightened by Israel's very high rate of consumption, far greater per capita than that of its Arab neighbours. Israelis use, for all purposes, 344 cubic metres per head per annum compared to 94 for West Bank Palestinians and 205 for Jordanians. The problem can only get worse as the population rises. Israel's current supply is some 2 billion cubic metres a year, including brackish water and retreated sewage, both used for agriculture. Domestic consumption is increasing by 30 million cubic metres a year.

There have been a number of plans for the use of the waters of the Jordan and Yarmouk. Chaim Weizman realised that water would be essential to any Zionist state and he called on the Paris peace conference of 1919 to include the Litani and the southern and western slopes of Mount Hermon in Palestine. David Ben-Gurion, Prime Minister 1948–53 and 1955–63, also wanted the Litani to be in Israel; there have been suspicions of Israeli ambitions ever since. In 1926 the British granted the Jewish Palestine Electricity Corporation the use of the Jordan and Yarmouk rivers at the expense of Arab farmers. In 1936 a hydrologist, Ionides, recommended the diversion of the Yarmouk and the Jordan into the Ghor Canal, which runs parallel to and east of the Jordan and is used to irrigate the Jordan Valley. His plan was frustrated by the electricity concession. Other plans were proposed: that of Walter Clay Loudermilk included the first suggestion for a canal from the Mediterranean to the Dead Sea, which is now being reconsidered.

In the 1950s President Eisenhower sent Eric Johnston as a special envoy to solve the water conflict. He proposed a plan prepared by Charles Main but this was rejected by both Arabs and Israelis who then proceeded to prepare their own proposals. Their two plans naturally favoured themselves and Johnston negotiated to take both into account. This resulted in the Main plan being altered in Israel's favour. While the Arab Technical Committee accepted the revised plan it was rejected by the Arab League for political reasons.

Israel has two main sources of water – the River Jordan and the West Bank aquifers. The Jordan is fed in the north by three sources: the Hasbani, which rises in Lebanon and discharges 150 million cubic metres a year; the Dan, which rises in the northern tip of Israel discharging 250 million cubic metres; and the Banias, which rises in Israeli-occupied Syria and discharges 110 million cubic metres. The Upper Jordan feeds the Sea of Galilee which is Israel's main reservoir and is also fed by its own springs, some of which are saline – the water from the latter is capped and led away. The Sea of Galilee loses between 160 and 270 million cubic metres a year through evaporation. Just south of the sea, the Yarmouk flows into the Jordan down the Syrian-Jordanian border. The Yarmouk discharges between 450 and 475 million cubic metres annually. Syrian plans to build a dam on the Yarmouk were frustrated by Israeli military action in the mid-1960s because the scheme included the diversion of water from the Banias. The Israelis attacked the Banias project sites in March and May 1965 and in July 1966. Israel takes between 350 and 500 million cubic metres annually from the Upper Jordan as it reaches the Sea of Galilee from where it is piped down as far as the Negev desert by the National Water Carrier, the construction of which was completed in 1964.

The importance of agreement on water resources was demonstrated by the inclusion of the Israeli commitment to concede a greater share of the Yarmouk to Jordan in the peace treaty signed in 1994. The agreement was for a finite quantity (40 million cubic metres annually) rather than a percentage and Israel was accused of violating the peace treaty when it found it was unable to provide the full amount due to the severe drought experienced during the winter of 1998/9 when allocations to Israeli farmers had to be cut by 25 per cent. No doubt water resources will also feature in any Israeli-Syrian and Israeli-Lebanese peace treaties. The commitment to cooperation in the field of water management is included in an annex to the Declaration of Principles on Interim Self-Government Arrangements signed by Israel and the PLO in Washington on 13 September 1993.

However, reaching agreement over control of the West Bank aquifers, on which both Israel and the Palestinian Authority depend, will be difficult. At present Israel gets about one-quarter of its water from the West Bank aquifers. The present arrangements are hardly fair to the Palestinian population but allowing uncontrolled drawing of water from the aquifers would lead to the salination of Israel's coastal aquifer. The latest estimates show that some 1.48 billion cubic metres are being taken from the aquifers each year but that replenishment provides only 1.25 billion cubic metres. Israel will want to continue its control of the West Bank aquifers and this will affect the amount of land it will be prepared to hand back to the Palestine Authority; hard bargaining lies ahead. One report claims that Israel must retain control of a western strip of the West Bank which at places will be up to 15 kilometres east of the Green Line.

The Dan Springs, Israel's source of the Jordan.

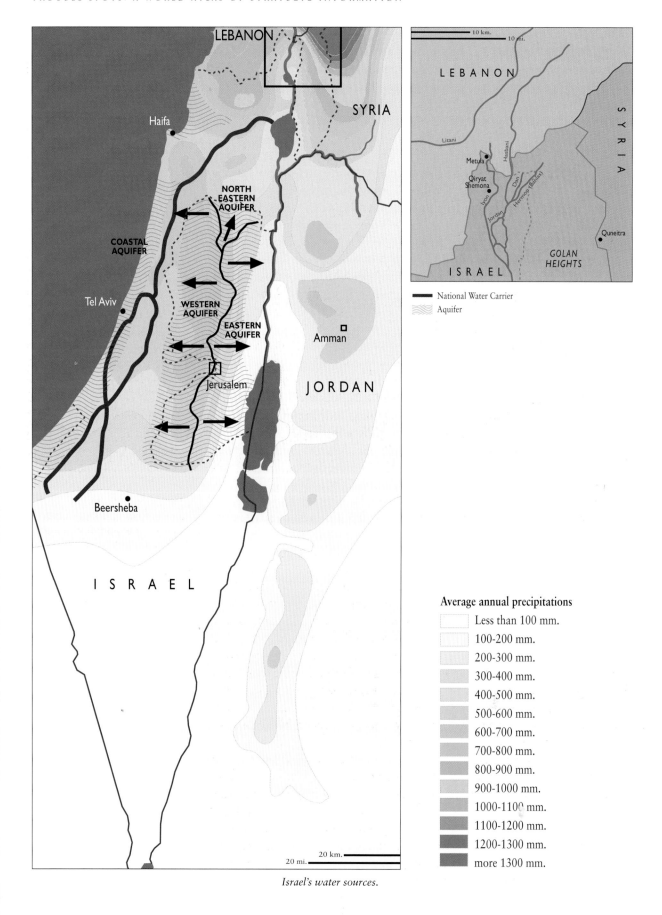

National Water Carrier

Aquifer

Average annual precipitations

	Less than 100 mm.
	100-200 mm.
	200-300 mm.
	300-400 mm.
	400-500 mm.
	500-600 mm.
	600-700 mm.
	700-800 mm.
	800-900 mm.
	900-1000 mm.
	1000-1100 mm.
	1100-1200 mm.
	1200-1300 mm.
	more 1300 mm.

Israel's water sources.

However, Israel has already withdrawn from some territory over the aquifers.

A number of ambitious schemes for solving the water shortage, not just for Israel but for the Palestinians and Jordan too, have been suggested. The simplest, but one that would be vulnerable to interference by Syria, is a 'peace pipeline' bringing water from Turkey. Water could also be brought from Turkey by large plastic dracones. Two canals to the Dead Sea, one from Elat on the Red Sea and one from the Mediterranean, have been proposed. The electricity generated by the drop of roughly 400 metres would be used to desalinate the water going through the system. Desalination employing a nuclear power reactor could be employed but the suspicions over any nuclear activity could preclude this option. It would be a prime strategic target should war re-occur. Plans are being prepared to desalinate 50 million cubic metres a year, but no plant will be operating before 2003.

The water requirements for both Israel and the territory of the Palestine Authority are rising yearly, mainly due to population increase. The most critical area is the Gaza Strip which has one of the highest population growth rates in the world. For peace to be sustained between Israel and the Palestinians water must be shared equitably and this will certainly mean finding new sources whether by desalination or large-scale imports. It is also clear that any attempts to reduce Israel's water supply from Lebanon or Syria could start a water war.

Looking south over Israel's water reservoir – the Kinneret or Sea of Galilee. (Zev Radovan)

Bibliography

Berschorner, Natasha, *Water and Instability in the Middle East*, IISS Adelphi Paper 273, 1992

de Villiers, Marq, *Water Wars: Is the World's Water Running Out?*, Weidenfeld & Nicolson, 1999

Elmusa, Sharif, 'The Jordan-Israeli Water Agreement: A Model or an Exception?' *Journal of Palestine Studies* XXIV (3), 1995

Kliot, Nurit, *Water Resources and Conflict in the Middle East*, Routledge, 1994

Soffer, Arnon, *Rivers of Fire: The Conflict Over Water in the Middle East*, Rowman & Littlefield, 1999

Low, Miriam, *West Bank Water Resources and the Resolution of Conflict in the Middle East*, Princeton University, 1992

IRAQ: AFTER SADDAM, CAN IT SURVIVE UNDIVIDED?

Iraqi population by race	
Arab	80 per cent
Kurd	20 per cent

Population by religion	
Sunni Muslim	45 per cent
Shi'a Muslim	55 per cent

Iraq has only been a state since the end of the First World War when the Ottoman Empire was broken up. The territory between the Euphrates and the Tigris has been important throughout history, whether as Sumeria, Assyria, Babylonia or Mesopotamia (the land between the rivers) in Alexander's empire and to the invading British forces during the First World War.

In the early third century AD the Persians forced the Romans west of the Euphrates. In 651 the Persians were defeated by the Arabs and Mesopotamia and Syria became a single Arab province. The Persians reoccupied Baghdad in 945 and Shi'a Islam dominated Mesopotamia until defeated by the Seldjuks, who had adopted Sunni Islam, in the eleventh century. They took Baghdad in 1055. Following a period of rule by the Mongol Tamerlane, the Persians took Baghdad and then Mosul in 1508 and an attempt was made to re-establish the Shi'a persuasion. In 1534 the Ottoman Sultan Suleiman failed to conquer Persia but, encouraged by a Sunni revolt, marched on Baghdad leaving only Basra and the extreme south to be occupied four years later. In the first three centuries of Ottoman rule the three provinces were governed as one entity from Baghdad, Mosul becoming separated in 1879 and Basra in 1884.

In 1865 the Turks attempted to gain more power in Arabia following a conflict over the Saudi succession, and Britain strengthened its ties with Bahrain. By the end of the century Britain, whose aim was to protect communications with its Indian empire and guarantee supplies of oil to fuel the navy, had realised the strategic importance of Kuwait and in 1899 signed an agreement to protect the Sheikh. He promised that neither he nor his heirs would in anyway hand over any part of the sheikhdom to another power without British consent. The seeds of the Iraqi-Kuwait dispute were sown.

The French and the British divided the Middle East between them in the Sykes-Picot Agreement of 1916, the provisions of which were kept secret from the Arabs who were being encouraged to revolt against the Turks. The British captured Baghdad in March 1917, and Kirkuk in May but withdrew two weeks later because priority was to be given to General Allenby's campaign in Palestine. Kirkuk was re-occupied in October 1918 and the Armistice came into effect at noon on 31 October. The Armistice terms included the surrender of all Turkish troops in Mesopotamia but immediately there was disagreement because the Turks claimed that the Mosul province was not part of Mesopotamia. At a conference held on 7 November the Turks reluctantly agreed to withdraw from Mosul.

The Cairo Conference of 1921 confirmed the basic elements of the Sykes-Picot agreement. Mesopotamia was renamed Iraq and Feisal, who had expected to rule Syria, agreed to be the Iraqi king under strict British supervision. The British retained full control over the Kurdish area that had been recognised as an independent state by the Treaty of Sèvres in 1920. Britain, and particularly the India Office, hoped to keep Iraq as a colony with a compliant ruler; the first Anglo-Iraqi Treaty was signed in October 1922. However, before the agreement there were numerous revolts and the British forces were too weak and too dispersed to defend all their garrisons. Then after reinforcement and using air power and gas the British crushed the revolt.

At the end of 1922 the Turks advanced into Mosul but were driven back by the British air force. At the Allied-Turkish Peace Conference at Lausanne the Turks made demands to recover Mosul; this was not agreed. In the Treaty there was no mention of Kurdistan and the Kurds were split between five states. Iraq was therefore formed by the Treaty of Lausanne from three Ottoman provinces: Mosul, Baghdad and Basra. In the south the population was mainly of the Shi'a persuasion while elsewhere there were Sunnis. In the north-east lived the hated Kurds, numbering some 700,000.

In 1925 the League of Nations, after a commission of inquiry whose recommendation was backed by the Court of International Justice, awarded Mosul to Iraq on condition that the British protected the Kurds until 1950. A second Anglo-Iraqi Treaty in 1930 allowed that Britain would continue to oversee foreign policy and army training. The Treaty protected British oil interests and allowed two military bases to be maintained. At the same time many of the mandatory responsibilities were dropped on account of their cost. In the 1930s there were a number of coups, culminating in General Nuri al-Said seizing power in 1938; he was pro-British and broke off relations with Germany at the start of the Second World War. In March 1940 Nuri was replaced by the anti-British Rashid Ali al-Gilani who refused to give Britain more bases in Iraq. In 1941 fighting broke out between the British and Iraqis, who had a small amount of German air support. Eventually Rashid fled to Iran and Nuri was reinstated as Prime Minister. He remained part of the government until 1958. Brigadier Abdul Karim Kassem had formed a 'Free Officers' organisation, similar to that in Egypt. On 14 July 1958 Kassem entered Baghdad, seized power killing both the king and Nuri and declared Iraq a republic.

The Ba'ath movement had been founded in Syria in 1947; it was devoted to the cause of pan-Arabism. The Iraqi Ba'ath Party was founded in 1951 but was slow to gain much support. In March 1959, with Syrian and Egyptian help, it fostered a revolt in Mosul that was brutally crushed by the Iraqi Army; this was not the only attempt at revolt between 1958 and 1963.

In June 1961 Kassem claimed Kuwait as a part of Iraq and demanded its return. Only the support given by other Gulf states and the deployment of British troops and armour ended Kassem's plan to invade Kuwait. Kassem was overthrown in February 1963 in a coup led by the Ba'ath

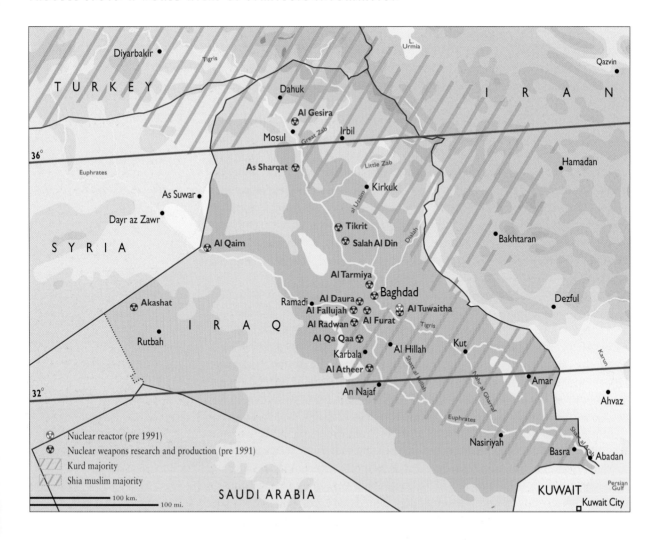

Iraq, showing its nuclear facilities and the areas populated by Shi'a and Kurds.

Chemical weapon production (as declared by Iraq)	
CW agent (in tons)	
Precursors (no evidence)	20,000+
Agents produced (no evidence)	3,850
Fired 1981–8 (no evidence)	2,870
Destroyed by UNSCOM	690
Claimed destroyed by bombing (no evidence)	290
Delivery munitions (quantity)	
Total produced (100,000+ not accounted for)	247,263
Total filled with CW	152,119
Expended 1981–8 (no evidence to support claim)	101,080
Unilateral destruction (15,260 not verified)	29,172
Destroyed by UNSCOM	38,537
Claimed destroyed by bombing (no evidence for 16,000)	78,264

Party accompanied by a wave of mass arrests and executions, particularly of communists. The new regime did not last long and was overthrown in an army coup in November.

Saddam Hussein had joined the Ba'ath Party in 1957; in 1958 he was a member of a team that attempted but failed to assassinate General Kassem. Saddam was wounded and escaped to Syria. He then remained in Egypt until 1963, returning to Iraq after Kassem's death. He went underground in November 1963 and was arrested and imprisoned in October 1964 but later escaped. By 1966 he had become the deputy secretary of the party and in 1968, after a second, this time successful, Ba'ath coup, he became Deputy Chairman of the Revolutionary Command Council responsible for internal security. As such, he built up a number of security organisations and organised a series of purges. Saddam declared himself President on 17 July 1979 and carried out a massive purge of the party.

At the end of the Gulf War, which broke out after Iraq invaded and occupied Kuwait in 1991, the people of Iraq were encouraged to rise up and overthrow Saddam and his regime. Initially the uprisings were successful both in the northern Kurdish area and among the Shi'a in the south, who it was suspected received help from Iran. But the rebels found that they had no support from the US whose President had encouraged them to overthrow Saddam. Saddam then brutally put down the insurrection, first in the south, where the rebels had managed to seize a number of cities, before turning to deal with the Kurds. The repression resulted in a mass movement of refugees. The Shi'a fled to Iran and into the marshes south-east of Basra. The Kurds fled in large numbers into the mountains on the Iraq-Turkey-Iran borders; the television pictures of their plight led to the deployment of an international force to establish 'safe havens' for them. After the force was withdrawn, Allied air units were based in Turkey to monitor a no-fly zone declared north of the 36th parallel. A similar no-fly zone south of the 32nd parallel is monitored by aircraft based in Kuwait and Saudi Arabia. Although the Iraqis were forbidden to fly in these two zones, protecting the populations from air attack, no action was taken against tanks and artillery used against them. The no-fly zones are still in force and Allied planes attack any Iraqi air defence elements that threaten them.

As part of formal ceasefire terms agreed at the end of the Gulf War Iraq had to declare the extent of its nuclear, CBW and missile programmes and facilities and allow these to be destroyed. Its compliance was to be monitored by teams from the International Atomic Energy Agency (IAEA) and the UN Special Commission (UNSCOM). Despite the success achieved by the IAEA and UNSCOM in eliminating Iraq's capability, now that UNSCOM no longer carries out its monitoring mission there are concerns that Iraq is attempting to reacquire CBW. The extent of Iraq's weapons of mass destruction programme is set out in the margin here and is discussed in the section entitled 'Military Reach: Too Late to Stop Proliferation' on pages 154–6.

While virtually everyone agrees that Saddam Hussein should be removed from office there is no one outside his own clique who could take over and hold the country together. And the replacement would, presumably, have to be even more ruthless than Saddam in order to establish his leadership. There have been reports of several attempted coups by generals but on each occasion they have been betrayed: it will be a brave man who tries again. There are numerous opposition parties, said to number ninety-one, all based abroad, but there is no agreement between them. Nor is there any leader with the charisma needed to mount a successful opposition campaign from abroad, despite the backing of $97 million in credit and surplus military equipment voted by the US Congress for this purpose. In November 1999 the US administration announced the provision of the first $5 million of military equipment and training for the Iraqi opposition. The Kurdish opposition though split has the greatest strength but it already has a virtually autonomous region and, given Turkish opposition to any Kurdish state, is likely to be content with that. For the moment it seems that Iraq and the world is stuck with Saddam Hussein and this is perhaps preferable to the conflicts that might break out should he lose control and the country break up into its three component parts. Iraq, though, is naturally keen to be reconciled with its Arab neighbours and to have sanctions lifted. The former could be achieved if Iraq was prepared to apologise for its invasion of Kuwait, accept the blame and pay the necessary reparations. It has been suggested that Iraq may make a number of symbolic moves to gain international approval and these would include: Saddam stepping down in favour of his son Qusai and liberalising its internal politics (neither likely to

---

Nuclear facilities pre-1991

Baghdad: research and development for lithium

Al Gesira: production of uranium dioxide, uranium tetrachloride and feed material for electromagnetic isotope separation (EMIS)

As Sharqat: EMIS

Tikrit: weapon components

Salah Al Din: weapon components

El Qaim: phosphate plant producing uranium concentrate

Akashat: uranium mine

Al Daura: reactor components and high pressure equipment

Al Furat: centrifuge production, planned site for experimental cascade

Al Fallujah: high temperature ovens

Al Radwan: weapon components

Al Qa Qaa: explosives, including exploding bridge wire detonators and storage of HMX

Al Atheer: main research and development site, computer simulation, uranium metallurgy

Al Tuwaitha: research reactor, enrichment research and development, experimental lithium production

Al Tarmiya: EMIS (8 units operational before bombing)

Opposition parties in exile (designated under the US Iraq Liberation Act)

Iraqi National Accord
Iraqi National Congress
Islamic Movement for Iraqi Kurdistan
Movement for Constitutional Monarchy
Kurdistan Democratic Party
Patriotic Union of Kurdistan
Supreme Council for the Islamic Revolution in Iraq

make much difference); and starting peace negotiations with Israel and taking in large numbers of Palestinian refugees. Lifting sanctions is a matter for the UN Security Council where three permanent members are in favour so long as a new arms inspection regime is accepted by Iraq.

Bibliography and Web Site

Longrigg, Stephen, *Iraq: 1900 to 1950*, Oxford University Press, 1953
Simons, Geoff, *Iraq: From Sumer to Saddam*, Macmillan, 1994

www.

The Iraq Foundation (Washington): www.iraqfoundation.org

IRAN: ARE THE AYATOLLAHS A THREAT?

Iran, or Persia as it was called before 1906, has a long history as an independent state. The Persians came from Central Asia at much the same time, the third millenium BC, as the Medes and the Hindus. The time of greatest Persian power was the fifth century BC when its empire stretched from the Indus in the east to Thrace and Cyrenaica in the west, and to Samarkand in the north and Elephantine, on the Nile, in the south.

The Persians were conquered by Alexander the Great and after his death Persia became part of the Seleucid Empire. The Roman Empire did not advance into Persia, which broke away from the Seleucids around AD 250. The Arabs conquered the Persians between 642 and 652. When the Persians were converted to Islam they were initially Sunni; in the early sixteenth century the Safavids, who followed the Sufi form of Sunnism, took power and adopted Shi'ism.

In more modern times Iran under the Shah was a strong supporter of the West. It was a member of the Central Treaty Organisation, with Turkey, Pakistan, the US and UK, which formed an eastern extension to NATO. The Shah was overthrown in 1979 and the rule of the ayatollahs began with the return from exile of Ayatollah Khomeini who led the country until his death in 1989. Khomeini instituted a new Islamic constitution that split power between the president and government and the Leader of the Islamic Revolution, who is also Commander-in-Chief of the Armed Forces, and Council of Guardians. Khomeini was succeeded by Ayatollah Ali Khamenei as Supreme Leader and Ayatollah Hashemi Rasfanjani as President, the latter being a pragmatist, who revised the constitution, creating more presidential power. The Supreme Leader remains head of the Revolutionary Guards. The election held in 1997 produced a landslide victory for Mohammad Khatami, a moderate cleric who gained the support of the young and of women. President Khatami has begun a movement to improve relations with both Iran's neighbours and the West.

Do the ayatollahs now in power in Iran present a threat and if so, to whom? The Gulf Arab states feel threatened both militarily and by the Islamic extremism of the Shi'a ayatollahs. The US and to a lesser extent Europeans see a threat from Iran's development of long-range missiles armed with nuclear and CBW warheads and from Iranian-inspired terrorism. The military threat posed by Iran's armed forces today can be overstated: the forces are large in number but as yet not equipped with modern armaments. The air force is credited with some 300 combat aircraft but serviceability is

Iranian population by race	
Persian	37,058,000
Azeri	17,439,000
Gilaki	5,813,000
Kurdish	5,086,000
Arab	2,180,000
Lur	1,453,000
Baluch	1,453,000
Turkmen	1,453,000

considered to be less than 50 per cent and there must be a grave shortage of spares for the 200 aircraft supplied by the US to the Shah over twenty years ago. The Gulf States have twice as many aircraft and these are more modern, better maintained and better armed. The three Iranian submarines acquired from Russia between 1992 and 1997 do represent a threat to shipping in the Persian Gulf and could make transiting the Strait of Hormuz dangerous. However, the Iranian Navy lacks the amphibious shipping to transport the size of force that would be needed to mount an invasion across the Gulf; at present it could lift no more than 1,000 men and 50 tanks. The Iranian Navy is the service that can best challenge the Gulf States but it can never match the force that could be deployed by the US. The conclusion that Iran has aggressive intentions can be drawn from the occupation of the Tunbs which belonged to Ras al-Khaimah in 1971. Iran, with the agreement of Sharjah, also occupied half the island of Abu Musa; in April 1992 it unilaterally took the whole island. During the Iran-Iraq war, begun by Iraq over the control of the Shatt al-Arab waterway, Iranian Revolutionary Guard naval units regularly attacked tankers, mainly those of Saudi Arabia and Kuwait, normally by laying mines in their path. In September 1998 Iran deployed as many as 270,000 troops and Revolutionary Guards on the border with Afghanistan in a show of strength after the murder of Iranian diplomats in Mazar-e-Sharif. Although Iranian troops clashed with Taliban forces, the deployment did not escalate into war.

The threat posed by Shi'a extremism is less easy to quantify. There are Shi'a majorities in southern Iraq and Bahrain and sizeable minorities in Saudi Arabia and Kuwait. There is evidence of Iranian support for Shi'a dissidents in Bahrain, Kuwait and Saudi Arabia but these have made little impact. Iran has had more success in supporting Hizbollah in Lebanon and Hezb e Wahdat in Afghanistan. It has rarely managed to forge alliances with Sunni movements, the only exception being the government of Sudan with whom it reached agreement in April 1995. The agreement included the supply of arms and assistance in training by Iran, the sharing of intelligence and an increase in cultural exchanges. Since the election of Mohammad Khatami as President, Iranian relations with Saudi Arabia are much improved.

At the time of the Iranian Revolution in 1979 the US embassy in Tehran was occupied and the staff held hostage for 444 days. The US mounted a rescue mission that went disastrously wrong. There is, therefore, no love lost between the Iranian regime and the US government, which invariably claims that Iran supports international terrorism (naming Mujahidin Khalq) and is actively developing weapons of mass destruction. It could be said that the US is more of a threat to Iran than Iran is to the US; America has imposed seventeen sanctions on Iran since 1979. The Iran-Libya Sanctions Act penalises foreign firms that invest more than $20 million a year in Iran's energy industry. The US has blocked the construction of an oil pipeline from the Caspian and opened a Radio Free Iran.

Iran's nuclear research programme is detailed at page 34; it is also known to have a CBW programme and was provoked into using CW against Iraq in retaliation for the more extensive use of such weapons by Iraq in the 1980–8 war. Iranian missiles were paraded for the first time on 25 September 1998 in Tehran. Three different, Iranian-built, short-range surface-to-surface missiles (SSM) were seen: all have solid fuel propellant,

Iranian amphibious forces			
Type	No.	Men	Tanks
Landing ship tank	4	225	9
Landing ship medium	3	140	9

Exiled opposition parties
Kurdish Democratic Party
National Council of Resistance
National Front (exile branches)
Republican Nationalists
People's Democratic Party
'Fedayeen Khalq' (Aksariat)
'Fedayeen Khalq' (Aghaliat)
Tudeh Party
The Constitutional Movement of Iran (Front Line)

two have a range of around 150 kilometres and all are available for export. Also on parade was the Shahab 3, successfully tested on 21 July 1998, with a claimed range of 1300 kilometres with a 1000 kilogram payload but with a likely CEP (accuracy) of only 4000 metres; the missile is probably not operational yet. A Shahab 4 is known to be under development, believed to be based on the Soviet SS-4 and with maybe a 2000 kilometres range; the US believes it could be operational within five years. Israel claims that versions with even longer ranges are being developed. The US has identified nine Russian institutes and firms that are assisting in the missile programme. Former Iranian President Hashemi Rafsanjani has claimed that Iran can now develop and manufacture missiles without outside help; it is more likely that some components still have to be imported in violation of the Missile Technology Control Regime (MTCR) regime. The official US position on the missile threat to America is that none is likely to emerge before 2010, but the Rumsfeld Commission believes Iran could be capable of deploying intercontinental missiles in five years.

Iran, showing nuclear plants and facilities.

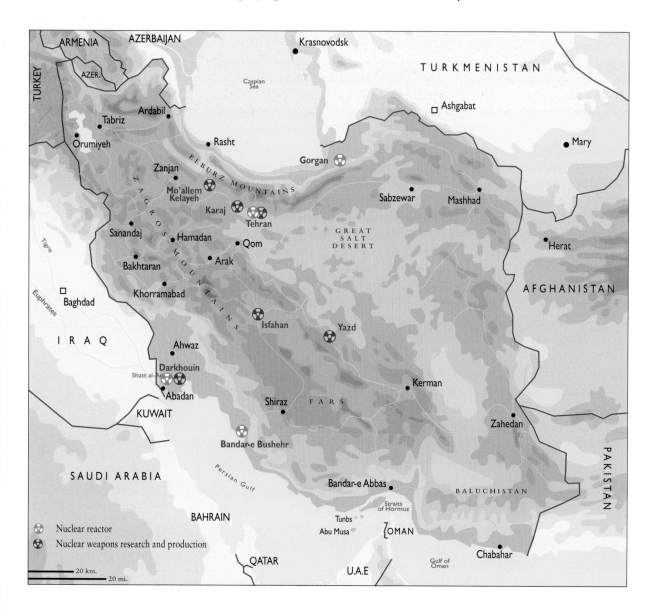

Once Iran has fully developed and deployed long-range missiles, with or without nuclear warheads, it will be able to threaten its neighbours more directly but at present they are making efforts to improve their relations with Iran. As great a threat could be Iranian backing for groups opposed to the feudal rulers in the Arabian Peninsula, but it is unlikely to support democratic groups and most extremist Islamist groups are Sunni rather than Shi'a. The US phobia regarding Iran will ensure that America will continue to protect the Gulf States for many years yet. The ayatollahs pose a threat but it can be overstated.

Iranian Shahab-3 missile on parade in Tehran, September 1998. (Associated Press)

Web Sites

Iranian Embassy London: www.iran-embassy.org.uk
Net Iran (Iranian News): http://.netiran.com

WWW.

SHIFTING SANDS: BORDER PROBLEMS IN THE ARABIAN PENINSULA AND PERSIAN GULF

In a region where for many centuries there have been no demarcated borders and where the sand seas of the desert make these hard to create even when agreement is reached, it is unsurprising that there are a number of unresolved issues. Often border disputes have centred on water and more recently on oil.

United Arab Emirates-Iran

The most serious issue does not concern the desert but islands in the Persian Gulf. In 1971, shortly after the withdrawal of British troops from the Arabian Peninsula, Iran occupied Abu Musa, which was then controlled by Sharjah, and the two Tunbs then controlled by Ras al-Khaimah. The islands are seen as having strategic value by the Iranians because they narrow the approach to the Strait of Hormuz. Both sheikhdoms had been under British protection since the 1820s; they are now both part of the United Arab Emirates (UAE), which was formed in 1971. In the case of Abu Musa the UAE claim to ownership is based on priority of occupation and the hoisting of the Sharjah flag there in 1903 when the island was unoccupied. The Qasemi (now Sharjah) rejects the Iranian claim, arguing that even though an Iranian Sheikh was Governor of Lengeh on the Iranian coast in the eighteenth century this does not entitle Iran to claim Abu Musa now. There are, however, numerous maps dating as far back as 1770 which show the islands to be Iranian.

A memorandum of understanding (MOU) was agreed between Sharjah and Iran in November 1971, splitting the island between the two and the sharing of oil revenue. The MOU opens with the statement that neither Iran nor Sharjah will give up its claim nor recognise the other's claim. Iranian troops deployed to Abu Musa twenty-four hours after the MOU was announced. Sharjah and the UAE have always considered the MOU a temporary arrangement and ownership of Abu Musa has been a source of dispute which has had implications for other Iran-UAE negotiations. The Ras al-Khaimah claim to the Tunbs also dates to 1903 when it occupied the islands, an occupation that Iran has objected to ever since. Iran recovered the Greater Tunb in 1935 but withdrew as a result of British pressure. It occupied both Tunbs at the same time as the occupation of Abu Musa. The UAE, as the follow-on state to Ras al-Khaimah, still claims the Tunbs.

Bahrain-Qatar

Bahrain and Qatar are in dispute over three areas: the Hawar Islands, the islands of Dibal and Jaradah, and Zubarah in north-west Qatar. Resolution of the dispute is made more difficult by the history of the two states which both declared their independence, after British protection, in late 1971. Bahrain and Qatar have agreed the limits of their continental shelves with Iran, Saudi Arabia and Abu Dhabi but cannot agree the limits of their mutual shelves because of the territorial disputes.

Bahrain has been identified as having been under Assyrian, Achmaeminian, Alexandrian and Sassanian rule and at one time included the eastern provinces of Saudi Arabia. Bahrain then came under Arab control until the Portuguese occupation in 1522. The Portuguese were driven out by the Iranian Safavids in 1602. In about 1710 the Utoobee tribe came from the interior of Arabia and settled in Kuwait. Fifty years later the head of the Al-Khalifah clan took his people to Zubarah in the Qatar peninsula to become pearl fishers. The Iranian governor mounted an expedition to bring the Al-Khalifah under control but his force was beaten off and the Al-Khalifah occupied Bahrain Island in 1783. The island changed hands among various Arab leaders between 1783 and the 1880s when Bahrain became a British protectorate. For most of this period Bahrain was ruled from Zubarah, which had always been the seat of government whether Iranian or Bahraini.

The origins of the state of Qatar are tied to the Al-Thani, a branch of the Bani Tamim tribe, who came to Qatar either in the seventeenth century or in 1750. There is Iranian evidence that at times in the first half of the nineteenth century the Al-Thani recognised Al-Khalifah supremacy and paid them taxes. The Al-Thani gained in wealth from pearling and aimed to be paramount on the peninsula. In 1861 the Al-Khalifah were defeated by the British when they attacked Zubarah and the Al-Thani took the opportunity to extend their authority in the peninsula. The population of Zubarah rebelled against the Bahraini Agent there in 1867 but this uprising was crushed by Sheikh Mohammed Kalifa with the help of the ruler of Abu Dhabi. The British then blockaded Bahrain, bombarded it, replaced the Sheikh with his brother, and signed a treaty that led to Bahrain becoming a British protectorate. The Al-Thani also signed a treaty with the British in 1868 that required them to pay tax to the Ruler of Bahrain. This is considered to be the foundation of the state of Qatar; it was recognised when the Sheikh signed a maritime treaty with the British in 1868.

Both the Al-Thani and Al-Khalifah continued to claim Zubarah but the dispute over territory was quiescent until the 1930s. Zubarah has an emotional value to Bahrainis as it is the burial place of the founder of Bahrain and was the headquarters of the Al-Khalifah between 1766 and 1870. The Al-Thani seized Zubarah, now ruined, in 1937. In the 1940s the British negotiated an agreement in which both Bahrain and Qatar undertook not to harm each others interests over Zubarah.

There is also a maritime dispute mainly concerning whether the median line between the two states should take into account the Hawar Islands. At the annual Gulf Cooperation Council summit in December 1990 it was agreed that, unless an out-of-court settlement could be agreed within six months, the dispute would be referred to the International Court of Justice. Qatar applied to the court in July 1991 but Bahrain claimed that a joint injunction was necessary. A joint injunction was submitted and the court decided in July 1994 that the whole dispute should be considered as the Bahrainis enjoined rather than in favour of the Qatar position which omitted Zubarah.

Yemen-Saudi Border

The border dispute between Yemen and Saudi Arabia originates from the 1934 war between the two when Yemen lost the provinces of Asir and

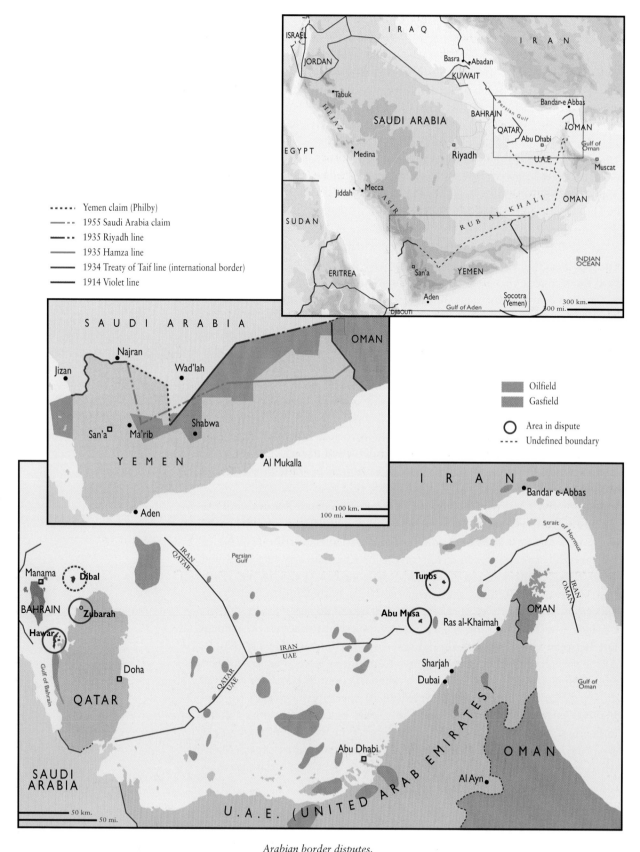

Legend:
- ······ Yemen claim (Philby)
- — · — 1955 Saudi Arabia claim
- — · · — 1935 Riyadh line
- ——— 1935 Hamza line
- ——— 1934 Treaty of Taif line (international border)
- ——— 1914 Violet line

- Oilfield
- Gasfield
- ○ Area in dispute
- - - - Undefined boundary

Arabian border disputes.

Najran. Yemeni nationalists still claim the provinces are theirs. The Treaty of Taif in 1934 demarcated the new border from the coast as far east as the town of Najran: from there to the junction with Oman the border remained undemarcated. Most of this border line was between Saudi Arabia and the British Eastern Aden Protectorate until South Yemen obtained its full independence in 1967. The importance of creating a demarcated border increased with the discovery of oil along its length. Over the years a number of lines have been drawn across the desert, none as yet accepted by either side. The Saudi claim, if upheld, would place a portion of the Marib, most of the Sirr Hazar and all of the North Sanaw oil fields in Saudi hands. There is also a maritime dispute over the position of the maritime border along the northern edge of the Antufash seabed oil field.

Bibliography and Web Site

Burrowes, Robert D., *Historical Dictionary of Yemen*, Scarecrow, 1996

Mojtahed-Zadeh, Pirouz, *Security and Territoriality in the Persian Gulf: A Maritime Political Geography*, Curzon, 1999

Schofield, Richard (ed.), *Territorial Foundations of the Gulf State*, SOAS/GRC Geopolitics Series, UCL, 1994

Gulf States News Letter: www.gulfstates.co.uk

www.

IS ISLAM A THREAT?

Professor Samuel Huntingdon, in *The Clash of Civilisations*, forecasts that future conflicts will be between the seven main civilisations he identifies in today's world: Western, Latin American, African, Islamic, Sinic, Hindu and Japanese. Although he does not say so overtly, the tenor of his analysis is that the most likely civilisation to indulge in conflict is Islam. He quotes various sources to show that a very high proportion of current and recent conflicts have involved Islam on either one side or both. He

The Islamic world.

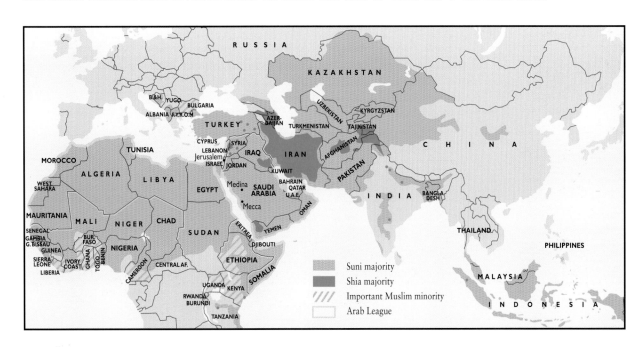

clearly sees Islam as a threat, pointing to its resurgence and the numbers of Muslims turning to a more Islamist way of life and eschewing secularism. Islam is the only religion that is also a political, social and cultural way of life. He also points to the growing success of Islamist movements in becoming the only alternative to existing regimes and, where they have taken power, to the reintroduction of sharia or Islamic Law. Islam is pro-modernisation but against Westernisation. Islam has its own international organisation, the Organisation of the Islamic Conference. No other religion has such a similar body; there has never been, for example, a conference of Christian Defence Ministers nor of Buddhist Agricultural Ministers.

The alternative view is set out by Professor Fred Halliday who considers the threat posed by Islam to be a myth. He acknowledges that there are two 'Islams' – the religion, and the social and political system. He clearly believes there is no unitary Islamist political force. He does not discuss the religion of Islam but states that it is not unitary: it may not be as fractured as Christianity but it is certainly not unitary as the different philosophies of the Sunni and Shi'a persuasions show. Which professor is right?

If Professor Huntington is right, to whom is Islam a threat and what is the nature of that threat? The answer, of course, is that there are many different entities which see Islam as a threat, and the threat to each entity is generally different. Most non-Muslims feel threatened by 'fundamentalism', probably without understanding what fundamentalism is. A better word is 'extremism' and the people most threatened by extremist Islam are those who are secular Muslims or less extreme. In most but not all intra-Muslim conflicts one side is more extreme in its pursuit of Islam than the other. Examples include the Iran-Iraq war, the Algerian and Afghanistan civil wars, the rivalry between Hamas and the Palestinian Authority, and Islamic terrorists in Egypt, Lebanon, Yemen and Karachi. The Iraqi invasion of Kuwait and its use of chemical weapons against its own people at Halabja, and the Syrian massacre of Muslim Brotherhood in Hama are examples of intra-Muslim conflict without religious connotations. In the Arabian Peninsula the contenders for power in place of the feudal rulers are democracy and Islam, with the latter being firm favourite. Certainly Islamic extremism is the enemy of true democracy. In Iran there is a growing split between the extremists and those looking for modernisation. So Islam is as much a threat to itself as to anyone else.

In the wider world there are many examples of Muslim versus non-Muslim conflict. However, a good many of these are more concerned with land than with religion. 'Natives versus immigrants' is the theme of the conflicts between Israel and the Palestinians, in Bosnia, Kosovo and East Timor. There are, of course, similar conflicts over land with no Muslim participation, as in Northern Ireland and Croatia for instance. The United States is an ally to some Muslim states but is opposed to the regimes in others. It feels threatened by Islam more on account of terrorism and the proliferation of weapons of mass destruction. It is true that Islamic extremists see the US as their major enemy and have carried out a number of successful terrorist attacks against American targets. However, a number of Muslim states feel equally or more threatened by the US and

---

Turkish Islamist groups

Militants
Hizbullah (predominantly Sunni)
Maybe up to 4,000 'fighters'. Breakaway group from Kurdish Islamist movement.

Islamic Great East Raiders Front
Attacks symbols of the secular state in west Turkish cities. Increased terrorist activity late 1999.

Islamic Movement Organisation
Few in numbers, supported by Iran.

Kaplancir (mainly in Germany)
Followers of Metin Kaplan

Other groups and political parties
Fetullah Gulen (broad-based group)
Followers of exiled Fetullah Gulen.
Controls schools and media outlets

Milli Gorus (National View)
Virtually all in Germany

Refah (Islamist Welfare Party)
Political party banned in early 1998

Fazilet (Islamist Virtue Party)
Successor to Refah

Muslims in Europe

Germany: 2 million (mainly Turks and Kurds, 250,000 Bosnians)
France: 5 million (mainly North African)
United Kingdom: 1 million (mainly from the Indian sub-continent)

Muslims in South-East Asia
Brunei: 71 per cent of 325,000
Indonesia: 87 per cent of 203 million
Malaysia: 54 per cent of 22 million
Philippines: 5 per cent of 75.6 million
Thailand: 4 per cent of 63.7 million

probably are. It has bombed Afghanistan, Sudan and Iraq and imposed sanctions on them and others. It has placed sanctions on Russian firms suspected of supplying Iran with nuclear and missile technology and has threatened companies against investing heavily in the Iranian energy industry. The world of Islam cannot understand the apparent unfairness of US policy at the UN in respect of their and Israel's non-compliance with UN resolutions. The US-Israeli strategic partnership is fine in theory but if the US should obtain Israeli military support or use Israeli facilities in any conflict then the whole Muslim world is likely to side with its opponents.

The likelihood of a pan-Islamic alliance being formed to confront one or other of the non-Muslim civilisations is very remote – the experience of Arab alliances is not encouraging in this respect. Examples include the Gulf Cooperation Council's consistent failure to implement the measures agreed for common defence, the split in the Muslim world of those supporting the US-led coalition and those more sympathetic to Iraq after its invasion of Kuwait, and Egypt's apparent deception of Syria over its true objectives in the 1973 Yom Kippur war. Then there is the split between those who actually make peace with Israel and those who remain implacably opposed to any concessions being made to it.

While the general public, and in some countries governments, undoubtedly see Islam as a threat it is very much a self-induced one brought about by ignorance and the bias of the media. Islam is far more of a threat to Muslims and Muslim states than to the West. Muslims who have experienced a degree of democracy and have enjoyed the fruits of modernisation are fearful of being resubjected to the rigours of sharia and the loss of freedom inherent in strict Muslim behaviour. The Islamic tendency is gaining ground in a number of previously secular states – in Turkey, Malaysia and Pakistan, for example – and the Islamic opposition appears to be being forgiven in Algeria. However, the development of missiles, chemical and biological weapons, and possibly nuclear weapons in a number of Muslim countries and the propensity for Islam to employ terrorism is threatening for non-Muslim states.

There will continue to be relatively minor clashes along the traditional fault lines of the world where Islam and other civilisations meet – in the Balkans, Caucasus, Central Asia, Middle East and the Indian subcontinent to name a few. There also appears to be a growing Islamist movement in far western China. However, a major war between Islam and, say, the West remains highly unlikely.

Bibliography and Web Sites

Dekmejian, R. Hrair, *Islam in Revolution: Fundamentalism in the Arab World*, Syracuse University Press, 1995

Halliday, Fred, *Islam and the Myth of Confrontation*, IB Taurus, 1996

Huntingdon, Samuel P., *The Clash of Civilisations and the Remaking of World Order*, Simon & Schuster, 1996

The Islamic Interlink: www.ais.org/~islam

The Wisdom Fund: www.twf.org

NORTH AFRICA: A THREATENING COASTLINE

The southern coast of the Mediterranean has provided a number of threats to the countries to the north of the sea over history. Examples include the Arab invasion of Spain in the early eighth century AD, the piracy of the Corsairs of the Barbary Coast in the sixteenth to early nineteenth centuries, and more recently the terrorism sponsored by Libya's Colonel Muammar Ghaddafi and his efforts to produce chemical weapons. The main threat from over the Mediterranean is no longer violence but demographic as the growing pressure of a population explosion encourages large-scale emigration to the north. In addition to examining this demographic pressure, this section looks at the civil war in Algeria and the long-standing problem of the Western Sahara.

NORTH AFRICA: DEMOGRAPHIC PRESSURE

The North African region has witnessed a continuing flow of immigration and emigration across the west Mediterranean over history. The first Europeans to colonise North Africa were the Romans in the second century BC who created 'a bread basket' for their empire on the Barce plateau. In the opposite direction, the Arab invaders of North Africa crossed into Spain in the eighth century AD and occupied the southern half of the country; they were forced back to North Africa by the end of the fifteenth century. Spanish and French colonisation of Algeria, Morocco and Tunisia took place during the nineteenth and early twentieth centuries and the Italians took Libya from the Turks in 1912. The last colonists, the 'colons' of Algeria, returned to Europe in 1962. Since then there has been continuing emigration by North Africans to southern Europe mainly to find work and a better standard of living.

The rate of population increase in North Africa has provoked fears of massive illegal emigration across the Mediterranean because Europeans believe that the North African countries are unable to support their estimated populations. Migration from North Africa began before its countries gained their independence; people left mainly during the First World War when some 175,000 North Africans joined the French Army and 150,000 went to work in French munitions factories. French labour shortages encouraged immigration both between the wars and after the Second World War. The Algerian community in France was a useful base for those working for Algerian independence; later, after independence, it became a haven for Algerian opposition groups. By 1970 North Africans had also penetrated into Germany, Belgium and the Netherlands; in 1979 there were 1.3 million workers in France and 180,000 in the other three countries. Immigrant workers, mainly Turks and Yugoslavs, were now also coming into Europe from the east. Also in the 1970s immigrants were allowed to bring in their families and so the immigrant population grew.

In the 1970s and '80s there was no common European policy on North African immigration: there was little control in Italy and Spain while France and Germany were increasingly concerned by illegal immigration. After 1989 western Europe also had to face a large inflow from the former communist countries and this led to further measures to slow down immigration from the Maghreb just when conditions there – population rise, unemployment and underdevelopment – increased the pressure for emigration. Emigration from the Maghreb became, therefore, a threat to employment opportunity and of increased Muslim militancy in Europe; in turn the existing migrant communities came to be seen as part of that threat.

European Union policy has been to focus on the whole Mediterranean rather than just the Maghreb and over the years a number of initiatives have been agreed. The most recent, the Redirected Mediterranean Policy, was instituted in 1994 but in the same year was overtaken by the Euro-Mediterranean Partnership that aimed to create a free trade area encompassing twenty-seven countries on both sides of the Mediterranean. Delegates from the twenty-seven adopted the Barcelona Declaration and Work Programme after a conference in the city in November 1998. The declaration covered a wide range of topics including human rights, terrorism, drugs and arms proliferation, as well as free trade and economic

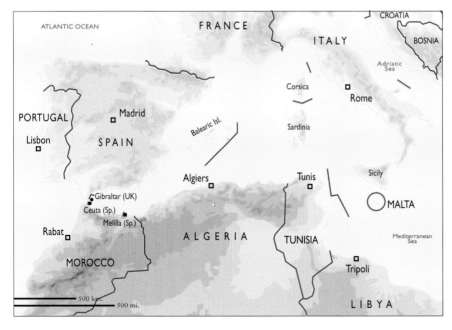

The western Mediterranean.

Demographic pressure and food dependency		

Size of Immigrant Population (in 000s)

	1975	1982	1990
France			
Algerian	711	805	615
Moroccan	260	441	573
Tunisian	140	191	206

	1985	1990	1995
Spain			
Moroccan	5.8	11.4	75
Italy			
Moroccan	2.6	78	94
Tunisian	4.4	41.2	40.5

Acquisition of Nationality

	1988	1990	1995
France			
Moroccan	4.4	7.7	12.2
Algerian	3.3	5.4	9.5
Tunisian	2.3	3.1	4.2
Spain			
Moroccan	3.1	1.6	0.7
Netherlands			
Moroccan	1.2	1.6	4.0

Population Expansion (millions)

	1980	1990	1999
Algeria	-	25.5	29.6
Morocco	24.8	29.8	-
Tunisia	-	8.0	9.8

cooperation. There were many criticisms of the declaration from both south Mediterranean countries and others who saw it as too European in content, objected to its description of the region as a 'crisis' zone, and, because of the perceived threat, allowed tighter immigration controls to be imposed. It was also argued that there could be no really free trade without free movement of labour. Free trade in agricultural products would only result in the North African countries being more dependent on imported food when their farmers turned to growing crops which would give them an advantage over European farmers. Some Europeans did not want to see this advantage, essential to the Maghreb suppliers, implemented.

North African immigration should be seen as a challenge rather than as a threat. Those who advocate investing in and improving living conditions in the Maghreb are more likely to reduce the flow than those who see increased trade in more nationalistic terms. The Maghreb needs aid and advice to improve state control of enterprises, industrial capability, service and banking industries and to cope with foreign debt. The Euro-Mediterranean Partnership has made some difference in these areas.

Prospects for the future, however, are not entirely negative. Already the birth rate has begun to fall, virtually by half as more people live in crowded cities and more women seek employment, though the population of the Maghreb countries is still estimated to rise from its present 70 million to perhaps 97 million by 2025. Growth rates have improved in Morocco and Tunisia, as has GDP, over the last ten years. The improved security situation in Algeria could see a rise in economic prosperity there. As the millennium ended, the UN prepared to publish a report which predicts that the European Union will have to take in over 1 million immigrants a year purely to keep the proportion of workers in the population level. If the ratio of active workers to older, retired people is to be maintained, as many as 135 million immigrants would have to be taken in by 2025. While workers continue to be available from across the Mediterranean, their arrival in Europe could fuel other problems concerning ethnic minorities and Islam.

Bibliography

Blank, Stephen (ed.), *Mediterranean Security in the Coming Millennium*, US Strategic Studies Institute, 1999

Collinson, Sarah, *Shore to Shore: The Politics of Migration in Euro-Maghreb Relations*, Royal Institute for International Affairs, 1996

Pierros, Filippos, Jacob Meunier and Stan Abrams, *Bridges and Barriers: The European Union's Mediterranean Policy, 1961–1998*, Ashgate, 1999

MOROCCO AND THE WESTERN SAHARA

The North African coastal region was conquered by the Ummayid Arabs and the population converted to Islam between AD 622 and 750. Until the twentieth century Morocco was inhabited by a collection of tribes with the Sultan only exercising real control over the towns and plains. The Spanish captured the Canary Islands in the first few years of the fifteenth century and their interest in the African coastline stemmed from their need for fishing rights and the opportunity to trade with Saharan caravans. After the Spanish-Moroccan war of 1859–60 the Moroccans conceded land on the Atlantic coast to Spain so that it could establish its fishing industry but this was not set up at Ifni until some years later.

Spain's negotiations with the French over Spanish control of the Western Sahara were dependent on the recognition of France's influence in Morocco. This was not finally given assent until the Franco-German agreement of 1911 and the Treaty of Fez of 1912 when the Sultan handed Morocco to French protection. A number of Franco-Spanish conventions in the early twentieth century demarcated the border between their areas of interest; the final convention of 1912 gave Spain only a small area of Morocco split from its enclave at Ifni. Saguia el-Hamra and Rio de Oro were recognised as Spanish colonies. However, Spanish control of the interior was not established until 1934.

As Africa became decolonised after the Second World War, both Morocco, from which France withdrew in 1956, and Mauritania, which had been a French colony from 1920–60, both claimed the territory of Western Sahara. At the same time the Popular Front for the Liberation of Saguia el-Hamra and Rio de Oro (POLISARIO) was formed; it claimed independence for the territory. When Spain finally withdrew in February 1976 the Djema (the Saharawi body formed by Spain in 1967 and named after the traditional djemas that had controlled tribal life) approved the reintegration of Western Sahara with Morocco and Mauritania. Serious fighting broke out between the POLISARIO and the forces of Morocco and Mauritania. The latter agreed that Morocco should have the northern two-thirds of the territory. The POLISARIO withdrew over the border into Algeria where it has had bases ever since. To defend against the POLISARIO guerrilla attacks that took place regularly in the years before 1982, the Moroccan government completed the construction of a 2500 kilometre earth wall (the *berm*) and deployed nearly half its army along it.

In 1979 Mauritania and the POLISARIO signed a peace agreement in which Mauritania, which had been driven out by POLISARIO, gave up its claims to Western Saharan territory. Morocco refused to recognise the treaty and its troops occupied the southern part of the country. The United Nations has been involved in Western Saharan affairs since 1963, and the General Assembly has on several occasions affirmed the right of the people to self-determination. In 1975 the International Court of Justice advised that although there were legal ties of allegiance to the Sultan of Morocco by some of the tribes (at the time of Spanish colonisation) and that there were some land rights between Mauritania and the territory, these did not establish any tie of territorial sovereignty. In 1979 the Organisation of African Unity (OAU) called for a referendum on self-determination and established a committee with the UN. At the OAU summit in 1981 King Hassan II agreed to a ceasefire and a referendum but would not talk directly to the POLISARIO. In 1982 twenty-six OAU members recognised the Saharan Arab Democratic Republic and admitted it to the Council of Ministers; Morocco withdrew from the OAU. After several years of negotiating by a joint UN-OAU mission of good offices, the UN appointed a special representative in 1988 who reported proposals for a settlement to the UN in 1990.

Morocco: Selected Chronology	
1966	UNGA anticipates Saharan self-determination after referendum
1974	UNGA asks for International Court of Justice to review status
1975	'Green March' by 350,000 Moroccans into Sahara
1976	Last Spanish troops leave
1976	Morocco and Mauritania sign 'sharing' agreement
1979	Mauritania in peace agreement with POLISARIO gives up claim to territory
1984	Morocco leaves OAU after admission of Western Sahara
1988	UN Sec Gen proposes peace plan to include referendum. Proposal accepted UNSC adopts resolution establishing Minurso. Registration of Saharawis eligible to vote begins
1995	POLISARIO suspends and resumes the identification process
1996	UN Secretary General cancels the identification process
1997	James Baker appointed UN Special Envoy

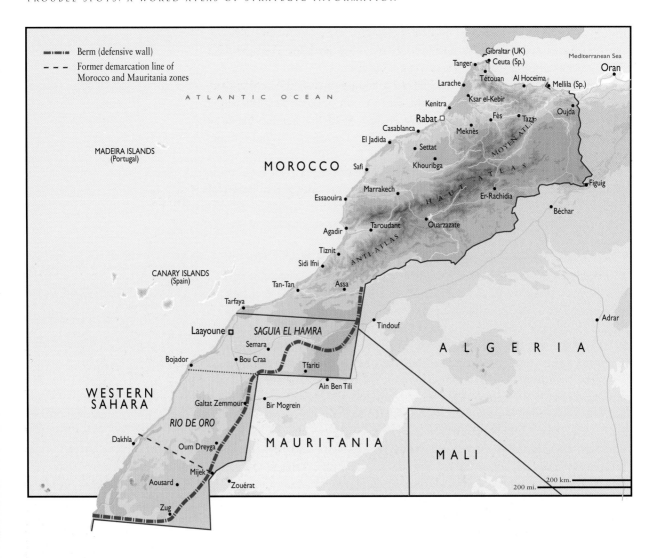

Legend:
- ▬▬▬ Berm (defensive wall)
- ▬ ▬ ▬ Former demarcation line of Morocco and Mauritania zones

Morocco and the Western Sahara.

The UN plan was for a UN Mission for the Referendum in Western Sahara (MINURSO) that would monitor the ceasefire, the reduction of armed forces and the confinement of those forces remaining in specified locations. It would also make the arrangements for the referendum, including the identification of those eligible to vote, and supervise a repatriation scheme for refugees. In April 1991 the UNSC decided to establish MINURSO and an agreed ceasefire was to come into effect on 6 September; however, a number of preliminary tasks could not be completed before this date. Fighting restarted after an unofficial ceasefire of two years; 228 UN monitors with helicopter support were deployed. While the ceasefire has held since September 1991, progress towards holding the referendum has been painfully slow with a number of interruptions caused by both sides. Timetables have been amended and MINURSO's mandate extended repeatedly. Disagreement continues over who is eligible to vote in the referendum with the Moroccan authorities arguing in favour of some 65,000 tribesman, who were not included in the Spanish census of 1974. The POLISARIO opposes this on the grounds that it is intended to increase the pro-Moroccan vote, a view UN officials tend to agree with. 150,000 Saharawi refugees and the POLISARIO guerrillas remain in camps in south-west Algeria.

Both Morocco and the POLISARIO have agreed that the referendum will now take place on 31 July 2000; they have also agreed a programme of preparation. Whether the agreement will be implemented this time remains to be seen.

Bibliography and Web Sites

Hodges, Tony, *Western Sahara: Roots of a Desert War*, Lawrence Hill, 1983

Moroccan Ministry of Communications: www.mincom.gov.ma
Western Sahara: www.arso.org

Algeria

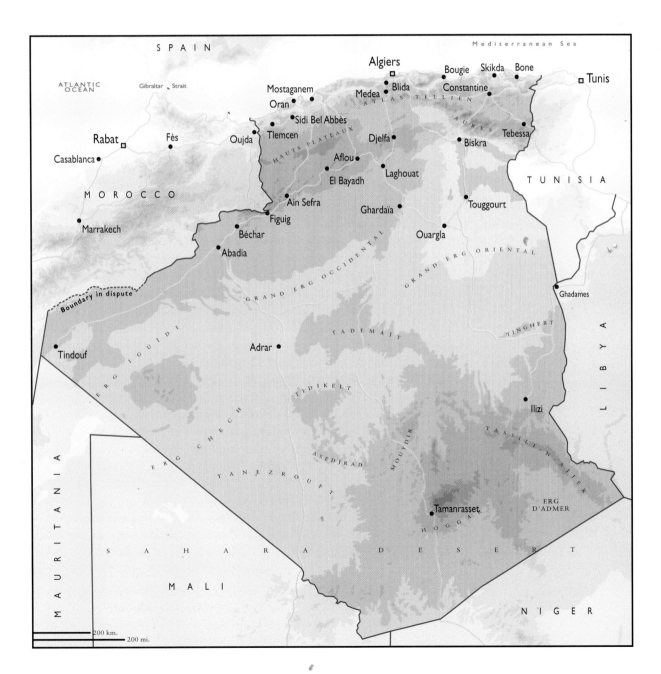

ALGERIA: WILL VIOLENCE EVER END?

Ever since the municipal and departmental elections in June 1990 – in which the Front Islamique du Salut (FIS) (Islamic Salvation Front) polled some 65 per cent of the votes cast, winning in 32 out of 48 provinces and in over half the municipalities, and which caused the Algerian government to postpone the national election due in June 1991 – Algeria has suffered an almost daily series of violent incidents. It is thought that some 75,000 have died.

Western North Africa was originally inhabited by the Berbers. It was part of the Roman and Byzantine Empires until invaded by the Ummayid Arabs in the seventh century AD when it was converted to Islam. After a brief period of Spanish rule in the sixteenth century it became part of the Ottoman Empire; the Ottomans formed the frontiers of Algeria. By the eighteenth century Ottoman rule was only nominal: Algeria had become a pirate state and its attacks on shipping invited a European reaction – an Anglo-Dutch fleet bombarded Algiers in 1816. The French captured Algiers in 1830 following a three-year blockade imposed after the French consul was assaulted. It then went on to occupy the whole North African region from today's Tunisian-Libyan border in the east to Agadir on the Atlantic in the west. The French introduced large numbers of settlers into Algeria; the European population, 109,000 in 1847, rose to 984,000, of whom 70 per cent had been born in Algeria, by 1954. The northern *départements* of Algiers, Constantine and Oran were incorporated into metropolitan France in 1881; the remainder of the country was under military control.

The Algerian War of Independence began with an insurrection in the Aurès Mountains on 1 November 1954. The Front de Libération Nationale (FLN) (National Liberation Front) was founded and offered to negotiate as long as the principle of self-determination for the Algerian people was accepted. The French responded that Algeria was the heart of the French republic and would be defended by all possible means. During the eight-year war some 1.5 million people are believed to have died.

From the start Algerian independence, gained in 1962, was marred by dispute. Its first president, Ahmed Ben Bella, was removed in a military coup after only three years. The army remained the main power throughout the next two presidencies because when the bulk of the French settlers left, so did most senior civil servants. The only political party – the Front de Libération Nationale, which had collapsed in 1962 – was revived but never gained the independent influence and power that could have united the country. A number of trends then emerged: modernisation, initially funded by oil revenue, took place but the agricultural sector was allowed to stagnate and Algeria had to import food to feed its fast growing population (by roughly 3 per cent per year). As oil prices fell so the new heavy industries became more of a burden on the state because they operated at a loss. Under President Chadli, Algeria became a multi-party democracy in 1989 and although a large number of political parties were formed the main threat to the governing FLN came from the Islamists in the form of the FIS, which had widespread appeal and was supported by over 10 per cent of the population within a year of its formation.

The FIS made substantial gains in the local elections of 1990, winning 54.3 per cent of the vote. Before the scheduled national election of June

Algeria: Selected Events

Jul 1992	700 Islamists arrested
Dec 1991	FIS wins first round of election
Jan 1992	Election annulled, FIS banned, martial law imposed, 300,000 demonstrate for democracy.
Feb 1992	State of emergency declared
Mar 1994	1,000 FIS prisoners escape from jails, President Zéroual begins talks with FIS
Sept 1994	FIS accepts conditions for talks
Oct 1994	Amnesty claims 20,000 killed since 1991
Dec 1994	French Airbus hijacked, stormed at Marseilles
Feb 1995	Government rejects Rome peace plan
Nov 1996	Referendum approves constitutional changes
Jun 1997	Elections preceded by massacres of villagers. Undecided whether these were carried out by GIA or government, 60,000 lives lost since 1992.
Apr 1999	Abdelaziz Bouteflika elected President
Dec 1999	4,200 rebels surrender, 1,500 may remain
Jan 2000	Army launches 'final' campaign

1991, the FLN-dominated National Assembly changed the election rules in order to weaken the FIS's chances and forbade electioneering to take place in mosques. In early June two squares in Algiers were occupied by several thousand Islamists; they were dispersed by troops who killed six and wounded over 100 more. The elections were postponed until December when the FIS gained 188 of the 430 Assembly seats and seemed certain to take control in the second round to be held in January 1992. These elections were never held as the army suspended them on the grounds that an FIS-controlled Assembly would mean the end of democracy. The FIS was banned in March and by the end of the month some 9,000 members had been arrested and sent to camps in the Sahara.

The following years have seen widespread violence with a breakdown of law and order. A splinter group of the FIS, the Groupe Islamique Armée (GIA), has emerged as the strongest element among the various Islamist guerrilla organisations. In 1993 the Islamist terrorists turned their attention to foreigners in an attempt to undermine the economy and a number were murdered, including engineering and electricity workers, priests and Russian military advisors. The murders have not deterred foreign investment in the oil and gas industries, which seem to have been spared from attack. Estimates of the number of dead, including soldiers, police, GIA and innocent civilians, vary but the figure could be as high as 75,000.

There have been two elections while the FIS has been banned. In 1995 a former general, Liamine Zéroual, became president in an election seen as an attempt to return to democracy. In 1997 the Rassemblement National Démocratique, a new party sponsored by the government and formed that year, won 38 per cent of the vote in national elections compared to the FLN's 16 per cent. It gained a higher percentage in the provincial and municipal elections. Soon after there came growing allegations of government involvement in a wave of killings in August and September said to have been committed by the GIA. The army claimed to have killed several hundred of the rebel GIA, but there were allegations that in fact the army had taken no action to stop some of the massacres.

In the presidential elections held in April 1999 Abdelaziz Bouteflika replaced Zéroual when the other six candidates withdrew immediately before the election. He has promised to continue to fight insurgency but has also invited Islamic militants to engage in political talks. He intends to end unemployment, corruption and inefficiency. The armed wing of the FIS, the Islamic Salvation Army, has said it is giving up the armed struggle; in return 3,000 imprisoned FIS members have been released. The amnesty ends in January 2000 and after that date Bouteflika has said every effort will be made to neutralise any rebels who have not given up the fight.

Bibliography and Web Site

Ageron, Charles-Robert, *Modern Algeria: A History from 1830 to the Present*, Hurst, 1991
Fuller, Graham, *Algeria: the Next Fundamentalist State?*, Rand, 1996
Quandt, William, *Algeria's Transition from Authoritarianism*, Brookings Institute Press, 1998
Shah-Kazemi, Reza (ed.), *Algeria: Revolution Revisited*, Islamic World Report, 1997
Spencer, Claire, *The Maghreb in the 1990s*, IISS Adelphi Paper 274, 1993
Willis, Michael, *The Islamist Challenge in Algeria: A Political History*, Ithaca, 1997

World Algeria Action Coalition (Washington): www.waac.org.

THE MIDDLE EAST–
AFRICAN INTERFACE

The four countries considered in this section have connections both with the Middle East and with Africa: all four are suffering violence. Sudan has been fighting a civil war for the last twenty-seven years; Somalia is ungoverned and the UN has abandoned trying to aid it; Ethiopia and Eritrea are at war with each other.

THE SUDAN: A DIVIDED STATE

Sudan has always been divided in two ways: by its people and their religions, and by the nature of the territory. In the north, covering roughly two-thirds of the country, it is dry; north of the capital, Khartoum, lies the Nubian Desert – the eastern end of the Sahara, which continues over the border into Egypt. The people here are largely of Arab descent and are Muslims; there are also Nubians, living along the Egyptian border, Bedouin tribes in the west, and Beja tribesmen in the Red Sea Hills to the east. The three southern provinces are quite different in terrain; they are mainly equatorial forests with the vast swamps of the Sudd. The people, who are either Christian or Animist, are of Nilo-Hamitic and Negro ethnicity and are closer in origin to the African peoples found in neighbouring Congo, Kenya and Uganda than to the northerners.

Accounts of the history of Sudan come mainly from the words of travellers. Nubia, in the north, was conquered by the Egyptians sometime after 2,000 BC. The Romans sent a small expedition that reached the Sudd and then reported that the country was not worth conquering. Around AD 1500 the north was converted to Islam though pockets of Christianity remained. The only interest in the south was in the search for ivory and slaves, both of which were ruthlessly extracted particularly after the Turkish-Egyptian penetration from 1820. The Egyptian conquest of Mohammed Ali in 1821 was driven by the lure of gold thought to be there and the desire to overthrow the last of Egypt's earlier rulers, the Mamelukes. After a short period of Egyptian rule the local tribal leaders were allowed to continue under the supervision of a governor-general in Khartoum. Taxation and corruption became excessive after General Gordon resigned as Governor-General in 1880, having failed to eradicate the slave trade, and became the causes of a revolution led by Sheikh Muhammed Ahmed, the Mahdi. After the Mahdi took control of

Sudan.

Kordofan and Dafur, a British force (Egypt was now a British protectorate while still nominally part of the Ottoman Empire) under General Gordon was despatched in 1884. But the garrison of Khartoum was overwhelmed and Gordon murdered; the Mahdi and his successor ruled Sudan from 1885 to 1898. After the battle of Omdurman in 1898 Sudan became an Anglo-Egyptian Condominium but was in effect ruled by the British governor-general. British interest in southern Sudan intensified as the French pressed eastwards from Central Africa, culminating in the Fashoda incident in 1898, a clash between British and French troops that nearly resulted in an Anglo-French war. During Kitchener's governorship the south was subject to missionary activity to convert it to Christianity which further separated the southern provinces from the north.

Sudan gained its independence on 1 January 1956. In 1958 a military coup took place but civilian rule was restored in 1964. Another military coup in 1969 led by Colonel Gaafar Mohammed el-Nimeiri established the Revolutionary Command Council; Nimeiri became President in 1971.

In August 1955 there had been an army mutiny at Torit, 100 kilometres east of Juba in Equitoria Province; the fighting that followed lasted only a few weeks and the mutineers fled to Uganda with only a few remaining in hiding in inaccessible areas. Insurgency then lay dormant until 1963 by when the old mutineers had been reinforced by students and young politicians forced into exile by the regime. The guerrilla force they formed was known as Anyanya but it was a fragmented organisation whose leaders spent as much time opposing each other as the Khartoum government. Military unity only came in the late 1970s when Israel decided only to arm Joseph Lagu's faction. This managed to unite the others and to bring the political wing under its leadership. This unification enabled talks to take place with the government and these led to the Addis Ababa agreement in 1972. However, the expectations from the agreement were not realised.

Opposition to Nimeiri's policies arose in both the north and the south and among Muslims and non-Muslims. And initially the Sudan People's Liberation Army (SPLA) addressed national rather purely southern Sudanese problems. Another change was that the dissidents in the south were now actively supported by Ethiopia following Nimeiri's support for anti-Derg forces there. As in 1963, the opposition was split into numerous groups but Ethiopian influence helped to bring them together, as did the cooperation of army defectors. In May 1983 two army battalions in Jonglei were persuaded to defect en masse with their arms and equipment. The SPLA emerged in July 1983 under the command of a former colonel, John Garang, who ensured that all operations were authorised and that all recruits were sent for training in Ethiopia. The late 1980s saw a series of SPLA victories as it grew in strength, captured smaller garrison towns, bottled the army up in larger ones and took control of much of the south. In 1985 Nimeiri was deposed and a year later Sadiq el-Mahdi, leader of the Umma Party, was elected Prime Minister of a coalition government. A peace treaty was signed with the SPLA, which split the coalition and led to another military coup. General Ahmed el-Bashir became President; the Umma Party was outlawed.

The SPLA suffered a major reverse in 1991 when the overthrow of Mengistu, the Ethiopian dictator, deprived them of Ethiopian support and the organisation fragmented again. There was a split between those, like Garang, looking to overthrow the Khartoum government and those who purely wanted independence for the south. The Upper Nile commanders complained of being isolated and last in line for supplies and reinforcements. In August 1991 they renounced their support for Garang and their aim of independence for the south. The dissidents did not receive the support they expected from the northern elements of the SPLA, and later accepted arms from the government, a move that further alienated them from the mainstream SPLA. They did, though, tie down numbers of

The Sudan

Population: 32,000,000

By religion
Muslim 70%
Christian 10%

By race
Arab 39%
African 52%

Garang's forces, which allowed the government to recover considerable territory during 1992 to 1994.

The SPLA recovered and by the end of 1995 was regaining lost ground; a number of factors helped to bring this about. New forces – the National Democratic Alliance in the north and the Sudan Allied Forces along the Eritrean and Ethiopian borders from Kassala to Kurmuk – allied to Garang and opened up new fronts against the government. The Sudanese government's support of Islamist dissidents led to the SPLA alliance gaining support from the Ethiopian, Eritrean, Kenyan and Ugandan armies. At the same time a regional intergovernmental body, formed originally to cooperate over drought and desertification and renamed the Intergovernmental Authority for Development, attempted to mediate in the civil war which was seen as destabilising the region. Among its recommendations was the separation of religion from the state in Sudan; the government was unable to accept secularism and remained committed to sharia. By now Sudan was host to a number of Islamist groups such as Hamas, Hizbollah, Islamic Jihad and some Egyptian terrorist associations, providing them arms and training camps.

The civil war continues and the SPLA's supporters are now concerned elsewhere – Eritrea and Ethiopia with their own war and Uganda having joined the civil war in the Congo. The government's finances will improve as oil starts to be exported. There are signs of a possible reconciliation; President Bashir and the Eritrean president have signed a treaty agreeing not to support each other's rebels and a senior Sudanese politician, Hassan Turabi, has held talks with former Prime Minister el-Mahdi who supports the SPLA from exile. The SPLA is demanding self-determination within Sudan, a split of church and state, equality for all, a share of the national wealth. If these requirements are not met then it will address the option of secession.

Bibliography and Web Sites

Clapham, Christopher (ed.), *African Guerrillas*, James Currey, 1998
Gurdon, Charles (ed.), *The Horn of Africa*, SOAS/GRC Geopolitics Series, UCL Press, 1994
Lesch, Ann Mosely, *The Sudan: Contested National Identities*, James Cirrey, 1999
Sidahmed, Abdel Salam, *Politics and Islam in Contemporary Sudan*, Curzon, 1997

Sudanese Embassy Washington: www.sudanembassyus.org
The Sudan Foundation (London): www.sufo.demon.co.uk

WWW.

THE HORN OF AFRICA: WAR RETURNS TO ETHIOPIA AND ERITREA

Ethiopia and Eritrea have suffered war almost continuously since 1970. There were five years of peace between the end of the civil war that overthrew the regime of Mengistu Haile Mariam and led to Eritrean independence in May 1993, and the renewed outbreak of fighting between the two countries in 1998.

The original inhabitants were the Agau, a Cushite people. Around 700 BC there was a wave of immigration of Semite people from southern Arabia who settled in what is now north-east Ethiopia and Eritrea. They established the kingdom of Axum which was converted to Coptic Christianity in the fourth century. Its power declined as that of Islam expanded and it became isolated from the Christian world. The region first became independent in the eleventh century. Between the fourteenth and seventeenth centuries the Christian state expanded after its conquest of the sultanates of the south-east escarpment, the Cushite Gibe region and Senaar in Sudan. In the late nineteenth century Menelik II took control of the area now constituting southern Ethiopia. As the kingdom of Abyssinia it suffered a number of invasions but never fell to European colonisation as the rest of Africa did. The northern province of Eritrea had fallen to the Turks in the mid-sixth century and was taken by Italy in 1889; it became a colony in 1900. The Italians invaded Ethiopia in 1935 and occupied it until they were defeated by the British in 1941 when Emperor Haile Selassie, who had first come to power in 1916, returned. After the war, the British administered Eritrea until 1952 when it became an autonomous part of a federal Ethiopia. In 1961 the emperor revoked Eritrea's autonomous status and disbanded its government; the resulting armed resistance continued inconclusively until 1991. The Ethiopian army deposed Haile Selassie in 1974 and the country became a socialist state ruled by the Dergue or military council.

A rebellion by the Oromo, a non-Amharic people, took place in 1964 as a result of governmental repression. The uprising spread and declared its aim of independence as Western Somalia; the revolt tended to merge with that in the Ogaden region of Somalia. It ended in 1970 but the Somali revolt continued. In 1977 another attempt to secure independence was made during the Ethiopian-Somali war but all resistance had petered out by the early 1980s.

Before Colonel Mengistu Haile Mariam took power in a coup in 1977, the Dergue had lost its first two leaders from assassination. After Mengistu came to power any rival or opponent suffered a similar fate.

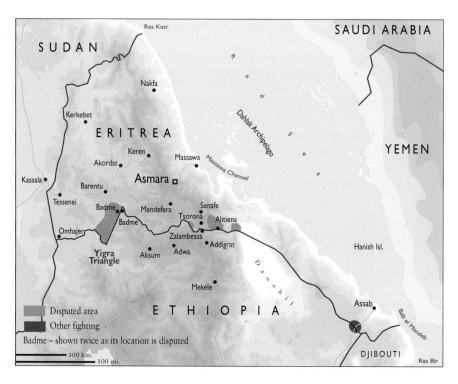

Eritrean-Ethiopian border fighting.

The Ethiopean Army patrols the front line of fighting with Eritrea, February 1999. (Associated Press)

Ethiopia moved closer to the Soviet block and was, with Soviet and Cuban help, able to repulse the Somali invasion of 1977. At their peak, Soviet advisers in Ethiopia numbered some 1,400 and Cubans over 11,000. The Soviet-Ethiopian agreement ended in January 1991 and Soviet military aid ceased; Mengistu had to flee the country less than five months later. The main opposition groups were the Eritrean People's Liberation Front (EPLF) and the Tigray People's Liberation Front (TPLF); they were allied against Mengistu but had different long-term aims – the EPLF aim of independence was not supported by the TPLF, though initially it was looking for autonomy for Tigray.

In May 1991 the EPLF defeated the Ethiopian Army at a battle some 50 kilometres south of Asmara which it then occupied and where a provisional Eritrean government was set up. At the same time the Army was also beaten by the Ethiopian People's Revolutionary Democratic Front (EPRDF) which installed a new government in Addis Ababa. Following an internationally monitored referendum, Eritrea formally declared its independence in May 1993. Earlier the provisional governments of Ethiopia and Eritrea had agreed to cooperate over security, trade and immigration; landlocked Ethiopian access to the port of Assab was guaranteed.

Border disputes between Ethiopia and Eritrea erupted in May 1998 after years of disagreement as to its legal line, which has never been officially demarcated. Fighting first took place over a barren 250 square mile area around Badme known as the Yigra triangle, which Ethiopia claims it had been administering for sometime but which Eritrea claims Italian maps show as its own. It is unclear which side began the fighting but both sent large-scale forces to defend their rival claims. By mid-June the war had spread to four other disputed zones, three to the east of Badme at Zala Ambessa, and one close to the Djibouti border where the main road to Assab crosses the frontier. Accurate reports of the fighting are scarce but all indicate a heavy toll of casualties on both sides. A three-day battle fought at Tsorona has been described as resembling the First World War with mass attacks being beaten off by machine-gun fire. The Eritreans claim to have killed some 10,000 Ethiopians and to have destroyed or captured some 80 of their tanks.

Armed forces 1999	
Ethiopia	
Men	350,000
Tanks	500
Artillery	?
Combat	70
Attack helicopters	24
Eritrea	
Men	180,000
Equipment numbers not known but include tanks, artillery and SAM	
Combat aircraft	20
Patrol craft	10
(all estimates)	

A moratorium on aerial bombing was agreed in 1998 but the Eritreans claim that Massawa was bombed in May 1999. The war continues, largely unreported, after a pause during the rainy season. The Organisation of African Unity has prepared a peace plan and is pressing to have it implemented.

Bibliography and Web Sites

Gurdon, Charles (ed.), *The Horn of Africa*, SOAS/GRC Geopolitics Series, UCL Press, 1994

Henze, Paul B., *The Horn of Africa: From War to Peace*, Macmillan, 1991

Iyob, Ruth, *The Eritrean Struggle for Independence: Domination, Resistance, Nationalism 1941–1993*, Cambridge University Press, 1995

Makinda, Samuel, *Security in the Horn of Africa*, International Institute for Strategic Studies Adelphi Paper 269, 1992

Woodward, Peter, and Murray Forsyth (eds), *Conflict and Peace in the Horn of Africa*, Dartmouth, 1994

WWW.

Eritrean Government: www.netafrica.org/eritrea

Ethiopia: www.ethiospokes.net/index

Ethiopian Embassy Washington: www.ethiopianembassy.org/conflict.net

SOMALIA: STILL UNGOVERNABLE

The Somali people were originally nomadic tribesman living on the east coast of Africa; they are now divided into clans which are grouped together in clan-families. It is claimed that they are descended from Noah's son Ham and that his son Cush founded the Cushite race, whose original kingdom was in northern Sudan. The Cushites migrated southwards after their defeat by the Auxumites around 300 BC. Legend has it that the Somali clans were formed by Arab settlers who intermarried with the local Oromo women. Two clans are still named after two of the settlers Darod and Isaq; the Hawiye and Gadabursi clans can be traced to even earlier settlers. Their traditional enemies are the Christian Amhara to the west of the Rift Valley who in the fourteenth and fifteenth centuries made efforts to control trade routes to the sea. The Somalis reacted to the increased extent of the raids in the sixteenth century by crossing the Rift and penetrating as far west as the Abyssinian highlands.

After European colonisation, the Somalis found themselves in five separate entities. In the north the French established the colony of the Isa, a Somali clan, and the Afars, an Ethiopian people; this has now become the independent state of Djibouti. To the south the British established the Somaliland Protectorate in 1884–5, signing treaties with the Isa and Gadabursi clans and the Habr Awal, Habr Garhajis and Habr Tojaala sub-clans. The area southwards to the border of the British colony of Kenya, in which a number of Somalis lived, became Italian Somalia. Inland to the west lay the Ogaden also populated by Somalis but claimed by the Ethiopians; the British agreed to drawing a boundary giving Ethiopia the northern Ogaden in 1897. Similarly, the Italians and Ethiopians came to an agreement but no official boundary was drawn.

British Somaliland and Italian Somalia gained their independence and merged as the Somali Republic in 1960. In 1969 the elected prime minister was overthrown in a military coup by the army commander, Mohamed

Siad Barre, who instituted a 'scientific socialist' state based on Marxist-Leninist principles that overrode the clan culture. A national security service was established to stamp out any opposition to the regime. One of the country's early aims was to create a greater Somalia embracing all the Somali people. In 1977 the Somalis invaded and overran the Ogaden but were beaten back by the Ethiopians after the latter received Cuban and Soviet support. The war caused several hundred thousand Ogadeni Somalis to become refugees in Somalia. The refugees formed 'militias' that committed atrocities against the Isaq population in the northern border region. This, coupled with the northerners' feeling of being left behind in terms of political and social development, led to the formation of the Somali National Movement (SNM). Other clans formed opposition groups.

In 1982 the north, or former British Somaliland, attempted to gain a degree of autonomy but was crushed by the central government: Hargheisa and Burao were bombed and badly damaged. In April 1988 Barre agreed an Ethiopian-Somali accord that called for the demilitarisation of the border area and appeared to give up Somalia's claim to the Ogaden. The Ogadenis, many of whom had joined the army, felt betrayed. In the north the SNM, encouraged by Ethiopia, was waging a civil war but now had to leave its bases in the Ogaden. It briefly captured Hargheisa and Burao but the government recovered them in 1989. At the same time the SNM received a substantial reinforcement from deserting troops.

In 1989 former General Mohamed Farah Aidid, after six years in prison and having been Ambassador in India, returned to the country and took charge of the Hawiye United Somali Congress (USC). Also in 1989 the US withdrew its military assistance on account of the regime's human rights record; other Western donors, except Italy, also cut their aid. The UNHCR, attempting to aid the many refugees, was ordered out after disagreements over the numbers of refugees and the routes for supplying aid; food supplies ended in November 1989. Somalia now suffered a widening civil war as the government was reduced to no more than Barre's clan militia. Starvation, caused by both the fighting and a drought, spread. By mid-1992 4.5 million people were threatened by starvation and some 300,000 may have died. Barre was forced out of office and left Mogadishu in January 1991. The interim President, Ali Mahdi Mohammed a Hawiye, was not supported by Aidid, the SNM or the Ogadeni group, the Somali Patriotic Movement (SPM); the country was ungovernable. In May northern Somalia announced its independence.

In March 1992 the UN brokered a ceasefire and embarked on a large-scale humanitarian relief operation. The United Nations Operation in Somalia (UNOSOM) was established but it took two months of negotiations before fifty unarmed observers to monitor the ceasefire could be deployed. It became obvious that aid convoys required military escort but, again, it took some months before the first troops, from Pakistan, arrived in September to guard the UN depot in Mogadishu. By September the UN had authorised a total of 4,200 infantry and logistical troops but only 900, including the Pakistani battalion, ever deployed. The UN situation in Somalia was untenable: its operations at the airport and seaport were fired upon and its aid convoys were increasingly being hijacked as UN supplies became the only acceptable currency.

Factions/links with clans

Somali National Movement/Isaq
Somali Democratic Alliance/Gadabursi
Somali Democratic Movement/Rahanwein and Digil
Somali National Democratic Movement/Darod
Somali National Front/Marehan (Darod)
Somali National Union/Rer Hamad
Somali Patriotic Movement/Darod
Somali Salvation Democratic Front/Darod
Southern Somali National Movement/Biyemal(Dir)
United Somali Congress/Hawiye (Ali Mahdi and Aideed)
United Somali Front/Issa
United Somali Party/Dulbahante and Warsangeli

Clans and sub-clans

DAROD

Abaskul	Omar Mahamud
Aulyehan	Rer Bidyahan
Dashishe	Rer Dalal
Dulbahante	Rer Hamad
Harti	Rer Ishak
Isa Mahamud	Rer Ugas Ner
Makahil	Siwakhron
Makhabul	Talamuge
Malingur	Usman Mahamud
Marehan	Warsangeli
Muhammad Zubeir	

DIGIL

Dabare	Gure
Jiddu	

DIR

Biyemal	Gadabursi
Isa	

HAWIYA

Abgal	Galjal
Ajuran	Habr Gidr Air
Auramaleh	Habr Gidr Saad
Awadleh	Habr Gidr Suleiman
Digodia	Murosada

IS'HAK

Eidagale	Habr Jaelo
Habr Awal	Habr Yunis

RAHANWEIN

Hadama	Luwai
Helledi	Maalwein

A 'technical' vehicle with militia of General Aidid. (The Hutchison Library)

In November the US offered to lead a force, the Unified Task Force (UNITAF), to create a secure environment for the delivery of human aid. On 2 December the UN accepted. The first US contingent landed on the beaches of Mogadishu on 9 December 1992. US forces were built up to a strength of 28,000 with another 17,000 troops being provided by 29 other countries. In January 1993 the UN Secretary-General chaired a meeting attended by 14 Somali political movements which agreed to a ceasefire, disarmament and the holding of a conference at Addis Ababa on national reconciliation.

UNITAF had always been a short-term mission and in May 1993 UNOSOM II took over the task. The US took on part of the logistics and provided a 'quick reaction' force that remained under US national command. Most UNITAF contingents remained as part of UNOSOM II. Serious fighting broke out in Mogadishu in June with twenty-five Pakistani soldiers being killed by Aidid's men and their bodies mutilated. The US began attacking arms depots, and street battles between Somali gangs and the UN took place. In the following three months the fighting escalated and efforts were made to arrest Aidid. On 3 October two US special forces helicopters were shot down; a relief column had great difficulty in reaching the survivors and suffered many casualties, as did a

The clan areas of Somalia and its neighbours.

second rescue column; 18 were killed and 75 wounded. The bodies of dead US soldiers were shown on television as they were dragged around the city. The US immediately reinforced their troops with tanks and armoured vehicles, at the same time announcing its total withdrawal by the end of March 1994. The incident was the first defeat of a 'high-tech' force by a 'low-tech' enemy. A number of countries withdrew their UNOSOM II contingents in late 1993/early 1994. UNOSOM II adopted a far less confrontational posture and although it remained on the defensive there was no reduction in the attacks on it or other international agencies.

UNOSOM II continued its mission in Somalia until March 1995 but without success in its aim of creating a secure environment. An international task force including US Marines covered the final withdrawal. UNOSOM II left Somalia with no central government and with the clans and their militia still competing for control of important assets, such as the port and airport, but with no ambitions to take control of the whole country. Attempts to broker a settlement were made at

Sodere in Ethiopia in January 1997 but the Somali National Association (SNA) did not attend, and in December the SNA and the National Somali Congress (NSC) met in Cairo.

Since 1995 Somaliland, which declared its independence in 1991, has enjoyed stability and security but has not yet received any international recognition, mainly because this is unacceptable to Somalia. There is a modest level of government, some rebuilding of the infrastructure, education has been organised, law and order restored and a degree of commerce achieved.

Northern Somalia is the most stable part of the country because it has strong clan leadership and no freelance warlords. The south remains in crisis; much of its land is still occupied by outside clans which weakens the influence of local clan leaders. There is a good deal of lawlessness with looting and kidnapping. Mogadishu remains split and four clans claim the airport, which remains closed. Hussein Aidid, leader of the SNA, has gained the support of Eritrea, while the NSC leader Ali Mahdi and Aidid's other opponents have the support of Ethiopia. Aidid and the Rahanweyn clan are fighting and Baidoa has changed hands several times.

Bibliography

Copson, Raymond, *Africa's Wars and Prospects for Peace*, ME Sharpe Inc, 1994

Gurdon, Charles (ed.), *The Horn of Africa*, SOAS/GRC Geopolitics Series, UCL, 1994

Henze, Paul B., *The Horn of Africa: From War to Peace*, Macmillan, 1991

Hirsch, John, and Robert Oakley, *Somalia and Operation Restore Hope*, US Institute of Peace Press, 1995

Lyons, Terence, and Ahmed Samatar, *Somalia: State Collapse, Multilateral Intervention, and Strategies for Political Reconstruction*, Brookings Institute, 1995

Sahnoun, Mohamed, *Somalia the Missed Opportunities*, US Institute for Peace, 1994

Woodward, Peter, and Murray Forsyth (eds), *Conflict and Peace in the Horn of Africa*, Dartmouth, 1994

Somalia: A Government at War with Its Own People, The Africa Watch Committee, 1990

SUB-SAHARAN AFRICA: THE IMPOVERISHED CONTINENT

Africa has now replaced Latin America as the most violent continent in the world. The reasons for this are set out below. Also in this section the civil wars and massacres that have taken place, and are still taking place, in Angola, Rwanda and Burundi, Liberia, the Democratic Republic of Congo and Sierra Leone are examined in more detail. There has been some good news, though: the civil war in Mozambique that lasted for over fourteen years has been resolved successfully with United Nations' assistance. Some smaller conflicts mainly in West Africa have also ended. Africans would not agree with those who congratulated themselves that the conclusion of the Cold War had made the world a safer place: in the period since it ended thousands in Africa have been killed by AK-47 rifles and machetes.

'The quality of the leaders, the misery they have brought to their people and my inability to work with them to turn the situation around are very disappointing. In many countries the wrong kind have made it to leadership. They see power for the sake of power and for their own aggrandisement rather than having a real understanding of the need to use power to improve their countries.'

Kofi Annan UN Secretary General, *The Sunday Times*, 9 April 2000

AFRICA: COLONIAL PAST, PRESENT LINKS

The first colonists to settle in Africa were the Dutch who established themselves at the Cape of Good Hope in 1652 until the British occupied the Cape Colony in 1806 and the Boers moved north to found the republics of Transvaal and the Orange Free State. The next state to be established was Liberia: it was not a colony but an area bought by the American Colonization Society in 1822 as a home for freed slaves. Although Britain and France had established some colonies earlier, the real race for Africa began in 1880 and continued until 1904 when the Entente Cordiale settled the final disputes between the French and British. The last territories to become European colonies were the French Protectorate of Morocco, and Tripolitania and Cyrenaica, captured by Italy from Turkey in 1912. Belgium, Germany, Portugal and Spain also had African possessions. The only countries to remain totally independent were Liberia and Ethiopia, though Italy occupied the latter in 1935.

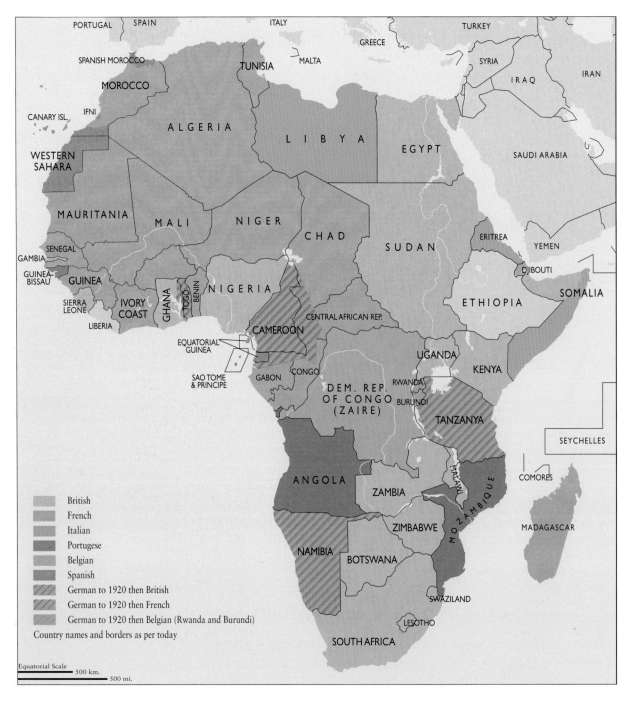

Africa divided between the Europeans after the Berlin Conference of 1884 and the Entente Cordiale 1904.

Before colonisation there were few African states as the term is now understood. Families coalesced into tribes and from time to time tribes were dominated by stronger neighbours; a number of kingdoms emerged. Today the term 'tribe' is seen as a relic of the past and so the term ethnic groups has been used to denote people with a common historic community. Colonisation took little account of the indigenous inhabitants and borders were decided largely on the whim of the colonisers and the bearing of a compass, though sometimes there was a conveniently placed river to act as a boundary. Colonial borders often split people of the same ethnic group, still a cause of discord today.

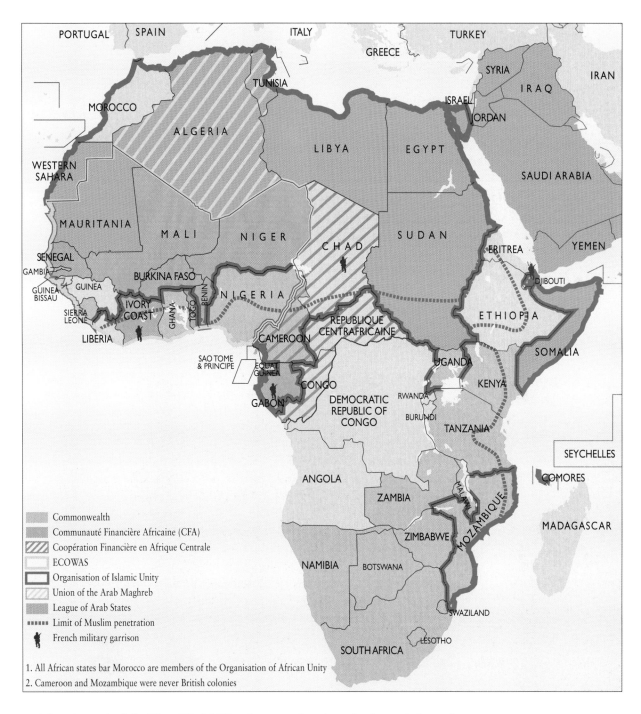

Legend:
- Commonwealth
- Communauté Financière Africaine (CFA)
- Coopération Financière en Afrique Centrale
- ECOWAS
- Organisation of Islamic Unity
- Union of the Arab Maghreb
- League of Arab States
- Limit of Muslim penetration
- French military garrison

1. All African states bar Morocco are members of the Organisation of African Unity
2. Cameroon and Mozambique were never British colonies

After the end of the First World War Germany lost its colonies and these were then administered under League of Nations' mandate by other European states. Similarly after the Second World War Great Britain administered Italian colonies until they received their independence. (The Italians were given back the administration of Italian Somaliland in 1950 under a UN mandate.)

The bulk of decolonisation took place in the 1960s and '70s. While most states gained their independence peacefully, a number dissolved into civil war soon afterwards. The worst of Africa's civil wars have occurred in the former colonies of Belgium and Portugal and in the never-colonised

African links, both internal and external.

Angola: Chronology

1975 Nov	Independence from Portugal achieved. MPLA, with Cuban military support, controls most of country and establishes republic.
1982	UN realises independence for Namibia. Requires Cuban withdrawal from Angola.
1983	Lusaka Agreement: South Africa to withdraw from Angola and SWAPO no longer to operate from there.
1986	South Africa re-commences raids into Angola
1988 Nov	Provisional agreement on Cuban and South African withdrawal
1989 Jan	UNAVEM begins deployment to verify Cuban withdrawal.
1991 May	Cuban withdrawal complete. UNAVEM II formed to monitor the disbandment of government forces and UNITA and formation of national army.
1992 Sept	Elections held observed by UN. UNITA resumes hostilities
1993 Oct	Lusaka talks begin, makes slow progress while fighting continues.
Nov	Lusaka protocol signed and ceasefire comes into effect.
1995 Feb	UNAVEM III established with wider mandate and to safeguard humanitarian efforts.
1997 Jun	UNAVEM III mandate ends and MONUA established as an observer mission.
1998 Jul	UNITA renews fighting
1999 Jan	Two UN transport planes shot down
Feb	MONUA and all other UN staff withdrawn

countries of Liberia and Ethiopia. Britain and France have maintained links with their former colonies. The UK has preserved contact through membership of the Commonwealth, which has been joined by two states that were never British possessions, Cameroon and Mozambique. France's links are both cultural and economic: francophone Africa operates two financial systems: the Communauté financière africaine and the Coopération financière en Afrique Centrale. France has defence agreements with eight francophone states and technical military assistance agreements with twenty-three others; French forces are still stationed in Chad, Côte d'Ivoire, Djibouti, Gabon and Senegal. In 1996 France announced plans to reduce its presence to only two or possibly three garrisons; it withdrew the garrison from the Central African Republic in 1998.

Africa is currently racked by violence with over a third of its countries involved either in civil war or in border disputes with neighbours. Like people throughout the world, the African considers his most prized asset to be his land, whether personal or communal. The value of the land is, of course, much increased if it lies above important minerals, including gems or oil, and much African conflict is focused on control of such assets. A growing number of states are, after European encouragement, providing peacekeeping forces but some of these are taking sides in the civil wars and are becoming part of the problem rather than helping to solve it. Many African leaders have become dictators, acquiring massive riches at the expense of their people – following the example of some of their former colonial masters. A number of the current civil wars are more about acquiring wealth than power.

In addition to war and civil war, Africa is beset by a further major problem: AIDS. It is claimed that as many as 22 million Africans are infected by HIV, the virus that causes AIDS. (The world's total of sufferers is over 33 million.) It is said that 5,000 are dying every day, a figure that could rise to 13,000 by 2005. Another horrific statistic is the estimate that there may be as many as 40 million AIDS orphans by 2010.

Few can afford the drugs necessary to attempt treatment. South Africa has passed a law to allow the government to manufacture drugs it deems too expensive to buy, and may suffer sanctions as a result. A UN pilot scheme is operating in Uganda where patients pay roughly half the European cost of the drugs. The scale of the disease is already affecting national economies.

Web Sites

www.

Africa News Online: www.africanews.org
Africa Policy Information Center: www.africapolicy.org

ANGOLA: CAN RECONCILIATION EVER BE ACHIEVED?

Portugal had already established trading settlements on the West African coast, notably at Luanda and Benguela, when it was allotted what is now Angola by the Berlin Conference of 1884–5, which divided African territory between the European powers. Portugal had long seen the

Catoca Diamond Mine in Lunda Sul province, Angola, August 1998. (Associated Press)

region as an economic replacement for its loss of Brazil. However, Portuguese interest in Angola was purely for trade and it only administered the hinterland after the conference, as it feared it would lose the colony.

Initially Portugal's colonies had a high degree of autonomy and were ruled dictatorially by governors who were free to gain investment from any source. After the appointment of António de Oliveira Salazar to organise Portugal's economy following the military coup of 1926 the colonies were brought very much under direct control from Lisbon; by 1951 they had become part of the Portuguese nation, just at the time when other European African powers were shedding their colonies.

Anti-colonial activity – attacks in Luanda and in the northern coffee-growing area – in early 1961 led to a new wave of development and investment, as well as a military clamp-down, in an attempt to both hold the colonies and maintain the Salazar regime in power in Portugal. The dominant sector of the Angolan economy was coffee and the demand for labour effected ethnic divisions between the northern people, Bakongo and Mbundu, and the southern Ovimbundo brought in to work on the new estates. The Bakongo were the most northern of the Angolan people; they also live in Zaire and the Angolan enclave of Kabinda. The Mbundu live along the River Kuanza which flows from the Cassanje Mountains to Luanda and was the main access route from the coast to the interior. A fourth group, the Lunda-Chokwe, inhabits the north-east and central parts of Angola.

In 1954 the rights of indigenous colonial populations were defined and two categories were given preferential treatment. 'Mestiço' were those of Portuguese-native descent and 'civilizado' was the status given to those who were literate, without criminal records, tax payers and had acquired an undefined degree of Portuguese culture; this process further divided the Angolan population. The first anti-colonial political movements were the Popular Movement for the Liberation of Angola (MPLA), established in 1956, which recruited 'Mestiço' and 'civilizado', mainly in the towns, and the National Front for Liberation of Angola (FNLA) supported by the unprivileged Angolans. The MPLA was supported mainly by the Mbundu, the FNLA by the Bakongo, and a third party, the National Union for the Total Independence of Angola (UNITA) led by Jonas Savimbi, represented the interests of the more populous Ovimbundo and Lunda-Chokwe. The ethnic make-up of the political movements was not absolute and there was some movement between the groups.

The war for independence began in 1961 but the Portuguese managed to maintain control of the whole country until the 1974 military coup in Portugal. Fighting continued for some weeks but the army was unwilling to continue the struggle and over the next six months ceasefires were signed with the three nationalist movements. In January 1975 the leaders of the three movements met and signed an agreement for independence from Portugal that set up a transitional government with the movement leaders forming a joint presidency alongside the Portuguese High Commissioner; independence would come on 11 November. Before November, fighting broke out between the movements, each of which had gained international support. The Soviet Union and Cuba, which sent several hundred military advisers during the summer, backed the MPLA which had become a Marxist organisation. The US naturally backed the other two groups. The West generally supported UNITA. The South Africans provided military support for the FNLA.

The MPLA as the strongest of the three groups established the government; the FNLA eventually disbanded but UNITA continued to fight and to control territory. In 1988 Cuban involvement reached its peak with some 50,000 troops deployed. Negotiating a peace settlement was made more difficult by the presence of up to 9,000 men from the South West African People's Organisation (SWAPO) who used Angolan territory as a base for their fight to achieve independence for South West Africa (now Namibia). The African National Congress (ANC) also had training bases there and, as a result, there were frequent incursions of South African forces from South West Africa. At the end of 1988 agreement was reached between Angola, Cuba and South Africa over the withdrawal of foreign troops and the UN was requested to monitor the process. (Namibia gained its independence on 1 April 1989.) The United Nations Angola Verification Mission (UNAVEM) of sixty observers from ten countries deployed in January 1989 with a mandate that was to last until August 1991, by which time the Cuban withdrawal would be complete. UNAVEM was concentrated at the ports and Luanda airport, and had two mobile teams checking that Cuban redeployment was taking place as agreed. The withdrawal was only interrupted twice by UNITA forces and after the second attack in January 1990 was suspended for one month.

Withdrawal was completed on 25 May 1991, just over a month ahead of schedule.

In April 1990 the government and UNITA began talks, mediated by Portugal with the US and Soviet Union as observers, that resulted in a peace agreement signed at Estoril in May 1991. The agreement provided for a ceasefire and the forces of both sides were to collect in agreed areas for demobilisation, with 20,000 from each side going to be trained as a new joint Angolan Army. There was also provision for a general election in which UNITA would participate. The ceasefire came into effect on 15 May 1991 and the UN was invited to monitor the demobilisation process. The first of UNAVEM II's 350 military and 60 police observers arrived on 2 June and

Angola, showing the sources of its riches.

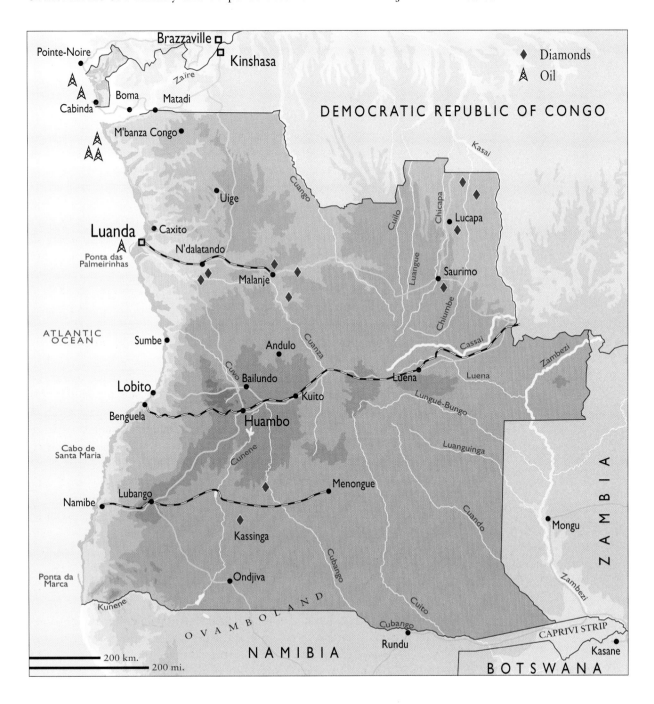

deployed to the 50 assembly areas and to ports, airports and border crossing points. While there were no violations of the ceasefire for 15 months only 45 per cent of the government forces and just 24 per cent of UNITA had been demobilised by September 1992, progress in forming the new army was behind schedule and there was a lack of food and transportation.

In September 1992 both sides announced the disbandment of their armies but neither had completed demobilisation and a much higher proportion of UNITA remained under arms. The elections took place at the end of September and the results, despite UNITA claims of widespread fraud, were declared by the UN monitors to be 'generally free and fair'. As neither side had got over 50 per cent of the vote, a second round was necessary. Fighting broke out again; another ceasefire was arranged but did not last long. Through 1993 and most of 1994 fighting continued and there was a series of peace talks, mostly held at Lusaka. At the same time a serious humanitarian problem had developed with many approaching starvation and UN relief efforts being halted from time to time by the war.

The Lusaka Protocol was signed on 20 November 1994, delayed by the continued fighting including the capture of Huambo, and a ceasefire came into effect on the 22nd. The protocol comprised ten annexes covering a wide range of topics including the ceasefire, the demilitarisation of UNITA, the disarming of civilians, the UN mandate and completion of the electoral process. A much stronger UN force, UNAVEM III, replaced the observers of UNAVEM II with an increased number of observers and police, and in due course formed units of infantry, engineers, transport and medical personnel were deployed. At its peak UNAVEM III numbered 6,500 troops, 336 military observers and 226 civil police. The UN also took on a new role, the clearing of mines; this is now mainly carried out by demining NGOs.

Until the summer of 1998 the ceasefire held with only minor local violations. Demobilisation took place but UNITA sent only the older men and young boys to the collection centres. UNITA representatives took their seats in the National Assembly. UNITA still held a number of strategic areas and some important diamond mines but it lost its main conduit for exporting these when President Mobuto lost control of Zaire in 1997. In July 1997 at the end of UNAVEM III's extended mandate a new UN force, the UN Observer Mission in Angola (MONUA), was formed. During 1998 UNITA failed to hand over a number of its strongholds and by October the civil war had re-erupted, this time with fears that it could spread over Angola's borders into the Democratic Republic of Congo (Zaire). All attempts to halt the present round of fighting failed and in February 1999 the UNSC voted unanimously to end its operations in Angola: MONUA and most other UN Agencies withdrew.

The war continued with no apparent end in sight. The government mounted a large-scale operation in September 1999 and recaptured a number of towns including Andulo which had been UNITA's military HQ for five years. The lack of damage in the captured towns has led to the belief that UNITA made a tactical withdrawal. Namibia, which, with Angola, is supporting Congolese President, Laurent Kabila, has agreed to allow the Angolans to use its territory to mount attacks against UNITA from the south.

Bibliography and Web Sites

Anstee, Margaret, *Angola: The Forgotten Tragedy*, David Davies Memorial Lecture
  published by International Relations, 1993
Guiarães, Fernando Andresen, *The Origins of the Angolan Civil War*, Macmillan Press, 1998
Klingshoffer, *The Angolan War*, Westview, 1986
Maier, Karl, *Angola: Promises and Lies*, Serif, 1996

Angolan Government: www.angola.org
UNITA Kwacha Press: www.kwacha.com

LIBERIA: LAND FOR THE FREE

The first American-freed African slaves landed on the coast of West Africa in 1822, sent by the American Colonisation Society. The society purchased 60 miles of coastline between Cape Mesurado (St Paul, now Monrovia) and the River Junk for $300 worth of trade goods. At that time the territory, now Liberia, was the home of sixteen ethnic groups. In the following years a number of other US states obtained land and sent freed slaves there; in 1827 Maryland had territory at Cape Palmas and Virginia between the Junk and Farmington Rivers, Pennsylvania in 1835 from Bossa Cove to the mouth of the St John River; and in 1838 Mississippi acquired the area from Greenville to the mouth of the Sinoe. In 1847 these territories united as the Republic of Liberia. The constitution and flag copied that of the US; of the population, 5 per cent were former American slaves. After the end of the American Civil War there were no further immigrants to Liberia. In 1883 the British annexed the territory north-west of the River Mano and in 1892 France annexed the land east of the River Cavallo; the French also annexed territory in the north of the country in 1911.

In 1912 the US sent three African-American former army officers to train the Liberian Frontier Force, responsible for defending the borders and suppressing internal opposition. In 1915 the Kru people who lived on the coast rebelled against the government and demanded that they be annexed by Sierra Leone. An American warship was diverted to assist in quelling the rebellion.

In 1944 William Shadrach Tubman became President and remained in power until he died in 1971. He was succeeded by William Tolbert who had been Vice-President for twenty years. His administration was corrupt and he was killed in a coup mounted by indigenous non-commissioned officers in the army led by Master Sergeant Samuel Doe in April 1980. The coup ended the rule of the 50,000 Americo-Liberians over the 2.5 million indigenous Africans. The Doe regime was notoriously savage, practising imprisonment without trial and summary execution for little reason. The US turned a blind eye to his excesses because it needed Liberia as an entry point into Africa to counter growing Soviet influence. Liberia was a conduit for US arms to the anti-communist forces in Angola and was the site for the Voice of America radio transmitters. Doe was re-elected in 1985 in a fraudulent poll that was in fact declared fair by the US Secretary of State.

Another army coup was attempted soon after the 1985 election but its leader was soon caught and killed. A number of opponents to Doe's rule

The armed forces, mid-1995	
Liberian	
Armed Forces of Liberia	2,000–3,000
ULIMO (Mandingo)	4,000
ULIMO (Krahn)	3,000
NPFL (Taylor)	8,000
NPFL (dissidents)	3,000–4,000
LPC	2,000
ECOMOG	
Nigeria	6,000
Ghana	900
Guinea	1,000
Sierra Leone	700
(all strengths estimates)	
UNOMIL	
70 observers from 11 countries	

found it necessary to leave the country; one of these was a notably dishonest junior minister, Charles Taylor, who fled to Burkina Faso and then received military training in Libya. At the end of 1989 a previously unknown group, the National Patriotic Forces of Liberia (NPLF) sent a force of 200 men over the border from Côte d'Ivoire to attack soldiers, police and other officials. They had assumed they would be supported by the people of Nimba Province but lost all support when Taylor assumed command of the NPLF. Taylor's men were mainly Gio tribesmen and they targeted the Krahn, Doe's group. The army was sent in and killed some 1,500 young men and caused 150,000 people to flee either to Côte d'Ivoire and Guinea or into the bush when their villages were looted and burnt. However, the NPLF was not defeated and Taylor with 10,000 men overran most of the country other than Monrovia where Doe remained in control.

Taylor's NPLF then split with Gio Prince Yarmie Johnson leading the breakaway group that entered Monrovia in February 1990, fighting both Taylor and Doe. In June Taylor captured the international airport, forcing Doe to barricade himself into his residence with several hundred bodyguards. The Economic Community of West African States (ECOWAS) held an emergency meeting attended by only seven of the sixteen member states who decided, calling themselves the Economic Community Monitoring Group (ECOMOG), to send in a peacekeeping force of 3,000 men to enforce a ceasefire and supervise elections. The force deployed in early September with contingents from Gambia, Ghana, Guinea, Nigeria and Sierra Leone. Taylor established himself in Kakata as a temporary capital from which virtually the whole Madingo population had been evicted or massacred.

ECOMOG arranged a ceasefire between Doe and Taylor. Doe, believing he was safe, left his residence to visit the ECOMOG commander. Johnson's men, the United Liberation Movement in Liberia (ULIMO) attacked and captured Doe, killing him and all his escort. ECOMOG did nothing to prevent the massacre. It was threatened by Taylor, and Johnson took prisoner 50 of its men. ECOMOG managed to evacuate around 1,000 of Doe's supporters and their families but several hundred stayed behind in the residence. This was attacked by both Taylor and Johnson but separately; they also attacked each other. The three groups met in Mali, agreed a ceasefire and later, in February 1991, signed a formal agreement to hold a reconciliation conference: the agreement made no progress. Doe's supporters were now known as the Armed Forces of Liberia (ALF). The rest of 1991 saw further fighting between the three factions and new attempts to broker a ceasefire; nor was any progress achieved throughout most of 1992. It was not until November 1992 that the UN imposed an arms embargo on Liberia and appointed a special representative.

In July 1993 a meeting was held at Cotonou, Benin, attended by the three Liberian factions, the UN Special Representative, the Chairman of the Organisation of African Unity (OAU) and the Executive Secretary of ECOWAS. A peace agreement was reached and signed. It allowed for a ceasefire from 1 August followed by disarmament, the deployment of a further 4,000 (non-West African) peacekeepers, and the establishment of a UN Observer

Force (UNOMIL). In 1994 some slow progress was made, further agreement was reached, the Council of State of the Transitional Government was installed, and three demobilisation centres were opened. ECOMOG and UNOMIL were deployed but not in all regions because of local resistance. A new faction, the Liberian Peace Council (LPC), emerged in the south-east of the country and opposed ECOMOG deployment there. Of the 60,000 soldiers in all factions, only some 2,000 were disarmed and demobilised in the first month.

Fighting broke out in May 1994 within the ULIMO between Krahn and Mandingo men and also in the east between the NPLF and the LPC. ECOMOG became increasingly mistrusted. A further agreement was reached at Akosombo, Ghana, in September but the military situation worsened. The Mandingo faction of ULIMO captured the NPLF headquarters and a coalition of the ALF, LPC and Krahn ULIMO attacked the NPLF in the northern and eastern regions of the country. The fighting created some 200,000 refugees and UNOMIL, unable to fulfil its mandate, withdrew to Monrovia. In December not just those who had signed at Akosombo but also the newly formed factions and breakaway groups approved another agreement in Accra. During 1995 the political stalemate continued and the attitude of the factions prevented essential relief from being delivered to the 1.5 million estimated to need it. Fighting still continued with four different

Liberia.

conflicts between differing factions across most of the country. Another meeting was held, this time at Abuja, at which most outstanding issues were settled. A new ceasefire was agreed, the humanitarian situation improved and a new council of state was installed – its membership plus some ministerial posts ensured that every faction and sub-faction was represented.

The situation deteriorated at the end of 1995. Disarmament and demobilisation were behind schedule as was the deployment of ECOMOG throughout the country. Interfaction fighting continued and in April 1996 major conflict broke out between two coalitions in Monrovia which was systematically looted by both groups and half its population made refugees. ECOMOG concentrated its forces in a number of locations but had to withdraw completely from several provinces. By now it was a mainly Nigerian force whose soldiers had been in Liberia for two years and were poorly paid; morale was understandably low and their effectiveness doubtful. US forces helped to evacuate foreigners from Monrovia. Another meeting produced another agreement in August signed by the four leading warlords including Taylor and Johnson. Heavy fighting resumed in Monrovia in May. In August ECOWAS imposed a number of sanctions on Liberia, the non-governmental aid agencies announced that they were curtailing their efforts to 'minimal life-saving activities' and the UN Secretary General warned that the international community would disengage from Liberia if the factions did not make peace.

By January 1997 the situation had changed dramatically. ECOMOG and UNOMIL reported that 10,000 men had been demobilised and over 5,000 weapons had been handed in. Following the end of the arms amnesty ECOMOG recovered nearly 4,000 additional weapons. By April the disarmament process was considered to be 90 per cent complete, though it was suspected that many weapons had been hidden. An election was held in July and was won by Taylor. His National Patriotic Party gained 21 of 26 Senate seats and 49 of 64 in the House of Representatives. UNOMIL's mandate ended on 30 September and ECOMOG began its withdrawal in December. Some 150,000 people are thought to have died in the civil war which was one of the first to see the large-scale employment of boys as young as twelve as soldiers: possibly as many as 3,000 were involved.

Violence re-erupted in August 1999 when rebels entered the country from Guinea taking hostages and occupying a number of villages. Liberia is likely to be unstable for several years to come.

Bibliography and Web Site

Nelson, Harold D., *Liberia a Country Study*, The American University, 1984

www.

Liberian Embassy Washington: www.liberiaemb.org

SIERRA LEONE: ANOTHER DISASTER ZONE

Sierra Leone as a territory was protected from early invasion by its geography. The coastal plain was thickly wooded and to the east are mountains. The rivers running from the latter were not navigable. The major African kingdoms did not penetrate into the area. The first Europeans to visit were Portuguese who named it Serra Lyoa because they believed the small mountainous peninsula that juts out into the Atlantic resembled a lion. The estuary of the River Scarcies provided a safe harbour for European ships which came for the gold, ivory and slaves that were offered and also the water and wood for fuel that was available.

An African people invaded the area in the 1560s and they captured the estuary but were unable to penetrate far inland. While Portuguese were the first settlers, the British too had begun to settle in the country south of the estuary by the early seventeenth century. The crown gave the Royal African Company a monopoly in 1663; it built two forts but health problems and the destruction of one fort caused the company to abandon Sierra Leone by 1730. There was no further British government involvement until it outlawed the slave trade in 1807 and took over the Sierra Leone Company which had been set up by individual traders, opposed to the slave trade, in 1791. Earlier Granville Sharp, an opponent of the slave trade, proposed founding a settlement of free slaves most of whom had escaped from America to Nova Scotia and New Brunswick and he persuaded the British government to transport them to Africa. There were clashes between the settlers and the local Temne people until a peace treaty was signed in 1807.

After the abolition of slavery the British government took over the colony and set up a Vice-Admiralty Court to try the crews of slave ships captured by the Royal Navy; the released slaves stayed to settle in the colony. They were educated and converted to Christianity by missionary societies funded by the government. Merchants replaced the slave trade with exports of timber, palm oil and groundnuts. The Creole (released slave) population wanted to see the colony expanded but the government opposed this until it realised that Sierra Leone was being hemmed in by the colonies that the French were establishing. So a protectorate was created in 1896 in the areas of British influence where the local chiefs advised by British District Officers would have autonomy. To pay for this administration, a tax, the 'Hut Tax', was introduced: it prompted an uprising of the Mende aimed at driving out the colonists completely. This was soon subdued by the military but many Creoles were massacred.

The movement for the end of colonial rule in West Africa began in 1920. A new constitution was introduced to Sierra Leone in 1924 that increased the number of indigenous people on the Legislative Council, including representatives from the Protectorate for the first time but still leaving British officials in control. After the Second World War decolonisation took on a new imperative and a new constitution was proposed. This was to treat the Colony and the Protectorate as a single entity and while the colonists would be given special representation the majority of voters would be from the Protectorate and so would hold power. The Creoles objected to this plan. A revised constitution was accepted in 1951 and slowly Sierra Leone advanced towards independence, which it gained in 1961.

The first two elections were won by the Sierra Leone People's Party. The All People's Congress led by Siaka Stevens won in 1967 but the army, disputing the result, took control. In a counter-coup the army then brought Stevens back as Prime Minister in 1968 and he was sworn in as President when Sierra Leone became a republic in 1971. Stevens remained in power and introduced a one-party state; he stepped down in 1985. His successor was the army commander General Joseph Momoh, who returned the country to multi-party politics in 1991 but he was attacked by the Revolutionary United Front (RUF) and the Sierra Leone civil war began. Charles Taylor in Liberia, where several Sierra Leone opposition parties were based, is seen as having had a hand in the rebellion. The RUF concentrated its operations in the south-east province. Corruption and appointments decided on political and ethnic grounds seriously weakened the army's capability – probably the most competent element had been

UNAMSIL contributors	
Bangladesh	Malaysia
Bolivia	Namibia
Canada	Nepal
Croatia	New Zealand
Czech Rep.	Nigeria
Denmark	Norway
Egypt	Pakistan
France	Russia
Gambia	Slovakia
Ghana	Sweden
India	Tanzania
Indonesia	Thailand
Jordan	UK
Kenya	Uruguay
Kirgyzstan Zambia	

	Authorised	Deployed
Troops	4,290	11,100
Police	220	260

sent to take part in the West African peacekeeping force in Liberia. Large-scale conscription of the unemployed took place but the new soldiers were poorly equipped and unpaid; they resorted to the same tactics as the RUF, using looting and intimidation to survive. The army stepped in again in 1992 to overthrow Momoh with Captain Valentine Strasser leading the interim National Provisional Ruling Council (NPRC). The RUF expected to make a deal with the NPRC but public opinion was opposed to this and so Strasser continued the war. A number of civil militia were formed because of lack of faith in the army, the most important being the 'Kamajors'. Strasser agreed to the involvement of the South African mercenary company, Executive Outcomes, which was brought in by two mining companies because RUF rebels were affecting their operations. The mercenaries teamed up with the Kamajors and made significant progress until Strasser was overthrown by his deputy, Julian Maada Bio. Bio opened negotiations with the RUF and a peace process involving Côte d'Ivoire, the OAU and UN was set in motion. The army aimed to achieve peace before holding elections but was overruled by popular opinion and an election was held in March 1996. It brought Ahmed Tejan-Kabbah, a former UN official, and the Sierra Leone People's Party into power.

Kabbah made a number of mistakes: he blamed the north for allowing former army corporal Foday Sankoh to start the civil war and calling for an apology; in an unpopular move he brought All Peoples Congress (APC) members into his administration; his liaison with Nigeria with whom he agreed a defence arrangement was equally unwelcome. His worst mistake was to end the contract with Executive Outcomes, the only disciplined force in the country. The Kamajors were greatly strengthened in numbers and their leader became Deputy Minister of Defence. The army was further disaffected and strengthened its alliance with the RUF. A peace accord was signed in Abidjan in November but it was upset by the overthrow of Sankoh as leader of the RUF and his arrest when visiting Nigeria. This was too much for the army, which saw a conspiracy to bring Nigeria in to destroy the RUF. In May 1997 an army coup released Major Johnny Paul Koroma from jail. He overthrew the government and Kabbah went into exile.

The new army regime faced both opposition from the population, the OAU meeting at Harare, and the Commonwealth, but little action was taken by its opponents. The RUF was brought into the government. Sankoh, though still in Nigeria, was appointed Vice-

Sierra Leone.

Nigerian troops of the West African peacekeeping force patrol the streets of Freetown, February 1998. (Associated Press)

President and was able to encourage his men to back the military regime. Kabbah now openly enlisted Nigerian support and at a meeting with the military junta and the British High Commissioner a date was set for the return of power to Kabbah. To emphasise their determination the Nigerians bombarded Sierra Leone from the sea. This provoked the capture of some 300 Nigerian soldiers who were assisting in the evacuation of foreign civilians. They were released but Nigeria was intent on intervention. ECOWAS was split with five members opposed to military action and Liberia refused to allow its territory to be used as a base for operations. Several reasons have been put forward for Nigeria's involvement – one being the need to keep its army occupied now that the Liberian operation was over, another the aim of the RUF and elements in the Sierra Leone army of gaining control of some of the country's natural resources, particularly the diamond mines.

At a meeting held at Conakry in October 1997 the junta agreed to the return of Kabbah to power by April 1998. ECOMOG would supervise the demobilisation of the forces and Koroma and his officers would not be charged with treason. Koroma then demanded that the army and the RUF men incorporated in it should not be disarmed, as they were the national army. He also objected to Nigeria's leading role in ECOMOG and demanded the release of Sankoh. The demands led the Nigerians to decide to remove the junta and they looked for an excuse to use force to do so. An attack on Nigerian troops was the excuse and the signal for an all-out attack on Freetown, which fell after three days fighting in February 1998; the army and the RUF fled into the countryside.

The RUF was not defeated and turned to a rampage of terror, mutilating hundreds of civilians. In July while feigning surrender they attacked the northern town of Kabala. The UN authorised a military observer force (UNOMSIL) to observe and report on the situation. In early January 1999 the rebels managed to fight their way into Freetown where they caused widespread damage. Kabbah and the still imprisoned Sankoh ordered a ceasefire which the rebels said they would honour once Sankoh was released. Kabbah said he would release Sankoh after the ceasefire had held for a week. ECOMOG troops were still attempting to clear Freetown of rebels two weeks later. UN observers reported that both sides had committed atrocities and that 150,000 refugees had been created. In July 1999 after several weeks of negotiations a power-sharing deal was agreed at Abidjan: the rebel leader, Foday Sankoh, will be Vice-President responsible for the mineral industry and for reconstruction. By October ECOMOG was planning the gradual withdrawal of its 12,000 troops and the UN had authorised the deployment of a 6,000-strong peacekeeping force that will help the disarmament and demobilisation of some 45,000 militia of both sides. The first UN contingent arrived on 30 November 1999.

The last few years of the civil war have seen a vast increase in the number of atrocities committed by the rebels and to a lesser extent by government forces. A worrying aspect of the civil war has been the large number of children who have been forced into the units of both sides. After such a long period of civil conflict it is too early to say whether peace really has been, or will be, maintained in Sierra Leone.

Bibliography and Web Sites

Fyfe, Christopher, *Sierra Leone Inheritance*, Oxford University Press, 1964

Sierra Leone Government: www.sierra-leone.gov.sl
Sierra Leone Web: www.sierra-leone.com

RWANDA/BURUNDI: TRIBAL GENOCIDE

The origin of the terms 'Hutu' and 'Tutsi' are unknown due to the lack of written records in ancient Africa. The Hutu are a Bantu people while the Tutsis, who are taller and have lighter skin, are thought to be a Hamitic people who probably came from Ethiopia in the sixteenth century. The original colonists, the Germans, followed by their successors after the First World War, the Belgians, considered the Tutsis more intelligent and as a result the Tutsis gained most of the jobs in the colonial administration and were also favoured by the educational system. There were, though, no tribal distinctions nor any traditional tribal lands: Hutus and Tutsis lived intermingled and often intermarried; they speak the same language. As the colonists 'separated' the two, so animosity developed and turned to enmity; what had previously been more a caste system became an explosive ethnic one. The first violence between the two took place in Rwanda, before independence, in 1959, when the Hutus, backed by the Belgians, threw out the Tutsi royal family and committed a number of massacres prompting large numbers of Tutsis to flee to Burundi and Uganda.

On independence in 1962 there was, for several years, a balance between Tutsis and Hutus in the Burundi government though 85 per cent of the population were Hutu. The Tutsis made every effort to control both the government and the army and ethnic divisions assumed greater importance following the assassination of Prince Rwagasore (a member of the Ganwa feudal elite) in October 1961. In 1965 there was an attempted coup by Hutu army officers which led to a purge of Hutu officers and the killing of several thousand Hutus, not just in the army but also most of their civil leaders. The same thing happened again in 1969. Widespread Hutu uprisings took place in 1972 and the army, now entirely Tutsi, is estimated to have killed 250,000 Hutus plus a number of rival Tutsis and to have caused 150,000 to flee the country. Incidents of Tutsi provocation in 1988 led to the massacre of hundreds of Tutsis in the north; the army responded by massacring 15,000–20,000 Hutus and driving many more into Rwanda.

A Hutu president was elected in 1993 and for the first time a Hutu government was appointed. A Tutsi military coup four months later failed to take power but it sparked an outbreak of ethnic violence in which 200,000 died and over a million people were driven from their homes. The next Hutu president was killed in a plane crash together with the Rwandan president. This set off the Rwandan crisis and led to a mass of refugees crossing into Burundi, but did not provoke a fresh outbreak of violence there. In July 1995 former President Buyoya, a Tutsi, regained power in Burundi in a military coup. Burundi has not agreed to any form of peacekeeping force deploying in the country but the UNHCR has played a major humanitarian role.

Until 1959 the Tutsis dominated political and economic life in Rwanda. When the King died extremist Tutsis attempted to fill the power vacuum but provoked a Hutu revolt. To avoid increasing ethnic violence a large number of Tutsis left the country, most going to Uganda. Rwanda gained its independence from Belgium in 1962. The Tutsis made a number of unsuccessful attempts to make an armed comeback but the Hutu remained in control of the country.

In October 1990 Rwanda was invaded by the Tutsi Rwandan Patriotic Front (RPF) from Uganda where it had been formed among the refugees. Many RPF members were serving in the Ugandan National Resistance Army. Although its advance into Rwanda was halted and pushed back, the RPF claimed to have taken control of the Rwandan-Ugandan border. After a conference at Dar-es-Salaam Rwanda agreed to accept back Tutsi refugees, scrap the one-party system and allow the Tutsi to form a political party. Fighting continued along the border and Tutsi gains created thousands of Hutu refugees. A ceasefire was agreed to in July 1992 and the Neutral Military Observer Group, supported by the OAU, monitored the agreement. Hostilities in the north resumed in February 1993 with the Rwandans accusing Uganda of assisting the RPF. As a result, in July the UN agreed to deploy a mission – the UN Military Observer Mission Uganda-Rwanda (UNOMUR) – along the border to ensure there was no reinforcement of the RPF. In August the Arusha Accords were signed and the UN agreed to deploy the UN Assistance Mission in Rwanda (UNAMIR) to maintain security in Kigali and establish a demilitarised zone incorporating UNOMUR.

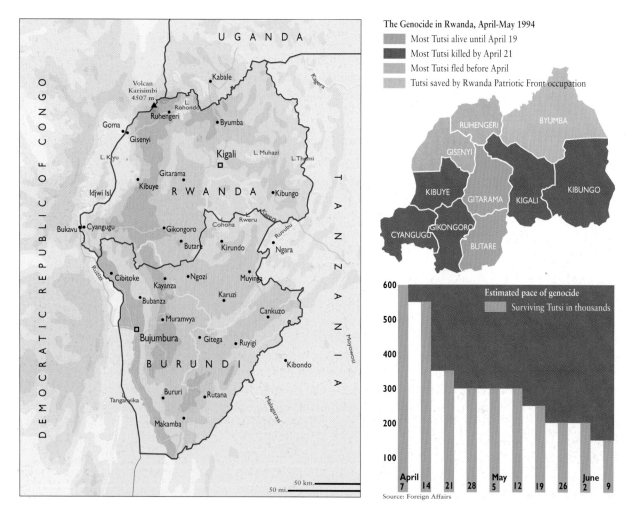

The Genocide in Rwanda, April-May 1994

Most Tutsi alive until April 19
Most Tutsi killed by April 21
Most Tutsi fled before April
Tutsi saved by Rwanda Patriotic Front occupation

Estimated pace of genocide
Surviving Tutsi in thousands

Source: Foreign Affairs

Rwanda and Burundi.

On 6 April 1994 the aircraft carrying the presidents of both Rwanda and Burundi crashed killing all on board. Two days later the RPF renewed its attacks. At the same time a series of mass murders of Tutsis amounting to genocide took place across the country. It was evident that the murders carried out by the Hutu army and militias known as the 'interahamwe' had been long prepared and only the signal to start had been awaited. At least 500,000 Tutsis and 'moderate' Hutus are known to have died. By the end of May the RPF had captured half the country and had surrounded Kigali. The Belgian government decided to withdraw its battalion from UNAMIR and the UN debated its future operations in the area, deciding that it should withdraw leaving only 270 men in Kigali to continue mediating between the two sides. The only alternative would have been to rush several thousand troops in with a Chapter VII enforcement mandate.

It was now the Hutus' turn to suffer and over 250,000 refugees crossed into Tanzania in twenty-four hours. At the end of May 1994 the UN Security Council was told that some 1.5 million people had been displaced in Rwanda and a further 400,000 refugees had crossed its borders. On 8 June the UNSC resolved to reinforce UNAMIR to 5,500 men. In the first week of July the French, in Operation 'Turquoise', established a 'humanitarian protected zone' in south-western Rwanda. By 18 July the RPF had taken control of virtually the whole country and unilaterally

Hutu refugees returning from Tanzania, December 1996. (Associated Press)

declared a ceasefire; on the 19th a broad-based government of national unity was formed. During July the refugee crisis grew and an estimated 1.5 million Hutus, often forced by the Hutu army, crossed into Zaire; they were followed by the remnants of the army.

In Zaire former Hutu officials and military forced the refugees to remain in the camps, were suspected of preparing for a counter-attack into Rwanda and were responsible for the state of lawlessness. The UN recommended deploying both police and military to control the camps but few nations were prepared to risk their forces in such an operation. The Zaire government and humanitarian agencies did their best; a number of nations sent military units to support humanitarian efforts, including the US, the UK, Australia and Israel. They concentrated on the supply of food and water, medical arrangements, road building and the repair of UN vehicles.

In August 1995 the Zaire government began the forced repatriation of refugees. By the time the policy was abandoned on account of international pressure some 13,000 had been returned to Rwanda but 170,000 fled into the forests to avoid repatriation. The UNHCR then took on the task of organising the return of refugees, but the results were too slow for the Tanzanian and Zairean governments. UNAMIR's mandate ended in March 1996 and UN troops withdrew from Rwanda. The total cost of UN operations there was over $4 billion.

www.

In October 1996 fighting in eastern Zaire between the government and the ethnic Tutsi Banyamulenge who have inhabited Kivu for many years led to panic in the refugee camps. Around 600,000 fled back to Rwanda and a further 300,000 went west deeper into Zaire. In December 1996 the UNHCR reached agreement with the Tanzanian authorities for the total repatriation of the remaining 540,000 refugees. On hearing of the plans most refugees attempted to hide in the bush but were turned back by the Tanzanian Army and then shepherded to the border.

In recent years there has been some admission that the genocide in Rwanda could have been prevented but for the lack of support, particularly from the US, for further action by the UN. In a visit to Kigali in March 1998 President Clinton apologised for not having 'fully appreciated . . . this unimaginable terror'.

Bibliography and Web Sites

Gourevitch, Philip, *We Wish to Inform You that Tomorrow We Will be Killed With Our Families*, 1998

Melvern, Linda, *The People Betrayed: The Role of the West in Rwanda's Genocide*, Zed Books, 2000

Prunier, Gerard, *The Rwandan Crisis 1959–1994: History of Genocide*, Hurst, 1995

Burundi Information: http://burundi@burundi

Rally for the Return of Refugees and Democracy in Rwanda: www.rdrwanda.org

Rwanda Information Exchange: www.rwanda.net

CONGO: NEARLY A PAN-AFRICAN WAR

This vast region of central Africa has had many names: originally the Kongo Kingdom, then claimed by Belgium as the Congo Free State until annexed as the Belgian Congo, after independence changing to Zaire and now called the Democratic Republic of Congo (DRC). The region had a complex pre-colonial history. A number of quite different societies lived there. Much of the area was inhabited by small-scale communities, originally based on villages that expanded by conquering neighbours and developing into tribes. The Mongo people of the central basin had no unifying political focus, nor did the 'gens d'eaus', living along the north of the River Congo. The people living between the Congo and River Ubangi had a more hierarchical system based on lineage. In the east there were Muslim/Arab traders and in the north-east, in the forest of Ituri, there were groups of 'hunter gatherers'. A number of kingdoms were formed over the centuries. In the late 1300s the Kongo Kingdom began expansion that continued until the mid-seventeenth century. The Lunda Kingdom was established in the late fifteenth century by a number of chieftains and in the sixteenth expanded to its west, east and south. In the late fifteenth century the Luba Empire was formed, around 1500 the Zande people appeared in the north and about 1630 the Kuba Kingdom was set up.

The first European explorers, the Portuguese, came in 1483. Dr Livingstone explored the Congo Basin between 1840 and 1872. In 1878 the Belgian King, Leopold II, formed a consortium of bankers to finance exploration and colonisation and by 1887 Sir Henry Stanley, under the auspices of the Belgian government, had obtained some 450 treaties with local chiefs. At the Congress of Berlin Leopold claimed the region as the Congo Free State and turned it into a private fiefdom taking the profits of the state for himself. The Belgian military expelled the Afro-Arab slave traders between 1890 and 1894 and slavery was banned. In 1908 Belgium annexed the territory as the Belgian Congo.

In the 1950s measures were introduced to allow Africans to own land, to have the right to trial and to participate in politics. In 1956 the Alliance of Congo People (Alliance des Bakongo-Abako) called for immediate independence. The Katangan independence party, the Confédération des Associations du Katanga, under the leadership of Moise Tshombe, was formed. By 1959 the Belgians had recognised the goal of total independence for Congo. In July that year the Congolese National Movement (Mouvement National Congolais) split, with Patrice Lumumba leading the radical group and in May 1960 he was appointed Prime Minister. Joseph Kasavubu, an Abako, was elected President and independence was gained on 30 June.

In July 1960 the army mutinied against its European officers and Joseph Mobutu, later to be known as Mobutu Sese Seko, became Chief of Staff. An unratified treaty allowed Belgium to maintain two military bases and, after disorder spread, the Belgian government, without the agreement of the Congolese government, ordered its troops to restore law and order and protect its nationals. A number of serious clashes between Belgian and Congolese troops occurred. Katanga declared its independence on 11 July and UN military assistance was called for. The UN Security Council agreed a Resolution on the night of 13 July that called on Belgium to withdraw its forces and authorised a peacekeeping force. Within forty-eight hours the advance party of the United Nations Operation on Congo (ONUC) had arrived. Within six weeks Belgian forces had withdrawn from the country but the secession of Katanga had not been resolved.

Following fighting between Baluba and Lulua tribesmen, the Southern Kasai seceded and there was increasing opposition to the government in the provinces of Equateur and Leopoldville. In September a constitutional crisis developed when President Kasavuba decided to dismiss the Prime Minister who refused to go and in turn dismissed the President. Mobutu mounted a not entirely successful coup and the army backed a council of commissioners that supported Kasavubu but was opposed by Lumumba. ONUC managed to remain neutral by guarding both leaders. It also negotiated an end to fighting in Katanga and set up a number of protected areas for both Europeans and Africans. Katanga's secession ended in February 1963; ONUC remained in the Congo until the end of June 1964 assisting with the reorganisation and training of the army and with the restoration of civil activity in a wide range of services.

In July 1964 Tshombe returned from exile and was appointed Prime Minister, and the country adopted the name of the Republic of Congo. Kasavubu and Tshombe were soon embroiled in a power struggle until Mobutu and the army intervened, establishing a 'second republic'. Mobutu was elected President in 1970, the country's name was changed to Zaire and all provincial names were also changed. Zaire suffered rebellions in Shaba in 1977 and 1978. The first was put down with the help of Moroccan troops and the second by French and Belgian soldiers.

MONUC contributors	
Algeria	Mali
Bangladesh	Nepal
Benin	Pakistan
Bolivia	Poland
Canada	Romania
Egypt	Russia
France	South Africa
Ghana	Sweden
India	Tanzanian
Italy	UK
Kenya	Uruguay
Libya	Zambia

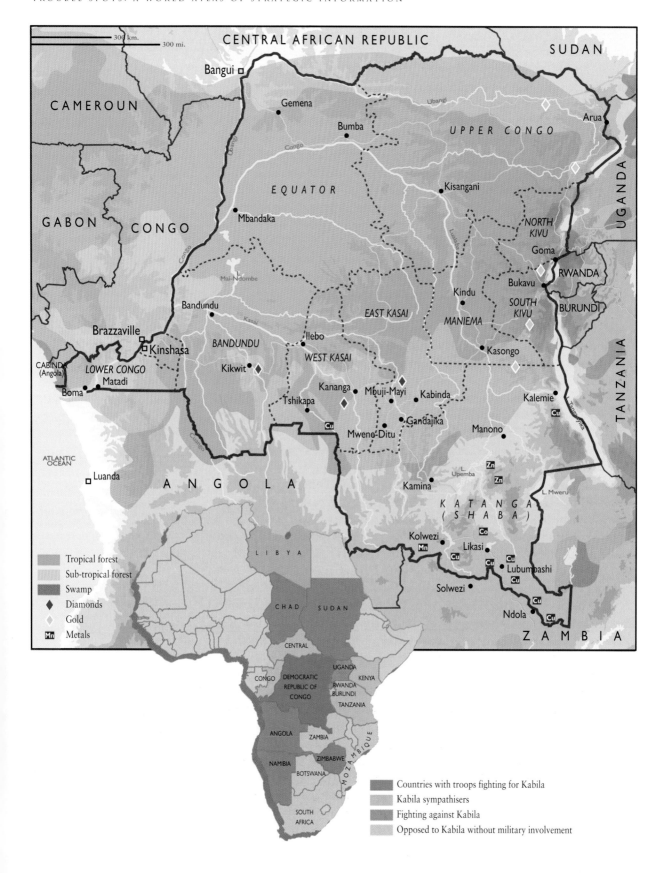

Democratic Republic of Congo.

Zaire is rich in natural resources with industrial diamonds, gold, copper, cobalt, manganese and tin. There is also offshore oil. Like his Belgian predecessor Mobutu built up a personal fortune while at the same time the country suffered from massive inflation and its infrastructure began to collapse through lack of maintenance. In 1994 close on a million refugees – Hutus from Rwanda – camped in eastern Zaire fed by the UN; among them were both Rwandan army and Hutu militiamen who both controlled the camps and mounted raids against Rwanda and Burundi.

A new rebellion broke out in late 1996 in Kivu Province sparked off by the attempted expulsion of the Tutsi population known as the Banyamulenge who had lived in Kivu for generations. They turned on the Zairean Army and beat them. They then turned on the Hutus, who had been encouraging the army and who fled their camps. Some 600,000 crossed back into Rwanda in a mass movement while another 300,000 went deeper into Zaire where thousands are thought to have been massacred in the forests. The rebellion was led by Laurent Kabila, a Luba from Shaba, who had taken part in earlier failed uprisings. The Zaire Army was unpaid and ill equipped and Kabila's men crossed the country remarkably swiftly, reaching Kinshasa in six months and taking it in May 1997. Kabila became President and Zaire was renamed the Democratic Republic of Congo (DRC).

The change of regime did not bring peace to the country. Both Uganda and Rwanda which were supporting Kabila were disappointed that he had failed to secure the east of the country, a failure that allowed insurgent Hutus to continue their cross-border attacks. The two countries therefore supported a new rebel force opposed to Kabila, the Rallye pour le Congo Démocratique (RCD). The Rwandan element of Kabila's forces left Kinshasa in July 1998 because they had been insufficiently rewarded and Kabila took the opportunity to replace senior army officers with his own men. This in turn led to a mutiny in Goma and elsewhere and the rebellious units soon took Kivu Province and most of Haut Zaire, and even threatened Kinshasa until Angolan troops drove them off. The RCD had active support from the Rwandan and Ugandan armies, while Kabila got military support from Chad, Angola, Namibia and, most importantly, Zimbabwe which supplied most of Kabila's air support.

In August 1999 the RCD split, with one faction supported by Rwanda, the other by Uganda. The troops of these two countries came to blows in three days of fighting in the city of Kisangani. A peace agreement has been ready for signing since July when it was drawn up by the foreign and defence ministers of the African countries involved in the war but the two factions of the RCD could not agree who should sign on their behalf. Eventually the agreement was signed by fifty founder members of the RCD on 1 September in Lusaka. It is too early to say whether the peace agreement will end violence in the DRC or whether the conflict will have a lasting effect on the relations between the other African countries that supported it.

Web Sites

International Crisis Group Central Africa Project: www.crisisweb.org/projects/cafrica
Republic of Congo and the Civil War (International Relations Security Network): www.isn.ethz.ch/congo

SOUTH ASIA: WITH NUCLEAR WEAPONS IN THE OPEN

That India and Pakistan had a nuclear capability came as no surprise but their tests have confirmed that capability and have given a new dimension to the situation in South Asia. In addition to considering the confrontation between India and Pakistan and the two countries' internal security concerns, this section also describes the background to the situations in Sri Lanka and Myanmar.

INDIA AND PAKISTAN: A NEW TEST FOR DETERRENCE

Indian and Pakistani enmity entered a new dimension when the two countries exploded nuclear devices in May 1998. However, the first Indian-Pakistani war erupted immediately after each received its independence on the British withdrawal and partition of the Indian Empire in 1947. The predominantly Muslim state of Kashmir opted for India and in response Pakistan occupied the north and western parts of it. There have been two wars since then, in 1965 and 1971. The two armies exchange fire over the line of control frequently. To the north-east, forces face each other over the Siachen Glacier, at 20,000 feet above sea level, where the line of control has never been delineated. Clashes began in 1984, when India deployed troops to the mountain passes, mainly because Pakistani maps showed the territory as theirs, and have continued ever since. The Indians see their possession of the glacier as essential on the grounds that with China now in control of both Shaksam Valley, ceded by Pakistan in 1963, to the west and Aksai Chin, taken from India in 1962, to the east, Pakistani control of the Siachen would threaten Ladakh and the route to Leh down the Nurba Valley. The Chinese have military roads connecting Siachen with Tibet, through Aksai Chin, and with Havelian. Neither side will allow the other to claim the territory that is still undemarcated. In February 1999 the two Prime Ministers agreed that the future of Siachen should be negotiated.

The world was taken by surprise when India exploded three nuclear devices at its Pokhran test site in the Rajahstan Desert on 11 May 1998. It was surprised again when India announced it had carried out two more tests two days later. It was no surprise, therefore, when Pakistan carried out five nuclear tests on 28 May and two more on the 30th. The Indian tests took place only two months after the Hindu nationalist Bharatiya Janata Party (BJP) government had been elected; they could probably have been conducted much earlier had a political decision to authorise tests been taken by the previous government.

International reaction to the tests centred on the implications for non-proliferation and whether they would encourage other states to embark on nuclear weapons programmes. The Comprehensive Test Ban Treaty (CTBT) was seen to be weakened by the failure of seismic stations to record India's tests on 13 May.

The real outcome of the tests is that the suspicion which had been strongly held for many years – that both India and Pakistan were pursuing nuclear programmes and were most likely to have all the components needed to produce nuclear weapons even if these had not already been assembled – was confirmed. In many ways the tests could have positive results: India and Pakistan have both said they will consider joining the CTBT and possibly support a fissile material production ban that is being discussed in Geneva. India has also said it might join both the Nuclear Suppliers Group and the Missile Technology Control Regime. Neither country can join the Nuclear Non-Proliferation Treaty that recognised five nuclear states when it came into force in 1970 as no other nuclear-armed state can be admitted. However there is no reason why some form of trilateral treaty with the United Nations could not be drafted which would legally and politically bind them to the same commitments to non-proliferation as the recognised nuclear states have undertaken.

In 1974 India exploded a so-called peaceful nuclear device and so was known to have the ability to make nuclear weapons. A study carried out by the Carnegie Task Force on non-proliferation and South Asian security ten years ago assessed that India could by then have produced sufficient plutonium to make at least twelve weapons and possibly as many as thirty-eight. Pakistan was thought to have sufficient fissile material to construct between one and seven weapons. These numbers will have increased since then even, when the material used in the tests is taken into account.

Both India and Pakistan are also developing surface-to-surface missiles capable of delivering nuclear warheads. India already has the Privthi with two versions: for the army a 150 kilometre range missile and for the air force a range of 250 kilometres. The Agni 1 was tested to a range of 1450 kilometres in 1994 and is reported to be ready for production. Agni 2 – a longer, 2,500 kilometre-range version – is being developed and was test fired on 11 April 1999 despite pressure from the US and China not to precipitate a missile race on the subcontinent. India is also developing a cruise missile and a sea-launched ballistic missile. Pakistan quickly responded to the Indian test by trialling its Ghauri 2 (HATF-V) missile on 14 April, achieving a 1120 kilometre flight; further

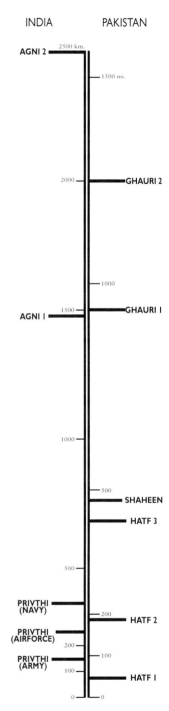

Ranges of Indian and Pakistani missiles.

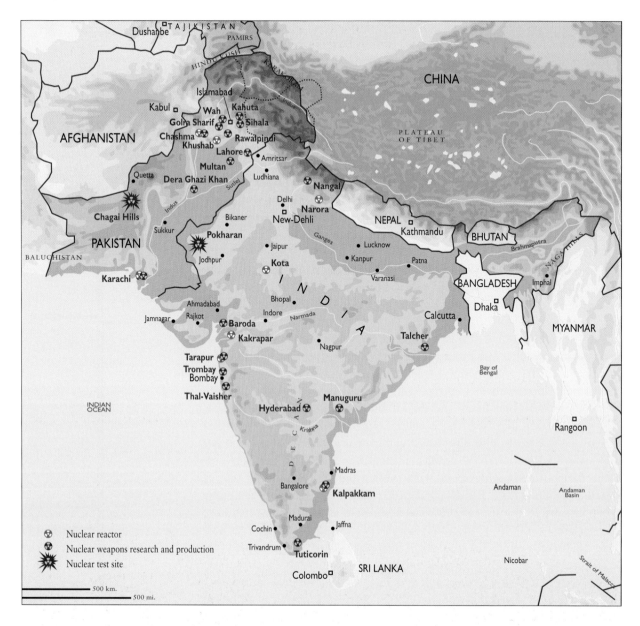

Nuclear weapons facilities in India and Pakistan.

full-range tests of 2320 kilometres are expected. Pakistan had tested the Ghauri 1, with a 1450 kilometre range, in April 1998; it also has three shorter-range versions of the HATF missile including the Shaheen (HATF-IV) which has a 600 kilometre range with a 1000 kilogram payload.

India maintains that its nuclear and missile developments are not designed to threaten Pakistan but are to be a deterrent to possible Chinese threats. Not that this is any comfort to Pakistan, which sees the developments as a distinct danger that it must counter with its own capability. There have been two positive developments: first, the Indian-Pakistani agreement not to attack each other's nuclear installations, reached in 1985 but not signed until 1988 nor ratified until January 1991. Secondly, in February 1999 the two Prime Ministers agreed a package of confidence-building measures that included an exchange of information on nuclear doctrine and on nuclear weapon and missile holdings and deployment. Advance warning of missile test flights would be given. The required warning was given by both states for the 1999 tests. Both countries' missiles will threaten other states: Agni 2 will be able to reach the south-east corner of Iraq and most of Iran but Israel will be just out of range of Pakistan's Ghauri 2.

After three wars over Kashmir where the issue is no nearer to being solved and where artillery fire is regularly exchanged, the possibility of a fourth war cannot be discounted. In August 1999 the Indians shot down a Pakistani surveillance aircraft which they claimed had intruded into Indian air space. The next day Pakistan fired on Indian military aircraft and helicopters, without shooting any down, close to where its plane had come down. Fortunately the incident did not escalate. Given India's preponderance in conventional strength, a future war could involve the use of nuclear weapons, perhaps first by Pakistan and then inevitably by India. However, the possession of nuclear weapons by both India and Pakistan could act as useful deterrent not just to nuclear war but to any war. In this light perhaps the tests could have served a useful purpose.

The nuclear tests, 1999

India
May: 43 kT thermonuclear device; 12 kT fission device; sub-kilo tonne device
13 May: 2 sub-kilo tonne devices (range 0.2–0.6 kT)

Pakistan
28 May: 30–35 kT fission device; four low yield tactical warheads.

Bibliography and Web Sites

Porkovich, George, *India's Nuclear Bomb*, University of California Press, 1999

Indian Ministry of Foreign Affairs: www.meadev.gov.in/
Pakistan Government: www.pak.gov.pk

Indian nuclear weapon test site, Pokharan, May 1998. (Indian Express)

KASHMIR: A CASE FOR INDEPENDENCE?

Kashmir has been claimed by both India and Pakistan since the end of the British Indian Empire on 15 August 1947. It is the main source of dispute between the two countries and has been the cause of three wars between them. Any fourth war is likely to be provoked by the continuing dispute over Kashmir. There is also an Indian claim to Aksai Chin which lies in north-west Ladakh and was occupied by the Chinese in 1962.

The Valley of Kashmir is bounded by three mountain ranges: the North Kashmir Range to the north, the Great Himalayan Range to the east and the Pir Panjal Range to the south and west. There are twenty passes leading into Kashmir over the mountains and so it is not invulnerable to hostile movement. Kashmir's independence rested on the strength of its king: under a strong monarch it remained secure from foreign intervention but under a weak one, who failed to guard the passes, it fell to conquerors. The original inhabitants were Nagas and other lesser tribes. In 800, Aryans from today's Uttar Pradesh became the dominant people in the region. Brahmin priests played an influential role throughout Kashmir's history.

The population is religiously mixed with Muslims predominant but also with Hindus and Sikhs, who live mainly in Jammu, and some Buddhists in Ladakh. Kashmir was originally Hindu, but Islam was introduced in the early fourteenth century. The persecution of Hindus began in the late fourteenth century when Genghis Khan demanded tribute of Kashmir. At first the Muslims were only of the Sunni persuasion but the Shi'a faith was introduced in 1492, further complicating Kashmir's religious tensions.

Kashmir's status as an independent kingdom ended in the mid-sixteenth century when it was brought into the Mughal Empire. As the power of the Mughals declined, Kashmir was ruled by tyrannical governors; this led to Kashmiri nobles turning to Afghanistan for help. The Afghans took over in 1751 but the Kashmiris soon found they were as cruel as the Mughals had been. After fifty years of rebellion and two unsuccessful attacks by Sikhs, Kashmir finally fell to the Sikhs in 1819. Sikh rule lasted for only twenty-eight years and was as harsh as that of the Afghans with the character of the governor determining the lot of Kashmiris.

Dogras, a hill Rajput people, ruled Jammu by the beginning of the nineteenth century but they lost it to the Sikhs in 1808. Gulab Singh was the great-great-nephew of the Dogra leader Ranjit Dev. He had fought against the Sikhs when only sixteen. He then joined the Sikh army and took part in the Sikh capture of Kashmir in 1819; after leading the Sikhs in putting down the revolt in Jammu in 1820, he was made the Rajah of Jammu. He and his two brothers acquired control of numerous small hill territories around Kashmir and in 1835 had made Ladakh a vassal to Jammu. Gulab deserted the Sikhs in their war with the British to avoid losing his domain should the British annex Sikh territories. After the British defeated the Sikhs at the battle of Sobraon in February 1846, they accepted Kashmir in lieu of the indemnity they demanded of the Sikhs; a week later the British had sold Kashmir to Gulab Singh for the same sum as the indemnity, one krore of rupees. Jammu and Kashmir remained loyal to the British during the Indian mutiny in May 1857. Dogra rule of Kashmir and Jammu was maintained until British rule in India ended.

At partition, rulers of princely states were asked to accede to either India or Pakistan; the ruler of Kashmir, who was a Hindu, despite British advice to consider the majority Muslim population chose to accede to India after attempting for two months to remain independent. The decision sparked off an immediate war between the newly independent states of India and Pakistan. If the former Viceroy Lord Wavell's advice had been taken, Britain would have retained control of the Muslim areas until agreement had been reached over boundaries when Britain would have withdrawn; the war would have been avoided and Kashmir might have survived in peace.

Fighting ended after the UN Security Council set up the UN Commission for India and Pakistan (UNCIP) which visited Kashmir in July 1948 and achieved the agreement of the Indian and Pakistani governments to order a ceasefire immediately before midnight on 1 January 1949. The ceasefire has been monitored by the UN Military Observer Group India and Pakistan (UNMOGIP) ever since.

Hostilities broke out in August 1965 after disagreements over claims to the Rann of Kutch. Fighting began along the Kashmir ceasefire line and by September had spread to the Indian-West Pakistan border. The UN adopted a number of resolutions and finally demanded in UNSC 211 that a ceasefire take effect from 0700 GMT and that all troops be withdrawn to positions held before 5 August. The UN established another monitoring mission, the UN India-Pakistan Observer Mission (UNIPOM), to monitor the ceasefire along the international border. Following a meeting in Tashkent, agreement was reached on troop withdrawal: it was effected by 25 February 1966. UNIPOM was disbanded on 22 March.

Hostilities broke out again in early December 1971, this time initially on the Indian-East Pakistan border. Both sides reinforced their presence in Kashmir in violation of the Karachi Agreement (reached in 1949) and fighting broke out there on 3 December. A ceasefire came into effect on 17 December, by which time a number of positions had changed hands. Pakistan continued to report Indian violations to UNGOMIP but India argued that the UN mandate had lapsed on account of the war and UNMOGIP had no responsibility for the new ceasefire line, which had come into existence in December. UNCIP was also responsible after the 1971 war ceasefire for assisting in the establishment of a ceasefire line that became known as the 'line of control'. Pakistan retained control of the Northern Areas (Baltistan and the Gilgit Agency) and a strip of land west of Pir Panjal Range now known as Azad Kashmir. In December 1972 the two governments agreed a new line of control which with some small differences followed the line of the 1949 ceasefire line.

The current uprising in Indian Kashmir began in July 1989 when bombs exploded in Srinagar, followed by sporadic outbreaks of violence. The revolt was prompted by the realisation that Pakistan was unable to hold and that India had no intention of holding the plebiscite on Kashmir's future as agreed by both countries at the 1949 ceasefire. The kidnapping of the daughter of the Indian Home Minister and her exchange for five Kashmiri militants from prison was the signal for demonstrations of victory throughout Kashmir. With weapons acquired from Pakistan and

---

Recent incidents in Kashmir

1999

May Large-scale infiltration (500 plus Afghan mercenaries and Pakistani Army) across some 80 km of line of control in the Kargil area. Infiltrators dig in in Indian Kashmir.
26: Indian Air Force attacks
27: two Indian MiG fighters shot down over Pakistan
Indian helicopter shot down

June 1: Indian casualties reach 46 dead. Both sides deploy armour to Punjab border.
Indian troops capture Tololing Ridge. 800 infiltrators said to be still in India.

July 12: Indian air attacks halted to allow withdrawal of infiltrators.
Kargil fighting ends. Casualties: Indian Army 410, Pakistan 698, mercenaries 135.

Aug 1: six infiltrators shot
Indian Army HQ shelled, 1 killed.
Indian Maritime patrol aircraft shot down.

Sept 5: land mine kills BJP candidate
9: Indian soldiers killed by artillery fire at Siachen glacier
14: Muslim militants killed.

Nov 9: one Indian and seventeen Pakistani soldiers killed in clash.

2000

Jan 1: 155 Indian airline hostages exchanged for three Kashmiri Muslim militants.

The contested region of Kashmir.

Princely State of Kashmir
Line of Control
Boundary claimed by India
Boundary claimed by China
Ceded by Pakistan to China in 1963
Occupied by India since 1983
(no defined boundary)

Afghanistan, a 'jihad' was launched against the Indian authorities. The Indians responded by appointing a hard-line governor with instructions to put down the revolt; he was sent some 250,000 men from the army and a number of paramilitary forces. Both sides have been guilty of atrocities and it has been estimated that as many as 20,000 have been killed since 1989.

Indian artillery engage Pakistani incursion at Kargil, Kashmir, June 1999. (Indian Express)

Indian and Pakistani troops still face each other all along the 776 kilometre line of control and regularly exchange fire across the line. In ten days in June 1998 it is estimated that some 400,000 rounds, including artillery, were fired killing about 100 people, some from each side of the line. In May 1999 the most serious clash for some years erupted when several hundred 'fighters' (the Indians claimed including Pakistani troops) occupied the mountains in Indian Kashmir around Kargil. Militants in Indian Kashmir get support from a number of Muslim countries including volunteer fighters. The Indians accuse Pakistan of actively supporting the militants.

While both India and Pakistan claim Kashmir, its inhabitants would prefer complete independence. UNSC Resolutions 38 and 39 of 1948 declare that Jammu and Kashmir are disputed territories whose final status has yet to be decided. Kashmir is one of the world's longest-lasting disputes and appears set to remain so.

Bibliography and Web Sites

Ganguly, Sunit, *The Crisis in Kashmir*, Cambridge University Press, 1997
Lamb, Alastair, *Incomplete Partition: The genesis of the Kashmir Dispute 1947–1948*, Roxford Books, 1997
Malik, Hafeez (ed.), *Dilemmas of National Security and Cooperation in India and Pakistan*, Macmillan, 1993
Schofield, Victoria, *Kashmir in the Crossfire*, Tauris, 1996
Wirsing, Robert, *War or Peace on the Line of Control? The India-Pakistan Dispute over Kashmir Turns 50*, International Boundaries Research Unit, 1999

International Boundaries Research Unit: www-ibru.dur.ac.uk/
India: www.meadev.gov.in/opn/kargil
Pakistan: www.pak.gov.pk/kashmir/index-kashmir

www.

INDIA'S CURRENT AND POTENTIAL INTERNAL PROBLEMS

India's chief security concerns are with Kashmir (see pages 242–5) and over nuclear and missile confrontation with China and Pakistan (see pages 238–41). In a state that was derived from the territories of 592 princes, that has nearly a billion population with four main religions (Hindu 80 per cent, Muslim 14 per cent, Christian 2 per cent and Sikh 2 per cent; there are also smaller numbers of Jains and Buddhists) and 15 major languages, it is not surprising that there are a number of internal issues with security connotations. Fortunately, a number of these appear to have been resolved but there is always a chance, given changes in government policy, that they might re-erupt. Currently the main region of concern is the north-east where there are continuing disputes with the Naga people, the Bodos and Assam.

Assam's importance lies in the fact that it controls the Siliguri corridor which links the north-eastern provinces rich in natural resources with the main body of India; losing Assam would mean the loss of the north-east. Historically Assam was never part of India and was only incorporated into India by the British after the Burmese invasion of 1874. Until then it had been independent for over 700 years despite numerous invasions from east and west. Originally it was an independent province but was merged with East Bengal after Bengal's partition in 1905; it regained its provincial status in 1911. It is the meeting place of three major ethnicities – Aryan, Dravidian and Mongoloid; its people are more ethnically varied than those in any other Indian state. Early causes of dissent were the introduction by the British of Bengali professionals and clerks to the administration, and the economics of the tea industry built by the British, who took the profits, and worked by labourers from north-east India, who sent their wages home.

Dissidence in Assam began as a student movement. It was highly successful and following the boycotted elections in 1983 it developed into a political wing, the Assam Gana Parishad (AGP) and a military wing, the United Liberation Front of Assam (ULFA). The ULFA made contact with the Pakistani Inter-Services Intelligence (ISI) and the Afghans and sent men for training in Myanmar. It gained considerable power when the AGP formed the government and used this to extract large sums from business. At its peak in 1990 its strength reached some 3,000. After Unilever decided to abandon its tea plantations rather than pay the ULFA's demands the Indian government decided to dismiss the state government and the army launched an operation against the ULFA. The army withdrew when the situation was considered stable enough to hold elections, which were won by the Congress Party. Immediately the ULFA kidnapped a number of managers and engineers of the oil industry. The army returned, conducted a more successful campaign, and the ULFA agreed in January 1992 to political talks. The state government also attempted a political solution, army operations were halted and 5,000 ULFA men who surrendered were allowed to keep their personal weapons and were given loans to pay for rehabilitation. The scheme was not a success and the loans were never repaid.

An AGP government was re-elected in 1996 but ULFA violence increased; in 1998 considerable progress was made in containing violence and UFLA groups withdrew across the border to camps in the jungles of Bhutan. The Indian government knows there is no military solution to the situation and has been encouraging the militants to join talks but they insist on three pre-conditions: talks to take place out of India; UN representatives to take part; and only the sovereignty of Assam to be discussed. These conditions are unacceptable; nevertheless the government has begun a development plan for the region. Its policy of continuing both military operations and economic development appears to be successful.

Another issue in Assam is the separatist movement of the Bodos, a major tribe living in the north of the territory; they claim to be the original inhabitants of Assam. They believe both the Assamese and the Indians are discriminating against them. They formed the National Democratic Front of Bodoland (NDFB) which claims the area north of the Brahmaputra for the six million Bodo people. In 1993 the governments of India and Assam signed an agreement with the Bodos creating an autonomous Bodo Council but its geographical boundary has not yet be decided on. The Bodo Liberation Tiger Force and the National Democratic Front of Bodoland still campaign for independence and have carried out some instances of ethnic cleansing. In 1996 the Bodos launched a campaign of violence, killing some 700 non-Bodos and attacking the railways.

To the east and south of Assam lie six states. Three – Nagaland, Manipur and Tripura – have a long record of insurgency; the first two are fighting for independence while the last looks for a separate tribal homeland. Insurgency in Arunachal Pradesh ended with the surrender of the leader of the United People's Volunteers of Arunachal Pradesh. The opposition movements in Meghalaya and Mizoram, both formerly part of Assam, currently operate within the Indian constitution.

The Naga National Council (NNC) was formed in 1946 when Nagaland was still part of Assam and under British rule. Nagas, immigrants from eastern Tibet, also settled in Manipur, Arunachal Pradesh and upper Myanmar. Before Indian independence an agreement was reached between the NNC and the Governor of Assam which recognised 'the right of the Nagas to develop themselves according to their freely expressed wishes'. The agreement was to be reviewed ten years later. The Nagas believed this would lead to independence while the Indian government saw it as leading only to a revision of administrative arrangements. When the NNC realised the situation it declared independence in August 1947. Negotiations between the Nagas and the Indian government continued for ten years without agreement and with security operations against the growing underground Naga army. In 1960 agreement was reached and by December 1963 Nagaland had become a state within the Indian Union.

The Naga dissident movement split in 1980 following an agreement with the government known as the Shillong Accord and the Nationalist Socialist Council of Nagaland (NSCN) was formed in the jungle of the Naga Hills where it assisted other insurgent groups with weapon training. Fighting continued between the NSCN and security forces and in 1986 a joint Indian-Myanmar offensive was launched but it did not break the Nagas. Peace talks were instituted but distrust and misunderstanding split the NSCN; the two factions became known by the initials of their rival leaders. The NSCN-IM, led by Isak and Muivah, and the NSCN-K, led by Khaplang, alleged that the NSCN had agreed to reach a solution within the Indian constitution – a charge rigorously denied. The government and the NSCN-IM agreed to a ceasefire in late 1997. Since then the insurgents have turned to crime. Talks between the NSCN and the government and between the two wings of the NSCN began in late 1998. It appears that the government while keeping Nagaland as part of the Union may be prepared to meet most of the NSCN's other demands.

Manipur, from which the Burmese were expelled in 1824 during the 1st Anglo-Burmese War, came under British rule in 1891 as a princely state after a conflict prompted by the execution of British officers. In October 1949 it became part of the Indian Union, gaining State of the Union status in 1972. In 1969 a group of about 200 Meitei youths travelled to East Pakistan (as Bangladesh was then called) in an

Indian para-military forces, showing controlling ministry	
National Security Guards	
7,400	Cabinet Secretariat
Anti-terrorism	
Special Frontier Force	
9,000, mainly ethnic Tibetans	Cabinet Secretariat
Rashtriya Rifles	
40,000	Ministry of Defence
Indo-Tibetan Border Police	
32,000	Ministry of Home Affairs
Assam Rifles	
52,000, (responsible for security in north-east)	Ministry of Home Affairs
Central Reserve Police Force	
165,000, (responsible for internal security country-wide)	Ministry of Home Affairs
Border Security Force	
185,000	Ministry of Home Affairs

attempt to obtain guerrilla training but the Pakistani authorities were unwilling to support the secessionists and handed them over to the Indians. Eight young men remained in East Pakistan: eventually they were given two years of training and took part in the Indian-Pakistani War. In 1975 another group of young dissidents made their way to Tibet where they received training and were also subject to political indoctrination. On their return to Manipur they began recruiting others and set up the People's Liberation Army, Eastern Region (PLA). Guerrilla operations consisted mainly of attacking police in order to capture weapons. Another underground organisation was the United National Liberation Front (UNLF); formed originally in 1964, it did not begin its campaign for independence until December 1991 when it attacked a police patrol.

A report in January 1999 assessed that four of the seven north-east states were seriously affected by insurgency, while in the other three there was simmering unrest. The Indian Home Ministry claims that there are ten

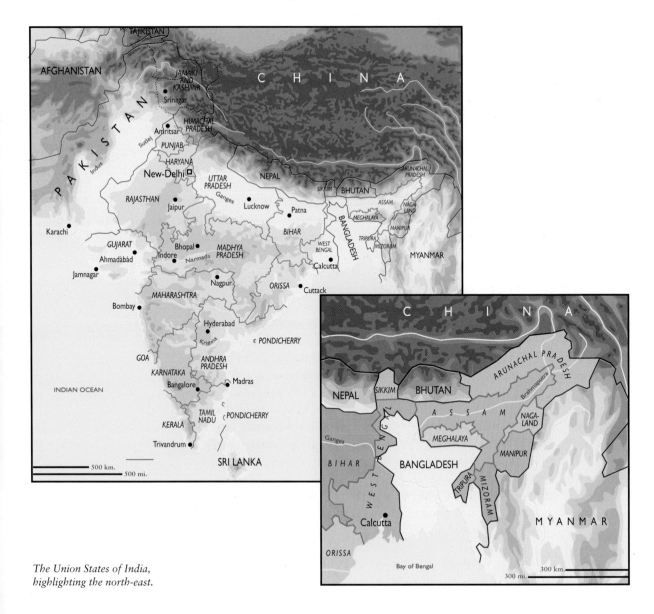

The Union States of India, highlighting the north-east.

dissident groups operating in Assam, Manipur, Nagaland and Tripura. Because of the long, hard-to-control borders with neighbouring countries, the groups have safe areas to withdraw to and in which they can acquire modern weapons. They also have contacts with the drugs trade. The dissident groups are concentrating on raising funds through extortion and ransom demands and on recruiting.

The Sikh religion evolved from Hinduism in the late fifteenth century when the Guru, Nanak, began teaching a faith that took in elements of both Hinduism (reincarnation and karma) and Islam (brotherhood). He was also much influenced by mysticism or the search for the heart of religion. Nanak was a Punjabi and it was in this area that the Sikh religion developed over some fifty-five years. It was recognised as a separate entity by the Mughal emperor who gave it land where the first shrine was built. This shrine developed into today's holy city of Amritsar. The fifth Sikh Guru, Arjun, became its first martyr when he was tortured to death by the then Mughal Emperor in 1606. His son raised a body of troops and the first of many clashes between Sikhs and the Mughal forces took place in 1628. Further battles took place in 1631 and 1634.

In 1672 the Mughal emperor ordered the forcible conversion of unbelievers to Islam and the Governor of Kashmir set about this with vigour. A group of Pandits, after one had dreamt that Lord Siva had instructed him to call for help from the Sikhs, appealed to the ninth Guru, Tegh Bahadur. Bahadur declared that if he could be converted to Islam then the Pandits should too and set out for Delhi where he was tortured and made to watch three of his followers brutally killed before being executed having continued to resist conversion. His son Banda Singh introduced the custom of unshorn hair and gave all Sikh men the surname Singh or Lion. From 1709 until his capture at the end of 1715 Banda Singh led the Sikhs in a campaign against the Mughals. He had many victories and several defeats from which, until the siege of Gurdas Nangal, he always escaped to raise another army. Mughal persecution of the Sikhs, who nevertheless had some successes, continued until 1748 when the Afghans invaded India.

They claimed the Punjab, which was now totally under Sikh control, as part of Afghanistan. Large numbers of Muslims and Hindus accepted the security offered by the Sikhs in Punjab. Fighting between the Afghans and Sikhs continued until 1799 with both sides suffering disasters. During this period an estimated 200,000 Sikhs were killed by the Afghans but the Sikhs remained in control of Punjab and other areas. The next Sikh leader, Ranjit Singh, extended the empire from Kashmir and the Chinese and Tibetan borders to the Khyber Pass and south-west to the border with Sindh. Sikhs were unable to penetrate to the south as the British were now in control there. They were defeated in the two Anglo-Sikh Wars of 1845 and 1848, though the British lost two battles during the conflicts. The Sikhs did not side with the mutineers in the Indian Mutiny of 1857 and soon became the backbone of the British Indian Army.

As independence approached, the Sikhs made it clear that they were opposed to the concept of Pakistan, the 'P' of which stood for Punjab, even though Muhammad Jinnah hinted that they would get full autonomy. The partition of Punjab was a disaster for the Sikhs: thousands in West Punjab were massacred both before and after partition and many more became refugees. The Sikhs in East Punjab turned on the Muslims in the area. The Sikh separatist movement was based on the religious political party set up in the 1920s, the Akali Dal. Its members realised that neither of the two options proposed for Punjab – partition or incorporation into Pakistan – was acceptable to Sikhs. It called for the creation of a Punjabi state but Nehru was opposed, seeing this as a communal demand not a linguistic one – the basis for the creation of other states in India. Indira Gandhi granted the creation of a Punjabi State in 1966 but at the same time created two other states from the original territory.

When Mrs Gandhi called an election in 1977 the Akali Dal formed a coalition government in Punjab with the Janata, a newly formed political coalition which came into power in Delhi. The forerunner of the 1984 battle at the Golden Temple was a plot engineered by Sanjay Gandhi, Mrs Gandhi's younger son, to create a split within the Sikhs and encourage opposition to the Akali Dal; Jarnail Singh Bhindranwale, a deeply religious teacher, led this opposition. His movement began to stir up hatred between Sikhs and Hindus but the government deliberately did nothing to stop him. The Sikh split did not materialise because the Akali Dal allied itself with Bhindranwale and the two causes merged. The Akali Dal called a meeting at the Golden Temple of Sikh ex-servicemen, at which 170 former colonels and more senior officers attended with at least 5,000 other ex-soldiers. Bhindranwale called for an armed uprising to achieve Sikh demands, decrying suggestions of more peaceful ways of persuasion.

After several months of terrorist attacks by Sikhs, the government imposed presidential rule on Punjab and gave the police greater freedom to enforce law and order. The new arrangements did little to halt Sikh terrorism. Eventually on 5 June 1984 the army was ordered to 'flush out the extremists from the Golden Temple using the minimum of force and causing as little damage as possible'. The temple area was strongly defended, tanks had to be brought in to effect an entrance and much damage was done. Army casualty figures were 83 killed and 249 wounded. There is no accurate estimate for losses on the Sikh side. The government figure was 493 killed. In fact, the total could have been as high as 1,500 but not the 5,000 claimed by one source. The aftermath of the assault included the mutiny of several Sikh army units and on 31 October 1984 the assassination of Indira Gandhi by one of her Sikh bodyguards followed by four days of anti-Sikh rioting in Delhi. Her son Rajiv, who succeeded her, quickly made a settlement with the Sikhs, giving them most of their original demands: the city of Chandigarh was given to Punjab, the water of the rivers remained shared until reviewed by a commission, and the Anandpur Sahib Resolution – a Sikh proposal to limit central government to only defence, currency and foreign affairs – was submitted to another commission. Sikh violence continued for a couple of years but by 1997 separatist Sikhs were mainly living in North America and the UK. Today the Punjab is as peaceful as it has ever been and there is no talk of Khalistan or a Sikh independent state.

Hindu militants destroy the mosque at Ayodhya, Uttar Pradesh, December 1992. (Associated Press)

There have been other separatist movements in other states, for instance in Tamil Nadu in the 1950s and early 1960s. The 55 million Tamils are descendants of the original Dravidian inhabitants, not of the Ayrans who arrived later. The movement for Dravidastan ended when the nationalist Dravida Munnetra Kazagham gained power in Tamil Nadu in 1962 only to find he had no support from other Dravidian people in southern India. Other movements calling for separate states based on language have had little success; neither in Maharashta where the Marathi-speakers demanded a Vidharba State nor in Andhra Pradesh where the Telegu speakers called for the creation of Telengana.

India is proud of the fact that it is religiously tolerant. Nevertheless, probably unsurprisingly, inter-faith violence does occur from time to time. An incident that still has to be resolved is the destruction of the mosque at Ayodhya in Uttar Pradesh. It is claimed that here 400 years ago the first Mughal emperor destroyed the Hindu temple commemorating the birthplace of the Hindu god Ram and replaced it with a Mosque. Hindu-Muslim clashes began in November 1989 and occurred regularly until Hindu extremists tore down the mosque in December 1992. Stonework for the new temple is being prepared elsewhere and the temple is being slowly constructed. Ayodhya is likely to witness further violence at the holy site though the government has said it will block construction.

A more recent feature has been the growing incidence of Hindu-Christian clashes which have taken place in Gujarat, Maharashtra, Orissa and Uttar Pradesh. The number of attacks on Christians has risen steadily since 1996, from only seven then to eighty-six in 1998. The attacks are blamed on missionary work which is concentrating on the poorest in the community and has had some success. The whole question of the growing gap between the rich and the poor is expected to result in unrest in the years to come.

Bibliography and Web Sites

Kaviraj, Sudipta (ed.), *Politics in India*, Oxford University Press, 1997

Rao, Krishna, 'Insurgency in the North East', *Journal of the United Services Institute of India*, April–June 1998

Singh, Patwant, *The Sikhs*, John Murray, 1999

Sinha, S.K., 'Insurgency in Assam', *Journal of the United Services Institute of India*, July–September 1998

Sinha, S.P., 'Insurgency in North-East India', *Journal of the United Services Institute of India*, July–September 1998

Tarapot, Phanjoubam, *Insurgency Movement in North Eastern India*, Vikas Publishing, 1993

Tully, Mark, and Satish Jacob, *Amritsar: Mrs Gandhi's Last Battle*, Jonathan Cape, 1985

www.

Indian Ministry of Foreign Affairs: www.meadev.gov.in

Indian Ministry of Home Affairs: www.nic.in

Institute for Peace and Conflict Studies (Delhi): www.ipcs.org

PAKISTAN'S CURRENT AND POTENTIAL INTERNAL SECURITY PROBLEMS

Pakistan's macro-problems are well known: the nuclear arms developments and the confrontation with India over Kashmir are considered elsewhere in this section. The latter was recently exacerbated by the incursion into Indian-held Kashmir at Kargil which was backed by the Pakistan military and the hijacking of an Indian airliner at Kabul over which the Pakistani authorities are accused of involvement. Of more general concern are the state of the economy and, since the military coup of October 1999, the re-establishment of democratic government. Pakistan is used to military rule. Field Marshal Ayub Khan governed the country from 1958 to 1969 and General Zia ul-Haq seized power in 1977 and ruled by martial law until 1985; he remained as President until his death in 1988. Nor has the record of civil rulers been a happy one; Zulfiqar Ali Bhutto, Prime Minister from 1973 until 1977, was hanged for murder, and his daughter, Benazir, Prime Minister from 1988 until she was dismissed in 1990, has been convicted of corruption. Now the recently deposed Prime Minister Nawaz Sharif is awaiting trial and his government is also accused of incompetence and corruption. There are, though, a number of internal issues that must give the government concern.

Pakistan is divided into four provinces: Baluchistan, North-West Frontier (NWF), Punjab and Sindh. All have at one time or another caused problems for the central government. Each province has its own linguistic group; the people of the NWF province are Pathans and speak Pushtun. A large number of Urdu and Gujarati speakers, known as Mohajirs, are Muslims who emigrated from India on partition; they mainly settled in Sindh. At the national level there are three main political parties. The Pakistan Muslim League (N) (there are several other Muslim League factions but none so successful electorally) whose heartland is the Punjab; it was led by the

Pakistan's population 144,350,000	
By religion	
Muslim	97.1%
Hindu	1.6%
Christian	1.3%

The provinces of Pakistan.

deposed Prime Minister, Nawaz Sharif. The Pakistan People's Party (PPP), the party of Benazir Bhutto, whose main support comes from Sindh, and Muttahida (originally Mohajir) Qaumi Mahaz (MQM) which is also strong in Sindh and in Karachi. There are another dozen smaller parties of which few gained seats in the 1997 National Assembly and few have representatives in more than one Provincial Assembly.

There have been separatist movements in three out of the four provinces; at various times these have aimed to form independent Baluchistan, Pushtunistan and Sindhudesh. The Baluchistan independence movement, actually more like tribal resistance to central government, was crushed by military force in the early 1970s after Prime Minister Bhutto was told that a Baloch Liberation Front had been formed and that the

Provincial Governor was plotting secession. The Russian invasion of Afghanistan and the arrival of 3 million Pushtun refugees in northern Pakistan halted the drive for Pushtun independence.

Karachi is the scene for political unrest that has descended into terrorism between the two factions of the MQM and a breakaway group the MQM-Haqiqi or Real MQM. Naturally the indigenous population and security forces became entangled. Violence began in 1994 and by mid-1995 was responsible for over 2,000 deaths. Over-reaction and suspected 'judicial' killings of MQM leaders by security forces led to the hardening of positions and an increase in violence.

Pakistan also suffers from religious intolerance – between Sunni and Shi'a Muslims and within the Sunni community between Islamists and Secularists. About 10–15 per cent of Pakistanis are Shi'a Muslims and their political parties have gained support and funds from Iran. Inter-faith violence was set off by the Iran-Iraq war and began with political assassinations. It led to the formation of terrorist organisations such as the Shi'a Sipah-e Mohammad Pakistan (SMP) and the Sunni Lashkar-e Jhangvi. Most of the inter-faith violence has taken place in Punjab, Karachi and the Kurram Agency on the Afghan border, where the Tori and Mangal tribes clash. The fighting in Afghanistan and Kashmir has both encouraged the resort to violence in Pakistan and made weapons easily available. There has been a large increase in the number of boys educated in madrassah or Islamic seminaries: several thousand have joined the ranks of Taliban and may well return to cause trouble in Pakistan as Taliban takes control of Afghanistan. Perhaps military government is just what Pakistan needs at this moment.

Bibliography and Web Sites

Cloughley, Brian, *A History of the Pakistan Army: Wars and Insurrections*, Oxford University Press, 1999
Rushbrook Williams, L.F., *The State of Pakistan*, Faber & Faber, 1962
Talbot, Ian, *Pakistan: A Modern History*, Hurst, 1998
Ziring, Lawrence, *Pakistan in the Twentieth Century: A Political History*, Oxford University Press, 1997

WWW.

Pakistan Government: www.pak.gov.pk
Pakistan; a country study: lcweb2.loc.gov/frd/cs/pktoc

SRI LANKA: NO LONGER A PARADISE

Sri Lanka, known as Ceylon during the British era, a beautiful island called 'the pearl of the Indian Ocean' and a popular tourist destination, has been plagued by a vicious civil war since 1983. There are two main ethnic peoples: the original inhabitants, the Sinhalese majority, who make up 74 per cent of the population; and the Tamils (18 per cent), most of whom migrated from southern India before the fifteenth century – others were brought in by the British after 1825 to work the tea plantations. The Sinhalese are mostly Buddhists, the Tamils are Hindu, and both communities have Christian minorities. There is also a Muslim population (about 7 per cent) who either came from south India or are the descendants of Arab, Persian and Malay traders and seamen.

Little is known of Sri Lanka's early history; first mentions of it came in Buddhist records begun in the first century AD. The island was divided into three kingdoms: Kitte on the west and south coast, Jaffna in the north and east, and inland Kandy; all were separated from each other by jungle. The Dutch and Portuguese colonised coastal strips between 1505 and 1796 after which the British governed the whole island until 1948 when it gained its independence. During all these years there was very little inter-community friction. The only serious clash was between the Sinhalese and the Muslims in 1915 and it was quickly crushed by the British. The British, who needed an English-educated administrative class, and the Christian missionaries, who also set up a number of schools teaching in English, created an educated elite in both the Sinhalese and Tamil communities. The latter, who came mainly from the relatively barren area in the north, were eager to gain 'white collar' work. The constitutions devised by the British were based on territorial and demographic considerations which gave the Sinhalese an electoral advantage.

It was only after independence that violence broke out between Sinhalese and Tamils. The first clash occurred in 1956 after the passing of the 'Sinhala Only Bill' and the announcement that the leading teacher training college would be reserved for Sinhalese only. A non-violent Tamil demonstration near the House of Representatives was broken up by force and was followed by riots. The next round of violence came in 1958 when the Tamils attempted to gain autonomy in a federal state. Tamils were attacked, mainly in Colombo. Prime Minister Solomon Bandaranaike was assassinated in 1959 and was succeeded by his widow Sirimavo. The name Sri Lanka meaning 'Resplendent Island' was adopted in 1972. In the elections of 1977 the Tamil United Liberation Front, formed in 1976, campaigned for an independent Tamil state of Eelam and again there were anti-Tamil riots. At the election Junius Jayawardene was elected President.

The long civil war began in 1983. The trigger is said to have been the ambush, killing and mutilation of thirteen soldiers on 23 July by the Liberation Tigers of Tamil Eelam (LTTE) in the Jaffna district and, after the bodies had been taken to and displayed in Colombo, there were widespread attacks on Tamils and their property in the city. Fifty-three Tamils were murdered in Colombo jail. The anti-Tamil attacks spread to other areas; the army and the police stood by and in some instances took part in the violence.

Sri Lanka.

In June 1987 the army mounted a successful campaign to clear the Tamil rebels from their strongholds and had reached the outskirts of Jaffna when India intervened because it feared a massacre of Tamils in the city. Sri Lanka was forced to accept Indian monitoring of an agreement for the army's withdrawal and the handing in of Tamil weapons. A referendum was to be held in the Eastern Province on whether it should join the Northern Province permanently, a vote which the Sinhalese majority was confident of winning. Tamil extremists murdered many Sinhalese in the Eastern Province with the aim of frightening them into voting for the union. The Indian Army presence, now over 30,000 strong, launched an attack on the LTTE in the north in October 1987. The Indians had some success but at the cost of a high casualty rate. The Sri Lankans now had also to contend with the anti-Indian Janatha Vimukti Peramuna (JVP) insurgency in the south of the island. The President demanded the withdrawal of the Indian force: India refused, having already made a number of phased withdrawals from territory that was re-occupied by the LTTE who now agreed to talks and to a ceasefire.

The Indians withdrew from Jaffna in January 1990 and their withdrawal from Sri Lanka as a whole had been completed by the end of March: they had lost more than 1,200 soldiers killed. In June a number of clashes between the Sri Lankan Army and the Tamil Tigers occurred. A ceasefire was arranged but was soon broken by the Tamils who captured an army base. The army launched a major offensive and managed to relieve the garrison of Jaffna Fort, which had been besieged for three months, but then abandoned it. The civil war has continued with breaks for talks ever since. The LTTE assassinated the President in May 1993 and the opposition candidate in October 1994. The Tigers managed to shoot down some air force planes and had considerable success against the Sri Lankan Navy. In December 1995 the army captured Jaffna but the Tamil Tigers continued to operate and carried out terrorist attacks in Colombo. Since May 1997 the army has been attempting to clear the 74 kilometres of road between Vavuniya at the southern end of LTTE-controlled territory and Elephant Pass just south of Jaffna so that it no longer has to be supplied by air and sea. On 27 September 1998 Kilnochchi was attacked and overrun by the Tigers who killed over 600 soldiers. In December 1998 the LTTE offered to restart peace talks but the government refused.

The conflict is now in its seventeenth year and has claimed over 60,000 lives. In December 1999, just before the presidential election, a bomb wounded President Chanrika Bandaranaike Kumaratunga, killed twenty-two and wounded another 110. After some 61,000 deaths no end to the war seems in sight.

Sri Lanka: Population 18,844,000	
By race	
Sinhalese	74 per cent
Tamil	18 per cent
Moor	7 per cent
By religion	
Buddhist	69 per cent
Hindu	15 per cent
Christian	8 per cent
Muslim	8 per cent

Bibliography and Web Sites

Tambiah, S.J., *Sri Lanka: Ethnic Fratricide and the Dismantling of Democracy*, Tauris, 1986

Tremayne, Penelope, *Tamil Terrorism: Nationalist or Marxist?*, Institute for the Study of Terrorism, 1986

Sri Lanka Ministry of Foreign Affairs: www.lanka.net/fn

Tamil Eelam: www.eelam.com

MYANMAR: DRUGS AND NO HUMAN RIGHTS

Myanmar, or Burma as it was once called, is a country with a number of ethnically different peoples. There is virtually no trace of the original population. The Burmese peoples came from eastern Tibet and western China and are believed to have come down from the Shan Hills into the plains of lower Burma in about AD 840. The largest non-Burmese groups are the Shan and the Karens, the former arriving by the thirteenth century while the latter had not completed their migration until after the British annexation of Bhamo in 1886. In many ways Burma is cut off from the rest of Asia by the mountains to its north-west and east, and by the sea; within Burma, the Arakan is similarly isolated. Burmese history is made

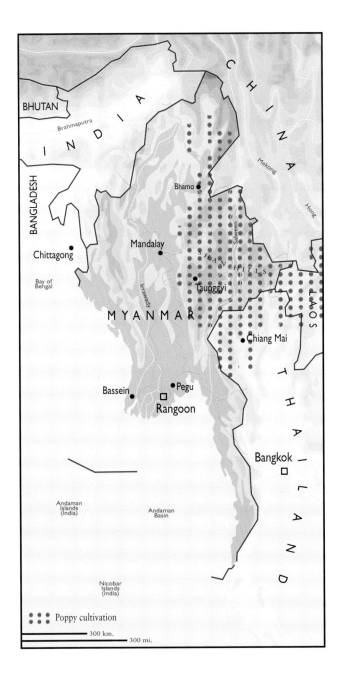

Myanmar, showing the areas of opium cultivation (left) and of the non-Burmese people (above).

up of a series of kingdoms, often at war, coalescing and then breaking up. The French and British started to take a hand in Burmese affairs in the eighteenth century with the British supporting Alaungpaya who had rebelled against the French-backed Talaing ruler. Alaungpaya united the country and was succeeded between 1760 and 1819 by his three sons. They invaded Siam twice, conquered the Arakan, repelled a Chinese invasion and took control of parts of Assam.

The 1st Anglo-Burmese War took place in 1824 and resulted in the Burmese being expelled from Assam, Manipur and Cachar and being forced to cede Arakan and Tenasserim, the southern coastal province, to the British. After the second war in 1852 the British annexed the remaining coastal province of Pegu. In the 3rd Anglo-Burmese War of 1885 the British completed their conquest of the country but it took five years and 35,000 troops to pacify Upper Burma. Burma became a province of the Indian Empire until 1937 when it was made a Crown Colony with a degree of self-government. Burma has nearly 4,000 miles of land border with five countries; the border areas are inhabited by a number of ethnic minorities.

During the 1930s the main opposition to British rule came from the Thakin movement led by Aung San and U Nu; it was violently opposed to the 1 million Indian population brought in as labour by the British. (There are still some 1.5 million Indians and Chinese in Burma.) At the start of the Second World War Aung San escaped British arrest and went to Japan where he received military training. The Japanese invasion led to the formation of a number of guerrilla groups among the tribes living along the borders with China and Thailand – the Kachins, Shans and Karens – who, with other minorities, continued the fight against the Burmese after independence was gained in 1948. During the Second World War when the Japanese reneged on their promise of Burmese independence to Aung San, he formed a coalition – the Anti-Fascist People's Freedom League (AFPFL) – fought the Japanese and then worked for independence from the British. Although Aung San was murdered in 1947 the AFPFL became the government in 1948.

The government's first act was to outlaw the Burmese Communist Party (BCP) whose 'White Flag' guerrillas were based along the border with China, which supported them, in Wa Province. The BCP launched a rebellion in 1948 and was joined by the Karens. At other times the Kachins and Shans have been in alliance with the BCP. All the non-Burmese minorities – the others being the Mons, Chins and Arakanese – have attempted to win some form of autonomy; they all considered the Burmese as much a colonial power as the British. The fortunes of the various dissident groups ebbed and flowed. In 1962 a military coup led by General Ne Win took power. Attempts to reach agreement with the minorities were unsuccessful, as were more determined military campaigns. The minorities were by now involved in drug production and trafficking. In 1980 an amnesty was offered but only a few thousand accepted its terms. Nine dissident groups formed the National Democratic Front (NDF) which never united with the BCP against the government. Today a third of the population, inhabiting about half the country, are from ethnic minority, communist and other opposition groups.

Myanmar	
Government forces	
Army	325,000
People's Police	50,000
People's Militia	35,000
Opposition	
Groups with ceasefire agreements	
Democratic Karen Buddhists	max 500
Kachin Independence Army	8,000
Mong Tai Army (Shan)	3,000
Mon National Liberation Army	1,000
Myanmar National Democratic	
Alliance Army (Shan)	2,000
National Democratic Army (Kachin)	1,000
New Democratic Army (Kachin)	500
Palaung State Liberation Army	700
Shan State Army	3,000
United Wa State Army	12,000
Groups still fighting	
All Burma Students Democratic	
Front	2,000
Karen National Liberation Army	4,000
Karenni Army (Kayah state)	1,000
(all strengths estimates)	

In 1988 Ne Win resigned after twenty-six years in power and was replaced briefly by a civilian government that was overthrown the same year by Saw Maung, a retired soldier. Fighting continued and also involved the Thai Army, which did not want the guerrillas to establish themselves on its territory. The new government named itself the State Law and Order Restoration Council (SLORC). Elections held in 1990 were won by the National League for Democracy (NLD) led by Daw Aung San Suu Kyi although she was under arrest at the time. The military regime annulled the elections and arrested members of the NLD. The SLORC, known as the State Peace and Development Council since November 1997 but without a change of leadership or policies, greatly expanded the size of the army and received large quantities of military hardware from China. It managed to agree terms with the expanding number of dissident groups. However, today there are still four groups continuing armed opposition with around 15,000 guerrillas all told.

The government's human rights record is one of the worst in the world. The UN Commission on Human Rights has appointed a Special Rapporteur but he has not been allowed to visit the country. His report contained a long list of human rights violations that included: arbitrary executions, political detentions (Amnesty International estimates there to be over 1,200 political prisoners in Myanmar), torture, rape, forced labour, forced relocation and no freedom of expression. Aung San Suu Kyi was released from house arrest in 1995 but her activities are still constrained. The European Union has suspended all non-humanitarian aid and imposed an arms embargo.

The Shan state is now the world's leading supplier of opium with a potential production in 1998 of 1750 tons. Drug production rose dramatically from 170 tons in 1980 to a peak 2790 tons in 1997 but has been reduced since then. In 1997 the government made an alliance with the drug warlord, Khun Sa, allowing him to trade in return for payment of tax on his profits. In 1998 the *Sunday Times* reported that the regime was expanding opium farming while claiming to be destroying it. In one instance some 5,000 villagers were evicted in the Arakan to make way for drug farmers.

Groups with ceasefire agreements

United Wa State Army
Kachin Independence Army
Mong Tai Army
Shan State Army
Myanmar National Democratic Alliance Army
Palaung State Liberation Army
New Democratic Army
Democratic Karen Buddhist Organisation

Groups still in opposition

Tai
Karen National Liberation Army
All Burma Students Democratic Front
Karenni Army

Bibliography and Web Sites

Carey, Peter (ed.), *Burma: The Challenge of Change in a Divided Society*, St Martin's Press, 1997
Christian, John, *Modern Burma*, University of California, 1942
Cocks, S.W., *A Short History of Burma*, Macmillan, 1910

Free Burma Coalition (Washington): www.freeburmacoalition.org
Myanmar: www.myanmar.com
SOROS Foundation Burma Project: www.soros.org/burma

EAST AND SOUTH-EAST ASIA

This section covers a wide area of the eastern world: its topics stretch from the possible future of the two Koreas in the north, down to Indonesia in the south. The analysis on China discounts the possibility that, despite the various pressures dividing its population, it will disintegrate. Nor is China likely to become a regional hegemon, as is feared, for some years and there is virtually no likelihood, in spite of its vast population and economic potential, that it will ever achieve superpower status to challenge the US. Other topics concern China; the status and human rights of Tibet; the question of Taiwan's status and independence; and the growing number of low-level clashes occurring in the South China Sea where competing claims over rocks and coral reefs and the sea surrounding them could escalate once the true value of the area's natural resources is proved. The piece on the Koreas covers both the continuing confrontation between North and South and the more widespread threat posed by the North's development of long-range missiles and unconventional warheads to arm them. The agonies experienced by Cambodia and the international community's efforts that failed to solve them are described. The internal problems facing the Indonesian government in widely separate areas of its vast Federation are discussed and the story of East Timor's fight for freedom told.

CHINA: APPROACHING HEGEMONY OR DISINTEGRATION?

There are those who consider China will soon be, if it is not already, a regional hegemon and one day may even be able to challenge the United States. The US believes it may be challenged by a regional power in fifteen or so years' time; it does not name China as that power but there are few other contenders. There are others, though, who forecast the break-up of China as democracy and prosperity replace communism and centralisation.

China has an ancient history but has not always ruled all of its present territory. The first Chinese dynasty, the Shang, emerged shortly after the start of the Bronze Age. Since then the central core of the country has been ruled by a succession of dynasties interspersed with periods of disintegration into smaller states before the next reunification. It has been

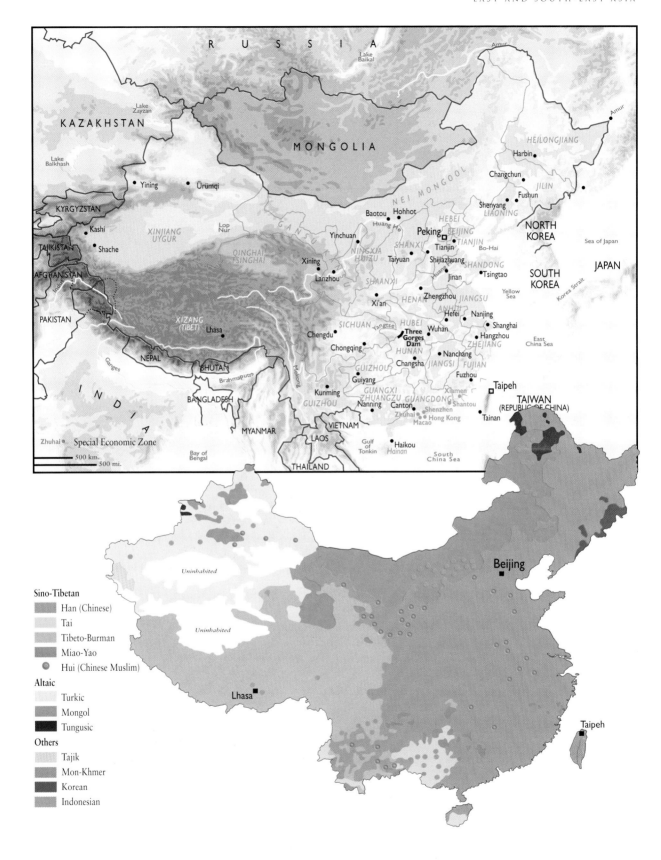

China, showing the provinces and the location of minority populations.

invaded and ruled by outside powers, the Mongols and the Manchus, and has expanded its borders on a number of occasions. At its peak, under the Ch'ing Manchu dynasty, China stretched in the north to the Argun River and the Altai Mountains, and included Outer Mongolia. In the west it reached Lake Balkhash and the Pamirs. Tributary states included Nepal, Burma, Siam, Laos, Tongking (Vietnam) and Korea. China's modern history has been equally violent with the revolution of 1911 when the country became a republic; fighting between the Communists and Chiang Kai-shek began as early as 1926. The Japanese invaded Manchuria in 1931 and then China in 1937. The Second World War was followed by civil war between the Guomindang under Chiang Kai-shek and the Communists that left the latter in control and the Guomindang withdrawn to Formosa. Communist rule has not been peaceful: 'the Great Leap Forward' cost some 20 million lives in floods and famine in 1959 to 1961. The Cultural Revolution between 1966 and 1969 was a period of chaos.

Of the Chinese population of 1,244 million, approximately 10 per cent are not Han Chinese; of these the most significant minorities are the Uighurs and Kazaks in Xinjiang, the Tibetans, and the Mongols of Inner Mongolia. The Tibetan question is discussed on pages 265–9. There is little separatist talk in Inner Mongolia, though the Mongols would prefer to be independent but not necessarily as part of what was called Outer Mongolia. Under 20 per cent of the regional population are ethnic Mongolians. Both the Uighurs and Kazaks are Muslim and Xinjiang has a record of revolt.

The earliest revolt in western China was in the 1860s when an East Turkestan authority ruled the region until it was defeated in 1878. The revolution of 1911, when Outer Mongolia gained its independence, had little impact in Xinjiang whose turn came in 1931 after the autonomous Khanate of Kumul had been annexed. Hui (a Chinese-speaking Islamic minority) troops from Gansu supported the rebellion but Kumul was destroyed with over 100,000 people killed. This was followed by a revolt in southern Xinjiang in 1933 when the Turkish-Islamic Republic of East Turkestan was proclaimed. The Soviet Union supported continued revolt in the north but feared that East Turkestan could encourage Muslim dissidents in Central Asia.

Another revolt took place in 1944 when Muslims again established an East Turkestan Republic and managed to drive Chinese forces out of the north-west of Xinjiang. As war with Japan was still in progress, the government negotiated with the rebels. It promised them self-government and undertakings were made in respect of religious and linguistic freedom; however, the reforms were never implemented. The Soviet Union had an interest in Xinjiang's natural assets during the Second World War and had a powerful influence there, at times backed by a military presence. Now that the Central Asian countries are independent, there are growing fears of the re-creation of an East Turkestan. However, the proportion of Han Chinese has risen from 10 per cent in 1954 to around 40 per cent by the 1990s. In February 1997 there were large-scale demonstrations in the Xinjiang city of Yining when, it is claimed, the authorities killed 100 Uighurs. There are Uighur Liberation Committees in Kazakhstan, Kirghizstan, Tajikistan and Turkey but if anything the Central Asians are more concerned by China than vice versa.

A more worrying factor than ethnic separatist issues, which can be controlled by military force and by increasing the Han population in minority regions, must be the growing divergence in the economic prosperity across China. People in areas such as the Special Economic Zones enjoy a far higher standard of living than those elsewhere and demonstrate the success of capitalism. Other factors that could lead to challenges to the government include civil rights, with the recent persecution of both Christian Chinese and cults such as the Falun Gong and the one child per family rule. Chinese communism sees religion as a threat to its monopoly of power. However, five religions are officially sanctioned: Buddhism, Islam, Catholicism, Protestantism and Taoism. Tibetans and Mongols are Buddhists and Uighurs and Kazaks are Muslims. Christianity was introduced by European missionaries and has been spread by foreign churches. In 1949 there were estimated to be 4 million Christians in China; today the number is thought to be between 30 and 40 million, most of whom worship in 'house' churches to avoid persecution. The law that outlawed the Falun Gong also declared ten Christian sects to be illegal cults. China challenged Christianity by appointing five Roman Catholic bishops without the Pope's authority. There is also a dispute over the reincarnation of the Panchen Lama: there are two, one recognised by the Dalai Lama and one by the Chinese. As it is the Panchen Lama who selects the next Dalai Lama, he too may be a Chinese choice.

The Falun Gong Buddhist sect claims to have 100 million members, though this may be an exaggeration, but it organised peaceful demonstrations in over thirty cities on a single day. It is a spiritual movement and claims to be apolitical. Its members are mainly middle-aged and many are women. The sect was banned in July 1999. A number of disillusioned officials and Communist Party members have been recruited by the sect and over 1,000 have been sent for re-education and self-criticism classes by the government. Some commentators have compared Falun Gong with the earlier T'ai P'ing and the Boxers. The former led a rebellion in 1850 that, after gaining control of much of the Chang Jiang valley, continued until 1864; its leader was a Christian. The Boxer rebellion in 1900 was aimed at the European community, and many Christian Chinese were murdered. Falun Gong is not the only large cult to emerge in China. There are many others but little information about them is available.

Another cause for discontent will be the relocation of over a million people by the Three Gorges Project (the Sanxia Dam on the Yangtze). They will join the other 10 million already re-located since 1950 by other river projects. A discontented population does not necessarily lead to civil war but could cause, over time, political change at national level.

To achieve a recognised hegemony, armed forces far stronger than any potential opposing alliance are needed as is the economic strength both to support those forces and to challenge opponents in the economic field. China's forces are certainly being modernised but progress is slow and there are a number of key items either missing or in very short supply. During the Cold War China anticipated that it was most likely to be attacked over its land borders and so defence doctrine was based on making use of its vast land space and huge manpower. An invader would be allowed to penetrate deep into the country and then be cut off from its supply lines and eliminated. Now the fear is more of airborne and seaborne attack. Since 1987 manpower has been scaled down in the active forces by 1 million men and by 3 million in the reserves. All arms are being modernised but priority is being given to elements that will facilitate an offensive strategy: attack on an opponent's strategic assets, his command, control and communications elements, logistic infrastructure and even population centres, all in an effort to avoid large-scale fighting between conventional forces.

When viewed as a proportion of the total inventory, China's development and purchase of advanced equipment is so small as to make little difference to its capability. For example, 50 Russian Su-27 fighters have been purchased, 200 more will be produced under licence and 50 Su-30 fighter ground attack aircraft have been ordered to join a total inventory of over 3,000 combat aircraft. There are as yet no airborne early warning aircraft and only a few in-flight refuelling tankers. The navy is also lacking a 'blue water' capability, being mainly a coastal defence force; there are no aircraft carriers and little replenishment at sea capability. The two Sovremennyy-class guided missile destroyers ordered from Russia will be armed with the 500 kilometre range SS-N-22 surface-to-surface missile and will be a step forward but only a small one. The submarine fleet is being modernised but will be more useful in defence than in attack. At present most other countries in the region are keeping pace and may even be ahead of Chinese equipment capability, whether in the air or at sea.

The nuclear missile arm (the second artillery) is also being modernised and longer-range and more accurate missiles are due into service in 2005, albeit in small numbers. A submarine-launched ballistic missile is also under development as is a nuclear-powered submarine from which to launch it; neither will be in service before 2008. It is not surprising that China is protesting against the US's plans to deploy an anti-ballistic missile system because this project could require China to deploy many more missiles than planned.

The Chinese defence budget has been rising by over 10 per cent for the last eleven years with a 13 per cent rise in 1999. Officially defence expenditure is put at $12.6 billion but many analysts believe the true figure is three times that amount; even the higher total is only a small percentage of the US defence budget of some $270 billion. It will take several years of greatly increased defence spending for China to achieve regional let alone global hegemony.

Three Gorges Project	
Height:	185m
Width:	2km
Reservoir:	600km upstream
Official cost:	$19 billion
Submerged:	13 cities, 140 towns, 1,350 villages, 650 factories

Bibliography and Web Sites

Goodman, David, and Gerald Segal (eds), *China in the Nineties: Crisis Management and Beyond*, Clarendon, 1991

——, *China Deconstructs: Politics, Trade and Regionalism*, Routledge, 1994

Heberer, Thomas, *China and Its National Minorities: Autonomy or Assimilation?*, ME Sharpe, 1989

MacKerras, Colin, *China's Minorities: Integration and Modernization in the Twentieth Century*, Oxford University Press, 1994

Shambaugh, David (ed.), *Greater China: The Next Superpower?*, Clarendon, 1995

Stokes, Mark, *China's Strategic Modernization: Implications for the United States*, Strategic Studies Institute, 1999

WWW.
Chinese Ministry of Foreign Affairs: www.fmprc.gov.ch/english

Inside China Today: www.insidechina.com

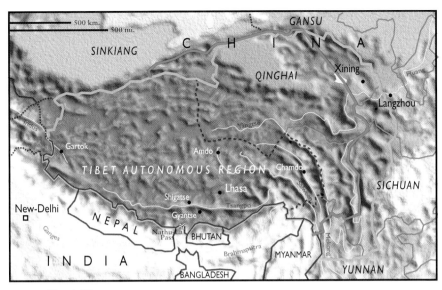

The borders of Tibet.

——————— Historic Tibet
——————— Simla Convention proposal, 1914

TIBET: WILL IT EVER BE INDEPENDENT AGAIN?

Until the seventh century AD Tibetans were a number of nomadic tribes living on the Tibetan plateau, today referred to as 'political Tibet'. They were unified under Tsanpo Songsten Gampo, who also either conquered surrounding countries or entered into matrimonial alliances, including with China and Nepal. The two brides introduced Buddhism to Tibet.

The Tibetans had expanded their empire to its greatest extent by the mid-eighth century. To the west it reached over the Pamir Mountains to Samarkand and the borders of the Arab and Turkic empires. In the south it took in Nepal and extended its influence to the banks of the Ganges and Brahmaputra. In the north it reached deep into Chinese Turkestan and in the east into Gansu and Sichuan, capturing the capital of the Tang dynasty, Changan (X'ian). Ethnic Tibetans inhabit a much wider area than the Chinese Tibetan Autonomous Region and more ethnic Tibetans live in the Chinese provinces of Qinghai, Gansu, Sichuan and Yunnan than in Tibet. They also live in the Indian provinces of Ladakh, Sikkim, Uttar Pradesh and Arunchal Pradesh, and in Bhutan and Nepal.

Buddhism was introduced into Tibet in the late eighth century and while the Tibetan Empire lasted for 200 years, it ended after the assassination of two rulers in 836 and 842 caused by the split between the adherents of Bon and Buddha and the persecution of the latter. By early in the tenth century Tibet had lost virtually all its conquests and was reduced to the Tibetan Plateau. The thirteenth century witnessed the rise and conquests of Genghis Khan and in 1240 Genghis's grandson made a treaty with a leading Tibetan Buddhist Lama in which the Lama was granted the nominal authority over Tibet. So began the tradition of relationships between Mongol, and later Chinese, emperors and Tibetan Lamas; the former protected Tibet and the latter became regent rulers on behalf of the Mongols and instructing them in religious affairs.

Though Tibet was dominated by the Mongols, it was never fully integrated into their empire and it regained its independence under a secular ruler in 1358. This development was accepted by the Yuan Dynasty, established by Kublai Khan when he conquered China in 1279 and by the ethnically Chinese Ming dynasty which overthrew the Yuans; Tibet remained independent for the next 300 years.

A tenet of the Buddhist faith is the belief that life consists of a sequence of birth, death and rebirth until one has achieved 'nirvana'. Reincarnation became the method of religious succession in Tibet as early as 1193. The tradition of the Dalai Lama began when Gyatso ('Dalai' being the Mongolian translation of 'Gyatso', the name of the second reincarnation of Gedun Trupa, a leading disciple of the Geluk Buddhist reform movement) visited the Mongol court and became the spiritual teacher of the Mongol emperor. The next reincarnation was found to be the great-grandson of the Mongol emperor; the next or fifth Dalai Lama became, after the Mongols defeated the rival Tibetan Army, both the spiritual and political head of Tibet in 1633. Tibet now became permanently involved with the Mongol-Qing Manchu dynasty rivalry.

The fifth Dalai Lama built a strong and united Tibet. He passed administrative power to a 'depa', who then concealed the Dalai Lama's death for fifteen years. The Depa encouraged the Dzungar Mongols to unify all the Mongols and they defeated the Qoshot Mongols in 1682. The Qoshot appealed to the Manchus, who had overthrown the Ming dynasty, for help. The Manchus, who founded the Qing dynasty, marched north and defeated the Dzungars at the Kalulun River. The Qing discovered the subterfuge of the Dalai Lama's death and were therefore supportive of Lhabsang Khan who staged a coup, executed the Depa and exiled the sixth Dalai Lama, who died or was murdered shortly after. Lhabsang was recognised by the Manchus as the ruler of Tibet and he agreed to pay tribute in return for their protection, thus placing Tibet in a subordinate position to China.

Over the next 100 years the Manchus had to send an army into Tibet on four occasions, each time at Tibetan request: in 1720 to evict Dzungar Mongols; after two internal revolts in 1728 and 1780; and to defeat a Nepalese invasion in 1793. On each occasion the administration of Tibet was revised to give the Manchus more authority. Also Tibetan-populated areas outside 'political' Tibet were transferred to Chinese provinces. The Qings drafted the 'Agreed Regulations for the Better Governing of Tibet' in 1793 which included the power to confirm the reincarnation of the Dalai Lama. The following 100 years saw a reduction in Qing influence in Tibet as the dynasty coped with other, more pressing problems. By the time the British became interested in Tibet towards the end of the nineteenth century, Manchu authority was purely symbolic.

British attention was drawn to Tibet in the mid-1800s as a result of fears of Russian infiltration but the Tibetans steadfastly kept them, and the Russians and British, out. The main result of Sir Francis Younghusband's expedition to Lhasa in 1904 and the subsequent Anglo-Tibetan Treaty – in which the Tibetans undertook to give no foreign power concessions nor allow them to intervene in its affairs without British consent – was to give Britain a hand in Tibetan-Manchu relations. The Manchus refused to accept the treaty and negotiations began to draw up an Adhesion Treaty, which was signed by Britain and the Manchu government in 1906. The treaty, which the Tibetans were not consulted about nor asked to sign, gave away much that the Younghusband treaty had gained for them. It shifted the

The Dalai Lamas	
Gendun Drup	1391–1474
Gendun Gyatso	1476–1542
Sonam Gyatso	1543–1588
Yonten Gyatso	1589–1616
Ngawang Lorang Gyatso	1617–1682
Tsangyang Gyatso	1683–1706
Kelsang Gyatso	1708–1757
Jampel Gyatso	1758–1804
Lungtog Gyatso	1805–1815
Tsultrim Gyatso	1816–1837
Khedrup Gyatso	1838–1855
Trinle Gyatso	1856–1875
Tubten Gyatso	1876–1933
Tenzin Gyatso	1935–

responsibility for implementing the Anglo-Tibetan Treaty from the Tibetans to the Manchus, who were excluded from the term 'Foreign Powers', and the British undertook not to interfere in Tibetan internal affairs.

In 1909 the Manchus invaded Tibet but neither Britain nor Nepal (also bound by treaty to aid Tibet) did more than complain to the Manchu authorities. The Dalai Lama was deposed and fled to India where he formally renounced all ties with the Manchus and their claim to suzerainty (not sovereignty) over Tibet. Within two years the Chinese revolution had taken place and the Republic of China had been established. In Tibet the Manchu troops mutinied, surrendered and left the country; the Dalai Lama returned and declared Tibet's independence.

In October 1912 Chinese troops entered eastern Tibet and British pressure on Peking led to the Three Power Conference, at which the Tibetan and Chinese positions on Tibet's status were far apart. The British devised a compromise dividing Tibet in two: in the eastern part or Inner Tibet the Chinese could establish a degree of control: in return they would play no part in the affairs of Outer Tibet and would allow direct Anglo-Tibetan relations. Although the Chinese envoy signed the convention, it was immediately repudiated by Peking and China lost an opportunity for its suzerainty to be internationally recognised. Britain went ahead to conclude the Anglo-Tibetan Treaty of 1914 which included the declaration that until China signed the convention it could not enjoy the advantages the agreement gave it, including the recognition of Chinese suzerainty over Tibet.

Until October 1950, when the People's Liberation Army (PLA) entered the country, Tibet maintained its independence from China, though the new Chinese constitution held that Tibet was a province of the Republic. The 40,000 strong PLA force soon defeated the 8,000 men of the Tibetan army but it did not enter Lhasa until September 1951. During this period a number of protests were made to the Chinese and the Dalai Lama was persuaded to accept the position of Tibet's supreme ruler. At the UN it was decided that the Tibetan appeal over Chinese aggression would not be debated, mainly because of the coincidental entry of China into the Korean War and because the Indians believed they could still negotiate a peaceful settlement.

Chinese troops occupied all Tibet's major cities but the Dalai Lama remained in Lhasa and the government continued to function at a local level. The Chinese embarked on a series of measures to downgrade Tibetan regional importance. Outer Tibet, the Tibetan provinces of Amdo and Kham were broken up into smaller entities and became parts of the Chinese provinces of Gansu, Qinghai, Sichuan and Yunnan. A number of Tibetan minorities, such as the Jangpas, Lhopas, Monpas, Sherpas and Tengpas, were reclassified as Chinese ethnic minorities. Unpalatable reforms were effected in Amdo and Kham which led to violent resistance and harsh repression; a number of religious and political figures disappeared. By 1959 there was a growing fear that the Dalai Lama might be taken to Beijing and a mass demonstration prevented him from attending a function at the Chinese barracks. In March fighting broke out, the Dalai Lama escaped to India and the Chinese dissolved the government of Tibet. Over the next eight months 87,000 Tibetan resistance fighters were killed, according to Chinese intelligence, and some 80,000 refugees managed to leave the country.

A chronology of Tibetan-Chinese relations	
632	First contact between Tibet and T'ang Dynasty
641	Srong-brtsan-sgam-po marries Chinese princess, Mun Cang. Introduction of Buddhism
670	Tibetan-Chinese War
710	Khri-lde-gtsug-brtsan marries Chinese princess, Kim Shang
821	Last treaty between Tibet and T'ang Dynasty
1207	Tibetan chiefs submit to Genghis Khan
1260	Kublai Khan as Chinese Emperor bestows title of Ti-Shih
1368	Yuan Dynasty falls, Tibet free of China
1578	Title of Dalai Lama given by Altan Khan
1642	Qosot Mongols installs Dalai Lama as King of Tibet.
1720	Ch'ing Emperor establishes his authority at Lhasa
1913	Chinese evicted from Tibet
1950	Chinese invade Tibet

The Potala Palace, Lhasa, Tibet.
(Barnaby's Picture Library)

The Chinese claim to sovereignty over Tibet began after the marriage in AD 635 of the Tubo (Tibetan king) to the Tang princess and the Tang-Tubo alliance which agreed 'that their two territories be united as one, have signed this alliance of great peace to last to eternity' (inscription on monument in Lhasa). The country claims that from the unification of China by the Yuan dynasty, Tibet has been an administrative region of China, citing the establishment of the office of the 'High Pacification Commissioner'.

India is the country most affected by Chinese occupation of Tibet for both military and environmental reasons. India sees Chinese missile deployment in Tibet as being aimed directly at it. The deforestation of Tibet has led to soil erosion and flooding; desertification has begun and the Indus and Brahmaputra are much more silted. The waste products from the Amdo uranium mine and the nuclear research centre and the possibility of nuclear waste dumping worry not just Tibetans but neighbours with rivers flowing from Tibet.

Bibliography and Web Sites

Anand, Kumar (ed.), *Tibet: A Source Book*, Sangam Books, 1995

Anand, R.P., 'The Status of Tibet in International Law', *International Studies* 10, No. 4, April 1969

Smith, Warren W., *Tibetan Nation: A History of Tibetan Nationalism and Sino-Tibetan Relations*, Westview, 1996

van Walt van Praag, Michael, *The Status of Tibet: History, Rights, and Prospects in International Law*, Westview Press, 1987

'Tibet – Its Ownership and Human Rights', *Beijing Review*, 35, No. 39, September–October 1992

International Campaign for Tibet: www.tibet.org

Tibetan Government in Exile: www.tibet.com

TAIWAN-CHINA: ONE COUNTRY – TWO SYSTEMS

Taiwan – known earlier as Yizhou, Liuqiu and Formosa – has belonged to China since ancient times. The earliest known Chinese settlement is that recorded in the Seaboard Geographic Gazetteer in the time of the Three Kingdoms over 1,700 years ago. Other settlements took place in the third and seventh centuries AD. The Chinese population was over 100,000 by the end of the seventeenth century and more than 2.5 million by the end of the nineteenth.

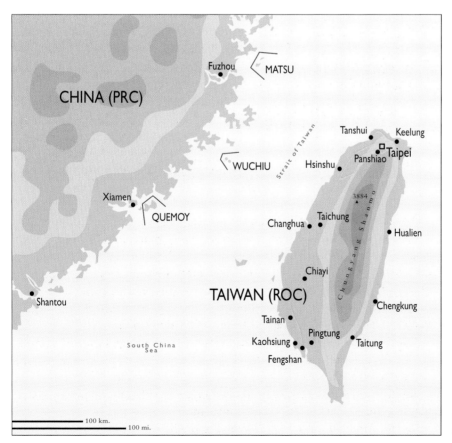

Taiwan (Republic of China) and the off-shore islands.

The first foreign invaders were the Dutch, who occupied southern Taiwan in 1624, and the Spanish, who seized the north of the island in 1626, only to be evicted by the Dutch in 1642. Mainland Chinese evicted the Dutch in 1662. After Chinese defeat in the war of 1894, Taiwan was ceded to Japan under the terms of the 1895 Treaty of Shimonoseki. There were regular popular uprisings against the Japanese until war broke out between China and Japan in 1937. China, then governed by Marshal Chiang Kai-shek, recovered the island in 1945. In the Chinese civil war that followed, the nationalists, the Kuomintang, were forced by the communists out of mainland China and withdrew to Taiwan with some 600,000 troops, hoping to regain the mainland that they still claimed as theirs. The US continued to recognise the Kuomintang as the rightful government of China and it held the Chinese seat at the United Nations until 1971 when it was expelled to be replaced by the People's Republic of China (PRC).

The Kuomintang also retained control of a number of offshore islands, notably Quemoy and the Matsu Islands, which became the scene of regular shelling from the mainland in 1958.

US naval forces protected Taiwan during the Korean War and the US and Taiwan signed a defence treaty in 1954. The US had to cancel the treaty and break off diplomatic relations with Taiwan in 1979 when the US and the PRC normalised their relations. Both the PRC and Taiwan agreed that there is only one China, at present under two systems; both claim sovereignty over the whole of China. Taiwan has declared that it will not use force to regain control of the mainland but the PRC as recently as July 1998 reaffirmed 'that it will not commit itself not to resort to force'. The PRC is concerned over any Taiwanese moves towards independence or membership of the UN – applications to join have been continually blocked. The Taiwanese President, Lee Teng-hui, said in July 1999 that bilateral talks could only continue on a state-to-state basis; the idea of one indivisible China had to be dropped. China immediately strongly warned Taiwan that it should not declare its independence. Independence is the goal of the Taiwanese opposition party, the Democratic Progressive Party, which is gaining support. The US accepts that the PRC has sovereignty over Taiwan, again on the principle of one country, two systems. It can be claimed that the 1979 Congressional Taiwan Relations Act, which was deliberately ambiguously drafted in an attempt to continue both ensuring Taiwan's security and following the 'one China' policy, commits the US to defending Taiwan.

After earlier military exercises, missile firing begun in July 1995 led to a US carrier group passing through the Taiwan Strait. In March 1996 the PRC conducted missile tests in two areas, both not far from the Taiwanese ports of Keelung and Tsoying, in a demonstration to show that these could be closed. The tests were followed by large-scale ground, sea and air exercises close to the islands of Matsou. These military moves were made in response to Taiwan's holding its first democratic presidential election. The US reinforced its carrier battle group deployed to the east of Taiwan with a second carrier group and the crisis did not escalate.

In February 1999 Taiwan claimed that the PRC had increased the number of missiles facing it by over 100: the US Pentagon acknowledges that the missiles have been modernised but not increased in number.

Nevertheless, a missile attack is the threat that Taiwan fears most as, to date, the PRC does not have the amphibious lift to mount a successful invasion of the island. The development of the Xiong Ying cruise missile means that targets in eastern Taiwan protected by the Chung Yang Shan Mountains could be attacked. Taiwan has purchased US Patriot missiles and is keen to acquire a missile defence system. The PRC objects to all purchases of US weaponry by Taiwan but particularly any type of anti-ballistic missile system.

While the PRC is unlikely to attack Taiwan deliberately, it is always possible that the use of military manoeuvres to back political pressure could get out of hand and escalate to conflict. Taiwan is unlikely to drop its application to join the UN or its fight to gain greater international recognition. (The establishment of diplomatic relations with Macedonia in early 1999 caused the PRC to veto the extension of the mandate of the UN force there.) Neither side will halt its arms build-up.

Bibliography and Web Sites

Lee, Bernice, *The Security Implications of the New Taiwan*, International Institute for Strategic Studies, Adelphi Paper 331, 1998

Republic of China Information Office: www.gio.gov.tw
Taiwan Security Research: www.taiwan security.org

Chinese amphibious capability		
Type	Number	Lift Men/Tanks
Yukan LST	8	200/10
Shan LST	3	150/16
Yuting LST	6	n/k
Yuliang LSM	32	100/3
Yuhai LSM	12	250/2
Quonsha Transport		400/-
Total capability		11,000/248

CAMBODIA: PEACE AT LAST?

The earliest state in the Mekong Delta was the Empire of Funan, thought to be the first Khmer Kingdom. Between AD 550 and 650 a number of small Khmer states to the north-west of the Delta emerged and overcame Funan; a period of chaos and decline followed. In the late seventh century another Khmer state, Chenla, was established. It soon divided into the upper or land Chenla and the lower or water Chenla; the latter was constantly harassed by Javanese pirates. In 802 Jayavarman II liberated the country from Java and unified it. Then followed the Angkorian period with the country being known as Kambusa. It reached its height in the twelfth century when it had expanded into Champa (northern Vietnam) and as far as the Irrawady to the west. The Muslim Cham destroyed the city of Angkor in 1177 but they were soon driven out. From the death of Jayavarman VIII in 1218 there was a period of slow decline and disintegration. In 1353 the Thais took Angkor and territory was lost to Laos. The late sixteenth century saw rule by the Thais and Vietnamese and by the end of the seventeenth century the Vietnamese controlled the whole coastal region. At the turn of the eighteenth and nineteenth centuries Thailand annexed three northern provinces.

The French first arrived in the region in 1862. They were invited to visit Cambodia and in the next year established a French protectorate. In return they received concessions to explore and to exploit mineral and forest resources. In 1887 the French established the Union Indochinoise to which Tonkin, Annam and Cochinchina joined, with Laos being added in 1893. Thailand returned the north-west province to Cambodia in 1907.

The now notorious image of the mass of skulls resulting from the Khmer Rouge massacres that took place in the 1970s. (Associated Press)

During the Japanese occupation, Vichy France was allowed to continue to administer Cambodia. But in March 1945 the Japanese dissolved the French administration and Cambodia's independence as Kampuchea was declared by Norodom Sihanouk, its 22-year-old king. The Japanese then recruited some 7,000 Khmer into a paramilitary militia to help repulse an Allied landing. However, the Allies occupied the country in October 1945 and the French returned to rule the country, though they allowed most of the laws and decrees enacted by Kampuchea during its nine months of independence to stand.

When the French withdrew in 1953 they left the country in an unstable situation that was accentuated by the spill-over from the war in Vietnam, which included bombing by the US. Sihanouk managed to keep the country out of the Vietnam War but a pro-American party led by General Lon Nol overthrew him in 1970. Lon Nol attempted to evict the Viet Cong sheltering in eastern Cambodia but they were better trained and equipped and, despite massive US air support, he failed to do so. In 1975 Pol Pot, leader of the Khmer Rouge, seized power and instituted a regime of social reconstruction that involved relocation, hard agricultural labour and political re-education. In the process, it is estimated that over a million people died. Pol Pot's reign ended with the Vietnamese invasion in 1978. It installed a communist government in Phnom Penh to rule the People's Republic of Kampuchea. An opposition coalition comprising Sihanouk's United National Front for an Independent, Peaceful and Co-operative Cambodia (FUNCINPEC), the Khmer People's Liberation Front (KPNLF) and the Khmer Rouge Party of Democratic Kampuchea (PDK) was formed in 1982. China, the US and the Association of South-East Asian

Nations (ASEAN) backed the coalition; it could muster some 50,000 to 60,000 troops, holding the area along the Thai border and north-west Cambodia. The government, backed by Vietnam and the Soviet Union, had some 50,000 troops.

The UN Security Council was unable to take any action because of the lack of agreement by the permanent members. The UN General Assembly called for the withdrawal of foreign forces and in 1981 established an International Conference and appointed a Special Representative for Humanitarian Affairs in South-East Asia. The Kampuchean Prime Minister, Hun Sen, met Sihanouk in 1987 and the next year the government and the coalition parties met informally. The

Cambodia.

Paris Conference was held in 1989 and Vietnamese forces withdrew. Negotiations continued, as did the fighting, while the four parties agreed to form a Supreme National Council, with three members from each party. It accepted a draft peace plan, agreed to a ceasefire and requested a UN survey mission. The UN Advance Mission in Cambodia (UNAMIC) deployed in November 1991, a further 1,090 personnel being authorised in December to include an engineering battalion and a mine-clearing training group. The Comprehensive Political Settlement of the Cambodian Conflict was signed in Paris in October 1991 after over ten years of negotiations involving the United Nations. Meanwhile, the Hun Sen regime, now the government of the State of Cambodia (SOC), remained in power.

The UN then embarked on its most ambitious operation. The UN Transitional Authority in Cambodia (UNTAC) was established with seven components: human rights, electoral, military, civil administration, civilian police, repatriation and rehabilitation. The military component had four main tasks: to verify the withdrawal of foreign forces; to supervise the ceasefire, including all aspects of demobilisation; to control weapons; and to assist in mine clearance. UNTAC strength was some 21,500 plus 4,800 local staff; of these 16,500 were troops and military observers with units from 22 countries and observers from 30 and 3,500 civil police from 32 countries. UNTAC's mission ended in September 1993 having cost a total of $1,621 million. The demobilisation process had not been completed as the PDK refused to join its second phase. Some 365,000 refugees were resettled and 37,000 land mines had been cleared from 4 million square metres of territory by the 2,300 Cambodians trained by UNTAC.

The UN-organised election took place between 23 and 28 May 1993. It was declared to have been free and fair and resulted in the new constituent assembly having 58 FUNCINPEC members, 51 from the Cambodian People's Party (CPP) and 10 from the KPNLF/Buddhist Liberal Democratic Party; the PDK had not registered as a political party and so had no candidates. After the election the CPP made numerous allegations of

UNTAC Structure

Special representative of the SG
Military force, contingents and observers
Civil police
Civil administration
    Human Rights Component
    Electoral Component
    Repatriation Component
    Rehabilitation Component

Contributing States

	Military	Police
Algeria	✓	✓
Argentina	✓	-
Australia	✓	✓
Austria	✓	✓
Bangladesh	✓	✓
Belgium	✓	-
Brunei	✓	✓
Bulgaria	✓	✓
Cameroon	✓	✓
Canada	✓	-
Chile	✓	-
China	✓	-
Colombia	-	✓
Egypt	-	✓
Fiji	-	✓
France	✓	✓
Germany	✓	✓
Ghana	✓	✓
Hungary	-	✓
India	✓	✓
Indonesia	✓	✓
Ireland	✓	✓
Italy	-	✓
Japan	✓	✓
Jordan	-	✓
Kenya	-	✓
Malaysia	✓	✓
Morocco	-	✓
Namibia	✓	-
Nepal	-	✓
Netherlands	✓	✓
New Zealand	✓	-
Nigeria	-	✓
Norway	-	✓
Pakistan	✓	✓
Philippines	✓	✓
Poland	✓	-
Russia	✓	-
Senegal	✓	-
Singapore	✓	✓
Sweden	-	✓
Thailand	✓	-
Tunisia	✓	✓
UK	✓	-
US	✓	-
Uruguay	✓	-

WWW.

electoral irregularity and demanded fresh elections in seven provinces but UNTAC maintained that the election had been fair. The SOC then declared the secession of the three south-eastern provinces. The Constituent Assembly gave Sihanouk full powers of head of state and he proposed the formation of an Interim Joint Administration of which Hun Sen and Prince Ranariddh would be co-chairmen. The CPP then acknowledged the election results, the secession collapsed and the PDK also accepted the election. UNTAC began its withdrawal and its mandate ended on 24 September 1993. On the same day Sihanouk was elected King of Cambodia and he appointed Ranariddh and Hun Sen as first and second prime ministers respectively.

The new coalition government soon became plagued by corruption; the army was grossly over-officered and its strength inflated to allow plundering of 'phantom' soldiers' salaries. The army failed to make any headway against the much-depleted Khmer Rouge forces that controlled several enclaves along the Thai border. In 1996 both Hun Sen and Ranariddh made overtures to different factions of the Khmer Rouge. The Khmer Rouge split with the faction led by Ieng Sary announcing that it was now committed to peace and democracy. Ieng Sary was granted amnesty and managed to continue his control of his territory. His forces gave their loyalty to Hun Sen. In July 1997 clashes between soldiers loyal to the two co-prime ministers occurred, allegedly over Ranariddh's attempts to bring the remaining Khmer Rouge guerrillas into his part of the army. A few days later the crisis had developed into a coup while Ranariddh was out of the country leaving Hun Sen in sole control. In the fighting that followed the Khmer Rouge sided with Ranariddh's forces. A ceasefire was agreed in February 1998 but it did not include the Khmer Rouge.

Fresh elections were held in July 1998, which resulted in a decisive vote in favour of Hun Sen and the CPP. In December the last guerrillas of the Khmer Rouge surrendered and were integrated into the army; they still control the region around Pailin. Of the last three senior leaders of the Khmer Rouge two, Khieu Samphan and Nuon Chea, are living protected by minefields close to Pailin while the military leader Ta Mok is under arrest in Phnom Penh. A further twenty or thirty guerrilla leaders are still at large but living outside Cambodia, probably in Thailand close to the border.

Bibliography and Web Sites

Chandler, David P., *The Tragedy of Cambodian History*, Yale University Press, 1991
Hendrickson, Dylan (ed.), *Safeguarding Peace: Cambodia's Constitutional Challenge*, Conciliation Resources, 1998
Khmer-Viet Relations and the Third Indochina Conflict, McFarland, 1992

Cambodian Embassy Washington: www.embassy.org/cambodia
International Crisis Centre Cambodia Project: www.crisisweb.org/projects/cambodia

INDONESIA: TOO LARGE TO REMAIN UNITED?

Indonesia is a huge archipelago. Its more than 13,000 islands stretch over 5,120 kilometres from east to west and 1,760 from north to south. There are five main islands: Java (the most dominant throughout modern history), Sumatra, Kalimantan (which is shared with Malaysia and Brunei and was earlier known as Borneo), Sulawesi (originally called the Celebes), and Irian Jaya (shared with Papua New Guinea and earlier known as New Guinea). The population of over 200 million is divided ethnically, by religion and by language. There are some 300 different ethnic groups in the population, the largest being the Javanese at 45 per cent, Sundanese 14 per cent, Madurese 7.5 per cent and coastal Malays 7.5 per cent. The majority of Indonesians, about 87 per cent, are Muslim; roughly 10 per cent are Christians, both Catholics and Protestants, 2 per cent are Hindu and 1 per cent Buddhist. Most provinces have Muslim majorities, the exceptions being Bali, which is overwhelmingly Hindu, and Irian Jaya, Nusa Tenggara Timur and Timor Timur (East Timor), which have large Christian majorities. There are roughly 70 million Javanese speakers, 25 million Sundanese and 10 million Malay; 13 other languages, out of the total of 669, are each spoken by over 1 million people. The national language is Bahasa Indonesian; it is spoken by about 6.7 million people. In addition, some 2 million speak one of the Chinese dialects.

The Indonesian peoples belong to a wider Indo-Malayan grouping that includes the Filipinos and Malays. From about 500 BC to AD 500 Indonesian contacts were primarily with south and east Asia. Only small indigenous coastal states existed at this time. Trade with India introduced both Hinduism and Mahayana Buddhism into the region and an element of Indian culture was acquired. The region became more organised and larger states were formed such as Srivijaya, which emanated from Palembang and gained suzerainty over most of Sumatra, western Java and the Malay Peninsula. Although trade with Muslim Arabs started much earlier, conversion to Islam began only in the late thirteenth century and spread slowly throughout the archipelago until some 87 per cent of the population were Muslim by the late twentieth century. Pockets of earlier religions held out and in the east of the archipelago there was strong competition from Portuguese priests.

The Portuguese were the first Europeans to come to Indonesia. They arrived in the early sixteenth century and established a chain of trading posts from Arabia to Japan. The Portuguese aimed to wrest the lucrative spice trade from the Muslims and Venetians. The Dutch first came in 1596. In 1602 the Dutch East India Company (Vereenigde Oost-Indische Compagnie or VOC) was formed and the Dutch colonisation of the archipelago began. The VOC was terminated in 1816 to be replaced by the Netherlands Indies government. The Treaty of London in 1824 agreed that the Malayan Peninsula should be a British and Sumatra a Dutch sphere of influence; it also provided for the continued independence of Aceh at the western end of Sumatra. However, the Dutch occupied it after a long and bloody war between 1873 and 1903. In 1840 the British established themselves in North Borneo and this alarmed the Dutch who began the colonisation of the eastern part of the archipelago but this was not completed until the early twentieth century. Gowa and Bone were only conquered in 1906, Bali in 1908 and the western half of New Guinea after the First World War. Dutch colonisation established the future borders of Indonesia.

Indonesian indigenous political movements started to form in the early twentieth century. In 1928 Achmed Sukarno and others founded the

Indonesian Nationalist Party (PNI) which had independence as its goal; he was arrested in December 1929 and sent to prison. His party was dissolved in 1931 and its successor, the Indonesia Party, which Sukarno joined, was suppressed by the Dutch and also dissolved.

The Dutch Indies supplied Japan with 25 per cent of its oil requirements but in 1941 they followed the US by imposing an oil embargo thus precipitating Japanese invasion. The Dutch surrendered on 9 March 1942 offering no resistance after the Allied Fleet had been defeated at the battle of the Java Sea. With the Dutch administrators and business community imprisoned, the opportunity was given to Indonesians to join the Japanese administration and a number of paramilitary forces that were formed. Sukarno cooperated with the Japanese. The Japanese realised towards the end of the Second World War that the archipelago was to become independent and in March 1945 a committee was formed that wanted to include East Timor, Borneo and Malaya in the new state – this was the forerunner of Sukarno's Greater Indonesia policy.

Japan surrendered on 15 August 1945 and Sukarno declared Indonesia's independence on the 17th. The Dutch were determined to regain their colony but were in no state to impose their authority. The priority of the Allied troops sent to Indonesia was to disarm and send home Japanese forces and to free European prisoners; they were less interested in Indonesia's future but the Indonesians believed they would attempt to reinstate the Dutch. The Indonesians hastened to take control, sometimes assisted by the Japanese who handed over weapons to the paramilitary groups they had formed – these became the basis for the Indonesian Army. During 1946 and early 1947 the Dutch negotiated the future of the archipelago, planning to establish a republic in Java and Sumatra and a Netherlands-Indonesian Union elsewhere; an agreement that pleased neither side was signed in May. The Dutch then attacked and managed to regain Sumatra and all of Java bar the Yogyakarta region; the UN sponsored negotiations and both sides agreed to a referendum being held in the areas retaken by the Dutch. The Indonesian Communist Party then took a hand but was defeated by the republicans who were now seen by

Indonesia.

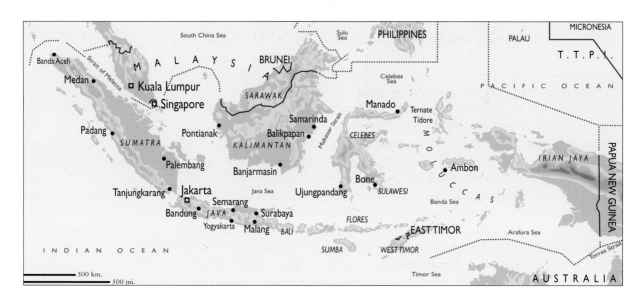

the US as anti-communist and not communist-inspired, as the Dutch claimed. The Dutch then captured Yogyakarta but they had lost the support of the international community and were forced to give Indonesia its independence as the Republic of the United States of Indonesia (RUSI) on 27 December 1949. By May 1950 all the federal states had been incorporated into the Republic of Indonesia. Only West New Guinea remained under Dutch control and East Timor under Portuguese (see pages 278–82).

General Suharto took charge after an abortive coup against Sukarno was put down in 1965. This was followed by a purge of suspected communists, in which as many as 500,000 may have died. Suharto became President in 1967 and remained in power until 21 May 1998, only two months after he had been re-elected for a seventh term. His downfall resulted from a combination of financial crisis, widespread unemployment and starvation in some areas. Large-scale rioting and looting broke out in Jakarta but when the army was sent in it was cheered by the rioters and stood by while the looting continued. Demonstrations by students took place across the country, the largest in Jakarta. Much of the looting was at the expense of the Chinese community. The Vice-President, B.J. Habibie was installed as an interim President until democratic elections could be held.

Political reform in Jakarta encouraged separatists, and Indonesia faces revolt or ethnic violence in a number of provinces. The Free Papua Movement was formed in Irian Jaya in the 1970s and it claims that since then some 42,000 have died in military operations against it. The independence movement in Aceh is the Gerakan Aceh Merdaka and there over 2,000 were killed in army repression between 1989 and 1992. Following the publication of a report by Amnesty International and Human Rights Watch on army atrocities in Aceh, the President apologised and ordered the army to withdraw. The withdrawal was halted in September 1998 when looting of Chinese shops broke out. Since then there have been continued attacks against the army. In December 1998 violence broke out in widely separated centres in Sumatra, Sulawesi and Kupang in West Timor where Christians burned four mosques in retaliation for the burning of over twenty churches in Jakarta in November. In West Kalimantan in February and March 1999 the indigenous Dayaks and Malays attacked Madurese settlers, who have been setting up farms there since the 1970s, leaving 90 dead and several thousand refugees; however, there is no independence movement in Kalimantan. In Ambon, capital of the eastern island province of Maluku, often referred to as the Spice or Molucca Islands, there have been clashes between Christians and Muslims since January 1999. In April 1999 there were Christian/Muslim clashes in Jakarta.

An election was held on 7 June. The army declared that it was neutral and the first genuine, and surprisingly peaceful, vote since 1955 took place. Counting was slow but it emerged that Megawati Sukarnoputri and the Indonesian Democratic Party had 34 per cent of the vote to the 21 per cent for Habibie's political alliance, Golkar. It was not at all certain that Megawati would be the next President; both elected and nominated members of the parliament choose the incumbent. Recent events in East Timor raised the spectre of another military takeover. In the event Abdurrahman Wahid, a respected Muslim scholar, was elected President; he chose Megawati as his Vice-President. In November, in an attempt to defuse the volatile situation in Aceh, he proposed that the region could hold a referendum, the question to be decided by Aceh, in June 2000. The army is bitterly opposed to any referendum and many Indonesians believe granting Aceh independence could signal the end of Indonesian unity as other provinces would seek to break away too.

Bibliography and Web Site

Indonesia: A Country Study, Federal Research Division, Library of Congress, 1993

Indonesian Department of Foreign Affairs: www.dfa-deplu.go.id

EAST TIMOR: THE PATH TO INDEPENDENCE

The first Portuguese conquest in the Far East was of Malacca in 1511. From there they developed contacts with the sources of spices at Amboina and Ternate where they built and occupied fortresses until they were driven out in 1575. Portuguese traders first visited Timor in 1514 and traded for sandalwood there. Dominican priests came in 1561 and set up a mission that successfully introduced Christianity. In 1602 the Vereenigde Oost-Indische Compagnie (Dutch East India Company) sent an expedition to the Moluccas that captured Tidore but never attempted to take Timor and Solor. By 1640, when Portugal had recovered its independence from Spain, the resistance of the Timorese and their priests had driven the Dutch from the north-east of the island. In 1859 the Dutch ceded the eastern part of the island to Portugal. By the beginning of the twentieth century Timor was prosperous: most Timorese were Christians and spoke a different language from that of their neighbours in Java and Bali.

Elsewhere in what is now Indonesia the Dutch had established colonies on the main islands and had captured Malacca from the Portuguese. In 1824 under the terms of the Anglo-Dutch Treaty the British withdrew from their colonies in Sumatra and the Dutch handed over Malacca and their remaining interests in India. In 1913 Portugal and the Netherlands agreed to split the island of Timor between them. During the Second World War the Japanese occupied the whole archipelago and later after the Japanese surrender their troops were employed by the British to help maintain law and order. The Portuguese recovered East Timor. In 1974 the Portuguese Army took over government and embarked on a programme of decolonisation. In Timor the Timorese Democratic Union (UDT) called for self-determination but federation with Portugal before independence. The other main political party, with a much younger membership, was the Timorese Social Democratic Association (ASDT); it called for gradual independence and then only after administrative, economic, social and political reform. There was also a pro-Indonesian party, Apodeti. The Indonesians were already planning to absorb East Timor, preferably without using force, and they were encouraged by the views of the Australian Prime Minister Gough Whitlam, who considered that an independent East Timor would not be viable and could destabilise the region.

In September 1974 the ASDT held a conference, where, bearing in mind the growing demand for independence and following the examples of the independence movements in Angola and Mozambique, it changed its name and objectives. The Frente Revolucionara do Timor Leste Independente (FRETILIN) was prepared to fight for independence. In October an Indonesian delegation to Portugal had convinced the government that the only viable future for East Timor was integration with Indonesia or self-government under Portugal: it argued that independence was not an option. The Portuguese sent a new governor to oversee the process of decolonisation. On arrival he found that his predecessor believed that the colony was to be integrated with Indonesia. There also appeared to be differences of opinion over East Timor's future under the new regime in Portugal.

A coalition of FRETILIN and the UDT was formed in January 1975 and called for a government in which FRETILIN, UDT and the Portuguese government would be equally represented and which would last for three years before independence. The Indonesians increased their claims that Apodeti was being persecuted and built up their forces in West Timor; they also began a campaign to win over the UDT by stressing the leftward movement of politics in Timor. FRETILIN demonstrated its growing popularity with large majorities in local elections. The Portuguese held talks with the coalition on transforming the administration into a transitional government; Apodeti would not attend the talks. The UDT had now become apprehensive of FRETILIN's strength and in May announced that it was leaving the coalition.

The Portuguese then held a conference in Macao intended for all parties to discuss decolonisation; FRETILIN would not attend the event, which went ahead without it. Apodeti was able to show that it was a viable political party and the UDT had its view of FRETILIN as a Marxist organisation confirmed. The Indonesians stepped up their propaganda campaign. In August, after two days of UDT demonstrations in Dili, they took over the police station and arrested FRETILIN supporters there and in other towns; there were rumours of executions. FRETILIN was handed the keys of the armoury in Dili and, with the support of two army garrisons, attacked the UDT. By 27 August it had gained control of Dili and driven UDT forces westwards. When some 500 soldiers and 2,500 refugees crossed into Indonesian Timor on 24 September they were forced to sign a petition calling for integration with Indonesia.

Indonesia now began a series of incursions, mainly with special forces, some disguised as UDT soldiers; these operations provoked little complaint from the Portuguese or from the Australians and the US. Indonesia next mounted an amphibious attack on Atabae, which they captured on 27 November; FRETILIN appealed to the UN. On the 28th the FRETILIN administration proclaimed the independence of the Democratic Republic of East Timor. In early December US President Gerald Ford visited Indonesia and the invasion of East Timor was delayed until he had left. In 1976 Indonesia annexed East Timor a move that was only recognised by Australia and not by any other country or the UN.

In late 1978 the FRETILIN leader Nicolau Lobato was killed by troops. Xanana Gusmão succeeded him until his arrest and sentencing to twenty

UNTAET contributors	
Argentina	Mozambique
Australia	Nepal
Austria	New Zealand
Bangladesh	Niger
Bolivia	Norway
Brazil	Pakistan
Canada	Philippines
Cape Verde	Portugal
Chile	Russia
China	Senegal
Denmark	Singapore
Egypt	Spain
Fiji	Sri Lanka
France	Sweden
Gambia	Thailand
Ghana	Turkey
Ireland	UK
Jordan	US
Kenya	Uruguay
South Korea	Zambia
Malaysia	Zimbabwe

	Deployed	Authorised
Troops	7,500	8,950
Police	933	1,640

East Timor

years' imprisonment in 1992. He was released from jail in September 1999. East Timor's campaign for independence gained momentum with the award of the Nobel Peace Prize in 1996 to Jose Ramos-Horta, an independence campaigner, and Carlos Felipe Ximenes Belo the Bishop of Dili. In June 1998 the new Indonesian government announced that it would give East Timor special status with a large degree of autonomy. Talks between Portugal and Indonesia under the auspices of the UN began in October. The Indonesian Army opposed the granting of independence and helped form and arm a pro-integration Indonesia militia. In January 1999 Indonesia said it was prepared to grant independence if autonomy was rejected. Gusmão, who had been transferred from prison to house arrest, authorised the resumption of the insurrection on 5 April after the integrationist militia killed seventeen people. The next two weeks witnessed further atrocities. An autonomy proposal was agreed and a UN monitoring mission was to supervise the referendum vote. Violence broke out again in the days before the vote, which was delayed by the UN until 30 August. The election was declared fair and free and when the result was announced on 4 September 78 per cent of East Timorese had voted for independence. Even before the results were known the militias turned against the UN staff and a number were killed. The result brought a much increased scale of violence, supported by the Indonesian forces in East Timor. Reinforcements were despatched but they were unable or unwilling to stop the militias from causing several hundred thousand to flee either into the hills and jungle or over the border into West Timor.

On 12 September President Habibie agreed to accept an international peacekeeping force and the UN mandated this on the 15th. Indonesian forces began to withdraw and the first elements of the peacekeeping force, provided mainly by Australia, began to deploy on the 20th. The world's press criticised the peace plan as too little and much too late. This is somewhat unfair and thanks to Australian planning and preparation the force was able to move swiftly once the UN had approved the deployment. Of course, a deployment before the referendum result was announced might have prevented the violence, the destruction of most of Dili and the

Opposite: *Destruction caused by pro-Indonesian militia at a village in East Timor, September 1999. (Associated Press)*

refugee crisis but at that stage there was no willingness on the part of Indonesia to accept foreign troops on what it saw as its soil.

The UN is now faced with having to replace the Australian-led peacekeeping force, to assist in the reconstruction of the country following the widespread destruction caused by the integrationist militia, and to help build up every institution needed by the newly independent state. It is estimated the task will take at least three years and that between $260 and $300 million will be needed to rebuild the country and to establish provision for health and education.

Bibliography and Web Sites

Taylor, John, *The Price of Freedom*, Zed Books, 2000

www.

East Timor International Support Center: www.easttimor.com
International Force for East Timor: http://easttimor.defence.gov.au/
UN Transitional Administration in East Timor: www.un.org/peace/etimor

THE KOREAS: WAR OR UNIFICATION

Korea claims to trace its history back to the Tangun Dynasty in 2333 BC. For many years it was a vassal state to China, the northern two-thirds of the country being part of both the Han and Ch'in Empires. Japan invaded and devastated the Korean peninsula on three occasions in the sixteenth century AD but the Japanese withdrew until their defeat of Russia in 1905 when the then independent Korea became a Japanese protectorate. It was annexed and Japanese settlers brought over in 1910. At the end of the Second World War the Russians declared war on Japan forty-eight hours after the first nuclear bomb was dropped on Hiroshima. The Russians marched into Korea and so were able to claim an occupied zone when the war ended. The dividing line between the Russians and the US was the 38th parallel. In 1948 the US military government handed over to the newly elected government of the Republic of Korea (ROK). In the north the Russians imposed the Executive Committee of the Korean People led by Soviet-trained Korean communists: it became the Democratic People's Republic of Korea (DPRK) in 1948, by which time the communist way of life was well established. The last Soviet forces withdrew in 1949 but an American garrison remains in the ROK.

The DPRK launched an invasion of the ROK on 25 June 1950 and had occupied some 90 per cent of the country, with only a small enclave around Pusan holding out, by August. The UN condemned the attack and, as the Soviets had walked out at that time, voted to provide forces to repel the invasion. General Douglas MacArthur, the US Commander-in-Chief in the Far East, made a large-scale landing at Inchon on the west coast just south of the 38th parallel in September. The North Koreans were forced to withdraw, first over the parallel and then further north as the UN advanced virtually to the Yalu on the Chinese border. The Chinese then attacked over the Yalu and the UN was driven south of the 38th parallel; the Chinese captured Seoul in January 1951. The UN managed to recover the territory south of the parallel and some way north of it on the eastern

side of the peninsula; the war reached a stalemate with both sides entrenched. Peace negotiations began in July 1951 but an armistice was not signed until two years later. A demilitarised zone was established as a buffer between the two sides and peace negotiations continued at Panmunjom without reaching a conclusion.

A strong UN military force remained in the south but, other than the US, all foreign forces had been withdrawn by 1958. Initially the US kept the ROK Army short of fuel and ammunition as it feared that the war might restart with an invasion of the north by the south. Over the years South Korea has become more and more prosperous while the North, through mismanagement and heavy military spending, has become poorer and poorer with starvation facing much of the population and causing perhaps over 2 million deaths. Following the unification of the two Germanys and the realisation of the cost to the West, South Korea became rather less keen on the aim of reunification.

The Democratic People's Republic of Korea (North Korea) announced in March 1993 that it was withdrawing from the Nuclear Non-Proliferation Treaty which it had acceded to in December 1985. The decision appears to have been provoked by the International Atomic Energy Agency's determination to inspect two undeclared waste disposal sites thought to contain nuclear waste, examination of which could show how much plutonium North Korea might have separated since

Kamak-San, 2,000 feet, dominates the way to Seoul. Gloucester Hill is on the right of the picture.

The Koreas, the demilitarised zone fence on the southern side.

1975. On 21 April 1994 North Korea announced that it was to replace the core of its 5 megawatt reactor. Despite several requests North Korea did not agree to allow IAEA inspection of the removal of the fuel until 12 May but then started the work before the inspectors arrived. The IAEA was unable to verify whether plutonium had been extracted from the reactor in previous years. The 8,000 fuel rods being removed could contain about 25 to 30 kilograms of plutonium, enough to make four or five nuclear weapons. The US and others felt their earlier suspicions were confirmed and that the North could have amassed sufficient fissile material to make up to five weapons. More recently there have been hints from US officials that North Korea has between two and seven nuclear warheads.

Following a visit by former US President Carter, North Korea agreed to resume negotiations and committed itself to neither reprocessing nor separating plutonium, not to restart the 5 megawatt reactor, to freeze construction of two gas-graphite reactors, to close and seal the laboratory suspected of being a separation plant, and to keep the spent fuel rods from the reactor in the cooling pond until their disposal was arranged. The US agreed to organise the financing and construction of lightwater reactors to replace the frozen reactors and to deliver 500,000 tons of heavy oil annually as an alternative source of energy. The Korean Energy Development Organisation (KEDO) is an international consortium, led by the US, Japan and South Korea, to implement the provision of lightwater reactors; KEDO and North Korea signed a contract for the construction of two 1,000 megawatt reactors with an aimed completion date for the first of 2003. Originally the North refused to contemplate a South Korean-designed reactor but agreed to do so with a US company supervising the project. Following the Asian economic crisis KEDO settled a new cost-sharing agreement for the reactor construction. The delivery of fuel oil has fallen behind schedule because the US Congress has not appropriated the necessary funds.

The US demanded access for inspectors to an underground construction site at Kumchangri about 40 kilometres north-west of the

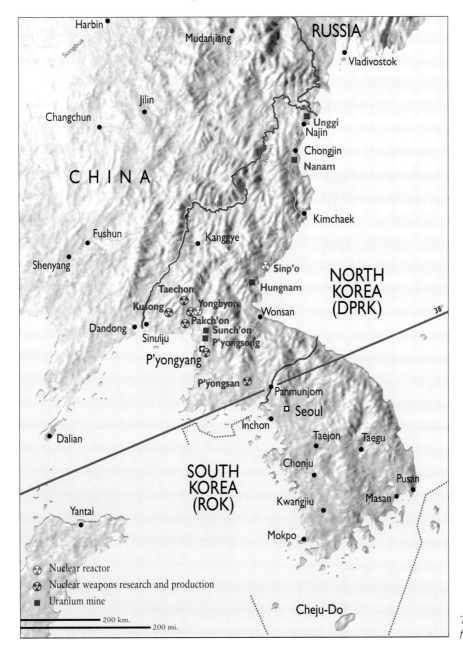

The Koreas, showing the nuclear facilities of North Korea.

nuclear plants at Yongbyon which it suspected had a nuclear weapons purpose. Access was at first refused and then offered at a price of $300 million which the US refused to pay; the US deny that the provision of 500,000 tons of food has any direct link to the visit. The site was visited in May 1999 and was found to be an extensive, but empty, tunnel system; the US has the right to return to the site. The contract to construct the two reactors was signed by South Korea and the US in December 1999 – North Korea did not attend the signing. South Korea is paying $3.2 billion of the $ 4.6 billion cost.

North Korea is also developing long-range missiles and has exported the technology for this, notably to Iran. The latest test flight was of a multi-stage missile that the Koreans described as a satellite launch. The missile was fired over Japan in August 1998. The first staged separated and fell into the sea 300 kilometres east of North Korea while the second stage crossed Honshu Island and fell 330 kilometres east of Japan. The test is believed to have been of the Taepo Dong-1, which could have a range of 2000 kilometres. When preparations for another missile test – this time probably of the Taepo Dong-2 that could have a potential range of up to 6000 kilometres – were spotted the US strongly warned North Korea against holding another trial. In September 1999 following North Korea's promise not to continue testing the US said it would lift a number of sanctions regarding trade which were imposed forty years ago. Japan also said it would lift sanctions and would consider resuming food aid deliveries that had been halted after the 1998 missile test.

There have always been small-scale incursions into South Korea from the north, sometimes through tunnels dug under the demilitarised zone. Agents are also delivered to the coast by submarines, one of which was caught in a South Korean fisherman's nets in June 1998. Shortly afterwards the body of a North Korean commando was washed ashore. There have also been confrontations at sea and in June 1999 a clash in the disputed sea buffer zone resulted in the sinking of a North Korean torpedo boat. The North does not recognise the sea demarcation line that curves up to the 38th parallel from the coastal border and runs between the North Korean coast and the Southern-held islands of Paengnyong Do. The North calls for peace and re-unification one minute and prepares for war the next.

South Korea, although its armed forces are smaller but better equipped than those of the North, fears a surprise attack employing short-range missiles, possibly with chemical and biological warheads, aimed at its capital Seoul and its million inhabitants. The city is only 50 kilometres from the border. South Korea with US support would be able to repulse any Northern attack but not before large-scale damage and many casualties were caused.

Opposing forces	
North Korea	
Men	1,080,000
Tanks	3,500
Artillery	±14,000
SSM (FROG, Scud)	54
Combat aircraft	590
Warships	180
Submarines	26
Amphibious	10
South Korea	
Men	672,000
Tanks	2,130
Artillery	± 8,000
SSM (NHK-I/II)	12
Combat aircraft	510
Warships	124
Submarines	19
Amphibious	14
US stationed	
Men	36,000
Tanks	116
Artillery	45
Combat aircraft	90

Bibliography and Web Site

Grinker, Roy Richard, *Korea and Its Future: Unification and the Unfinished War*, Macmillan, 1998

Oberclonfer, Don, *The Two Koreas*, Little Brown, 1998

www.

South Korean Ministry of Unification: www.uinkorea.go.kr

SOUTH CHINA SEA: A MULTI-NATIONAL PROBLEM

The Spratlys and Paracels are two groups of small islands, reefs and sandbanks, spread over some 800,000 square kilometres of the South China Sea. China, Taiwan and Vietnam make rival claims to the Spratlys (or Nansha Islands); the Philippines and Malaysia claim parts of the island group. Brunei claims the Louisa Reef, which lies in an extension of its maritime boundaries. The Paracels (Xisha Islands) occupied by China are also claimed by Vietnam. The distances involved are vast; the Union Reefs, roughly in the centre of the Spratlys, lie 350 kilometres from the Philippines, 450 kilometres from East Malaysia, 650 kilometres from Vietnam and 1200 kilometres from China (Hainan). Few of the Spratlys are inhabited and those that are, are inhabited only by the military, oil exploration staff and fishermen. There have been wildly different estimates of the oil and gas potential of the Spratlys ranging from 1 to over 17 billion tons: at present about 1 million tons is being extracted a year. The Spratlys are also rich in fish; 2.5 million tons were caught in 1980.

The Chinese claims, both those of the People's Republic (PRC) and the Republic of China (ROC, Taiwan), stem from ancient history and they maintain the Chinese discovered the islands as long ago as the Han dynasty in the second century BC. The Chinese claim is for territorial waters covering the whole South China Sea extending to within 50 miles of the Philippines, East Malaysia and Vietnam. The evidence of Chinese occupation is dependent on the acceptance of Chinese maps drawn in the eighteenth and nineteenth centuries. The Chinese claim that their fishermen have lived and fished there for centuries. When the Japanese, who controlled the islands after 1937 and during the Second World War, surrendered, General Chiang Kai-shek's forces took over from the Japanese, carried out surveys and set up stone markers. In 1947, China published its boundaries in the South China Sea.

The Vietnamese claim is also based on history. A seventeenth-century atlas reported annual visits to the Paracels to salvage the cargoes of ships wrecked there. The Paracels were shown as dependencies of Annam in a French publication in 1834 and a Vietnamese map of 1838. However, the French recognised Chinese claims in 1887, 1921 and 1929; but in 1931, when Japan was attacking China's north-east provinces, France backed Annam's claim to the Paracels and in 1933 occupied nine islands in the Spratlys. In 1946 a French warship placed markers claiming the islands of Spratly and Itu Aba. In September 1957 the South Vietnamese government claimed both the Spratlys and Paracels in continuation of earlier French demands. After Vietnam claimed its territorial waters, contiguous zone, exclusive economic zone and continental shelf in 1977, Hanoi published 'Vietnam's Sovereignty over the Hoang Sa (Paracels) and Truong Sa (Spratlys) Archipelagos' in 1979, that contained all the documentary evidence supporting the Vietnamese claim.

The Philippine claim is based on treaties signed between the US and Spain in 1898 and 1900, and the US and UK in 1930. It is also founded on the Philippines' right to an economic exclusion zone that it claims covers

The Spratlys	
Geographic Board Name	*Chinese Name*
Occupied by China	
Subi Reef	Zhubi Jiao
Gaven Reefs	Nanxun Jiao
Fiery Cross Reef	Yungshu Jiao
Cuarteron Reef	Huayang Jiao
Johnson Reef	Zhuying Jiao
Chiqua Reef	Dongmen Jiao
Mischief Reef	Meizo Jiao
Occupied by Malaysia	
Mariveles Reef	Nan Hai Jiao
Swallow Reef	Dan Wan Jiao
Ardasier Reef	Andu Tan
Occupied by Philippines	
Commodore Reef	Siling Jiao
Nanshan Island	Mahuan Dao
Flat Island	Feixin Dao
West York Island	Xiyue Dao
Northeast Cay	Beizi Dao
Thitu Island	Zhongye Dao
Lankiam Cay	Yangxin Shazhou
Loaita Island	Nanyue Dao
Occupied by Taiwan	
Itu Aba Island	Tai Ping Dao
Occupied by Vietnam	
Ladd Reef	Riji Jiao
Spratly Island	Nanwei Dao
West Reef	Xi Jiao
East Reef	Dong Jiao
Central Reef	Zhong Jiao
Amboyna Cay	Anbo Shazhou
Barque Canada Reef	Bai Jiao
Pearson Reef	Bisheng Jiao
Cornwallis South Reef	Nanhua Jiao
Alison Reef	Liumen Jiao
Pigeon Reef	Wumie Jiao
Len Dao	Qiong Jiao
Collins Reef	Guihan Jiao
Sin Cowe Island	Jing Hong Dao
Namyit Island	Hongxiu Dao
Sand Cay	Dunqian Shazhou
Petley Reef	Bolan Jiao
South Reef	Nailou Jiao
Southwest Cay	Nanzi Dao
Union Reefs	Jiu Zhang Qunjra

the eastern part of the South China Sea. The Malaysian claim is also based on its economic exclusion zone under the UN Convention on the Law of the Sea.

The view of most impartial observers is that most of the claims of sovereignty are weak and would not be upheld at the International Court of Justice; few claims can be supported by the necessary evidence of continuous and effective control. Nor, once sovereignty is agreed, do many of the small islets qualify to have economic exclusion zones because to be so designated they would have to be able to sustain human occupation. The area of the largest island is less than half a square kilometre and only the next six largest are more than 100 square metres in size. Claims based on continental shelves are more likely to succeed than those founded on other evidence.

South China Sea.

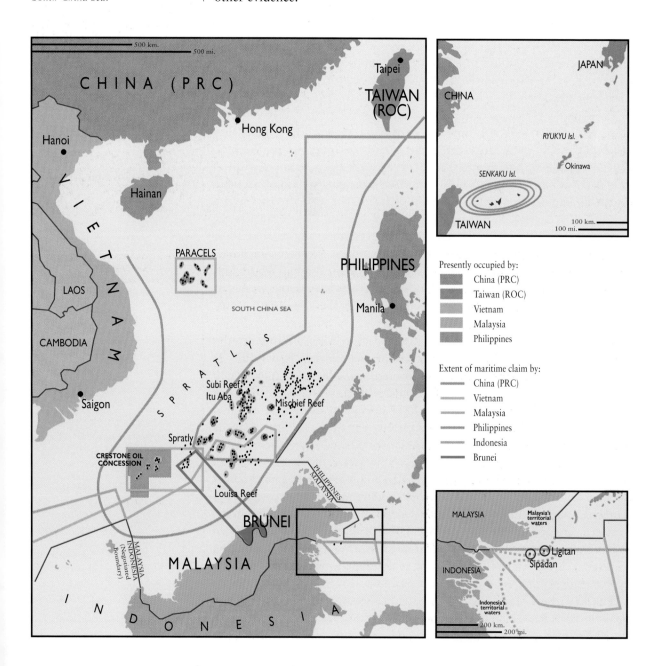

Presently occupied by:
- China (PRC)
- Taiwan (ROC)
- Vietnam
- Malaysia
- Philippines

Extent of maritime claim by:
- China (PRC)
- Vietnam
- Malaysia
- Philippines
- Indonesia
- Brunei

Chinese building and helicopter pad on Subi Reef, Spratlys, April 1997. (Associated Press)

Until 1974 the Paracels were occupied by both the PRC and South Vietnam but in 1974 the PRC took advantage of the collapse of South Vietnam to seize the western islands; as North Vietnam was being supported by the PRC it declined to question the takeover but in 1988 Vietnam renewed its claim to both the Paracels and Spratlys. The ASEAN countries with claims in the South China Sea would prefer to see the whole question settled by an international conference, while the PRC is only prepared to engage in bilateral negotiations. All the claimants have taken possession of a number of islands with the PRC occupying the remainder over the last ten years. In 1995 it took Mischief Reef which is clearly in the Philippine economic exclusion zone and in 1998/9 it increased the construction of facilities there. Oil exploration began in 1992 when the PRC granted a concession to Crestone in the Vanguard Bank area. Soon after Vietnam gave a Japanese-US consortium concessions in the nearby Blue Dragon field. There have been isolated clashes between rival claimants, the most recent being the sinking of two PRC fishing boats by the Philippines in May and July 1999.

Conflict over the Spratlys would be hard to sustain given the distances involved and the lack of aircraft carriers and in-flight refuelling capability by the claimants. Even maintaining large numbers of naval craft would prove difficult as few local navies have developed at-sea replenishment ships and tankers. Only the PRC could maintain naval forces continuously in the Spratlys and then with only very limited air cover. Malaysia is capable of defending its relatively limited claims off the East Malaysian coast. The Philippines are the militarily weakest of the claimants and could not mount an effective defence of the islands they presently occupy; the US has made it clear that it is not prepared to become involved in militarily supporting Philippine claims.

There are other island disputes at the northern and southern ends of the South China Sea. Japan, the PRC and the ROC all claim the Senaku (Diaoyus in Chinese) Islands, which are 100 miles north-east of Taiwan and 200 miles west of Okinawa. The uninhabited islands became part of Japan in 1895 and China recognised this when Taiwan (then Formosa) was ceded to Japan. The Chinese claim was renewed in 1992 when it passed its law on Territorial Seas and Contiguous Zones. The Philippines and the PRC both claim and had a confrontation at Scarborough Reef in 1997. In the south, Malaysia and Indonesia both claim the islands of Sipedan and Ligitan which lie due east of the Malaysian-Indonesian border; both countries have agreed to refer the dispute to the International Court of Justice.

Bibliography and Web Sites

Dzurek, Daniel J., *The Spratly Islands Dispute: Who's on First*, International Boundaries Research Unit, Maritime Briefing, 1996

Garver, John, 'China's Push Through the South China Sea: The Interaction of Bureaucratic and National Interests', *The China Quarterly*, 1992

Kien-hong Yu, Peter, *A Study of the Prats, Macclesfield Bank, Paracels and Spratleys in the South China Sea*, Critical Issues in Asian Studies Monograph Series, 1988

Politics and Concepts Regarding the South China Sea, Issues and Studies, September 1993

Energy and Security in the South China Sea (University of Oslo):
www.sum.uio.no/southchinasea

South China Sea Informal Working Group (University of British Columbia):
http://faculty.law.ubc.ca/scs

www.

LATIN AMERICA: OUTSIDE THE MAINSTREAM

Only some twenty years or so ago Latin America was the continent most at conflict, with virtually all its states ruled by military dictators or juntas. In the south Argentina and Brazil were engaged in an arms race that included developing nuclear weapons and the missiles to deliver them. Argentina and Chile were confronting each other over claims in the Beagle Strait, and Peru and Ecuador were engaged in a mini-jungle war over border claims. Honduras was threatening Belize, and Argentina invaded the Falkland Islands in attempt to, as it claims, regain them. Further north, internal strife was the order of the day with civil wars in Guatemala, Nicaragua and El Salvador. Colombia was racked, as it still is, by the violence of the drug-trafficking cartels.

Most of these troubles are now thankfully over and democracy has been restored more or less throughout the continent. Argentina and Brazil have renounced their nuclear and missile programmes and have joined the rest of the continent in forming a nuclear-weapon free zone. Border problems have been resolved, most civil wars have ended with the UN supervising the process and verifying disarmament. The five topics included in the section begin with the future of the Panama Canal handed over by the US to the Panamanian Government at the end of 1999. The history of the Falkland Islands and the events leading to the Argentinian invasion are described. Three long-standing conflicts examined here are the continuing civil war and drug-trafficking in Colombia, the terrorism of the Shining Path in Peru, and the Zapatista rebellion in the Chiapas region of Mexico.

THE PANAMA CANAL: A WATERWAY AT RISK

The Panama Canal is one of the two most important inland waterways in the world. It stretches 51 miles from the Caribbean Sea to the Pacific Ocean and takes about thirty hours to transit; the alternative route round Cape Horn is over 10,000 miles from either end of the canal and the journey takes, on average, thirty days. Since it was opened in 1914 the waterway has been administered by the Panama Canal Commission, a branch of the government of the United States.

The Panama Canal and some possible alternative routes.

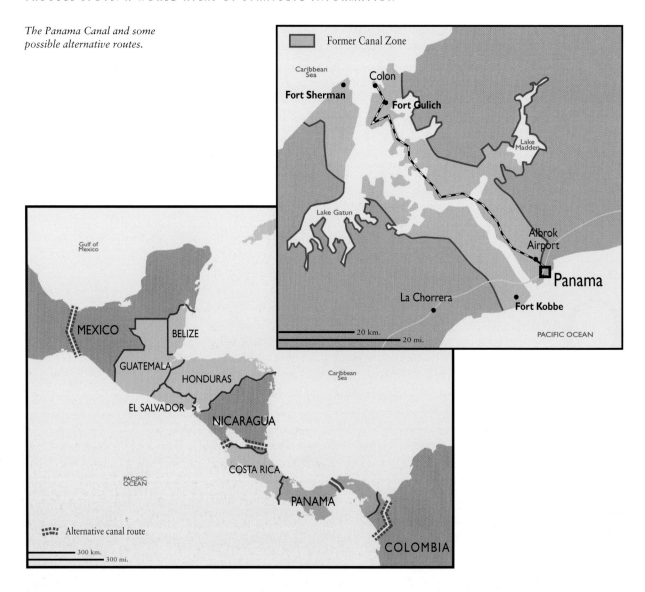

In 1821 Panama declared its independence from Spain and became a province of Gran Colombia; during the next eighty years it made a number of unsuccessful attempts to gain its independence. The US and Colombia signed a treaty in 1856 that gave the US transit rights across the Panama Isthmus by any existing or future means of transportation, the first being the Panama Railroad which was opened before the trans-US railway. The first French attempt to build a Panama Canal began in 1880 but ended in failure nine years later.

In 1903 the US negotiated a treaty with Colombia to build a canal across the narrows between Colon and Balbao; the US was to lease for 100 years a strip of territory 8 kilometres either side of the canal route. The Colombian Senate refused to ratify the treaty and this led to US support for Panamanian secessionists, who, with the assistance of the US Navy and Marines, gained independence. The US agreed to guarantee Panama's independence and was given the right to intervene militarily to protect the canal. The US sent troops into Panama on nine occasions between 1903 and 1936, when a treaty of friendship and cooperation was signed, to put down unrest. The first was in 1904 after which a new constitution gave the US the right to intervene in any part of Panama to re-establish peace and constitutional order. The 1936 treaty did not contain provisions for the US to guarantee Panama's independence nor the US's right to intervene in Panama except to defend the canal. A fresh treaty was agreed in 1977 to transfer the canal and canal zone to Panama by the end of 1999; it also established and guaranteed the canal's neutrality so that it will 'remain secure and open to peaceful transit by the vessels of all nations on terms of entire equality'.

A planned expansion of the canal's capability to allow the US Navy's new and much larger battleships and aircraft carriers, known as the 'third locks' project, was begun in 1939 but abandoned in 1942. The US acknowledged that the canal could not be protected from an all-out attack and could be closed by nuclear weapons. Naval ships transiting the canal would be vulnerable to air attack and to submarines as they reached the open sea. Despite the US's downgrading of the canal's strategic value, the protection of the integrity of the canal treaty was one of the stated reasons for the US invasion of December 1989 – the twentieth US intervention. The other reasons given were to safeguard US lives, to defend democracy in Panama and to combat drug trafficking.

> **Statement of Understanding appended to the Panama Canal Treaty (1977)**
>
> That [Panama and the US] shall ... defend the canal against any threat to the regime of neutrality....This does not mean, nor shall be interpreted as, the right of intervention of the US in the internal affairs of Panama. US action ... shall never be directed against the territorial integrity or political independence of Panama.

Miraflores Locks on the Pacific side of the canal. (US Department of Defense)

Panama Canal traffic		
	Transits	Cargo Tonnage
1989	13,389	151,868,626
1990	13,325	157,322,924
1992	14,148	159,615,224
1994	14,029	170,836,012
1996	15,187	198,488,502
1998	14,244	192,188,728

Distances to the Canal (nautical miles)	
Hong Kong	9,195
New Orleans	1,444
New York	2,018
Rotterdam	4,842
San Francisco	3,245
Yokohama	7,682

The canal can accommodate ships with up to 106 foot beam, 39.5 foot draught and 965 foot length. The number of ships transiting the canal has risen steadily over the years, from nearly 13,400 in 1989 to just over 14,200 in 1998. Cargo traffic rose from nearly 160 million long tonnes to over 192 million and toll charges from about $330 million to $546 million over the same period. Flags of convenience (Panama, Liberia, Bahamas and Cyprus) use the canal most, followed by Germany, Greece, Philippines and USA. The canal needs to be modernised and its locks to be enlarged if it is to be able to handle today's larger ships. In 1998 the Canal Capacity Project Office was established to assess the long-term options for improving the canal and its water supplies that have already been affected by El Niño.

In the build-up to the handover of the canal to the Panamanian authorities on 31 December 1999, there was a flurry of press reports over US concerns for the future. Most can be discounted, such as the worry over Chinese influence because of the leasing to a Hong Kong company of the container ports at either end of the canal; in any event China needs an efficient canal as much as the US. More serious was the attack on a Colombian naval base close to the Panama border at Jurado by FARC (Communist Armed Forces of the Colombian Revolution) rebels; forty-five marines were killed. This could be a foretaste of things to come as the FARC and drug traffickers attempt to spread their areas of operations and control. However, there are 300 kilometres of thick jungle between the Colombian border and the canal.

Fears that the Panamanians will be unable to operate the canal efficiently are unfounded and the plans to get private enterprise to invest in improving its capacity have more chance of success than relying on government funding. The main concern must be the likelihood that the canal's revenue from tolls may be used for purposes other than the canal's well-being.

Bibliography and Web Site

Conniff, Michael, *Panama and the United States: The Forced Alliance*, University of Georgia Press, 1992
Weeks, John, and Phil Gunson, *Panama: Made in the USA*, Latin American Bureau, 1991
Panama Canal Commission: Annual Report

www.pancanal.com

THE FALKLANDS OR ISLAS MALVINAS

British naval Captain John Strong made the first landing on the islands, which were uninhabited, in 1690 and he named them The Falklands after the then First Lord of the Admiralty, Viscount Falkland. The Islands were visited during the eighteenth century by French seal-hunters, who named them Les Iles Malouines; in 1764 a small French colony was established on East Falkland which was sold to the Spanish in 1767. The settlement became known as Puerto de la Soledad and 'Malouines' was translated to 'Malvinas'.

A British expedition took possession of West Falkland in the name of George III in 1765 and a settlement was established in 1766; the settlers were driven out by the Spaniards in 1770, nearly bringing Spain and Britain to war. The settlement was returned to the British in 1771 but the presence had to be withdrawn for financial reasons in 1774. However, the British claim they never gave up their sovereignty. In 1811 the Spanish settlement was also withdrawn and the islands were uninhabited until 1820 when an American, Colonel Daniel Jewitt, claimed possession of the islands for the government at Buenos Aires (which had become independent from Spain in 1816 but was not yet recognised by other powers). He only remained there for a few days and the islands remained uninhabited until a settlement was established in 1826 under an Argentinian governor, despite the protests of the British government.

In 1825 a United States warship destroyed the Argentinian fort as a reprisal for the arrest of three US ships and the captain declared the islands free from all government. The Argentinians appointed a new governor in 1832 but mutineering soldiers murdered him shortly after he arrived. The British then sent a warship in 1833 whose captain claimed the right of sovereignty and required the Argentinian commander with his troops and most of the settlers to withdraw. There has been a British population on the islands since then.

Argentina renewed its interest in the islands, and in South Georgia and the South Sandwich Islands which it also claims, in 1963. In 1964 it raised its claim to them with the United Nations Special Committee for implementing the Declaration of the Granting of Independence to Colonial Countries and Peoples. The UN General Assembly invited Argentina and the UK to negotiate and talks were held during 1966. The UK's initial position was that the question of sovereignty should be 'frozen' for thirty years, after which the islanders could decide on their future; this was rejected by Argentina. In March 1967 the UK said for the first time that it would give up sovereignty subject to certain conditions and to the wishes of the islanders and the UK parliament. The islanders saw and objected to a draft memorandum of understanding in February 1968. In 1971 an agreement on communications between the islands and Argentina was made, without sovereignty being mentioned, and air and sea services from Argentina were instituted.

The situation became more intense after the military coup in Argentina in March 1976. That the UK's interest in protecting the islands had diminished was seen in the withdrawal of the Royal Navy frigate stationed there, the ending of the Simonstown Agreement and the decision not to lengthen the airstrip. In the Defence Review of 1981 it had been decided to sell the aircraft carrier *Invincible* and to withdraw the ice patrol ship *Endurance* from service. Talks continued in 1976 and 1977 and in 1978 a number of working groups were established. After the Argentinian elections Argentina called for a more dynamic pace to the negotiations.

The Argentinians invaded the islands on 2 April 1982; within two months the UK had assembled a naval task force which sailed to the Falklands and British troops landed on 21 May 1982. The Argentinians surrendered on 14 June: they had lost about 750 men and their cruiser the *Belgrano* had been sunk. The British suffered men 256 killed; naval losses

---

The Falklands or Islas Malvinas: recent chronology

1975 Shackleton Mission to investigate natural resources. Argentina protests

1976 Argentina withdraws ambassador

1979 Diplomatic relations re-established

1980 FCO gives up initiative in talks. Invites Argentina to make proposals

1982 February: Agreement reached to establish permanent negotiating commission

March: Argentine workers land in South Georgia. UK dispatches HMS *Endurance*

April: Argentine troops invade Falklands. US President declares support for UK

May: British troops land.

June: Argentine troops surrender

1983 Argentine election restores civil government

1989 Carlos Menem elected President

1990 Diplomatic relations re-established

1994 Argentine constitution amended: claims to the islands to be pursued in accordance with international law.

1995 Cooperation over off-shore activities agreed.

1999 Ban on Argentinian visits lifted.

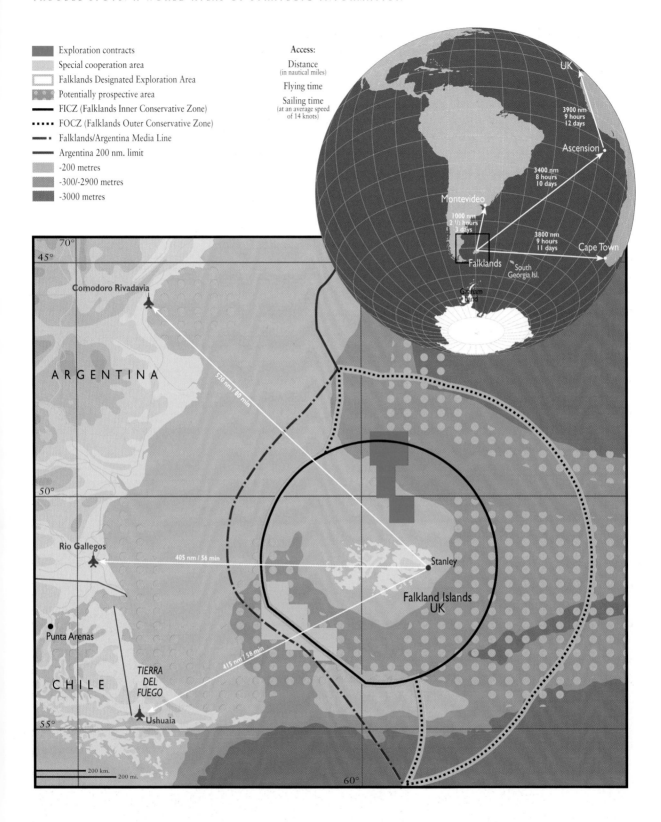

Exploration contracts
Special cooperation area
Falklands Designated Exploration Area
Potentially prospective area
FICZ (Falklands Inner Conservative Zone)
FOCZ (Falklands Outer Conservative Zone)
Falklands/Argentina Media Line
Argentina 200 nm. limit
-200 metres
-300/-2900 metres
-3000 metres

Access:

Distance
(in nautical miles)

Flying time

Sailing time
(at an average speed
of 14 knots)

The South Atlantic.

were substantial. After the war the British constructed an airfield and deployed aircraft and a military garrison. In Argentina the military junta was disgraced and replaced by a democratically elected government.

In 1987 Britain established the Falklands Islands Interim Conservation and Management Zone with a radius of up to 150 miles from the centre of the Islands and the Falkland Islands government began issuing fishing licences. Following a meeting with the Argentinians, the British-Argentinian South Atlantic Fisheries Commission was set up to ensure the preservation of stocks. The Falklands Outer Conservation Zone extends conservation control up to a further 50 miles beyond the interim zone. Between 250,000 and 300,000 tonnes of fish are caught each year, generating £15–20 million annually in licence fees.

Argentina amended its constitution in 1994 to allow the pursuit of its claim to the Falklands in accordance with International Law. Earlier in talks in Madrid the two sides had agreed a formula protecting their respective positions on sovereignty: this has allowed substantial progress to be made in a number of fields.

Argentina and the UK signed a joint declaration on cooperation on hydrocarbon development in September 1995 and set up the South West Atlantic Hydrocarbons Commission – neither development affects either side's position over sovereignty. So far seven licences to explore areas, all north of the islands, have been awarded. Six wells, in four of the blocks, were drilled during 1998 and although traces of oil and gas were found, none was in commercial quantities.

Falklands, British ships in San Carlos Water shortly after the British landing, June 1982. (Associated Press)

Despite the cooperation achieved between Argentina, the United Kingdom and the Falklands, the former has not dropped its claim to the islands. The islanders remain determined to stay British.

Web Sites

Argentine Embassy London: www.argentine-embassy.uk.org
Falklands-Malvinas Forum (Inter-Mediación): www.falklands-malvinas.com
UK Foreign Office: www.fco.gov.uk/news/briefs

COLOMBIA: FORTY YEARS OF CIVIL WAR

For many years Colombia has been one of the most dangerous countries in the world. The Spanish conquered the Chibcha Indians in the sixteenth century and Colombia formed part of the colony of New Granada, which also contained Panama and most of Venezuela. The problems caused by its large area and the distance between centres of population meant that central government was hard to exercise and vast estates had a high degree of independence. Government was corrupt, inefficient and abusive, but then it was so in most of the world at that time. These conditions led to a tradition of violence in Colombia caused not by government, as elsewhere in Latin America, but by lack of it. In 1819 Ecuador was added to the country's territory and its name was changed to Gran Colombia; it became independent under Simón Bolívar. Ecuador and Colombia split in 1830. Little was done to create a strong administration: Colombia's leaders had witnessed other new states losing their democracy to powerful institutions such as the army, nor did they want to pay the high taxes needed to develop a national army and police force. Colombia's leaders preferred to provide their own security. Leadership was divided between anti-church radicals and defenders of the faith who became Liberals and Conservatives respectively.

After independence from Spain in 1819, the country suffered seven civil wars between the Liberal and Conservative factions, the last being between 1899 and 1902 which the Conservatives won. The next forty-five years were peaceful. The Liberals gained power in the 1930 elections when the Conservatives were split. However, violence re-emerged in 1946 when the re-united Conservatives regained power. 'La Violencia' was ten years of near civil war between Liberal/left-wing guerrilla groups, infiltrated to some extent by communists, and Conservative militias formed to protect themselves and to retaliate. Some 250,000 people are thought to have died.

In 1958 the political parties joined to share government through the National Front constitution, which required the presidency to alternate between Liberals and Conservatives and for the two parties to share posts in the bureaucracy and legislature. The military assumed the leading role in ending La Violencia; it received US aid and training and trebled in size in twenty years. The power of the army grew and it was authorised to try suspected guerrillas. The military was brought into anti-drug operations but that led to corruption, the bribing of officers and the misuse of US funds given to aid the campaign against drugs being spent on the war fought with the guerrillas.

The formation of the four guerrilla groups stems from the final years of La Violencia. The first to be formed, in 1962, was the pro-Castro Army of National Liberation (Ejército Liberación Nacional) (ELN) composed mainly of university students. Next, in 1966, the Communist Armed Forces of the Colombian Revolution (Fuerzas Armadas de la Revolución Colombiana) (FARC) was created. A pro-Chinese group, the People's Liberation Army (Ejército Popular de Liberación) (EPL) was founded in 1974. The best-known guerrilla movement the M-19 (Movimiento 19 de Abril) first appeared in 1974; it was formed from factions of both the FARC and the political National Popular Alliance, of which it claimed to be the military wing. The Liberal president ended the National Front arrangements in 1986.

In addition to the guerrilla problem Colombia has had to contend with a large-scale drug industry. The production of marijuana escalated following the major campaign launched against drug trafficking in Mexico in 1975. In addition to processing its own coca crop, Colombia also refines and exports most of the coca grown in Peru and Bolivia. The Colombian drug barons accumulated massive wealth and power and were seemingly above the law. They formed their own paramilitary groups. The Attorney-General, who favoured extradition for trial in the US, was assassinated in 1988 as were more than fifty judges over a three-year period. Two cartels, the Cali and the Medellín whose rivalry has added to the Colombian death rate, dominated the drug trade. The cartels have subsidised guerrilla groups but the tendency of the FARC to kidnap leading drug traffickers and hold them for ransom led to fighting between the two organisations.

Threatened by both guerrillas and drug cartels, it is not surprising that a number of self-defence paramilitary groups were formed to provide some protection for business concerns and peasant communities. The army created a number of special units to combat the guerrillas, employing the same vicious tactics, and this led inevitably to human rights abuses, torture and illegal killing.

In recent months a form of peace process has evolved. It is driven by the increasing strength and capability of FARC and the ELN, which specialises in harassing the activities of foreign oil companies, and by the general public's weariness after so many years of civil conflict. President Pastrana agreed to the establishment of a zone from which all army and police were withdrawn, leaving FARC in complete control. FARC also wants the disbandment of the paramilitary groups who are now more centrally organised, opposes negotiation with the groups and intends to continue to fight them. The government appears unable, or unwilling to counter the paramilitary groups' activities.

A more worrying factor is the possibility of the insurgency spreading to Colombia's neighbours. Panama, Ecuador and Venezuela have been used both as safe havens and training grounds for FARC and as refuges for Colombians attempting to escape the fighting. Colombia processes most of Peru's coca crop, while Panama is an essential link in the smuggling out of cocaine and smuggling in of arms for FARC. The worst case scenario is for a return to a New Granada or Gran Colombia run by drug barons.

Meanwhile, the peace process is stalled with, according to Colombian Army intelligence, the FARC taking advantage of the demilitarised zone to

Colombia: drug statistics (in hectares)

Potential harvest	1989	1998
coca	42.4	101.8
opium	1.3	6.1
cannabis	2.3	5.0

Eradication	1989	1997
coca	6.4	19.0
opium	1.16.9	
cannabis	0.1	na

Seizures (metric tonnes)

heroin/		
morphine base	0.05 (1992)	0.32 (1998)
opium	0.43 (1992)	0.1 (1998)
cannabis	708 (1989)	69 (1998)
base and basuco	5.8 (1993)	29 (1998)
cocaine HCl	47.2 (1990)	54.7 (1998)

Colombia, showing the areas of drug cultivation.

build up its strength to 17,000 men and to carry out raids against the army outside its boundaries. At the same time, cocaine production has increased by 28 per cent and is set to continue to grow.

Bibliography and Web Sites

Kline, Harvey F., *State Building and Conflict Resolution in Colombia, 1986–1994*, University of Alabama Press, 1999

Maullin, Richard, *Soldiers, Guerrillas and Politics in Colombia*, Lexington, 1973

Amnesty International: www.amnesty.org/ailib/countries

Colombian Ministry of Foreign Affairs: www.minrelext.gov.co.english

www.

PERU: WAR WITH THE SHINING PATH

The first act of violence committed by the Shining Path, or Sendero Luminoso (officially the Communist Party of Peru), was the burning of the registry and ballot boxes at the electoral registration office in Chuschi on

17 May 1980. The Shining Path formed in 1969 in the Ayacucho Department; its founder leader was a philosophy professor, Manuel Rubén Abimael Guzmán. It was a rural organisation whose aim was to restore the traditions of the Quechua Indians using Maoist and Marxist principles; it employed assassination and mutilation of victims to increase the terror effect of its operations. Although the Shining Path advocates a rural, peasant revolution it is led by middle-class intellectuals who employ indoctrination, particularly of the young (12–15-year-olds) in their recruiting and motivation practices.

The Shining Path originated in Huamanga University as an elitist group but it soon spread throughout the educational system to both urban secondary and village single-class schools. Its strategy is based on the uniqueness of the Andean environment with its three ecological floors at different altitudes. The Andes have always been a refuge for the underprivileged and 50 per cent of Peru's population lives there, existing on labour-intensive farming. The region has little importance to the government and it has not made the investment needed to maintain effective control. It is an ideal area for a patient communist organisation

Peru, showing the areas of drug cultivation.

with very long-term aims. The Shining Path exploits the disparities between the lives of the urban and rural populations, exemplified by the difference in prices, with as much as a 200 per cent mark-up in some Andean markets. Land ownership has long been a source of peasant anger. Initially the best land was in the hands of the hacienda owners. They were then replaced by the cooperatives which, in their turn, were broken up. Subsequent land redistribution was both arbitrary and chaotic; it favoured neither local communities nor the landless peasants.

The Shining Path has made widespread use of violence both to intimidate the peasant population and to undermine government efforts. It aims to disorganise politics and create a vacuum by murdering the most unpopular and by persuading the most respected to leave. The Shining Path has both an authoritarian and a cell structure, which has made it hard to infiltrate.

The Andes and the Amazon jungle form the base for Shining Path operations. It is an area measuring some 750 by 200 miles, over which the government cannot maintain law and order. From it the Shining Path can strike west to the Pacific coast. The organisation has survived as a terrorist/guerrilla organisation because of its ideology, and its use of violence both to ensure loyalty and to disrupt any form of authority. Its alliance with the drug cartels has provided much of its finance. It has never been strong enough to win the war against government but has been content to wait until corrupt authority destroys itself.

In September 1993, from his prison cell Guzmán called on his followers to abandon the armed struggle and to turn to political activity. There followed a period of reduced terrorist attack and several thousand of guerrillas surrendered in response to President Fujimori's 'Repentance Law'. Estimates vary between 25,000 and 30,000 for the number who died during the fifteen-year civil war. The tactics adopted by the army to counter the guerrillas were as brutal as those of the rebels and many of the casualties were the innocent caught between the two. Fujimori's suspension of the Congress and the introduction of 'faceless judges' to try terrorists removed many of the restraints on army activity. The US found it hard to support anti-drug operations while condemning the human rights abuses of the counter-guerrilla war. At roughly the same time, US and Peruvian government efforts to eliminate the drug trade from which the Shining Path acquired much of its finance had a high degree of success. The rate of production dropped dramatically – some 65,000 hectares, about 56 per cent of the total, being eradicated – while the air force shot down any aircraft suspected of drug trafficking. But the Shining Path, though much reduced in size, did not give up completely and in 1996 there was a resurgence of terrorist attacks against government targets. The movement's current leader, Oscar Ramirez Durand, was arrested on 14 July 1999. Though this was a major blow to the organisation, it is not expected that the Shining Path will collapse. However, its strength, probably about 1,000 fighters, is much reduced from the 10,000 it had in the early 1990s.

The Shining Path is not the only rebel movement the government has to contend with. The Tupac Amaru Revolutionary Movement (MRTA) is a smaller and less vicious organisation than the Shining Path. It began its campaign of terrorism in 1984 by attacking targets that would attract

---

Peru: armed forces

Army
Men: 75,000 (52,000 conscripts)
Divisions: 13 (including 3 armoured, 1 cavalry, 7 infantry, 1 jungle, 1 airborne)
Helicopters: 60
Attack Helicopters: 23
Transport Helicopter:86

General Police
Men: 43,000

Security Police
Men: 21,000

Technical Police
Men: 13,000

Rondas Campesinas (peasant self defence force)
About 2,000 groups, strength varies from probably 20–30 each, some small arms.

Opposition (estimates)

Sendero Luminoso
Maximum 2,000 'fighters'

Movimiento Revolucionario Tupac Amaru
Maximum 600 'fighters'

maximum publicity, such as the US Embassy and American business interests. It probably numbered some 3,000 guerrillas in the mid-1980s. It inevitably clashed with the Shining Path over the sharing of drugs-trafficking profits. Its boldest moment came when it managed to take control of the Japanese Ambassador's compound while a diplomatic cocktail party was in progress on 17 December 1996. The 72 remaining hostages were only freed in an assault made on 21 April 1997 in which all 14 terrorists and one hostage were killed. MRTA has gained no publicity since then.

Bibliography and Web Site

Clawson, Patrick, and Rensselaer Lee, *The Andean Cocaine Industry*, Macmillan, 1996
Scott Palmer, David, *Shining Path of Peru*, Hurst, 1992

Peruvian Ministry of Foreign Affairs: www.rree.gob.pe/ing

WWW.

MEXICO: THE ZAPATISTAS AND CHIAPAS

The province of Chiapas was originally populated by Mayans, one of the pre-Spanish civilisations of Central and South America. Today some one million Mayan Indians live in Chiapas province, the poorest in Mexico, separated from the rest of the country by mountains and the Lacandon Forest. It was conquered by the Spanish between 1524 and 1527 and was then part of Guatemala. The diseases brought by the Spanish decimated the indigenous population except in the cooler highlands. Dominican monks who followed the conquest were instrumental in ending slavery and gaining permission for the Mayans to control their own community affairs. Chiapas became a province of Mexico in 1824.

Throughout the last decades of the nineteenth century the number of private estates in Chiapas steadily increased from about 1,000 in 1880 to 6,800 in 1909, all established at the expense of the Indian community. The counter-revolution that began in 1911 was set off by the government's decision to abolish debt servitude and to grant workers the right to a minimum wage: this was violently opposed by the landowners. They managed to coerce the Indians into joining their private armies but they were defeated. When Alberto Pineda reorganised these armies in 1915 the Indians did not support him and by 1917 they had joined the government forces. They retook their communal lands as plantation owners were forced out. Unfortunately, Pineda managed to defeat the government army: by 1920 the Chiapas had regained its autonomy under the landowners and labour reform was halted.

In the 1960s there was widespread clearance of the rainforest to provide more land for farming and to ease the problem of overpopulation. Thousands of acres were deforested. However, the farming methods used elsewhere in Mexico were unsuitable for this area; after only a few harvests the farms collapsed and the land fell into the hands of the old established owners of large estates. The Mayan peasants once again became impoverished labourers.

Armed rebellion in Chiapas broke out in January 1994 when Indian peasants seized four towns and six villages and kidnapped the state

governor. The rebels were led by the Ejército Zapatista Liberación Nacional (Zapatista National Liberation Army) (ZNLA). The name Zapatista comes from that of the hero of Mexican revolution fought between 1911 and 1915, Emiliano Zapata, whose aim was to recover communal land for the peasants from the rich landowners. The ZNLA was formed in 1983 after the violent eviction of three peasant communities from the Lacandon Forest; it was a self-defence force rather than a revolutionary one. By 1986 it still had only twelve members but recruiting campaigns in 1988 and 1989 brought numbers up to about 1,300 and arms began to be obtained secretly. It is still not clear how much the origins of the ZNLA are owed to other revolutionaries from northern and central Mexico, nor, as the government claims, how much it is supported by Mexican volunteers who fought in Nicaragua's and El Salvador's civil wars. The ZNLA is primarily a Mayan peasant force. The rebellion that began in 1994 was prompted by a combination of human rights abuses, failure to bring in adequate land reform and the effect of a 50 per cent drop in world coffee prices on the many small holders.

The Mexican Army swiftly recovered the six captured towns. ZNLA melted away into the forests and intimated that it was ready for negotiations. The government initially over-reacted and committed acts of indiscriminate violence and violated human rights, executing suspects and employing torture during interrogation. However, it quickly showed it too was ready to negotiate. The Zapatistas' demands included the relief of peasant poverty, an end to racism and the introduction of democracy throughout Mexico. They have promised to continue the war as long as their demands are not met, and indeed have done so.

The August 1994 election replaced the authoritarian President Carlos Salinas with Ernesto Zedillo, who is more committed to political and

Opposite: A typical view of the Chiapas region, Mexico. (Photographers Library)

Mexico, showing the areas of drug cultivation.

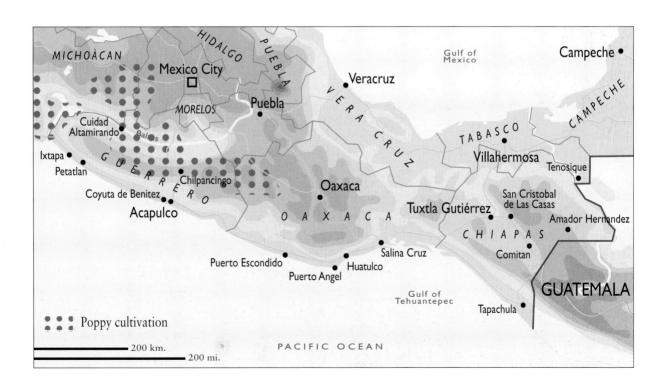

economic reform. In February 1995 the army entered Chiapas in strength with the aim of capturing the ZNLA leader, known as Sub-commandante Marcos and now thought to be Rafael Guillén Vicente who had taken part in the Sandinista uprising and had had military training in the Soviet Union. The goal was to crush the revolution. As before the ZNLA did not stand and fight an obviously superior force but retired into the mountains. Marcos' main aim, to gain worldwide publicity and sympathy for the cause, was achieved. A military zone was established. Talks between the ZNLA and the government were held between April and July 1995 without agreement being reached. However, some progress was made: extra funds were allocated to the region and a food distribution programme for children was to be set up. In February 1996 after a further six months of negotiation an agreement covering the rights of indigenous natives was signed; other issues, land, democracy, and justice, remained unresolved.

In September 1996 the Zapatistas, claiming that the government had not followed the agreed agenda, refused to attend further talks. In fact it was the emergence of another revolutionary party, the Ejército Popular Revolucionario (EPR) that led to the change of tactics. The EPR was formed in Guerrero province, has similar aims to the ZNLA but is considered a more terrorist-oriented organisation. Its first round of attacks in August 1996 took place against army and police posts in four provinces. A further problem for the Mexican government was the discovery that General Gutiérrez had been collaborating with drug traffickers responsible for the transit of 70 per cent of the cocaine that reaches the US through Mexico.

Bibliography and Web Site

Harvey, Neil, *The Chiapas Rebellion: The Struggle for Land and Democracy*, Duke University Press, 1998

www. Mexican Presidency: www.presidecia.gob.mx/welcome

SPACE: THE NEW BATTLEFIELD

The first part of this section defines the terms used later, the second describes the military uses of space involving satellites and the third covers anti-satellite warfare. While space has several positive uses, such as for scientific research and improved communications and meteorology, it is also of great value to the military. In peacetime satellites collect vital intelligence and in wartime space is the route for long-range missiles.

DEFINING SPACE: AN ILLUSTRATED GLOSSARY

Space. Space is divided into layers based on distance from the earth. Diagram 1 shows the terms used and the altitudes involved. Atmosphere is the gaseous envelope that surrounds the Earth and provides the oxygen needed for humans to breath and engines to function. The further away from Earth, the thinner the atmosphere, so that humans normally need oxygen supplies above 10,000 feet and jet engines cease to function much above 20 miles. Space has also been divided into regions. Region I is the Earth and the space for near-Earth orbit; it extends to 22,400 miles, the height required for geosynchronous orbit. Between there and the orbit of the Moon is Region II, also known as Cislunar space, while beyond the Moon's orbit is Region III or Translunar space.

Orbits. An orbit is the path of any object as it flies through space. Spacecraft that orbit the earth must have sufficient velocity to balance the pull of gravity; too great a velocity causes the spacecraft to leave its intended orbit. An **elliptical orbit** is a non-circular flight path; extremely elongated or squashed ellipses are known as **eccentric orbits**. The **apogee** of an elliptical orbit is the furthest distance the spacecraft reaches from the Earth, while the closest it gets is its **perigee**. A **low earth orbit** is one of between 60 and 300 miles' altitude. Depending on altitude, one orbit will take between 90 minutes and a few hours. A **geostationary orbit** is one in which the spacecraft remains above the same point on Earth, above the equator, as it travels at the same speed as the earth rotates. A **geosynchronous orbit** is one where the spacecraft makes a figure of eight 22,294 miles above the equator and so circles the earth once every twenty-four hours. In a **semi-synchronous orbit** the spacecraft orbits the earth twice in twenty-four hours at an altitude of 12,400 miles. The **molniya orbit** (named after the codename of the first

The theoretical height for geosynchronous orbit is 29,400 miles or 35,900 kilometres. In practice, satellites orbit at either 20,800/33,500 kilometres or 22,230 miles/35,800 kilometres.

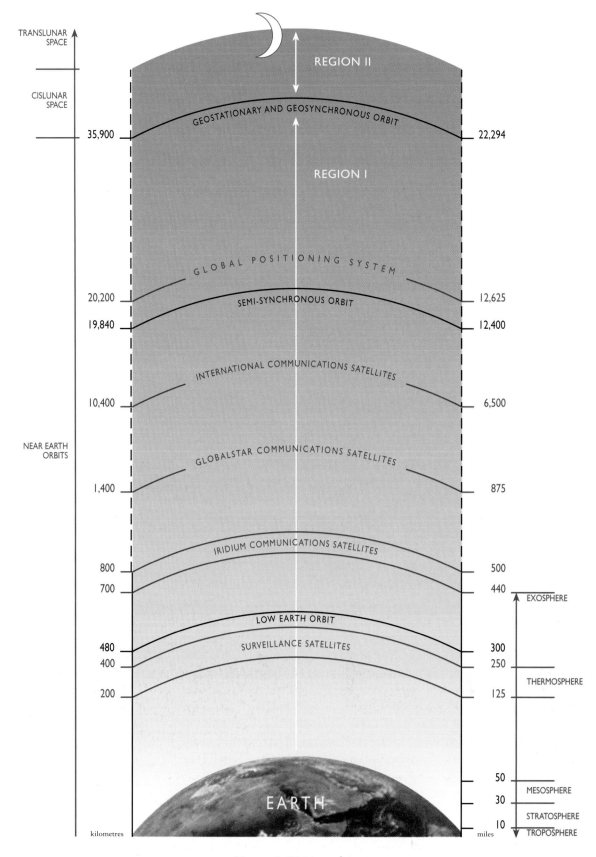

Diagram 1: Divisions of space.

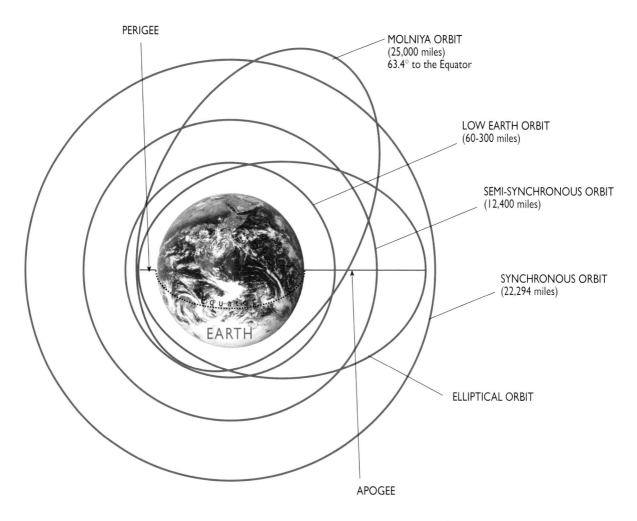

PERIGEE

MOLNIYA ORBIT
(25,000 miles)
63.4° to the Equator

LOW EARTH ORBIT
(60-300 miles)

SEMI-SYNCHRONOUS ORBIT
(12,400 miles)

SYNCHRONOUS ORBIT
(22,294 miles)

ELLIPTICAL ORBIT

APOGEE

Diagram 2: Types of orbit.

Soviet communications satellite that employed this orbit) has an inclination of 63° and is used by Russians for their surveillance satellites because its path takes it over North America for most of its orbit. A spacecraft due to go into orbit higher than 250 miles' altitude is often launched first into a low earth orbit, known as a **parking orbit**; then, after dropping its launch vehicle and when the requisite window appears, it is transferred to the required altitude thus using less propellant than in direct ascent. **Orbital inclination** is the angle of the flight path relative to the equator. Paths flying east over the equator have 0° inclination, those flying west 180°; polar paths have a 90° or 270° inclination. **Sun-synchronous orbit** is inclined at about 98° to the equator and constantly maintains the same position relative to the Sun. Satellites on this orbit pass over the same points at the same local time each day and so changes in shadow length can indicate changes on the ground. **Perturbations** are natural forces – such as luni-solar gravity, solar winds, and electro-magnetic forces – that cause spacecraft to deviate from their ideal flight path. Diagram 2 illustrates the various orbits.

Flight. The **launch window** is the period when a spacecraft or missile can be launched to achieve its intention, taking into account launch and destination sites, gravity and atmospheric drag. **Atmospheric** or **aerodynamic drag** is the force that slows flight – the closer to Earth, the greater the drag. Above 60 miles, drag is virtually insignificant. The earliest phase of flight is the **boost phase** when the rocket motor is burning. A missile then enters its **mid-course phase**. The **re-entry** or **terminal phase** is the spacecraft's or missile's return flight through the Earth's atmosphere: it must be designed to survive the intense heat of re-entry. During powered flight a spacecraft's course can be controlled by correcting its attitude and direction: this is known as **thrust vector control**. **Ground track** is the path traced by the satellite under its orbit. **Period** is the time taken to orbit the earth once.

Vehicles. A spacecraft is any manned or unmanned vehicle intended to operate above the Earth's atmosphere. A **surface-to-surface missile** (SSM) is a projectile launched from Earth aimed to hit a target also on Earth. A **ballistic missile** is a projectile launched from land, sea or aircraft whose trajectory, after its power source is used up, is determined by its velocity, gravity and aerodynamic drag. Mid-course corrections can be made and terminal guidance ensures greater accuracy. A **rocket** is a projectile that can continue to be propelled outside the Earth's atmosphere because it carries an oxidiser in addition to fuel. A rocket can have several stages that can be separated after they have completed their task; each stage has its own engine. **Bus** is the name given to that part of the projectile that carries the payload which can comprise **warheads** (the projectile's weapons) or **penetration aids** to complicate the task of interception. The latter include **decoys**, which simulate the weapons and attract the enemy's countermeasures, **spoofers**, devices which transmit false electronic signals, and **jammers**, transmitters which degrade or swamp enemy radar or radio signals. Sensors can be active, which transmit signals to gain a reflection from the target, or passive, which rely purely on intercepting signals (electronic, seismic, infrared, magnetic, radioactive, etc.) to locate the target.

Bibliography

Collins, John M., *Military Space Forces*, Pergamon-Brassey's, 1989
Outer Space-Battlefield of the Future?, SIPRI, Taylor & Francis, 1978

MILITARY USE OF SPACE

Space has become an essential area of operations for the military. There are several advantages in utilising space for military purposes. First, it belongs to no one so there is no problem regarding entering another country's air space, as the US U-2 spy planes had to do during the 1950s. Secondly, only three geostationary satellites on a circular orbit over the equator at an altitude of 22,300 miles are needed to be able to communicate between any two points on earth. The main disadvantages are the difficulty of hiding in space and probably more serious is the growing reliance of the military on space-based aids whose loss could seriously impede operations on Earth. Space is the best place for military eyes and ears to operate from.

The US, naturally, has the widest space-based inventory; it cannot be matched, for reasons of cost, by any other country or alliance. Originally satellite-derived imagery, known as Imint, was only available to the US and the Soviet Union but now there are an increasing number of commercial satellites that can be tasked by anyone to obtain the imagery they require. Commercial satellites obviously cannot react to new requirements as quickly as military ones and, so far, the resolution of their imagery is far inferior to that obtainable by US military satellites. At present the US has two satellite systems providing imagery; the Improved Crystal or advanced KH-11/12 can generate both optical and infrared imagery with a resolution of as little as 15 centimetres. The other system is the Lacrosse radar imaging satellite, which has a resolution of between

Satellite photograph of Washington Airport taken by an Ikonos 2 camera with a resolution of 1 metre orbiting at about 680 kilometres. (SPOT image)

1 and 2 metres. An example of the commercial satellite pictures available is that provided by Space Imaging which has launched two IKONOS satellites, orbiting at 425 miles' altitude and delivering imagery with a resolution of 1 metre.

In addition to imagery, satellites also provide valuable intelligence by intercepting communications (Sigint) and other electronic transmissions (Elint), such as radar emissions. The US is believed to have at least seven such satellites. While both Sigint and Elint can be collected by ground and seaborne intercept stations and by specially equipped aircraft, satellites are ideally suited for the task. Satellites in low to mid-Earth orbit (500–700 miles' altitude) are used to intercept air defence and early warning radar signals, and can track ships by their radar signatures. Satellites in geostationary orbit at a 22,300 mile altitude orbit at the same speed as the earth revolves and so remain over the same area continuously; they are ideal for gathering UHF and VHF signals whose interception requires line of sight. Satellites in elliptical orbit can, depending on their inclination, spend most of their orbit as they move towards and from their apogee over their target area. The US Trump system has an elliptical orbit, as do several of the Russian satellites. One of the problems of employing both Imint and Sigint satellites is that the volume of material intercepted is vast and so must be filtered by computers programmed to identify messages containing keywords that can be analysed further. There is no shortage of raw data but, and this was brought out during the Gulf War, there is a shortage of analysts.

Satellites also produce valuable early warning. The US Defense Support Program (DSP) employing infrared sensors is used to detect missile launches (in their boost phase), nuclear detonations and other infrared events. The satellites spot a missile plume or aircraft afterburner and then alert the appropriate ground-based early warning and missile tracking radar. The US is currently developing its next generation Space-Based Infrared System (SBIRS), the first part of which will be launched in 2002. The system will employ both geosynchronous high altitude satellites and twenty-four in low Earth orbit tasked to track missiles for both National and Theatre Missile Defence.

France, Italy and Spain cooperated in the production of two Helios 1 satellites, the first launched in 1995 to provide imagery with a 1 metre resolution. France, Germany and Italy have agreed to fund jointly the French-designed Helios 2 satellite, which will also have an infrared capability, and the Horus radar satellite; the former will be launched in 2001 and the latter sometime between 2002 and 2004. The Western European Union (WEU) has established a Satellite Centre at Torrejón in Spain where satellite imagery interpretation takes place. At present it relies on Helios and commercial imagery because there are no WEU satellites.

Communications are vital to any military operation and the introduction of satellites has greatly eased the problems of long-range communications. There are a great number of both military and civil systems operated by a number of countries; this was well demonstrated in the Gulf War when both special forces patrols and television camera crews were equipped with satellite ground stations. During the Gulf War the US

Some optical commercial satellites

Country	Satellite	Resolution	Launch date
France	SPOT 4	10 P 20XS	1998
	SPOT 5	2.5 P	2000
India	ISR-1C	5.8 P 24 XS	1995
	IRS-1D	5.8 P & XS	1997
	IRS-P6	2.5 P	1998
Israel	Eros 1 & 2	1.5 P 5 XS	1998
	David	5 P	1998
US	Landsat-7	15 P 30 XS	1998
	IKONOS-1	1 P	1997
	ORBVIEW-3	1 P	1999
	QUICKBIRD-1	0.82 P	1998

P= Panchromatic XS = Multiband.
Resolution in metres

Source: UNIDIR Disarmament Forum

Indian Ocean satellite of the Defence Satellite Communications System (DSCS) was soon overloaded. The Eastern Atlantic satellite had to have its antennas realigned and a reserve satellite over the West Pacific was repositioned (an operation that took a month to complete) so that the system could cope with massive communications traffic. The US has ambitious plans for upgrading its satellite communications capability over the next ten years.

Finally, the military is becoming reliant – as also are yachtsmen, for example – on the Global Positioning System (GPS) for knowing where its units are and for guiding a number of airborne weapons, including cruise missiles. The US Navigational Satellite Timing and Ranging (NAVSTAR) system comprises twenty-one satellites plus three in-orbit reserves placed in six orbital planes at 20,000 kilometres' altitude. They transmit two signals. One is encrypted so that only military users can receive and decrypt it to give a positional accuracy to within 15 metres. Civilian users access an uncrypted signal that gives their position to within 30 metres. However, this facility can be degraded to allow only a 100 metre accuracy so as not to aid an enemy. NAVSTAR allows a minimum of four satellites to be accessed simultaneously from any point on earth.

Space-based systems are well suited to verify arms control treaties. When the first treaties were negotiated there was still a coyness about admitting the use of space to spy on one's enemies and so the anodyne phrase 'national technical means' (NTM) was crafted to cover Imint and Sigint. Most treaties include a clause forbidding the interference with NTM. Apart from these clauses, there are few legally binding restrictions on Anti-Satellite (ASAT) warfare. The Partial Test Ban Treaty prohibits nuclear explosions in the atmosphere and outer space. In the context of a general war these restrictions are unlikely to be respected.

Bibliography and Web Sites

Levine, Alan J., *The Missile and Space Race*, Praeger, 1994

Federation of American Scientists Space Policy Project: www.fas.org/spp
Space Imaging: www.spaceimaging.com

ANTI-SATELLITE WEAPONS: WAR IN SPACE

Anti-Satellite (ASAT) weapons have been and are being developed. Three main types are envisaged: steerable killer satellites that would be manoeuvred alongside the target and then exploded; rocket-propelled missiles that would destroy the satellite by smashing into it; and laser or high energy beams. The US first tested an ASAT weapon in 1959 with a nuclear-armed rocket; the test was successful but the radioactive fall-out and electro-magnetic pulse side effects were so serious that the project was abandoned. Since then the US Air Force has developed a Miniature Homing Vehicle that would be launched from an airborne platform and would destroy the satellite by the force of impact. A successful test (the

'The space "playing field" is levelling rapidly, so US forces will be increasingly vulnerable. Additionally, though adversaries will benefit greatly from space, losing the use of space may be more devastating to the United States. It would be intolerable for US forces, modeled along the lines of a Joint Vision 2010 force, to be deprived of capabilities in space.'

US Joint Vision 2010 concept, 1995

www.

only one conducted) was carried out in September 1985 using an F-15 fighter as the launch vehicle. The army was developing a similar weapon that would initially be launched by a Pershing II missile which would double the range of the aircraft-launched ASAT. This programme was terminated in 1993. One problem with developing ASAT is that they could also be used as anti-ballistic missile weapons, which are currently banned by the ABM Treaty the Russians are determined should not be amended.

The Soviet Union developed its own ASAT, a co-orbital weapon, between 1968 and 1982: it was tested at least twenty times. In 1983 the Soviet Union announced a unilateral moratorium on developing ASAT but failed to get the US Administration to join as the latter was then embarking on the Strategic Defence Initiative (SDI). However, the US Congress restricted ASAT testing for five years, which led to the cancellation of the F-15 associated programme. In 1992 a display of aircraft for the Minsk summit meeting of the Commonwealth of Independent States included a MiG-31 armed with what was claimed to be an ASAT weapon.

In December 1994 a senior research fellow at Stanford University claimed that a space-based laser, known as Alpha, was virtually ready for deployment. The Alpha project was part of the Strategic Defense Initiative programme. It was also claimed that a force of twelve laser-armed satellites could engage five ballistic missiles per minute when they were still over the launching country's territory. The Soviet Union had been conducting laser development at a site in the mountains of Tajikistan.

On 17 October 1997 the US tested its ground-based Mid-Infrared Advanced Chemical Laser (MIRACL). The chemical laser is produced by the combustion of hydrogen and fluorine. The aim of the tests was to examine the effects of 1 and 10 second bursts of the laser beam on the target satellite's imaging sensors. The trials raised a number of objections and criticisms. The Russians said that 'laser programmes may become a step towards creating an anti-satellite potential', something that the Soviet Union and Russia have opposed since attempts to negotiate an ASAT Treaty in the 1970s. US Democrat Senators had tried to get the test postponed on the grounds that it should not take place before the whole question of ASAT had been properly debated and that demonstrating a capability could encourage others to embark on ASAT development. Other critics claimed the tests could just as well have been conducted on the ground. The ABM Treaty bans space-based missile interceptors, including lasers.

If ASAT is a feasible military operation then the next development must be protection and counter-measures for satellites and an anti-ASAT weapon. Given the many difficulties in negotiating an ASAT treaty, war in space looks a more likely option. Certainly the loss of intelligence-collection and communications satellites would be a major setback in any conflict situation.

Web Site

www. Federation of American Scientists Space Policy Project: www.fas.org/spp

STOP PRESS

This section describes the main events that took place across the world between the end of the drafting of *Trouble Spots* in December 1999 and its dispatch to the printer on 1 June 2000. All the topics included here, bar three, have been covered in the book and so only a brief statement is needed. The three new subjects are Fiji, the Philippines and Zimbabwe. The first is experiencing repetition of a previous trouble; the next has had troubles for a good many years but appeared to have solved them. The violence in Zimbabwe and the occupation of white-owned farms is a new development but perhaps not an unexpected one. A short background brief on these three is included.

GLOBAL CONCERNS, PAGES 3–8

No new wars have begun nor have any new UN peacekeeping missions been deployed.

CYBER-TERRORISM, PAGE 22

The saga of the 'I love you' virus that infiltrated 45 million computers in April 2000 was followed by a number of 'copycat' attacks. It showed what could potentially be achieved by an attack on military computers in a crisis or war situation.

NUCLEAR ARMS CONTROL, PAGES 31–5 AND 37–42

Shortly after the installation of Vladimir Putin as President, the Russian Duma ratified two long outstanding treaties. On 21 April 2000 the Comprehensive Test Ban Treaty was ratified with a vote of 298 to 74, further embarrassing the US whose Senate refused ratification on 13 October 1999. A week earlier, on 14 April, the Duma had ratified the Treaty on the Further Reduction and Limitation of Strategic Offensive Arms or START II which was signed in January 1993. However, a number of caveats must be met before the treaty can come into effect. First the US must ratify the Agreement on Confidence-Building Measures Related to Systems to Counter Ballistic Missiles other than Strategic Ballistic Missiles, agreed in September 1997. The US Senate is unlikely to vote in favour of this measure as it sets limits to the capability of defences against theatre ballistic missile attack and the Senate is determined to support the deployment of National Missile Defense against the possibility of long-range missile attack by states such as Iran or North Korea. The ratification legislation also gives Russia the right to withdraw from START II should the US withdraw from the Anti-Ballistic Missile Treaty. The ratification of START II was approved by the Russian Upper House on 19 April. When, or if, the treaty comes into force, then agreement can be reached on START III (see page 39).

RUSSIA, PAGES 74–7

The new President Vladimir Putin wasted little time after his instalment on 26 March 2000 in taking action to gain greater control over Russia's regions and republics. On 10 April he suspended local laws in Amur and the Ingush Republic which conflicted with federal law and Bashkortostan was ordered to bring its constitution into line with that of the federation. Next, on the 13th, he issued a decree that created seven districts to which all eighty-nine regions and republics will be subordinate; each district is to be headed by a federal governor-general with strong powers, replacing the regional governors that coordinate federal affairs in each region at present. Then on the 17th he announced a reorganisation of the Federation Council or Upper House to remove the regional governors from it. He also said he would seek the legal authority to dismiss any governor who flouted federal law.

NATO ENLARGEMENT, PAGES 87–91

On 19 May 2000, at a meeting in Vilnius, nine Central and East European states agreed a common policy on seeking an invitation to join NATO at its summit meeting to be held in 2002. The countries are: Albania, Bulgaria, Estonia, Latvia, Lithuania, Macedonia, Romania, Slovakia and Slovenia. There have been sympathetic comments on the proposal but it is thought to be unlikely that NATO members will be ready to discuss its implementation in time for a 2002 entry date.

NORTHERN IRELAND, PAGES 105–10

In February 2000, the Secretary of State, Peter Mandelson, suspended the the Northern Ireland Assembly and Executive after receiving a report from Canadian General John de Chastelaine regarding the likelihood of IRA arms decommissioning. It concluded 'to date we have received no information from the IRA as to when decommissioning will start'. The suspension was made in part to pre-empt a decision by the Unionist leader, David Trimble, to resign and by the Unionists to withdraw from the Assembly. Many commentators took the opportunity to say that they had never expected the IRA to decommission its weapons and that it never would. On 6 May the IRA made an unexpected statement that included 'it will initiate a process that will completely and verifiably put IRA arms beyond use'. It proposed that Cyril Ramaphosa, a leading ANC figure, and Marti Arhtisaari, a former President of Finland, should be shown a number of weapons' stores and then regularly re-inspect them to confirm that none had been removed. The suspicious have pointed out that: no weapons are to be destroyed, not all weapons are necessarily being put in stores and that the IRA statement also included 'that the full implementation [of decommissioning] depends on a political process that would remove the causes of conflict, and in which Irish Republicans and Unionists can, as equals, pursue our respective political objectives peacefully'.

The Unionists are under pressure from the British government to agree to return to the Executive with Sinn Fein; for their part, the Unionists are looking for concessions over the reorganisation and renaming of the Royal Ulster Constabulary. On 27 May the Ulster Unionist Party voted (53 to 47 per cent) to return to power-sharing government. However, anti-agreement Unionists will outnumber those in favour of it in the Assembly. Still no IRA arms have been decommissioned nor yet put beyond use. The fear is now of renewed terrorism by extremists of both sides.

CENTRAL ASIAN OIL, PAGES 138–40

A consortium of Western oil companies has revealed a new Caspian oilfield off the coast of Kazakhstan that could have reserves of up to 50 billion barrels. This figure has not yet been confirmed. The new field, the Kashagan, will heighten the competition between Russia and the US over the choice of pipeline routes. The proposed Baku–Ceyhan (Turkey) route would be more cost effective if it transhipped the oil from Kashagan.

LEBANON, PAGES 160–3

The long-awaited withdrawal of the Israeli Defence Force from Lebanon was completed on 21 May 2000. It had begun in a low key way some weeks earlier but for the final few days it took place under widespread media coverage. The South Lebanon Army disintegrated. A number of its members surrendered and others deserted, while some 6,000 soldiers and families were allowed into Israel. The withdrawal was closely followed up by Hizbollah and by the original Lebanese inhabitants returning to the villages they had been forced to vacate, some as long as eighteen years previously. For some time the IDF and UN officials have been redemarcating the international border between Israel and Lebanon because over the years Israeli border defences had encroached into Lebanese territory.

Both sides claimed victory. Israelis in northern settlements now wait to see whether Hizbollah will abide by its agreement not to attack Israel so long as Israel refrains from attacking civilian targets in Lebanon. The Israelis have made it clear that they will hold Syria responsible for any future attacks over the border.

One small area of contention remains. The Shebaa Farms (Har Dov to the Israelis) in the Mount Hermon range is claimed by Hizbollah to be Lebanese territory while the Israelis maintain it is part of occupied Syria.

THE HORN OF AFRICA, PAGES 207–10

The war between Ethiopia and Eritrea, which had been dormant since February 1999, re-erupted in May 2000 with a successful Ethiopian outflanking movement over difficult country. The Ethiopians captured the towns of Shambiku, Barentu and Omhajer in the south-west corner of Eritrea before advancing in the central sector and taking Zalambessa. As before, both sides claimed to have inflicted massive casualties on the other, but observers saw little evidence of this.

ANGOLA, PAGES 218–22

The civil war in Angola continued unabated. In April 2000 the Security Council debated a report, prepared by a panel organised by the Canadian UN representative, that revealed a number of sanction breakers who were

TROUBLE SPOTS: A WORLD ATLAS OF STRATEGIC INFORMATION

trading with UNITA. Bulgaria was accused of selling UNITA arms and the Belgian Diamond Authorities were criticised for inadequately monitoring operations that had allowed UNITA to sell its diamonds in Antwerp. Several African countries (Burkino Faso, Cote D'Ivoire, Republic of Congo, Rwanda, Togo, Uganda, Mobuto's Zaire), or their heads of state, were accused variously of providing petroleum, allowing the transhipment of arms, providing financial services and allowing UNITA officials to hold meetings on their territory, all being violations of UN-imposed sanctions. All those accused have denied the accusations and have complained of the disclosure, in variance with UN custom, of the accusations before they had been properly investigated. The UNSC sanctions committee will collect more evidence over the next six months and the UNSC has warned that any country guilty of violating the sanctions will have sanctions imposed on it.

SIERRA LEONE, PAGES 226–30

UN peacekeepers deployed to Sierra Leone during the first months of 2000. By April their strength had reached 7,400 and they had begun the process of disarming the estimated 45,000 armed combatants. On 2 May things started to go wrong: seven UN soldiers were shot dead and forty-eight others were taken hostage by the Revolutionary United Front (RUF) led by Foday Sankoh. Further UN hostages have been taken including over 200 Zambian soldiers who were ambushed, disarmed and lost a number of armoured personnel carriers. The total captured by the RUF may have been as high as 500. Following mediation by Liberian Charles Taylor, all the hostages have now been released.

An incorrect report by the UN that the RUF was advancing on Freetown caused panic there; the United Kingdom deployed a battalion, which had been pre-positioned earlier in Senegal, to protect the airport and to cover the evacuation of European civilians. On 17 May Sankoh was found hiding in Freetown and was arrested. Eventually he was flown under British guard to Lungi airport. The British presence has given the government army a new confidence and it has made some progress against the RUF.

SRI LANKA, PAGES 254–6

The Tamil Tigers took the opportunity of the absence of President Chandrika Kumaratunga, who left the country in April 2000 for medical treatment, to launch an attack on Elephant Pass, which controls the land access to Jaffna. After heavy fighting the army abandoned its base there and government troops, said to number up to 40,000, were cut off in the Jaffna Peninsula.

The government does not have the shipping necessary to evacuate the force and has appealed to India for help, while the airport is under fire from Tamil artillery. India has said it will help with an evacuation but only if both sides agree a ceasefire.

COLOMBIA, PAGES 298–300

At the end of April 2000 the government, in an attempt to end the many years of fighting, announced that it would establish a second demilitarised zone, this time for the smaller dissident group, the National Liberation Army (NLA). The new zone is smaller than the first, 4,800 square kilometres as opposed to 42,000, but NLA strength is around 5,000 compared with FARC's 17,000 men. The zone is around San Pablo some 200 kilometres north of Bogota. The establishment of the zone is opposed by the right-wing militias.

FIJI

A coup attempt is still in progress in Fiji as this book goes to print.

The Melanesian Islands became a British colony in 1874. As elsewhere, the British brought in Indian workers. Fiji gained its independence in 1970. The Indian population grew until it formed 44 per cent of the country's 805,000 people; indigenous Fijians form 51 per cent.

Colonel Steve Rabuka led two army coups in 1987 after Indians formed the government and in September declared himself head of state; Fiji became a republic in October of that year. The constitution instituted then barred Indians, who dominate the business sector, from holding major political posts or having a parliamentary majority. In the 1999 elections an Indian, Mahendra Chaudhry, was elected Prime Minister of a coalition government. On 20 May 2000 a group of gunmen led by George Speight stormed the parliament building and held the Prime Minister and his cabinet hostage. The President, whom the rebels called on to resign, declared a state of emergency, agreed to dismiss the government and to grant the rebels immunity in the hope that this would end the coup peacefully. The Great Council of (Tribal) Chiefs has also sided with the coup plotters. However, unlike in 1987, the majority of the army has not backed the coup. Initially there was little violence but the security forces did little to stop it. After the television centre was ransacked martial law was declared and the army enforced a curfew. The President has now resigned leaving the army in control. The hostages had not been released by 30 May.

The Philippines

PHILIPPINES

Fighting broke out again between the government and Islamist separatists in the southern island of Mindanao in April 2000.

Islam was brought to the Philippines by early Arab traders but was replaced as the national religion by Catholicism after the Spanish conquest in 1565. The Sultanates of Sulu and Mindanao resisted Christianity and remained predominantly Muslim. During the Spanish-American war the Spanish fleet was sunk in Manila Bay in 1898 and the Filipinos declared independence, only to be put down by the US with some 200,000 killed. The islands were ceded to the US by Spain and a form of self-government was introduced.

The Philippines became fully independent in 1946 following the end of the Japanese occupation. Ferdinand Marcos gained power in 1965 and ruled the country until 1986 – by martial law from 1972 to 1981 on account of insurgency by both communists and Muslim separatists. The government of Corazon Aquino survived a number of attempted coups and tried to end the insurgency in the south. The Communist Moro National Liberation Front and the government began talks in 1995 and reached a human rights accord in 1996. The government proposed

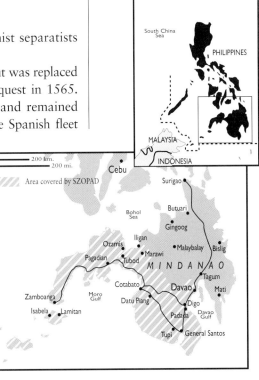

establishing a Special Zone of Peace and Development (SZOPAD) that would give a degree of autonomy to the fourteen provinces with Muslim populations. The Moro Islamic Liberation Front (MILF) held peace talks with the government in late 1997 and agreed a ceasefire. No further progress was made and clashes occurred from time to time. Serious fighting erupted in March 2000 and the army counter-attacked strongly. Some 100,000 people were made refugees.

The situation was complicated by the kidnapping by another Muslim group, Abu Sayyaf, of twenty-three tourists from the Malaysian island of Sipadan. Other hostages have been taken by the MILF which called a unilateral ceasefire in early May; the government suspects this is a purely tactical move. At the end of May the hostages held by Abu Sayyaf had not been released.

Web Site

Philippines News-Link Online: www.philnews.com

ZIMBABWE

In February violence broke out in Zimbabwe as supporters of President Robert Mugabe began to occupy white-owned farms and to attack their political opponents in the Movement for Democratic Change (DMC).

Zimbabwe means 'stone house' in Bantu and was the scene of an early African civilisation. Ruled first by the Shona and then the Rwozi it was annexed and colonised by the British in the late nineteenth century. Mashonaland, Matabeleland and what is now Zambia became Rhodesia in 1895. In 1923 the part south of the Zambezi became the self-governing colony of Southern Rhodesia. By then there was a large white population which had established a thriving tobacco farming economy. A number of African nationalist political parties were formed and campaigned for independence; the white leadership refused British terms for independence that would have led to majority rule and in 1965 declared unilateral independence.

The first guerrilla incident took place in July 1964 and the two main black opposition parties formed military wings which engaged in guerrilla warfare with the Rhodesian Security Forces for fifteen years. At the same time, numerous attempts were made to achieve a settlement, UN resolutions were adopted; selective and then comprehensive sanctions were enforced. By 1980 the civil war was costing some 37 per cent of government expenditure. Finally, at the Lancaster House talks in December 1979 agreement was reached and a British-led Commonwealth Force supervised a demilitarisation process.

Independence as Zimbabwe was achieved in April 1980 with Robert Mugabe as Prime Minister. Land reform and redistribution was part of the agreement but little was achieved and those white farms that were taken over were presented to members of Mugabe's elite.

Following the referendum of February 2000, which resulted in a vote against a proposed new constitution, attacks on white-owned farms and against DMC supporters began, encouraged by Mugabe who was soon to face an election that the referendum result showed he could lose.

GENERAL BIBLIOGRAPHY

Books

Dictionary of World History, Hutchinson, 1998

Dupuy, Trevor (ed.), *International Military and Defense Encyclopedia*, Brassey's (US), 1993

Roberts, Adam, and Benedict Kingsbury (eds), *United Nations, Divided World: The UN's Roles in International Relations*, Clarendon, 1993.

Stack, John, and Lui Hebron (eds), *The Ethnic Entanglement: Conflict and Intervention in World Politics*, Praeger, 1999

Wiberg, Hakan, and Christian Scherrer (eds), *Ethnicity and Intra-State Conflict: Types, Causes and Peace Strategies*, Ashgate, 1999

Journals

Arms Control Reporter, Institute for Defence and Disarmament Studies

Arms Control Today, US Arms Control Association

Disarmament Diplomacy, The Acronym Institute

Foreign Affairs

Foreign Policy, Carnegie Endowment for International Peace

International Affairs, Royal Institute of International Affairs

Report to The President and The Congress, US Department of Defense

SIPRI Yearbook, Stockholm International Peace Research Institute

Strategic Assessment, US National Defense University

Strategic Comment, International Institute for Strategic Studies

Strategic Survey, International Institute for Strategic Studies

Survival, International Institute for Strategic Studies

The International Security Review, Royal United Services Institute

The Military Balance, International Institute for Strategic Studies

Today, Royal Institute for International Affairs

Web Sites

Amnesty International:www.amnesty.org/ailib/countries

Arms Control Association: www.armscontrol.org/

British American Security Council: www.basicint.org/

Central Intelligence Agency Fact Book: www.odci.gov/cia/publications

Defense-Aerospace (Briganti et Associés): www.defense-aerospace.com

International Boundaries Research Unit: www.ibru.dur.ac.uk/links

International Institute for Strategic Studies: www.isn.ethz.ch/iiss

Library of Congress Studies: http://lcweb21oc.gov/frd/cs/atmtoc

Perry-Castañeda Library Map Collection: www.lib.utexas.edu/lib/PCL/Map collection

Royal Institute for International Affairs: www.riia.org

Royal United Services Institute: www.rusi.org

Cartography

Atlas of World History, The Times, 1999

National Geographic Atlas of the World, seventh edition, 1999

Grosser Historischer Weltatlas, Bayerischer Schulbuch-Verlag, 1995

Ade Ajayi, J.F., and Michael Crowder, *Historical Atlas of Africa*, Longman, 1985

Bahat, Dan, *Carta's Great Historical Atlas of Jerusalem*, Carta, 1989

Crampton, Richard and Ben, *Atlas of Eastern Europe in the Twentieth Century*, Routledge, 1996

Duby, Georges, *Atlas Historique*, Larousse-Bordas, 1998

Vidal-Naquet, Pierre, and Jacques Bertin, *Histoire de l'Humanité*, Hachette, 1987

Cartographic Web Sites

Australian Defence Forces Academy: www.adfa.oz.au

Central Intelligence Agency: www.odci.gov/cia

Chechen Republic Online: www.amina.com

Foundation for Middle East Peace: www.fmep.org.

Rainforest Action Network: www.ran.org

Slavic Research Centre, Hokkaido University: www.src.home.slav.hokudai.ac.jp

Swedish Armed Forces: www.swedint.mil.se

The Latin American Alliance: www.latinsynergy.org

United Nations: www.un.org

University of Texas at Austin: www.lib.utexas.edu

University of Virginia: www.lib.virginia.edu

World Resources Institute: www.wri.org

INDEX